The Literary Vocation of
H E N R Y   A D A M S

For discourse
(and, therefore, for man)
nothing is more frightening
than the absence of answer.
—*Mikhail Bakhtin*

The Literary Vocation of
HENRY ADAMS

William Merrill Decker

The University of North Carolina Press
Chapel Hill and London

© 1990 The University of North Carolina Press
All rights reserved
Manufactured in the United States of America

The paper used in this book meets the guidelines for
permanence and durability of the Committee
on Production Guidelines for Book Longevity
of the Council on Library Resources.

94 93 92 91 90   5 4 3 2 1

Library of Congress Cataloging-in-Publication Data

Decker, William Merrill, 1951–
   The literary vocation of Henry Adams / by William Merrill Decker.
     p. cm.
   Includes bibliographical references.
   ISBN 0-8078-1874-7 (alk. paper)
   1. Adams, Henry, 1838–1918—Philosophy.   2. Adams, Henry,
1838–1918—Literary art.   I. Title.
E175.5.A2D43   1990
973.07202—dc20   89-36157
                                                            CIP

In Memory of My Father
Harold Albert Decker
1908–1986

Contents

Preface

MY INTEREST in Henry Adams dates from my first contact with the *Education*, which I read in January 1976 as a beginning graduate student at the University of Iowa, enrolled in Sherman Paul's celebrated course, Literature and Culture of Twentieth-Century America. Mine is not the first book that locates its origin in horizons opened by his lectures or that would catch in its tone and ultimate commitment the mentor's resonant voice. I know that I am in good company to consider his instruction and friendship to have been (and to continue to be) an incalculably enabling good fortune.

Scholarship thrives by virtue of a community of interest. No one who writes on Henry Adams can fail to be aware of his or her work's enormous indebtedness to William H. Jordy, Ernest Samuels, and J. C. Levenson, the creators of the field's seminal scholarship; or to the scholarly, bibliographical, and editorial labors of Earl N. Harbert, who through the Library of America has made Adams's *History* newly available to a broad readership; or to the editorial work of Levenson, Samuels, Charles Vandersee, and Viola Hopkins Winner, whose six-volume *Letters of Henry Adams* will confirm Adams's candidacy for the title of most fascinating of American correspondents. Increasingly, students of Henry Adams will feel themselves likewise beholden to the editorial and biographical research of Edward Chalfant, whose work has considerably enriched my sense of the young Adams. More particularly, I am indebted to Ernest Samuels for answering my somewhat arcane inquiries and to Charles Vandersee for cheerfully arranging on short notice the duplication of page-proof from the last three volumes of the *Letters* so that I might have the advantage of the new edition before its general publication.

I thank James M. Cox as well as Earl N. Harbert for reading the manuscript and for offering criticism and encouragement. To Iris Tillman Hill, editor-in-chief at the University of North Carolina Press, I am grateful for befriending this book when it existed as no more than a conference paper and a prospectus. I thank Paula Wald for her expert scrutiny of the completed manuscript and Ron Maner for his unfailing helpfulness.

Former colleagues of mine at the University of Wyoming, where I taught from 1983 to 1986, were extremely helpful during the manuscript's most formative stage. Keith N. Hull, acting chair of the Department of English from 1985 to 1987, fashioned a teaching schedule that allowed me to write, while Lewis M. Dabney carefully read and critiqued a draft of the first chapter. My friend of many years, John Lo Vecchio of Boston University, facilitated research conducted over long distance. My wife, Elizabeth Grubgeld of Oklahoma State University, closely read large portions of the manuscript, commenting with the eye for detail and the grasp of scale that have always made her my best reader.

To my in-laws, Dr. Lester E. and Jane S. Grubgeld of Palo Alto, California, I am grateful for lively interest and for considerable moral and material support. To my sons, Edward and Robert (the latter, as I write, too young to be aware of what I do in the time I spend away from him), I am grateful for that pressure to finish which from their standpoint has been simply their desire for my company. To my father, Harold Decker, who died soon after I broke ground on this book, and to my mother, Marion Decker, there is so little for which I am not ultimately indebted that I might labor for pages and still not come to my gratitude's proper statement.

December 26, 1988

The Literary Vocation of
HENRY ADAMS

Abbreviations

EDITIONS OF Adams's works that are cited frequently in the text and notes have been identified by the following abbreviations. In citations, page references appear after the abbreviations.

A I   *Democracy, Esther, Mont Saint Michel and Chartres, The Education of Henry Adams, Poems.* Edited by Ernest Samuels and Jayne N. Samuels. New York: Library of America, 1983.

A II   *History of the United States during the Administrations of Thomas Jefferson.* Edited by Earl N. Harbert. New York: Library of America, 1986.

A III   *History of the United States during the Administrations of James Madison.* Edited by Earl N. Harbert. New York: Library of America, 1986.

ASCL   "Anglo-Saxon Courts of Law." In *Essays in Anglo-Saxon Law,* edited by Henry Adams. Boston: Little, Brown and Co., 1876.

D   *The Degradation of the Democratic Dogma.* Edited by Brooks Adams. 1919. Reprint. New York: Peter Smith, 1949.

DNEF   *Documents Relating to New-England Federalism, 1800–1815.* Edited by Henry Adams. Boston: Little, Brown and Co., 1877.

G   *The Life of Albert Gallatin.* 1879. Reprint. New York: Peter Smith, 1943.

GSW   *The Great Secession Winter of 1860–61 and Other Essays by Henry Adams.* Edited by George Hochfield. New York: Sagamore Press, 1958.

LHA   *The Letters of Henry Adams.* 6 vols. Edited by J. C. Levenson, Ernest Samuels, Charles Vandersee, and Viola Hopkins Winner. Cambridge: Harvard University Press, 1982–88.

NAR   *North American Review* (various unreprinted works and earlier versions of works later revised and reprinted).

R   *John Randolph.* Boston: Houghton Mifflin, 1882.

Sk   *Sketches for the North American Review.* Edited by Edward Chalfant. Hamden, Conn.: Archon Books, 1986.

T   *Tahiti: Memoirs of Arii Taimai e Marama of Eimeo, Teriirere of Tooarai, Terrinui of Tahiti, Tauraatua i Amo.* Edited by Robert E. Spiller. New York: Scholars' Facsimiles and Reprints, 1947.

Introduction

SOMETIME IN early 1886, Henry Adams, an inveterate poseur, committed himself to the pose that has since been associated with his name: neglected patrician, sangfroid doomsayer, literary man whose virtue and bereavement had fatally deflected him from the pursuit of an active public life. It was a pose, to be sure, of multiple guises: not only Adams the scientist and avant-garde artist, but also Parisian cosmopolite and Polynesian primitive, statesman's companion and votive of the Virgin imaged in several centuries of French stained glass. All such guises came back perhaps to something of a single posture: an aloofness in which Adams, laying claim to his defeats, defined himself as other than his contemporary America and thus reserved the right to be whom and say what he wished. Yet his aloofness remained ever studied, peculiarly incomplete; manifestly he meant it as a form of participation. If he played at being a twelfth-century monk, he cast himself also as the Republic's last true patriot; all of the earth's hemispheres are compassed in his later correspondence, yet the Washington address recurs at the head of his letters, marking an always ultimate point of return. Beneath the reticence and evasiveness of the *Education* lies the implicit proposition that he was the one man who could save America—if only his voice were heard.

Yet his writings of this period seem equally to question whether he can be heard and whether, in any case, America is worth saving. *Mont Saint Michel and Chartres* (1904) and *The Education of Henry Adams* (1907) won for Adams a kind of symbolic status as America's Great Naysayer, an accolade from the standpoint of many young intellectuals in the decade following World War I, although readers have often differed as to how legitimately Adams came by his right to say nay. T. S. Eliot found in Adams a morbidly detached, convictionless temperament casting the world in the image of its own malaise; Van Wyck Brooks admired the intellect that saw through to the meanness of the Gilded Age but deplored what he took to be the fatalism and passivity that kept Adams from assuming the public role for which he was qualified by force of mind. The more programmatically tradition-seeking Granville Hicks all but dismissed Adams as a thinker who self-indulgently plunged from adolescence to senility.

For such readers, Adams's negation, at most partly earned, had been largely misspent. Their view would find confirmation in William H. Jordy's *Henry Adams: Scientific Historian*, the first major book-length appraisal of Adams's work. Primarily, however, those scholars who established Adams's academic reputation in the decades following World War II concede their subject's social narrowness and spiritual hypochondria yet applaud what they view as his intellectual heroism and artistic achievement. This is not surprising, for Robert E. Spiller, R. P. Blackmur, Ernest Samuels, and J. C. Levenson all start (more or less consciously) from the assumption that the intellectual is divorced from his society and that the highest achievements of mind are rather defiantly aesthetic ones. Splendid as their studies have been, these writers have tended to celebrate Adams's isolation as the condition of his greatness and to perceive his denunciatory habit as a sometimes unhealthy but serviceable defense mechanism in behalf of a sustained life of the mind. Inevitably, perhaps, academic intellectuals have found in Adams a magnified image of their own scholarly compulsions and social disaffection.

Blackmur, Samuels, and Levenson have all sought to adjust the extreme assertions Adams made of his isolation and neglect; they have demonstrated Adams's involvement in and complicity with the events of his day even as they have presented him as a historically transcendent thinker and artist. Despite their close attention to historical context—their admirable sensitivity to Adams the calculating rhetorician—they have promoted a reading of Adams's achievement as an allegory of the (necessarily) isolated modern artist. Although they and, more recently, John J. Conder, Earl N. Harbert, Charles Vandersee, and Carolyn Porter have explored the relation Adams attempted to establish between himself and his audience, no work has appeared thus far that systematically addresses the uniquely rhetorical dimensions of his work—the audiences Adams meant to be read by, the aims of his work as intended public discourse, the peculiar ways in which that work internalized Adams's diminishing confidence in a broad, intelligent readership. In this study I attempt to view Adams from such perspectives. My immediate purpose is to examine Adams's works (the early polemical essays, the biographies and novels, the nine-volume history and speculative essays, correspondence and poems, as well as the late masterpieces) as the diverse products of Adams's lifelong effort to realize, in the face of changing conditions, some signal public purpose as an Adams and, more specifically, a decisive social office as an author.

But my reader will perceive that in conducting this investigation I have embarked on another project as well—that I have begun with certain assumptions regarding the text as public discourse and that my inquiry into Adams the rhetorician has led to an allegorical reading of my own. Of the many curiosities of Adams's career, none repays consideration more than the variety of forms in which he wrote: polemical essay, scholarly monograph, scholarly and popular biography, grand narrative history, novel, art history, autobiography, philosophical essay, poem, and—most constantly of all—the familiar letter. His long-standing commitment to personal correspondence suggests that the immediate and responsive attention of contemporaries stood chief among his authorship's objects, but his otherwise wide-ranging efforts show that he could never permanently identify that authorship with any established public mode. His failure to do so is attributable less to an inability to find or to invent the genre most compatible with his imagination than to the fact that no one genre ever afforded him the sensation of public influence that he sought. His restlessness with literary form is largely to be explained by his recurrent unrealization of a more than literary motive; and although at times he seems to write to no end but to annoy, his work always betrays the wish to be dialogically placed in a purposive and sophisticated national discussion. It always reveals the hope (or the equally significant despair) that it may contribute to an American civilization that would vindicate the aspirations of the country's fathers, among whom an Adams had conspicuously figured. In short it seeks a generative relation with its readership, even as it speculates upon the sterility of the world to which it must be consigned.

As he turned from one genre to another, Adams could expect to be read by different if often overlapping readerships, yet in preparing all but his more scholarly works he nearly always had in view a broad, educable, general readership—one that might receive from his text a clarified sense of the American past and a chastened, if also exhilarating, notion of the national prospect. To invoke Aristotle's famous distinction, Adams was always more rhetorician than dialectician. In curbing the vitriolic moralizing of *John Randolph* for the scientific restraint of the *History*, or in laying aside the "science" of the latter for the metaphysical speculation of *Esther* or the prophetic forecasts of the *Education*, he may have thought of himself as pursuing different orders of truth. *Mont Saint Michel and Chartres* in particular becomes a locus of contention between science and sympathy (the way of art and popular religion)—between truths that can only be coldly seen and truths that can be felt; and early readers conventionally regarded Adams the historian as disjunct from Adams the literary artist. Adams the self-consciously scientific historian would not, perhaps, have relished being told that his magnum opus is manifestly poetic in structure or that the paradoxical valence of its verbal impression renders impossible the extraction of a clear, Hegelian thesis. Yet he was painfully aware during the composition of the *History* that his generalization resisted mathematical statement, and long before he adopted the guise of Conservative

Christian Anarchist he had come to the conclusion that discourse, however "scientific" or "rational," did not in practice conform to dialectics—whether those of Aristotle or of Hegel. However serious his pretense to science, however obsessive his later pursuit of monist explanations of all phenomena, his writings proceed in the more or less conscious conviction that their validity lies not so much in their approximate arrival at ultimate truth as in their power to focus, critique, and (however remotely) direct the moral evolution of the national community.

As he composed his more conventionally historical texts, Adams must at some level have been aware that the history he wrote lived by virtue of the language he invented for the occasion of its telling. The *History* may have its arid stretches, but its archly satiric and stunningly lyric passages betray the mark of the conscious performer who gloried in the *poesis*—the verbal inventiveness—from which his masterful effects patently derived. Neither in the *History* nor in his eclectic later works would Adams ever quite succeed in freeing the poetic bearing of his writing from his Comtean aspiration to create a science of history, to which he clung (as we shall see) with a highly rhetorical insistence; but that need not keep us from approaching his corpus as an essentially literary enterprise. In *Metahistory: The Historical Imagination in Nineteenth-Century Europe* (1973), Hayden White credits Nietzsche with dissociating the writing of history from any possible, positivist pursuit of objective truth and with locating the origins of historical consciousness "in a specifically poetic apprehension of reality."[1] White's work, building principally on Northrop Frye's *Anatomy of Criticism* and Kenneth Burke's *A Grammar of Motives*, has itself done much to reinforce the view that historical writing is *writing* and as such is governed by structures more conventionally associated with "literary" texts. If the recognition of the fundamentally poetic or textual nature of historical writing is still far from supplanting the notion that history, unlike "imaginative" literature, describes objectively "real" events, it cannot surprise us that Adams never entirely achieved a Nietzschean sense of the constitutive role of the historian's language. A tortured adherent to the nineteenth-century historicist view of human experience—the view that human experience must be seen as progressing toward some culmination, some ultimate disclosure of that experience's unitary meaning[2]—he could not abandon the notion that meaning is determined by something outside that experience, some "transcendental signified," to borrow Jacques Derrida's well-known phrase. "Always and everywhere the mind creates its own universe, and pursues its own phantoms," Adams wrote in "The Rule of Phase Applied to History" (1909), "but the force behind the image is always a reality" (*D* 310). Without such a hypostatized reality (to be assumed if not proven), Adams could not imagine the possibility of even a minimally stable and hence shareable language—the indispensable thread of social consensus.

If the view of historical writing as writing (poesis) helps prepare us for a Henry Adams whose science is always that of the nonmathematical literary man, the view of literature as social discourse keeps us from approaching him as a literary artist necessarily divorced from the public currents of his day. This is all the more important insofar as even in his most mandarin pretense to the "privacy and *abandon*" (*LHA* 6:63) of the nineteenth-century aesthete and even in what Ernest Samuels has distinguished as the symbolist character of his late style, Adams maintained an eighteenth-century sense of "literary language" as the medium of rational, purposive, public discussion.[3] Although I am indebted to Derrida for certain features of my operative notion of the "text," more importantly I think my analysis reflects the suggestiveness of Michel Foucault's conception of language as *discourse* and Mikhail Bakhtin's conception of language as *dialogic*: both serve to focus attention on the culturally engaged, pragmatic activity of language—a step crucial to any proper understanding of Henry Adams's vocational project.[4] In defining that project, I have also found useful Sacvan Bercovitch's recent redefinition of that peculiar ritual, the American jeremiad, for Adams's rhetoric is patently if inconclusively jeremiadical; yet I venture that Adams, caught so squarely in the late nineteenth-century "crisis of historicism," is ultimately more interesting for those rituals of affirmation that he developed outside of the jeremiad, which affirms as he finally could not the ultimate coherence of historical life.[5]

Following previous scholarship, my study takes the *Education* as the culminating moment of Adams's career, but my discussion of that work is aimed less at articulating the text's rich symbology (a task brilliantly performed by such commentators as Blackmur, Levenson, and, more recently, John Carlos Rowe) than at reading the text as a reflection of Adams's lifelong courtship of an audience. I treat the *Education* as at once the autobiography of Adams's literary vocation and that vocation's valedictory enactment. I define that vocation as one that compelled Adams to retain as his chief object the political and spiritual redemption of his American readership, even as the increasingly problematic nature of writing and publishing—the primary activities of authorship—complicated any simple, pragmatic intentionality that Adams might bring to his text. His "failure" in the *Education* to arrive at a redemptive reformulation of historical experience is bound up with his by then accustomed doubt of his ability to claim a readership and through it make a historical difference. Voiced throughout the *Education*, this doubt is dramatically reflected in the volume's peculiar publishing history: circulated privately in 1907 and

1908, it was withheld from general publication until after Adams's death in 1918. Still, I argue that Adams's acts of publishing the *Education* affirm his redemptive conception of authorial purpose, and that they do so precisely by placing that conception in jeopardy.

Espoused with frank idealism in young manhood, Adams's vocation was never unproblematic. In the post–Civil War years he clearly wished to work for the success of the democratic American experiment, but it was a success that he tended to envision in millennial terms whose bold outlines served to obscure details. Beyond the reform of Grantism (for an Adams simultaneously the eradication of Jacksonism), he was never entirely certain of his vocation's exact bearings: his intellectual, classically republican preference for strictly constitutional government and a primitively capitalist economy coexisted perilously with a desire that his country prosper materially and expand into a world presence. His recognition of the need for a distinctly American expression translated into little actual sympathy with nineteenth-century efforts to create a native culture. His earliest essays are divided between denunciation and affirmation, between the elegizing of lost enthusiasms and the projection of a future rectified American order. The work of his middle years would hazard the proposition of a visionary America shimmering above the mire of the (always) present crisis. His vocation however became increasingly unsupportable as the nineteenth century drew to a close: more and more, the polemicist who would purge public life of its interim corruptions and the historian who would celebrate the American emergence of a new human order found himself cut off from the ruling coteries of the new capitalist state and from an American public that seemed incapable of responsive readership and renovating initiative.

Still, we must not let Adams the ironist keep us from duly recognizing the major if always tentative project of his early middle years: to create a symbology by which the "national mind" might receive the impress of ideals and accept a vision of cultural possibilities that could be pragmatically applied to the task of creating a high national culture. The particular failures of *Esther* and the *History* to find a broad responsive readership lie at the center of Adams's vocational crisis, a crisis compounded, although certainly not caused, by Marian Hooper Adams's suicide in December 1885. Again, Adams's desire for a high visionary American civilization never translated into a precise vision of what, socially and economically, such a civilization might be, and in projecting the objects of American ambition he was never consistently able to distinguish possession of power from achievement of community. But he had never set out single-handedly to project the millennial America. Seeing always his task as collaborative, undertaken "in full partnership with the society of his age" (A I 724), and hence transcending his own necessarily incomplete efforts, he had counted upon his contemporaries and the coming generations to join in the projection and its realization: What else was there, wondered the visionary in him, for a young, rich, idealistically minded country to do? Increasingly he became aware that a visionary Adams—the Henry Adams of the optative mood—was mostly lost upon his own generation.

In midcareer he could hardly have foreseen that he would enter the American canon as one who helped clarify for the disaffected readerships of the early and middle twentieth century the repressions and impoverishments of an America made overly of money, the increasing perils of the technocratic will-to-power. Yet almost from the first Adams vacillated between two conflicting attitudes toward history: one that looks upon the human order as susceptible to high ideals and renascent cultural energies and one that regards that order as entrapped by its base impulses and therefore spiritually stultified, socially inert, and chaotic in proportion to its intellectual development and technological advance. Each view implies a different position and program for the historian-novelist-autobiographer. The first encourages him to envision and engender ideals among his audience and so participate in the creation of the new, millennial American order. The second promotes the detached observation of the "scientific" historian and designates, ultimately, the dying social organism as its object of study. Both attitudes are present in all of Adams's works, although the second, of course, gained ascendancy as he grew older. American democracy, much as Tocqueville ambivalently defined it, remains ever the central unknown of these alternate views of history. In the first, generative view, it figures as the liberation of natural genius suppressed by Old World class structure; in the second, it appears as the degradation of artistic capacity and the heroic ideals of a romantic individualism. Yet American democracy, for Adams, always constituted more than a historical force of undetermined character: it was the rhetorically determining condition of his literary effort, the audience to which he must ultimately publish his work or from which specifically withhold it.

Adams's late writings betray great anxiety with regard to historical continuity and democratic readership—a fear that the breaks in historical sequence must tear asunder text, author, and audience, revealing the inability of language to preserve the possibility of common social purpose. To read the *Education*, the "Rule," and *A Letter to American Teachers of History* is to be aware that Adams all but comes to disbelieve in the continued existence of such common human ground as the author-reader relation minimally requires. Inevitably we must ask: Who, in the last decades of the twentieth century, reads this work and to what purpose? No reader perhaps becomes interested in Adams who does not already feel the vertigo of historical experience or who has not known the sensation of residing at the margin of cultural participation or who has not felt other than his or her own contemporary society.[6] Some readers may well accept Adams's crisis of historicism as their own. More, perhaps, regard Adams's pursuit of unity in the cosmos and directionality in history to be dated or simply fruitless—a totalizing project that reflects Adams's legitimate fears of social disintegration but that also gives rise to that strain in his writing that is willing to deny legitimacy to those who fall outside of his kind of people or to thinking that does not coincide with his version of the march of Western thought. Perhaps what is most oppressive in Adams's thought is best read as rivaling, and so unmasking, the totalizing projects of the finance capitalist or political tyrant. Yet, as I shall argue, there are limits to which Adams's work may be celebrated as the demystifying satire of the prevailing discourses of power.

Both destructive and constructive responses to the problems of Western imperial culture are to be found in the Adams corpus: his lesson resolves into multiples at the last. For American readers, among the most compelling of his works' lessons must be those that address the difficulties of living with the failure of a peculiarly American historicism. The collapse of the grand designs that were his as an American, an Adams, an heir to Enlightenment thought, may have led to a rather vengeful monism, but it also made intermittently possible his sympathetic apprehension of that life which existed outside the bounds of the historicist frame: that of the gifted American woman, the colonized non-"Aryan," the common European "multiple," whose one comfort lay in the Virgin's unqualified love. His espousal of such may be cited as examples of a fundamentally humane imagination. And a persistent, indeed heroic, affirmation may be felt in the wonderfully self-regenerative (if "perverse") manner by which he came to dwell as *other* committed to addressing the "great problems" of the society that he rightly perceived had gone off after idols antithetical to his own. But his lesson as a permanently marginal voice also drives home the perilous tentativity of our accustomed sense of historical placement. If our continued reading of his texts refutes his worst suspicions of the disintegrative tendencies of modern life, it cannot help but deepen our awareness of the historical continuities we affirm as we read and of the disciplined deliberation this activity requires.

It is my own conviction that any conscientious life finds itself at least some of the time on the margin and hence able to benefit from an encounter with Henry Adams. My desire for an audience is not therefore materially different from Adams's: like him I write with the hope that my work will prove useful not only to a specialist audience but to a general educated readership. The drama and moment of the life of the mind have never been confined to the academy. My inquiry into the rhetorical dimensions of Adams's vocation is (unavoidably) also a narrative of what I believe to be a singularly illustrative instance in the nation's intellectual history. If that history has been typically one of ambition and disappointment, it has also been one of improvisation and renewal—the more impressive for coming unforeseen. It is therefore no accident that my narrative begins and ends with Adams's retirement from all set forms to which literary ambition had in his time been conventionally held.

1

Retirement from Authorship

Outward-Bound

WHEN HENRY ADAMS embarked upon a year-long tour of the South Seas in August 1890, he had reason to consider his public duties discharged and his life, for all but personal purposes, behind him. Judged by the number of volumes he had authored, that life had been an unusually productive one. Two biographies, the nine-volume *History of the United States during the Administrations of Jefferson and Madison,* and a collection of historical essays made up his avowed literary contribution. With such accomplishments, the question of whether he should ever receive credit for his two novels—the first published anonymously, the second under a pseudonym—could not have been urgent. In fact, his peculiar wish with regard to the fiction was that it not be identified as his while he was still alive, lest he should have to answer, as a living author, for texts that touched a period of his life from which his wife's death had left him estranged. The prospect of his already massive correspondence becoming available to general readership probably did not often cross his mind; when it did, it must have seemed preposterous or remote.[1] Aware in 1890 that his departure from Washington marked a great turning point, he yet could barely make out the longer itinerary that lay before him, much less foresee the two masterworks upon which his fame would most rest in the century to come.

From our vantage late in that century, we can contemplate this outward-bound Henry Adams with retrospective foreknowledge of what was to follow the apparent hiatus of 1890 to 1904, the year *Mont Saint Michel and Chartres* first appeared. We can see that this fourteen-year period would be one of constant literary activity—an authorship that would document, frequently against an exotic setting, a chaotic emotional and intellectual passage. Viewed retrospectively, the varied departures that characterize this period draw ironic attention to all that he could not put behind him: his pen, his Adams identity, and his desire for a responsive, national audience. Of his active if ambivalent return to such apparently fixed principles of himself *The Education of Henry Adams* constitutes the lasting monument, and with this book in our possession it is only too easy to ascribe a false inevitability to the completed sequence of its author's work. Not to do so, however, is crucial to an appreciation of his early as well as his later writings, the continued freshness of which lies in their unforeseeability, their responsiveness to what they take as their historical condition, their increasingly desperate enactment of the desire that history be determined by our discussion of it. Although Adams's work always took unpredictable turns, the late texts come particularly unforeseen, the writings through the *History* only sketchily intimating the achievement's final shape. To be sure, the fascination with the "eternal woman" that he had cultivated as historian and novelist anticipates *Mont Saint Michel and Chartres* and pivotal features of the *Education*'s symbology. But these late works take their distinctive tones from the circumstances contemporaneous with their composition: the economic fluctuations that rocked America in 1893, the intensification of imperialist rivalries, the mood of fin-de-siècle Paris. As for the *Education*, although Adams had established in a January 1884 letter to John Hay that he meant to write and thereby "murder" his own life, he could hardly then anticipate the full motive or the means by which he would make good the intention.[2]

Yet to say that in 1890 Henry Adams could not foresee the books to come does little to recapture the poise of the man who in August of that year gazed at the blank Pacific from San Francisco Bay and who would spend the next year and much of the next decade gazing at an ocean horizon between landfalls. If his course proved unforeseeable, it was largely because he willed it to be so. By choosing to leave his Washington residence for indefinite wanderings in the world's far corners, he sought to remove himself from a routine of set sorrows and a life whose main burden, the completion of the *History*, had absorbed the last energies of an outworn ambition. But from our viewpoint, the earliest specific anticipation of Adams's later career lies in a statement through which he wills a change more fundamental than travel per se could bring on. The statement is his renunciation, upon completing the *History*, of authorship itself.

"With the year 1890," he declared to Henry Holt five months prior to departure, "I shall retire from authorship" (*LHA* 3:225). Since its occasion was the tedious final preparation of the manuscript for press, the statement even more profoundly signals the author's withdrawal from twenty-five years of expectations and disappointments centering upon what he could and could not do as an Adams who had taken up the pen. What, for Adams, was authorship? What, by 1890, had become of a calling from which he needed to retire in order to keep his life open, his pen active? What new life, education, writings were made possible in direct consequence of his retirement? These questions will be with us for the length of the study, but we begin to address all three the moment we take on the first, for "authorship" is the one term that comprehends a long and otherwise fragmentary life. Authorship is the vocation Henry Adams assumed in youth, the work chosen with specific, albeit shifting, personal and social aims. Although his first published articles generally serve a distinctly polemical purpose, and although his mature historical writings aspire to a severe scientific aesthetic, he understood from the start the poetic nature and license of literary discourse, and in his earliest surviving correspondence demonstrates to himself the paradoxical tendencies of language. He was always aware that authorship gave itself to a multitude of rhetorical possibilities. From the start Adams seems subconsciously to have recognized that authorship, much more than statesmanship, compelled ongoing invention, that of a speaker and that of the world he would address.

If in choosing the pen he diverged from the legal and statesmanly calling of his male ancestors and brothers, the texts he produced reveal vigorous acceptance of family doctrine and social imperatives. Yet almost from the first, Adams's authorship was characterized by tensions between his various, largely inherited vocational aims and the texts that he dispatched to bring about the realization of those aims. Nearly always the text seemed inadequate, given the evident obtuseness of readers or the simple absence of a readership and given Adams's own consequent suspicion of his aims as an author. Early and late Adams's self-suspicion is present in his work as an ambivalence embracing contradictory motives— one that affirmed the Enlightenment aspiration to master the course of history and one that denied it—and that ambivalence always arose from and returned to the question of audience. As much as he came to affect the alleged detachment of scientist and artist, a readership was ever a necessity; his sense of audience always determined his idea of himself as author and so served as the principal factor shaping his texts. This, as we shall see, holds true whether his audience is the imagined intelligent readership of a still-young republic or an aging fellow of his own moribund generation. In fact, we find Adams's sensitivity to his reader even more acute after retirement from authorship had become for him the private metaphor of his life, the new discipline that opened his self-styled "posthumous" existence to the possibilities of fresh and (again) unforeseeable creation.

By retiring from authorship in 1890, Adams withdrew from a vocation whose doctrines and enthusiasms the completed text of the *History* had variously consumed. Brought to a close five years into Adams's widowerhood, amid the death of his mother and an isolation relieved only by companions with whom he shared no forward-looking ideal, the *History* betrays an anticlimax that Adams freely admitted. Although the tone of the last chapters does little to suggest it, the nine-volume work had been conceived twelve years earlier as a high contribution to a future national order. Like the biographies and novels, it had emerged from the premise that authorship, alternatingly castigating and celebratory, could serve as a form of statecraft—one that proceeded at a decided remove from the political arena that had drawn and disappointed four generations of Adamses. As political journalist, Henry Adams himself had skirted the edge of that arena. He had prepared annual reviews of Congress; authored, with his brother Charles, exposés of Grant-era corruption; and served the reform cause as editor of the *North American Review*. He and some friends twice attempted to acquire controlling interest in a Boston newspaper. The abrupt reversals to which the collaborative effort of politics is prone frustrated Adams in the long run, while the solid gains of the reform movement appeased his activist impulse. As an assistant professor at Harvard from 1871 to 1877, he found himself increasingly drawn toward the less immediately public questions of historical scholarship. Freed financially by his marriage to Marian Hooper, he was able in 1877 to withdraw from university teaching and establish himself in the nation's capital as an independent scholar, as a society man with invisible political leverage, and as a concealed novelist free to project horrific, if also exalted, versions of the national destiny. At his most sanguine, he was able to imagine himself as a charter member of an emergent American intelligentsia, one of several prophetic sources "of that great light which is to dazzle and set the world on fire hereafter" (*LHA* 2:326). As he conceived it in the expansive moods of his early middle age, Adams's vocational aim was to help father what early in the *History* he would call "the America of thought and art": the secular, millennial order of which Jefferson and Gallatin (but also John and John Quincy Adams) dreamed and whose partial realization Henry Adams saw as his post–Civil War generation's supreme task.

To realize "the America of thought and art" would be to establish the United States among what for Adams were the elite civilizations of Western history: Greece, Rome, and England. To be sure, the ambition partook of the current enthusiasm for America's prospective emergence as a world power. Yet Adams had serious, republican qualms over the imperialist implications of such an emergence. Power, a hegemony exceeding continental bounds, great material wealth—these could exist independently of a high intellectual and moral order, and it was ever Adams's worry that they were likely to thrive at the higher order's expense. American nationality remained an inalienable, if troubled, article in Adams's system of belief, one that retained a reflex allegiance that his eventual disillusionment could never quite root out. Because of this allegiance, Adams's thought could never work free of the conflict implicit in his demand for public morality and his suspicion that power relations follow an inevitable, amoral course—one, after 1898, troublingly favorable to American supremacy. His ambivalence here lays bare the innermost workings of conservative American ideology in its transformation from republican doctrine to aggressive capitalist practice, and the contradictions comprise for Adams a kind of ideological subconscious, constantly flickering at the edge of recognition, receiving only momentarily the attention of his whole mind.

Contradiction and disillusionment are more commonly associated with the elderly Adams, but his idealistically conceived nationalist vocation was troubled from the start. No unshakable faith in American character and progress abides beneath Adams's satire of post–Civil War Washington in *Democracy* or beneath the now tragic, now sickly light reflected in the mirror for magistrates that he created in his studies of Gallatin and Randolph. Certainly Adams felt the recurrent appeals of national faith, but he compelled himself to earn and re-earn that faith intellectually. Even in the young man, faith had to answer to "science," a positivism that reinforced ironic and reductive perspective, encouraging him to think in terms of an inevitable course of events. Not surprisingly, as his historiography became more aspiringly scientific, it tended to curb what may be called the poesis of his national desire, and intellect and faith fell into an increasingly rigid antithetical relation. Beyond the first six (prologue) chapters of the *History*, "science" steadily deflated the human drama of the *History*, voicing Adams's deep suspicion of the moral and imaginative capacity that alone could foster an "America of thought and art."[3] Only with the *History* behind him did Adams begin to see through the disguise of scientific history and to perceive that aspects of his temperament, and an experience touched by bereavement and isolation, contributed to the loss of his vocational vision. Still, he could never become absolutely impervious to that vision's appeal. After he had lost sight of that "great light which is to dazzle" the modern world, he retained a certain dry ambition for the masterwork of his middle years that matched his tired allegiance to his country. Having written consciously for "a continent of a hundred million people fifty years hence," Adams could believe that he had at least established a "foundation" on which future historians could effectively build (*LHA* 2:535; 5:39).

Retirement in some form might well be the natural outcome of any such monumental achievement as the *History*. A certain fatalism is bound to accompany the completion of a work whose success (however measured) lies beyond its immediate reception, in an epoch the author is obliged to fix beyond his life expectancy. The rhetorical appeal to an audience "fifty years hence" finds its "scientific" rationale in Adams's contention that one must wait that long before drawing conclusions with respect to the democratic experiment. The appeal, however, cannot but project the historian's absence; in so doing, it confirms that author and completed text have fallen out of living relation—that Adams is "dead" to his creation. The "death of the author" has become a commonplace of postmodernist criticism, one that has usefully challenged the practice of viewing the literary personality—romantic poet, Victorian sage, or modernist artist—as the origin and ultimate substantiation of discourse.[4] Adams's middle-to-late authorial pose incorporates elements of artist and sage yet intuits the textual dispersions of ego that theorists have only recently explored. No doubt his intuitions came to him in part as the bearer of a name that preempted even as it signified him; a name by which (in the case of his novels) he could significantly decline to sign his text, and one that in any case he could never simply inscribe. But Adams's retirement from authorship reflects more than his frustration in bearing a name that suggested increasingly vague public claims upon him, more than the experience of creating texts that took on, in the course of their production, an independent life. For reasons that we shall soon explore, the "science" of the *History* would in almost any event have had to negate Adams's expansively envisioned literary vocation. Still, the peculiar course of Adams's retirement traces its strongest impulse to an event that Adams the author eventually did everything he could to live down: the suicide of Marian Hooper Adams in 1885.

In one way or another, Marian Adams's death has always been seen as the principal determinant of Adams's later development. His elaborate and protracted mourning, his conceit that, from the moment of his wife's death, he could lead only a posthumous life, have done everything to encourage such a view. What we know about Clover Adams and her troubled relationships with father and spouse subjects her suicide to endless if always inconclusive speculation. Yet we can see how her death serves as key to Henry Adams's full development only insofar as we can grasp Adams's widowerhood in terms of the symbology he himself created from it. Specifically, in this study I wish to see the event in relation to Adams's self-identity as (retired) author and to discover its place in the long drama of his recovered authorship. From the first months of his bereavement, Adams was given to viewing his widowerhood in metaphors that drew upon his practice as author, even as he assessed his future possibilities as author with reference to his widower status. Although these possibilities are depicted as essentially lost, the loss is expressed in a paradoxical language that prefigures Adams's restored activity.

In a letter dated March 8, 1886, Adams responds to a condolence letter from Henry Holt, who as the publisher of *Democracy* and *Esther* was one of the few who knew the novels' authorship. In characterizing his bereavement, the historian and novelist speaks of a now bygone sensitivity to reviewers: "Thanks for your letter. I am almost amused at the idea of my caring now for anything that so-called critics could say. When the only chapter of one's story for which one cares is closed forever, locked up, and put away, to be kept, as a sort of open secret, between oneself and eternity, one does not think much of newspapers" (*LHA* 3:5). The date of this letter surely identifies that "only chapter . . . for which one cares" as one whose closure corresponds to Marian Adams's death and its abrupt abrogation of the thirteen-year marriage. Yet the moment we inquire after that chapter's specific content we must pause. Although for Adams it clearly possessed particular features and an overriding urgency, to the degree that it remains unwritten the chapter can hardly be said to have outline, much less closure. Inasmuch as Adams's mention of "the only chapter of one's story for which one cares" occurs in a letter to Holt and inasmuch as he alludes to newspaper reviewers, *Esther* certainly figures in the correspondence to which this letter belongs.[5] Yet Adams significantly does not equate "the only chapter" with *Esther*; he speaks, rather, of his life as a book made up of chapters—a book whose evident moral is that Adams (as mortal) could not sufficiently author it. "The only chapter" was not a particular text but a term Adams used to designate that which he considered unwritable yet which alone had value for him. It represented the possibility of a story that would have meaning to the degree that he could share it, and, although he looked upon it as an aborted possibility, he never left off pursuing its rescue. He could never abandon his pen, making good his vows of silence; the unwritable therefore always to some extent eventually appeared in print.

The first designation of "the only chapter," however, did take the form of an already established text—Adams's second novel written two years before his bereavement. The heroine, drawn in part from Marian Hooper Adams, represents visionary American possibilities traduced by the conservative American male who will not marry the heroine on her terms.[6] Since Marian's suicide in 1885, *Esther* had become for Adams a sacred object, shared exclusively and perhaps only through correspondence with Clarence King, John Hay, and Elizabeth Cameron. In an 1891 letter to Mrs. Cameron from Tahiti, Adams claimed that he cared "more for one chapter, or any dozen pages of Esther than for the whole History, including maps and indexes; so much more, indeed, that I would not let anyone read the story for fear the reader should profane it" (*LHA* 3:409). This statement bears striking resemblance to what he had written in his letter to Holt. In both letters, Adams claims that a slender portion of (variously) a long life or a vast output means more to him than all else and that the value of "the only chapter" may be preserved only as he can withhold it. Beyond the heroine's clear resemblance to Marian Adams, there are other reasons that *Esther* might be the first designated textual incarnation of "the only chapter." The established text allows him to share it with such reverence and exclusivity as can serve to affirm its sacral qualities. And by confining it to an established text, he can possess that chapter as a suppressible article; one that, having been significantly shared, he can withhold if not unwrite. In the letter to Mrs. Cameron, Adams marks the early phases of a retirement in which he was anxious to view his life up to 1890 as a closed book. Yet he was never able to cite a text without opening it. Taken together, the two letters suggest that "the only chapter of one's story for which one cares" is at most written in part and anything but closed.

When Adams put his life in sequence in the *Education*, he supposedly left twenty years unwritten: the long period of sustained authorship he compressed into a few misleading sentences, while of his married life and bereavement he says nothing—directly. Before, however, we inquire after what the *Education* specifically withholds, we should observe the extent to which that book reverses the abdications of authorship found in the letters to Holt and Mrs. Cameron. As do all his writings dating from 1890, the *Education* enacts Adams's continued authorship, but with a self-consciousness commensurate with the book's manifest public directedness. Adams's continued authorship may have been always shadowed by the moral that he could never sufficiently author his life, but his ongoing activity implies that he did have a chapter—perhaps many chapters promising to cohere in a unified story—for which he cared sufficiently to write. And write, moreover, with specific audiences in mind: upon the *Education*'s completion, the author circulated a "private" edition among an elite that included the president of the United States, and before his death he duly prepared an edition that could serve as the basis for the book's posthumous release to the general public. As we shall see in Chapter 2, Adams's profound ambivalence toward his multiple projections of audience appears at times to threaten the text's very existence. But here let us note that whereas the specific content of an unwritten, closed chapter must be fundamentally unrecoverable, such is not the problem that materially confronts Adams's reader. By the time he came to write the *Education*, the opening and enlargement of "the only chapter" had become the retired author's central activity. The omission of twenty years could suppress little more than the ostensibly literal and private origins of what Adams saw as his great public lesson: that the best education, most privileged social rank, most idealistically conceived vocation and energetic pen may come to nothing in a world where a dehumanized pursuit of power has spent society's renascent capacities—capacities evidenced by such communal initiative as built the cathedrals and launched the American experiment.

Adams's twenty-year omission discourages the reduction of his lesson to private biography; our being thus discouraged is crucial to his success in persuading us that his singular life story possesses extraordinary public relevance. In part, the *Education*'s success lies in making us see that Marian Adams's death could only anchor Adams's pen in the darker courses already open to it. Perhaps such anchorage imposed the discipline that kept Adams from becoming the mere creature and victim of the forces with which he had contended since young manhood. In any case, it was only with the *History*'s completion that Adams could permit himself to meditate at length upon the difficulties of sustaining a public authorship when the content of his text was so bleak. Only then could he suspect his own complicity in the dehumanization of the historical subject; only then could he admit intuitions that were his as party to a frustrating and tragic marriage. The *Education* would constitute the valedictory, agonized, and evasive statement of his belated authorial self-consciousness. Yet, in the discussion ahead, we shall see that marital failure and the progressive vitiation of national ideals had assumed central and analogical, if not yet fully stateable, placement in Adams's thought long before Marian's death. An author given more to vital recognitions than plain affirmation, the retired Adams would come to see and gradually measure the extent to which death had begun to possess his thought, which had once moved to the appeal of generative myths and possibilities. Such recognitions would become the substance of "the only chapter of one's story for which one cares," elaborated through a sequence of writings whose insistent materialization must have surprised him. Whatever his ambivalence toward public authorship, Adams could not keep these writings from becoming public testimony.

The extent to which death possessed his thought and threatened his continued authorship is particularly visible in the chilly subtext of the *History*'s final pages. The principal (but unstated) question of the magnum opus had been whether society evolves in response to creative human initiative or in accord with immutable physical law. Among the philosophical inquiries that Henry Adams inherited as an Adams, this question had assumed special urgency in the light of nineteenth-century science and politics; it figures as centrally in his earliest correspondence as it does in his late speculative works. Although he might try to approach it in a spirit of neutral inquiry, subjecting it to the alternate hypotheses of his historical science, the issue could never be purged of its moral dimensions.[7] The tension between a view of history as (within limits) free, creative, and morally answerable and one that reduces human experience to a mechanistic evolution is subtly reflected in the famous sets of questions the historian asks of American destiny at the commencement and close of the *History.* With a detachment that cannot conceal his own visionary appreciation of human initiative—his own sense of participation in a large national task—Adams had asked, at the end of "American Ideals" (the last in his sequence of prologue chapters), the following of the American nation ushered in by Jefferson's 1801 ascendancy: "Could it transmute its social power into the higher forms of thought? . . . Could it give new life to religion and art? Could it create and maintain in the mass of mankind those habits of mind which had hitherto belonged to men of science alone? . . . Could it produce, or was it compatible with, the differentiation of a higher variety of the human race? Nothing less than this," he appended pointedly, "was necessary for its complete success" (A II 125).

If the closing stipulation of the prologue chapters was not without a certain measure of foreboding, the questions that conclude the last six epilogue chapters imply that, by the end of the second Madison administration, a drastic revision of expectations was in order. By 1815, Adams affirmed, Americans had shown themselves to be distinctly "scientific"; but "what control would their science exercise over their destiny?" This question acquires urgency from two others which focus skeptically on the nation's moral will. In certain respects, the historian concedes, it had been advantageous for the American people to have become religiously mild, "but what corruption" he asks with the seventy intervening years clearly in view, "would their relaxations bring? They were peaceful, but by what machinery were their corruptions to be purged?" In the end, the historian who nine volumes earlier had written glowingly of Jefferson's and Gallatin's conception of an "America of thought and art" found himself reduced to asking, "What interests were to vivify a society so vast and uniform? What ideals were to ennoble it? What object, besides physical content, must a democratic continent aspire to attain?" (A III 1345).

In the *History*'s final sentence, Adams declares that a full century must elapse from 1815 (the year that marked the country's emergence from the War of 1812) before history could treat such questions. Yet a question's treatment begins with the way it is phrased, and the analysis that forms the context of Adams's questions can leave little doubt as to the tendency of his thought. "The inertia of several hundred million people, all formed in a similar social mold, was as likely to stifle energy as to stimulate evolution" (A III 1335). From the perspective of 1890, twenty-five years short of the full century mark, the stifling of the higher expressions of energy appears foregone, and Adams's susceptibility to the myth of cosmic de-creation presents itself decidedly. He is still a long way from the entropy thesis of *A Letter to American Teachers of History*, but the valedictory rhetoric by which he would habitually separate himself from the age of the dynamo in the twenty-eight years left to him makes its first solemn appearance. "No historian," writes Adams, more or less consciously bidding adieu to the orthodox writing of history, "cared to hasten the coming of an epoch when man should study his own history in the same spirit and by the same methods with which he studied the formation of a crystal. Yet history had its scientific as well as its human side, and in American history the scientific interest was greater than the human [for] nowhere could [the student] study so well the evolution of a race. The interest of such a subject exceeded that of any other branch of science, for it brought mankind within sight of its own end" (A III 1334).

The leave-taking is complex, compelled as much by the moral degradation his object of study implicitly manifests as by what Adams sees as the increasingly austere course a scientific historiography must pursue. The specific opposition the passage turns upon is that of "scientific" to "heroic" history. In the heroic historiography of the Old World, the powerful individual was treated as the representative of his rigidly hierarchical society; he was a colorful, if generally immoral or amoral, figure. As the artificial barrier of class falls away and the natural tendency of the race is released through the democratization of institutions, heroic and poetic historiography becomes obsolete. In Adams's judgment, it ought and will unquestionably be replaced by a scientific historiography equipped to focus on the broadest human grouping—the race. What about his own practice in view of this great transition? As Adams himself points out, the *History* is the product of an eclectic methodology, partly poetic, partly scientific. Given the state of historical discourse, he has had no choice but to proceed with a transitional historiography. Yet he suggests that such a historiography has served well the task of depicting a transitional period in which "national character" evolved from a population whose traits (as Adams claimed in the prologue) could be best read in the features of its leaders. "For that reason," Adams explains, "in the story of Jefferson and Madison individuals retained their old interest as types of character, if not as sources of power" (A III 1335).

Yet Adams's transitional historiography is more than merely serviceable: it subtly depicts the *History*'s central moral drama. At some level, the historian must have felt personally the clause, "if not as sources of power." American society had permitted the emergence of men who were at once moral and able, but their practical influence had been limited by regional rivalries, the jealousies of party politics, and, most of all, the narrowly self-interested movements of a largely unconscious electorate. When the able man's power dissolves and becomes the property of a democratic commons, human history becomes subject to scientific treatment. But for Henry Adams it also marks the point at which practical democracy (as opposed to the visionary republicanism of Jefferson or John Adams) loses its great moral opportunity. With Nathan Gore, the patrician historian of his first novel, Adams could affirm that democracy, notwithstanding its corruptions, was the one human experiment currently worth making, but its tendency to frustrate the same able men whom its deliverance from Old World class structure had allowed to rise was to be lamented. In the stultification of such gifted individuals as Gallatin and Jefferson much was lost to the public realm. For the insurgents of 1801 (as well as for John Quincy Adams twenty-five years later) it meant no centrally planned internal improvements, no national university. For Jefferson as for his historian, another gifted man promoted and yet marginalized by the long-term operations of American democracy, it meant no imminent "America of thought and art." Beyond the Republic's founding and the excitements of early nationhood, which lent so much credence to the idea that a people properly guided could create the history it desired, the democratic order appeared to move autonomously, in accord with no able man's, no natural aristocracy's, vision and will and in flagrant disregard of the supposedly binding principles articulated in that most sacred of secular texts, the U.S. Constitution.

Such autonomous movement, Adams thought, could and should be treated as a natural phenomenon. But to treat it as such, as he had begun to appreciate fully perhaps only as he brought the *History* to a close, had devastating consequences for the historian. As the ultimate object of historical knowledge, "national character" comes to represent more than the mere collectivization of the individual, more than the dilution of the able man submersed in the mass of the all-too-human mob. It is the first step in the dehumanization of the object studied, a dehumanization reinforced in such notions as "race" and in such phrasings as the "inertia of several hundred million people" and "democratic ocean."[8] According to this line of thought, democratization culminates when its ablest men conceive human progress after the model of the crystal, whose illustrative paradox is that it is dead and yet capable of growth. From the knowing subject's standpoint, the supreme tragedy in viewing history as determined lies in the coercive methods by which one must study the human crystal's formation. Authorship as creation, as contribution to a human social organism susceptible to intelligent shaping, becomes extinct. To the historian there remain only the tasks of formulation and prediction, the refinement of a history that is known before the fact—a master text that discourages intervention in the course of events it allows us too perfectly to foresee. Of course Adams no more than any historian could care "to hasten the coming of an epoch" that would put humanity "within sight of its own end." American teleologies, whether articulated by Cotton Mather, John Adams, or Walt Whitman, always throve on the bright mist in which the imagination gladly lost sight of the New World's latter days. The aforequoted passage from the *History*'s conclusion is true to a pattern that recurs throughout Adams's later correspondence and books: valediction delivered in the face of an apocalypse that has not quite yet arrived (and for Adams will never definitively arrive) but is expected at any moment.

Travels

As metaphor, retirement from authorship serves as a kind of specific clause to the larger metaphor by which Adams defined his life as widower—that he was dead to the world insofar as it solicited his active interest and participation, however much he might appear to go through the forms of his old existence. He considered the completion of the *History* just such a fulfillment of form. If the writing of certain episodes (particularly the naval campaigns of the War of 1812) rekindled a semblance of former enthusiasms, the project as a whole belonged, as he wrote Elizabeth Cameron from Tahiti in 1891, "to the *me* of 1870" (*LHA* 3:408; unless otherwise noted throughout, italics appear as in original). Retiring from authorship meant withdrawing from the role of public author and from the illusion of a responsive readership. It meant the discontinuation of what had become a bleak testimony to a vague public, one whose very readership that testimony had come to dismiss. Retirement permitted Adams to shed his professionally grave attire as a public historian with an inherited mandate, give up his classical restraint in the face of an America that was going bad. What it at no time meant was any actual abandonment of the pen; in time, of course, that pen would recover its bleak testimony and mandated solicitudes. But retirement from authorship did mean changing the terms, purpose, and audience of his writings. And to the extent that it entailed such change, retirement constituted the focal gesture of an elaborate ritual of rebirth.

Between the completion of the *History* and composition of *Mont Saint Michel and Chartres*, Adams's achievements are those of correspondent, ghostwriter of *Memoirs of Arii Taimai*, poet of "Buddha and Brahma," and president of and preceptor to the American Historical Association—his address, "The Tendency of History," delivered to his colleagues in characteristic absentia. The titles and occasions of these texts (as well as of *Mont Saint Michel and Chartres,* the first of the two masterworks they would prepare for) articulate Adams's incessant state of transit. The travels of Adams's widowerhood became compulsive, motivated by his dual need to break through to fresh and revitalizing realities and to absent himself from old and deadening ones, where his continued existence could be only too "posthumous." His travel motive may have been at first simply recuperative, but from the start choice of itinerary and travel terminology make his movements an ironic commentary upon the broad patterns of Puritan and American emigration.[9] In the summer after his wife's death, Adams spurned the well-known ocean to the east, which he had crossed and recrossed in Marian's company, and took the more pioneer departure west to Japan. As the *History* remained unfinished, this first journey to the Far East could be only a trial run. But the trial, uncomfortable and unsuccessful in its pursuit of nirvana as Adams observed upon his return, did make him "earnest to close up everything here, finish history, cut society, foreswear strong drink and politics, and start in about three years for China, never to return. China," he proceeded to gloss, "is the great unknown country of the world"; he meant "to enter the celestial kingdom by that road" (*LHA* 3:49, 44).

With his long New England genealogy, he ironically assumed the role of pilgrim. Yet beneath his compulsive quest for "amusement" there subsisted a genuinely religious drive to confront ultimate realities, although one peculiarly Victorian in its agonized agnosticism. Adams's correspondence reveals that travel for him held out the possibility of metaphysical transport beyond the accustomed skepticism and "science" of his mental reflex. Travel constituted the otherworldly escape for the American historian whose last professional tasks lay in demolishing the basis of belief in an American exceptionalism, in grimly yet dutifully hastening the arrival of that "epoch when man should study his own history in the same spirit and by the same methods with which he studied the formation of a crystal." Freeing himself, through his "death," from an America with which history and death had caught up, Adams "set out, after the manner of Ulysses, in search of that new world which is the old" (*LHA* 3:53).

The Ulysses whose manner he would adopt owes much to Tennyson, who invested the Greek hero with a restlessness particularly British and imperial: an adventurer-in-decline driven to seek "a newer world." Equipped with the Homeric texts, Adams did attempt to recover the antiquity of Odysseus upon arrival in Samoa. Comparing the islanders to the lost heroic races of the Mediterranean, he concluded that South Seas culture represented an even more archaic stage, and, beneath his quasi-scientific posture, the retired historian began his investigations into the cosmo-

gony of the old, matrifocal worlds. Samoa particularly offered a broad
field for ethnographic observations and speculation concerning the birth
and archaic virtues of the human family. Having in the *History* recently
projected the frigid "end" of human movement in the New World, he now
sought in the non-European Old World the warm origins of human time.
His long diary letters to Elizabeth Cameron and John Hay show that the
journey, undertaken in the company of the artist John La Farge, proved
immediately restorative.[10] The delight Adams took in the exotic surfaces
of these far-flung worlds, in their social orders and histories as he came to
know them, and in the frank eros of the native dance of which he was a
welcomed spectator, is manifested by the sheer volume of correspondence
he produced. No author upon completion of a major project could hope
for a more thorough rebirth than that which compelled Adams's pen in
the South Seas, where it was not unusual for him to write in three-hour
sittings nor too inconvenient for him to transcribe his impressions while
tossing in a native canoe amid the reefs. Nevertheless, a persistent plain-
tive note sounds beneath the rich compilation of observed detail, one
which registers boredom with remote surroundings, a failure to let go of
the old life, and an inability to sustain the figure of bachelor tourist.

There was no stepping out of time, no earthly ultimate haven. As he
concedes in his poem "Buddha and Brahma," written on board ship during the return journey, he could not yet be claimed by such renunciation of
self and world, such cultivated immunity to historical process, as the Ori-
ent had attractively symbolized from afar and as he himself had asked
Augustus Saint-Gaudens to capture in the monument for Marian's grave
during his absence. His life would remain agonizingly but also vitally dual:

> . . . we, who cannot fly the world, must seek
> To live two separate lives; one, in the world
> Which we must ever seem to treat as real;
> The other in ourselves, behind a veil
> Not to be raised without disturbing both.
>
> (A I 1200)

His attempt to fly the world would of course never so nicely subside in
the resolution to seek and support two separate lives. The world of historical being and becoming, of bright surface and mysterious generation,
retained ever an erotic interest, one sustained and yet finally dissipated
in the traveler's perpetual motion. As he had no wife to hold him to a
particular place, his wanderings might go on forever, a continual pilgrimage to the globe's scattered nuptials, at which he should never count as
anything more than a welcomed guest. His impossible love for Elizabeth
Cameron, the increasingly estranged wife of Senator Donald Cameron of

Pennsylvania, confirmed the permanence of his solitary existence. Incapable of asceticism, he allowed the world to draw him on and yet keep him miserably at one remove within its circles of intimacy. Only with his arrival at Chartres would his career as roving celibate-observer find some mitigation.

In journeying to the South Seas in 1890, Adams entered a world upon which the hammerlock of European colonialism had long been fastened. Except in Samoa, where Adams's attendance at the *siva* was permitted only after his repeated assurance that he and La Farge were not missionaries, native expression had been suppressed as part of a total subjugation of the islands. Decline of births and the outlawing of traditional dance suggested to Adams the particularly sexual repression of the colonial regimes. Evidence of the European dominion over these islands provided substance upon which Adams's discontent could work openly. While he had always possessed the ability to free one foot and take a half step away from the broadly Western ideology of manifest destiny, in the South Seas he spent considerable time with both feet nearly out of the mesh. Never before had Adams so strongly felt the appeal of the cultural other, an appeal made the more urgent by that other's visible perishability. In the *History* he had observed, with something of the social Darwinist's detachment, that "no acid ever worked more mechanically on a vegetable fibre than the white man acted on the Indian" (A III 343). Yet nothing had heretofore so driven home the scope of the West's acculturation of its subject peoples or the death and corruption colonialism brought. To the isolated islands the European had introduced "virulent diseases which had been developed among the struggling masses of Asia and Europe" and which rapidly killed off the native population. "For this," wrote Adams for Arii Taimai, "the foreigners were not wholly responsible, although their civilization certainly was; but for the political misery the foreigner was wholly to blame, and for the social and moral degradation he was the active cause" (T 137).

Drawing upon his own chronic state of bereavement, Adams's observations of a vanishing native order released his elegiac sympathies, especially as that native order was personified in Arii Taimai, the "archaic woman" herself and matriarch of the Tevas, the displaced ruling clan. Acquaintance with the family rescued Adams from a boredom that threatened to become neurasthenic during his last weeks in Tahiti. His admission into their circle culminated in their formal adoption of him, an affection he returned by writing, based on Arii Taimai's oral accounts, *Memoirs of Marau Taaroa, Last Queen of Tahiti* (1893; later revised, retitled *Memoirs of Arii Taimai*, and privately printed in 1901), which traces the family's history and documents the island's decline. The voice of island tradition that Adams endeavored to translate into English (the work was meant in part to keep Tahitian history from being lost along with the native tongue) distinctly anticipates the uncle in *Mont Saint Michel and Chartres*, Adams's proper elegy for his own lost ancestress prepared for members of his own dispersed clan. His feelings of personal bereavement in Polynesia found more direct utterance in his letters home. Certainly Adams intuited that, as the missionary followed in the wake of the trader and military ruler, so the roving elegist, with his lush imagination of once-blessed isles, followed the missionary. What the retired and increasingly elegiac historian could rescue from a Western onslaught with which he could not help but be in complicity will be defined later. Here we should observe the ways in which his fieldwork altered his view of the world, diminishing his sense of the emigrant's opportunities. By the time he was in striking distance of it, the China he had spoken of as an ahistorical Cathay had become a confirmed part of the temporal realm due to an intensive colonialization that had begun to provoke the Chinese against the whites. Prudent travelers did well to consider those borders closed. The world had indeed grown small.

What he read in the American papers reinforced his sense of the world's shrinkage. That American papers got through to him and were met by his eager consumption suggests that the world could never have been large enough for him to have lost sight of his homeland. Although it is impossible to measure Adams's restoration except by reference to the writings of the next fifteen years, we may note the beginnings of a reclaimed interest in America toward the close of his journey and efforts on his part to redefine himself as an American author. As is often the case with Adams, the surest clues are paradoxical: we can best gauge the absorption of his attention by the renunciations and dismissals he was given to make throughout these years of transition.

From Sydney, approaching his journey's end, he wrote Charles Francis Adams, Jr., his brother and former collaborator in the reform movement, a paragraph whose rhetorical paradigm would appear frequently throughout the next decade: "I have followed American affairs, in the newspapers, out here, much more carefully than I have done at home for many years. Everywhere I have been, I have found the world going to the devil, and am the less troubled to observe that America seems well on her way to the same destiny. At our age we can afford to take it coolly. If America likes it, it suits me. Only I no longer feel the ardor of twenty years ago to set it right, and I opine that even you must by this time have come to the resigned conclusion that the planetary dance had better go its own cussed way" (*LHA* 3:517). Since the end of 1890, the newspapers had for Adams's purposes been dominated by the failure of the London Barings and the beginnings of recession in America. In Samoa, he had read about Charles's inability, as the director of the Union Pacific, to refinance the railroad, and his consequent surrender of the post to his old nemesis, Jay Gould. Such, Adams implies, is proof positive that their reform writings had been in vain. But against his explicit statement, we may note that Adams writes as though fundamentally unresigned to the notion that "America seems well on her way to the same destiny": the frustration implicit in his remark suggests the continued habit of viewing America as an exceptional historical possibility. This, at least on the surface, is highly inconsistent with the bleak prophecy and evident resignation with which the *History* concludes. It is even more specifically inconsistent with Adams's contention, illustrated throughout the long narrative, that America had never been able to remain aloof from the common experience of nations, despite the fact that its average popular intelligence and morality were patently superior to all such averages in the Old World.[11]

Yet it is highly consistent with his writing's tendency to reflect specific rhetorical contexts and meet particular, present exigencies. Whereas the *History* addressed an audience whose remoteness eventually passed the vanishing point, the letter to Charles, alive if disgruntled in Boston, negotiates what to the still live author is a sequence of possible, portentous events. The paragraph quoted registers the imminence of homecoming and establishes contact with the current family elder, the older brother to whom Henry's early vocational identity was closely tied. Whereas it engages Charles on the now common ground of retirement, it nonetheless protests against the spectacle of America succumbing to such Old World practices as the international conspiracy of the "gold bug." Insofar as it attempts to justify resignation, it does so by citing the apparent failure of the moment to rouse scruples at home. This is revealing in that the early careers of both men had been given literally to the rousing of the public's scruples.

From his vantage in Sydney, Henry could support the pretention of viewing the drama as pure "planetary" spectacle, especially given his own "escape from being stranded penniless" in the Southern Hemisphere (*LHA* 3:381). But insofar as he was acutely aware (as his close following of American affairs demonstrates) that the "dance" must drag him with it, we must read ambiguity, if not antithesis, into each of the paragraph's positive assertions. As the world's remote paradisaical islands fell to capitalist hegemony, he was all the more troubled to observe America on her way to a destiny that some of her founders (Jefferson and John Adams among them) had sought to avoid. At ages fifty-three and fifty-six respectively, Henry and Charles could not afford to take too coolly a "destiny" that threatened havoc to the investments on which their lives (and Henry's purported coolness) were based. Neither morally nor financially could such a destiny suit Henry; it could only suit an America that had broken faith with what to the Adams brothers remained the old, true ideals. The ardor of twenty years earlier certainly had fled. But, as so often would be the case, Adams's attempt to close a former chapter and repudiate a motive—to reclose a presumably closed chapter and re-repudiate a repudiated motive—keeps the chapter open and the motive in some form alive. His letter to Charles betrays his still vital concern for what they had tried to accomplish in the name of reform.

His 1891 New Year's letter to Elizabeth Cameron demonstrates just how deeply Adams responded to the 1890 recession as erstwhile reformer and retired author recalled to former interests. This is a document of primary importance to any understanding of the dialectic through which Adams would pass in his effort to redefine himself as public author. The panic's course, Adams wrote, "would be a delight if I were twenty years younger, for, if you happen upon my new volume of Essays . . . you will see that I wrote the first chapter of this story in an article called the 'Gold Conspiracy.' The second chapter has been my brother's administration of Union Pacific, and its foredoomed failure. The last chapter—in my lifetime—has still to come, but is close at hand. I do not know the climax, but am devoured by curiosity" (*LHA* 3:381). Again, Adams employs the word "chapter" to designate that which is at once closed and somehow to be continued. In so using the word, he reveals himself to be engaged in a significant act of revision; here specifically he uses "chapter" to project a sequence of events in an ironically collaborative narrative. In the course of that narrative his own position changes from that of active, reform-motivated writer (as author, with Charles, of the 1871 volume *Chapters of Erie and Other Essays*) to that of reader passively "devoured by curiosity"—the one form of cannibalism (one of the traveler's comic fascinations) Adams encounters in the South Seas. His brother's supposedly "foredoomed failure" implies that Adams's "first chapter" was similarly foredoomed, notwithstanding the bygone "delight" of preparing articles in the belief that they could effect reform. The author of the last chapter, Jay Gould, "too is foredoomed to failure," but not without instruction for the thoughtful reader, for "Gould has much to tell us" about "where American democracy was coming out" (*LHA* 3:381, 382).

The passage culminates with Adams's perhaps unconscious parody of the questions that conclude the *History*: "If I am right, and if Gould must fail, I see the most splendid possibilities of a climax. Will he subside quietly? Will he break down? Will he be hung on a lamp-post? Will government and society stand under the shock?" (*LHA* 3:381). The sequence must end, Adams asserts, with Charles living "to write the story and the epitaph of Jay Gould," a moral victory of sorts for the House of Adams. But how such moral victories—or such thumbnail parodies of the Adams vocation as Henry has here written—figure in the larger national narrative he cannot say. If, he writes, in twenty-five years he were alive and in full possession of his powers, he would continue his *History* with a view to summarizing the democratic experiment. But fitness for such a task, he concedes, requires moral sympathy with the subject, lest (we may infer) the historian be reduced to describing the inorganic formation of a crystal. "Unfortunately," he writes in the same letter to Elizabeth, "I am cursed with the misfortune of thinking that I know beforehand what the result must be, and of feeling sure that it is one which I do not care to pursue; one with which I have little or no sympathy, except in a coldly scientific way; and a man cannot with decency or chance of success take a part in a stage-play when he cannot help showing the audience that he thinks the whole thing a devilish poor piece of work" (*LHA* 3:382). Here Adams establishes as an ethical basis for his retirement his reluctance to take a part in the historical process that (as a defense mechanism) he inveterately represented as a play—shifting, however tentatively, the focus of his disaffection with America from the likes of Jay Gould to himself. He would not often make such concessions, but he no doubt knew better than anyone how crucial they were to the preservation of the life of his mind. His emergence from retirement would not, of course, entail a complete triumph over his coldly scientific view, but it would involve some cultivation of his sympathies and a rather significant concession that he might not know beforehand what the result would be.

The New Year's letter to Elizabeth Cameron constitutes a capsule apologia; an attempt to explain autobiographically the alienation with which he now mostly regarded American affairs. He quite frankly submits his life as the text behind the "more critical—deliberately fault-finding" later volumes of the *History*, "written . . . in a very different frame of mind from that in which the work was begun." The coldly scientific view, if valid, should be exempt from autobiographical explanation. Contemplating the course his magnum opus took, Adams is yet driven to remark that between the first volume and the ninth his reader must feel that "the light has gone out. I am not to blame. As long as I could make life work, I stood by it, and swore by it as though it were my God, as indeed it was." Without any signal of a change in subject he goes from speaking of his book to speaking of his life. While it absolutizes the break with his past and candidly mourns the loss of youthful ardors, the letter nevertheless plots a return to his diminished American circle. It petitions Elizabeth, his specific auditor, to rescue one who "like the unfortunate Robinson . . . cannot get back to land." Toward that return he is willing to make a major concession: namely, to absolve himself of particular sexual motive, to be his auditor's "tame cat, after the manner of Chateaubriand. . . . Please," the entry in closing implores, "say yes" (*LHA* 3:382).

A year later he was in Paris undergoing dental work, recuperating from minor surgery performed in London, and recovering from a November reunion with Elizabeth that had found the parties shy of the intimacy that had marked their correspondence of the preceding year and a half. Alone in London, he had had to contend with a thick atmosphere of association, the memories of his 1872 wedding trip and of his young manhood spent in the American legation making him feel ancient. Still, among the ghosts of statesmen and old friends, he registered the "queer sensation" of "coming to life again in a dead world" (*LHA* 3:603). He dismissed a European civilization that had "vulgarized" and had made no progress beyond electric light. He ridiculed the morass of British politics and complained of the degraded sexuality of the Paris theater and the new French literature. Fin-de-siècle despair was too demonstrative, voluble: "The mark of real despair," he wrote with such tacit reference as his correspondent could be trusted to pick up, ". . . is silence" (*LHA* 3:592). His own vows of silence, however, had been ever violated in his compulsive annotation of them. Now, prior to binding himself "beyond recall, to a week's misery, and the new world" (*LHA* 3:607), he loosely sketched in a letter to John Hay a project with which his own scattered and voluble energies, as well as those of the somewhat retired Hay, might be engaged to beguile the ennui that awaited him in Washington. It would consist of a collaboration, "under any assumed name or character" that might suit Hay, in "a volume or two of Travels"; an improvisatory "ragbag" that would allow Adams and Hay (if he wished) to escape the constraints of orthodox history, to combine history with speculation concerning psychology, poetry, and art, and "to grill a few literary and political gentlemen to serve with champagne" (*LHA* 3:598, 599). As Ernest Samuels has suggested, this proposition broaches the hybrid thought that would lead to *Mont Saint Michel and Chartres* and the *Education*.[12]

The letter more immediately looks ahead to the uncertainty that awaited his appearance, redivivus, in Washington. With vengeful comedy its posture combines an aristocratic cannibal who grills his old enemies (certain literary and political enmities apparently very much alive for Adams) with a resigned idealist who sips champagne in his moral superiority. But Adams's self-satire betrays more than he could have recognized. To the degree that we are alert to his fiction of self-sufficiency and to the broken state of his professed silence, the satire serves to unmask Adams's defensive and monied aloofness. His appeal for a collaborator reveals the social support his vulnerable aloofness always required. As much as he would celebrate the moral virtue and tragic dignity of "standing alone" in the *Education*, Adams never relished being a party of one. Just as he preferred companionship in travel, so in authorship he preferred community, dialogue, to break the silences into which his monologue must otherwise lapse. Yet the form of his aloofness—his retirement, his "death"— must remain intact. "I have said and stick to it," he reminded Hay, "that I will never again appear as an author, but I don't mind writing anonymously" (*LHA* 3:599).

To write anonymously means writing to be read; why else the precautionary concealment? Anticipating his return to America, Adams may seem willing to hazard no more than a narrow projection of audience but it is one decidedly closer than "fifty years hence"; he may be anonymous, but as author he is still in life, able to take pleasure in watching his victims squirm. But to what other effect would he be so read? In retrospect, we may watch the ragbag cohere in such books as *Mont Saint Michel and Chartres* and the *Education*. As we shall see, these works reveal self-consciously high and solemn motives behind Adams's authorship, despite the *Education*'s tendency to problematize and ridicule them and despite Adams's refusal to appear as live author before the large audience whose consideration his works require if they are to be more than the satire of his (continued) sense of high calling as an Adams and as public author. The ragbag's coherence entailed an evolution from an intended sequence of marginal and abusive sallies to two books of grave concern, communicable only as they dignify a potential American audience. While we can scarcely trace all the particulars of that evolution, Adams's correspondence reveals that the emergent cohesion of his late work paralleled his country's metamorphosis into a world power. It paralleled his own sense of coming into and falling out of relation with a country that was becoming an international and ultimate force whose course at best threatened to negate the citizen's exercise of educated choice and at worst already had. Adams's late works, the *Education* in particular, occupy the space of that uncertainty—a space dramatically narrowed by the ultimate disappearance that Adams enacts through the *Education*'s genuinely posthumous release to the general public.

At the Fair

As the *Education* explains it, the genesis of the late work lay in those events that drove home to the retired author his economic nexus wherever, in his voyages, tidings of panic happened to catch up with him. The collapse of the Barings while he was in the South Seas had given Adams some mildly anxious moments, but the *Education* places his first major scare in 1893, the summer of the Chicago Exposition, while he was vacationing with the Camerons in Switzerland. Arriving at Lucerne one July afternoon, he found "letters from his brothers requesting his immediate return to Boston because the community was bankrupt and he was probably a beggar" (A I 1028).

"As a starting-point for a new education at fifty-five years old," he continues, "the shock of finding one suspended, for several months, over the edge of bankruptcy, without knowing how one got there, or how to get away, is to be strongly recommended" (A I 1029). Upon reaching Quincy, he found the family assets riding out the storm. Beyond the immediate call to inventory the loss and restructure investments he fell into intense dialogue with his younger brother Brooks, then at work on *The Law of Civilization and Decay*. In his first sustained contact with Brooks in many years, Adams saw that his brother's unfolding theory of history confirmed many of his own intimations while it provoked and offered to serve as the basis for further thought. At the time, Henry's pessimism drew upon a complex experience in which disappointment as a public author was inextricably caught up in the collapse of his domestic life—an experience he was unprepared to vent except in a "ragbag." Brooks, on the other hand, with an experience intensely but more simply disappointing and a temper much less given to paradox, had moved beyond the sensation of pessimism to a systematic analysis of historical decline.[13] Decline, in that analysis, was traced to usurious economic practice. In the final chapter of the *History* Adams had predicted that American democracy was as likely to stifle itself as to continue responding to the peculiar stimuli that had accompanied Jefferson's ascendancy. Now, the efficient cause of stagnation had become clearer, appearing in the personally assailable form of the international finance capitalist.

In the Quincy household, the banker had long been an object of antipathy, and Adams had recently reasserted in the *History* the thesis that State Street pursued its self-interest unto treason. Since the Civil War, largely on the basis of a jealously guarded single gold standard, the financial guild had consolidated into a truly leviathanic force; a decision in London's Lombard Street could rapidly contract American currency, suppressing agriculture in Iowa and mining in Montana. Joining a chorus variously made up of populists, conservatives of an antiquated republicanism, and the ranks of a growing anti-Semitic contingent, Adams fumed over the world's "infernal Jewry" and audibly wished "to sink Lombard Street and Wall Street under the ocean" (*LHA* 4:157). In a less vitriolic mood, he marvelled to Charles Milnes Gaskell, his longtime British friend, that "in this young, rich continent, capable of supporting three times its population with ease, we have had a million men out of employment for nearly a year, and the situation growing worse rather than better." Speaking in 1894 as one for whom the New World slenderly retained its right to moral and economic exemption, he remarked that "Europe and Asia are used to accepting disease and death as inevitable, but to us the idea is a new one. We want to know what is wrong with the world that it should suddenly go to smash without visible cause or possible advantage" (*LHA* 4:185). The international fluctuation of capital, which Adams understood well, did not sufficiently account for the suppression of American fecundity. There had to be a moral, amoral, or perhaps even occult force behind it, one that Brooks's *Law* was not equipped to detect.

Adams's dismay over the evident stagnation of so young a country, whose resistance to accepting the inevitability of disease and death he himself confirmed in his efforts to arrive at an explanation for it, articulates the claims his country retained upon him. The coldly scientific view, which aligned itself precisely with an acceptance of death, consumed neither that dismay nor his long-dormant patriotism, which was awakened in the first moments of the Spanish-American War. Nor had his science erased his capacity for such renewed agonizing over American political morality as was occasioned by the country's postwar imperial course. After his return from the South Seas, travel kept him detached and yet curious, studious, susceptible. From 1893 to 1896, the retired historian divided his time between residence at Washington and varied adventures. In later years he would vacillate regularly between 1603 H Street and his Paris "attic," from which he would reconnoiter the cathedral country and other European points. But the midnineties saw Adams afoot on a number of strenuous American tours (the Rockies, Mexico, the West Indies) in addition to his annual trips to Europe. What he observed in his tours of the Americas provided some contrasts—in Mexico, a seemingly well-employed labor force that threatened to keep its northern counterpart out of work; in Cuba, a country "totally ruined and on the verge of social and political dissolution" (*LHA* 4:251). With eyes that had received political as well as aesthetic education in his recent circumnavigation of the globe, he now saw everywhere "the trader and the money-lender . . . exploiting the tiller of the soil" (*LHA* 4:259). The United States, in the midst of a prolonged agrarian crisis, remained the chief example; what was true of the farmer counted equally for the industrial operative. Until the Spanish-American War, Adams perceived little by which to anticipate America's vigorous entry into the twentieth century. But certain harbingers of the new America did meet his eyes, and the strongest took the form of an event that still marks a watershed in the country's historical self-consciousness: the 1893 World's Columbian Exposition.

The depression that had come to a head the same year guaranteed that the fair would not escape ironic perspective. There was, however, a host of such assurances. The appearance of the neoclassical White City within the precincts of the heartland's sprawling metropolis and the conjunction of high culture with carnival, learned conference with commercial enterprise, old art with new technology, represent some of the immediately visible tensions. Less obvious were the tensions inherent in celebrating a national identity conceived in terms of an agrarian past while welcoming a national destiny that would be urban and industrial in its domestic configuration and assertively international in its activity.[14] The impasse to be reached along these lines was adumbrated in Frederick Jackson Turner's "The Significance of the Frontier in American History," which first appeared at Chicago in July 1893 in the form of an address to the American Historical Association, convened as a part of the exposition's World's Congresses program. What Turner cast historiographically had been stated repeatedly in the nation's literature: that American character represents the rebirth of a European populace transformed by its contact with American nature, that this rebirth has restored the individual's native sovereignty, and that the fundamental mandate of American institutions has been to preserve that sovereignty's restoration. Although Adams found in diplomatic history more comprehensive explanations of American development, the *History*'s prologue chapters may be said to contain a frontier thesis in partial agreement with that of the younger historian from Wisconsin. Turner's address is important as the public witness to the passing of an era, even though the substance of his argument was not new, and, as Henry Nash Smith writes, "the real end of the frontier period" had been brought on by an economic crisis to which the myth of the garden had succumbed long before the Columbian observance.[15] The frontier thesis confirmed the increasingly cherished myth of a "first period of American experience" while it looked, with evident and disconcerted inconclusiveness, upon the beginning of a sequel in which "American energy [would] continually demand a wider field for its exercise."[16]

Demand for a wider field would in five years take the form of the Spanish-American War. An honored presence at the fair because of her sponsorship of Columbus, Spain would find herself expelled from the New World and stripped of her South Pacific possessions at the end of the war. Thus would pass the last of the Columbian celebration's irenic pretensions, most of which had perished amid the civil strife that visited Chicago the year after the fair. Yet for some, those pretensions had always been suspect, given the European and imperial associations of the architecture that by all accounts had been the exposition's most impressive feature. Of the beaux arts mode adopted by the board of architects, Louis Sullivan, the contributor of the eccentric polychromatic Transportation Building, was the first and ever the harshest critic. The White City (Court of Honor) represented feudalism, the Old World, the East Coast; it usurped the rightful place of the Garden City of a democratic order in that order's appointed home, the American heartland. The influence of the exposition's style dealt, in Sullivan's estimation, a nearly fatal blow to a newly emerging American architecture. Lewis Mumford, also in the name of democracy, amplified this view: to the calculated, frigid dazzle of the exposition mode, America's "native" and "organic" civic architecture temporarily succumbed, reviving only with the maturity of Frank Lloyd Wright. Wright himself vented considerable spleen on the subject of the fair's buildings, again on democratic grounds.[17] The question of the New World's historical exemption, over which Adams had freshly brooded as an American in Polynesia, Asia, and Europe, was focused for the younger generation by the international event in the country's heartland. For them, it was no less a cause for alarm that the exposition represented the United States as a contender in, rather than the victim of, global involvement.

Because of the exposition's corporate nature, its mandate to affirm a necessarily select set of doctrines in the name of the United States and the world, one cannot pursue the art far before tumbling into the web of power relations that largely determined the form that the art would take. As a predominantly conservative expression, the fair resisted the diverse social reality of the host city. However much Adams and other easterners might associate it with the rural heartland, Chicago had come by the nineties to display the most advanced conditions of the American urban scene. It occupied the center of a world whose existence Adams suspected but refused substantially to know; it was another America—an America of others—that existed for him as the half-visible agent of his progressive alienation, merging his America with the old, polyglot, irredeemable world. By the nineties Chicago was the second largest American city, absorbing a destitute rural population as well as a flood of European immigrants. In no other American city had social lines been defined more militantly; in 1877, 1886, and again in 1894 labor unrest erupted into open riot for which federal troops were called out. Providing employment and a fragile psychological unity to the city's diverse classes and interests, the exposition offered a year's holiday to Chicago. After it closed in October 1893, the city fell back into its old polarities with a vengeance, one to which the empty exposition buildings lent their final spectacle. During the harsh winter of 1893 and 1894, the buildings, surviving vandalism and minor fires, served as impromptu tenements for the Chicago homeless. (Would Turner have appreciated the ironies of such urban homesteading?) The following summer, at the height of the Pullman strike, the defaced structures, ignited by rioters, went up in flames.

Exempt, during the summer of its run, from the tensions of a country undergoing economic collapse, the exposition proved a financial, if not for all visitors an artistic, success. Yet its power as spectacle may be seen in the emphatic responses of Henry Adams, who as global traveler and habitual ironist should have maintained perhaps as much distance from the event as any American. Indeed in 1895, from Saint Thomas, Virgin Islands, he would dryly suggest that the "negro, the half-breed, and the broken planter are the results of Columbus and the five hundred years of triumphant civilisation which we celebrated at Chicago the other day" (*LHA* 4:259). Yet, in the exposition's presence, he must have been struck by something that recalled "the America of thought and art" that he had described in the *History*'s prologue as the vision of his republican idealists. Stunned, as were most visitors, by the relentless virtuosity of the architectural performance—one that, as any photograph will confirm, abhorred a void, moving to subdue the least space with some stock gesture—Adams wrote John Hay: "I like to look at it as an appeal to the human animal, the superstitious and ignorant savage within us, that has instincts and no reason, against the world as money has made it. I have seen a faint gleam of intelligence lighten the faces even of the ignorant rich, and almost penetrate the eyes of a mugwump and Harvard college graduate, as he brooded, in his usual stolidity of self-satisfaction, on his own merits, before the Court of Honor. Never tell me to despair of our goldbugs after this; we can always drown them" (*LHA* 4:134–35). Seldom had he allowed himself to be so beguiled (or at least to represent himself as such). He had quite rigorously kept up a measure of resistance to the charms of Polynesia, and even after his first real discovery of Chartres in 1895, he would record along with his raptures the suspicion that the Gothic church "exploits the world, and makes profits," that the art was "false," and that the pointed arch was "cheap" (*LHA* 4:321–22).

Perhaps it cannot greatly surprise us that Adams should so miss the complicity of the exposition's artists in the (Chicago) goldbug's ideology. Although he had made himself uncommonly familiar with the mountain West, his perception of Chicago as western was tinged by his easterner's condescension toward the westerner's supposedly deprived culture. Retaining ever certain Bostonian perspectives on the world, he tended to underestimate the sophistication of the newly rich, particularly that of the newly rich westerners (John Hay was the great paradox here) in their purchase of culture. The White City was precisely the world as money had made it; the fair discovered the taste of well-to-do Chicago. Awry as Adams's first impression may have been, it was one that served to reawaken his interest in his country, even as it reinforced other incentives to set about framing a historical sequence capable of divining the world's perilous future course. Recalling him to his avowedly avocational literary pursuit, the exposition, he assured Hay, was worth "a volume or two" of their projected "Travels."

In chapter 21 of the *Education*, Adams would in fact come to give the fair its due, qualifying his initial enthusiasm by seeing the event in the context of the 1893 depression, the silver question, the gold standard's ultimate triumph, "McKinleyism," the Spanish-American War, and the haunting precedent of imperial Rome. As is so often the case in the *Education*, the qualification is largely implied, even in conflict with particular statements: although this book represents Adams's attempt to arrive at definitive positions, his perceptions and judgments as of 1906 approach closure little more decidedly than they did in his fin-de-siècle years of transition. In his most colorful and frequently quoted remark about the fair (is he not also speaking of the undecided carpetbag of mid-nineties America?) he asserts that "since Noah's Ark, no such Babel of loose and ill-joined, such vague and ill-defined and unrelated thoughts and half-thoughts and experimental outcries as the Exposition, had ever ruffled the surface of the lakes" (A I 1031). Such a description no doubt accounts well for the comic mélange of the exposition considered in toto: the White City and midway; the sprawling, "western," socially unstable workaday city of Chicago, to which the Court of Honor must have seemed as exotic as Versailles; the prairie and lake in which the promise of a now scarcely virgin continent abode as a faded suggestion.

Adams's reading of the exposition's art takes its own tack. Having registered the comedy of the architects' attempt "to impose classical standards upon plastic Chicago" and conceded the architecture's lapses by commenting that "all trading cities had always shown traders' taste," he still wishes to honor, as he can, the artistic achievement. The magnificent pseudobuildings, in the presence of which Adams pondered "on the steps beneath Richard Hunt's dome almost as deeply as on the steps of Ara Coeli, and much to the same purpose," suggested breach of historical continuity. "Was it real," Adams asks, "or only apparent? One's personal universe hung on the answer, for, if the rupture was real and the new American world could take this sharp and conscious twist towards ideals, one's personal friends would come in, at last, as winners in the great American chariot-race for fame" (A I 1032). As in his letter to Hay more than ten years earlier, Adams seems to recall "the America of thought and art" that he had proposed in "American Ideals" as the unarticulated vision of Jefferson and Gallatin, even as, by undertaking the *History*, he had identified the creation of such an America as his own generation's great task. In this passage from early in the second half of the *Education*—a part of the book particularly given to nostalgic and wistful utterance—he appears willing to imagine that "Hunt and Richardson, La Farge and St.

Gaudens, Burnham and McKim, and Stanford White" would live in the national mind when the patrons whose tastes they flattered were forgotten. That he wishes to see these men vindicated is understandable: he speaks here of the work of a generation, not merely the achievement of the fair. La Farge's presence at the exposition was limited to the exhibition of some watercolors.[18] Richardson had died in 1886; his vigorous Romanesque would have clashed with the academic refinement of the beaux arts mode. But as generously as Adams wished to speak of his generation's artistic achievement, "chariot-race for fame" cannot but suggest that high aspiration had to make do with compromising conditions. The invocation of Ara Coeli sounds a more deeply somber note. Given the associations that the *Education*, by this point, has invested in "Rome," this parallel proposes that the fair's art at best constitutes an abortive achievement: the happy product but ultimate victim of historical "rupture" and an ideal that human depravity will pull down as certainly as it subverted the millennial promise of Rome.

This would appear to be the kindest light by which Adams in 1906 could read the exposition's art and the artistic achievement of his generation that he permits the fair to symbolize. Although his text invites the reader to infer that the achievement had been bought, had lent itself wholly to the world as money had made it, Adams does not, and cannot, say that directly. By the light of *Mont Saint Michel and Chartres*, which (following Ruskin) indicts Renaissance art as the expression of commerce, the exposition's architecture ought instantly to be condemned as the goldbug's bought pageantry and as testimony to the true artist's death. Well might Adams have dismissed the White City's comparatively cheap, meretricious pretense to the millennial (American) city. Had he been abstractly consistent, he would have had to: in Chicago, plaster masqueraded as adamant. Mary's cathedrals, he had surely not forgotten, had been built to last forever. His consistency lies rather in his effort to modulate or suspend his judgment in view of a particular audience: the *Education* readership of 1907 to 1909 included survivors of his own generation as well as that generation's familial and social heirs. With them he had been, and continued to be, in partnership. That he dismisses their art tentatively and by implication is significant: whatever he may actually concede in granting the benefit of the doubt, he signals his reluctance to score a direct hit when so much of himself stands in front of the target. It is in moments like these, scattered throughout the *Education*, that we are aware of a voice emanating from a subject position that is emphatically still in life.

For Adams to write with such a clear sense of partnership suggests that he could not but return on occasion to the live rhetorical position to which he had aspired in choosing a literary career. Such instances in the

Education may in themselves seem rather tentative, sabotaged (as we shall see) by other passages that appear to reject the possibility that anyone may read, let alone heed, the book or that the volume could have a lesson to which it would be worth anyone's time to attend. Yet the case must be made that the text as a whole—that is, as a discrete and deliberately published *book*—constitutes return. By considering further what came to be his "Travels" chapter on the fair, we may see more deeply into those tensions against which, in returning, he had to contend.

Adams had felt ambivalently close to the art as a member of the generation of whom the White City plausibly represented the artistic flower. When it came to the dynamos and kindred exhibits, however, the reading was different. Such prodigies seemed the property of another, more advanced generation. For all his efforts to contribute to a scientific history, Adams in 1893 was no scientist, and the scientific and technological exhibitions at Chicago and seven years later at Paris remained for him technically unreadable.[19] His was the "historical mind," not truly the scientific, even though he instantly sensed that the dynamos "gave to history a new phase" (A I 1033). The ignorance that he felt when confronted with the dynamo impeached his authority as a historical scholar and reinforced his retirement as public author; in the *Education*, he cannot speak of the new science and technology without referring to himself as an eighteenth-century anachronism. Yet since 1893 he had invested many hours in what he called his "pursuit of ignorance in silence" (A I 1115). He had developed ways as a nonscientist to negotiate his exasperated nescience, bringing the chaos of new thought to account before the social values that motivated his never very silent pursuit. His formulation of history as the sequence of force available to and reactive upon a dynamically evolving human community finally emerged as the convenient fiction by which he would read his world.

With this formulation in hand, he was able around 1906 to look back on the fair paradoxically. Whether or not Americans were deliberately "driving or drifting unconsciously to some point in thought" that could be determined "if relations enough could be observed," Adams was willing to venture that "Chicago was the first expression of American thought as a unity; one must start there" (A I 1034). If the scientific exhibits impeached his once comfortable authority and made him "aghast" at what he and the liberally educated class of his time "had said and done in all these years" (A I 1033), the sequence-of-force formulation could do little to enlighten technically. But it did serve to focus his ignorance, clarify the moral problem, and raise the issue to a philosophical level at which Adams could assume the ironic authority of Socratic inquiry. One cannot assume a Socratic role without being at odds with (if not, like Socrates, strictly

condemned by) the society one would dialectically and/or rhetorically engage, and it was under such conditions that Adams, in the *Education*, came to address his people.

But, for the retiree ashore in a new America after slow circumnavigation of the world, this would be a long time coming. Called upon by the American Historical Association to serve as president in 1893, and hence address the membership at the next annual meeting, he displayed an unreadiness to speak publicly, however much the remarks he did prepare anticipate the conditions of his eventual return to public authorship. "The Tendency of History," the address that Adams delivered by proxy, fell back upon the thesis that had informed the concluding pages of the *History*. Although it lacks the epilogue's implicit suggestion that human history admits of scientific treatment only in consequence of a crucial historiographical shift—the reconception of society as a natural, rather than a personal, imaginative, and potentially moral, force—the "Tendency" is nevertheless a cry of one in the wilderness, preparing the way for the "great generalization" that will "reduce all history under a law as clear as the laws which govern the material world" (*D* 127). A "science of history," Adams warns, "must be absolute, like other sciences, and must fix with mathematical certainty the path which human society has got to follow. That path can hardly lead toward the interests of all the great social organizations." Rather, it is sure to run afoul of church, state, property, and labor. And as it "must exclude the idea of a personal and active providence," this science assumes veto power over not only orthodox religious teachings but any conception of history as morally directed or directable, whether by "God" or by a people whose invocation of Providence is the enabling ritual of its attempt to impose its own design on historical life (*D* 129).

On the surface, Adams's address would seem to do no more than define the ideological dilemma that the supposedly disinterested scientific historian soon must face.[20] Yet in so doing, it could not but adumbrate for Adams's colleagues the crisis that had stilled his practice as a professional historian. The "Tendency" goes beyond the concluding pages of the *History* by opposing "science" not only to an older historiography built upon the assumption that history reflects the character of its leading personalities but also to the rival forces of a mass society, as though it were in the historian's power to unleash an absolute and vengeful truth upon a people locked in extortionist faction. The jeremiad of the fathers is present here, although in a peculiarly inverted form.[21] As historiography, "scientific" or (through a distinctly allegorical reading of its supposed science) moral, the address is most striking in that it compels the historian to disappear—as one whose moral wisdom is ostensibly overruled by the "generalization" his discourse has caught and as one proscribed by the

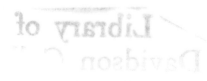

society that refuses the "truth" that he cannot in honesty soften. And, as Adams's 1891 New Year's letter to Elizabeth Cameron makes clear, there is a third motive for disappearance as well: the moral indecency of the "coldly scientific" view, which Adams could never be absolutely sure was not an outlook he had perversely chosen. As anything more than the record of a world progressively emptied of its human face, history at this point was lost to him. In these straits, the widower as historian and the historian as widower converge upon the single formula for all bereavement: "Silence is best. In these remarks, which are only casual and offered in the paradoxical spirit of private conversation, I have not ventured to express any opinion of my own; or, if I have expressed it, pray consider it as withdrawn" (D 133). But once opened, the chapter could not be closed; his opinion *had* been implicated in his foregoing "remarks," as his disclaimer, offered in the "paradoxical spirit," confirms. They would not admit of easy erasure; nor could Adams let such a paradox be.

Still, the "Tendency" would appear to plot anything but a return. Prepared months ahead of time, it named Guadalajara as its point of origin. At the beginning of the address, Adams assured his colleagues that he was, at the moment it would be read, "believed to be somewhere beyond the Isthmus of Panama," outward-bound (D 125). He thereby positioned himself, as absent speaker, in what the historians assembled back in Washington would have literally seen as a wilderness. Could he be thus obliquely commenting upon whatever knowledge may have come his way respecting Turner's paper, which by missing the Chicago meeting of 1893 he did not hear? But surely it had been his long-standing practice to promote the myth of himself as one who crossed frontiers. From the countries he penetrated, be they nations mapped from antiquity or uncharted inner isles, he had always written back. Yet it is only retrospectively that we may say that his departure presaged return. Neither Adams nor the historians listening to his paper could have ventured that his departures would not take a turn toward the permanent disappearance of one specific historian.

Whatever the risks, it was ever beyond the Isthmus of Panama, or amid his more or less scholarly visitations of a pre-Renaissance Europe, that Adams escaped the constraints of scientific history and the oppressiveness of its bleak gospel. Having arrived at an idea of what compelled Adams's retirement, we must now turn to what impelled his ongoing activity—what his retirement allowed him to say, what it is about those remarks, "offered in the paradoxical spirit of private conversation," that has so far caused his presence to endure. For answers, we shall first look into the varied motives, rhetorical strategies, publication, and audience of the *Education*—Adams's elaborate and, even as he lived, lingering valediction.

2

The Education of Henry Adams: Return and Valediction

Proofsheets

WITH THE EDUCATION OF HENRY ADAMS, Adams would succeed in fixing a monitory voice in the sphere of his nation's self-scrutiny, but not without preserving the form of his retirement, the withdrawal in which he continued to brood upon what had always seemed to be his voice's muffled resonance. Although the book's existence in itself proclaims Adams's deep need to speak publicly, he holds throughout to a certain tentativity, reserves his right to disappear—indeed promotes the notion of his bygone departure. If he has returned, it is to linger at the threshold; if he reopens old matters, it is to do so with an eye to closure—for him the definitive closure of Henry Adams's death. The artifice Adams invested in the fiction of his own lingering decease is doubtless much more evident to us than it could have been to him. Although by 1907 he had sustained (and strained) the conceit of his posthumous life for over twenty years, he entered his sixties with genuine uneasiness, alert to signs of frailty, failing memory, and declining vigor.[1] *Mont Saint Michel and Chartres* abounds in suggestions that it, in its author's view, could well be his last performance. How much more valedictory the *Education*, then, must have seemed to him. Perhaps more than his age, his catastrophic view of the 1907 historical present may have served to make improbable to him the nearly fourteen hundred letters and two essays he would survive the *Education* to write. Although in practice it would remain urgent, the motive for authorship seemed to diminish with every year. The essays, if not the letters, would on the surface do little more than refine the catastrophic theme.

Although he lived some thirteen years beyond its composition, the *Education* would remain Adams's last major effort to reestablish his voice as a persuasive moral presence in his country's public discourse, and the effort stands despite the text's famous self-deprecation. Inasmuch as it has been and continues to be read critically, the *Education* must be judged to have succeeded. And it has done so not only in spite of but because of its apology, its insistence that we attend to the likelihood and nature of its (and our) failure. The failure of which the book and its author stand self-convicted proceeds from the protagonist Henry Adams's failure: his inability, as student, reformer, author, to make headway against the irrational course of history. The more specific failure of Henry Adams, the author of the *Education*, is defined by Adams in a variety of ways. Equally important, it is defined on a multitude of occasions, ranging from the 1907 preface and the personal letters that prefaced the book as it was circulated in 1907 and 1908, to the letters in which Adams reflected back on the *Education* from several years' distance, to the final reassessment of the 1916 so-called editor's preface. Throughout Adams's commentary on his book, within or without the text proper, there runs a deep suspicion of the book's implicit claim to derive a public authority from a particular ego's experience, from the language that ego has fashioned to mediate an experience it cannot presume to be shared. Adams concedes that the problem as it relates to his project may arise from the singularity and comparative antiquity of his story, not to mention the evident obsolescence of his values; but the ultimate focus of his suspicion is the "new American" whom he cannot trust to share some common human ground by which such a story as his must be approached. Quite certain that the future reader should fail him as much as he should fail the reader—that no language existed to bind them in transgenerational sympathy—Adams nevertheless wrote and published (even if only by failing to suppress) the *Education*. By so doing, he submitted the autobiographical text, and hence the language of the private ego, as a redemptive social resource.

We speak of the *Education* as autobiography against Adams's express wishes, but insofar as "education" is offered as his life's story we may think of the book as a specialized autobiography. The life Adams submits to us is much more complicated than "education" of course can suggest; well might we agree with William James that the word is "stirred in too much."[2] As the existence of the *Education* itself proposes, Adams pursued education with authorship ever in view, an authorship that sought to alter the conditions amid which his texts appeared. Hence the *Education* really seeks consideration as the autobiography of Adams's vocation, and, at the same time, as that vocation's valedictory enactment. The book therefore requires consideration as text and act, "act" referring to the text as published in a particular mode to a particular audience. We may distinguish two deliberate "initial" publications of the *Education*: the "private" publication from 1907 to 1909 to a readership Adams selected and the posthumous release of a trade edition in 1918 to the public at large. The 1918 text remains essentially the same as that of 1907: it picks up, in addition to innumerable minor corrections (some of them reflecting the thought of the later "Rule of Phase Applied to History"), only the substantial supplement of the editor's preface, written by Adams although signed by Henry Cabot Lodge. Nevertheless, given the vast differences between the modes of publication and the author-audience relationships that the two publications assume, we do well to begin by approaching the *Education* as two distinct books.

The initial circulation of 1907 to 1909 itself came in two stages: a first printing of forty copies that went out to family, friends, and former associates mentioned in the *Education* and a subsequent printing of sixty more, sent to some readers for specific consultation and to others because they requested it. The ambition, the generational and class dynamics, and above all the genuine desire for dialogue implicit in this "private" publication have never been adequately addressed. Seldom perhaps has a book's release proceeded with such deliberation, with such clear eagerness for direct and personal response. The first recipient was Charles Francis Adams, Jr., and symmetry dictated that he head the list. Older brother, family elder, and former collaborator in reform, Charles had edited and seen to the publication of Henry's youthful dispatches from Italy, Washington, and London and therefore counted as the first reader of Henry's vocational writing.[3] Requesting that Charles review the "personal allusions" to him, Henry asked that he draw his pen through "any phrase or expression" to which he might object and return the volume (*LHA* 6:48). In lieu of the volume, he received from Charles a letter recording the older brother's raptures over chapter 1, "Quincy (1838–1848)," a response that emphasized the emotive and private dimensions of the text: "Lord! how you do bring it all back! and you and I alone of all living, recalling it all . . . Oh dear! Oh dear!! I'm a boy again!" An often harsh critic of his brother's prior work, Charles had never let Henry off so easily.[4]

Other recipients of the first printing included Theodore Roosevelt, Henry Cabot Lodge, and Charles William Eliot. Each was instructed, as Henry's brother Charles had been, to strike out inaccurate or disagreeable material and to return the volume. As the *Education*'s portraits of Adams's still-living contemporaries were often far from flattering, Ernest Samuels is right to call the initial circulation "a gesture of conciliation"; but we should qualify his observation that Adams had "devised a formula that almost none of the recipients would be bold enough—or so careless of their prize—to adopt."[5] That only four recipients are known to have returned copies would seem to bear out this view. But one, James Ford Rhodes, appears to have been asked to comment as a Civil War specialist on the chapters that deal with the war; the return of his copy would have been largely a matter of professional courtesy. Even the book's submission to those whose portraits contain materials that proved personally objectionable to their models must have been aimed at more than mere appeasement. Much more than a personal apologia given to settling old scores (the grilling of "a few literary and political gentlemen"), the *Education* is intended as the story of a particular generation. Adams knew that the book could possess lasting value only as the articulation of a common if dated experience, and his dispatch of copies to members of his own generation must have come from a real need to test his story's commonality, which was backed by a willingness to adjust in the interest of a broadened consensus.

A number of his recipients were bold men from whom he could reasonably expect bold responses. He was particularly anxious as he awaited word from Charles William Eliot, president of Harvard from 1869 to 1909, who was certain to take offense at what Adams had written about the university despite Adams's admission that, of American institutions, Harvard alone had been kind to him and despite Adams's commendation that Harvard "redeemed America, since it was true to its own" (A I 999). If his family objected, he wrote to Roosevelt, "I can happily suppress the whole thing, as is my wont; but Charles Eliot's sentence will be damnation forever" (*LHA* 6:52). Eliot did return his volume, evidently leaving Adams's strictures intact. As he was later to call the man and the book "overrated," it may be that his "sentence" lay in his refusal to contribute in any way to the book.[6]

The 1907 to 1909 readership includes some of the period's most enduring names. In addition to Roosevelt, Lodge, Eliot, and Henry's brothers, the *Education* went out to Oliver Wendell Holmes, Jr., Henry and William James, Bernard Berenson, Augustus Saint-Gaudens, and John La Farge. The recipients also include a number of public men no longer well known but powerful at the time. It was dispatched to Charles Milnes Gaskell, author, sometime member of Parliament, and Adams's oldest surviving nonfamily intimate. The book was also circulated among the upper-class women who preponderated in Adams's select social circle: wives of old friends and the "nieces," a group of now mostly married younger women, some of them nieces in fact, whose companionship was a central feature of his half-year Washington residency. Within limits the readership is a diverse group. One finds representatives of Adams's own generation and the generation that succeeded it, politicians, university administrators, academic historians, artists, and the exceptional women—class sisters of Esther Dudley—whose social position promoted the languishing of their gifts. New Englanders were amply represented on his list, yet the readership was chosen without regional bias. Although sent in some cases to men who were not friends as much as colleagues, the book did not go out to strangers; hence the exclusion of the Wall Street crowd, self-tutored industrialists, and new millionaires with whom Adams would not have mixed socially. Neither Samuel Clemens nor William Dean Howells, Adams's fellow members of the newly instituted American Academy of Arts and Letters, received a copy. As the aspiring spokesman of a generation, Adams would appear to have excluded from consultation many of those to whom the Gilded Age owed its tone and direction. Conscious no doubt that his book should constitute a minority statement, he writes as one who occupies what he, for one, would regard as his country's (bygone) moral center. Yet as one never fully confident that he has indeed achieved that center, he is in need of genuine consultation. Given the delicacy of such a need, not to mention the author's temperamental exclusivity, it would be surprising if Adams had gone to readers with whom his past had not been shared, personally or professionally.

The criteria by which Adams conferred respect and, more rarely, extended friendship were exorbitant. His readership, with all of its impressive variations, was apt to unite on several counts. Personal distinction was certainly important, as was possession of power, be it political influence, artistic genius, or social charm. Yet just as important was a conservatism that resisted the new America of the financier, the immigrant, and the industrial city; that appreciated old art, shrank from the full, brutal exercise of power, and clung to an old, genteel vision of a natural aristocracy. It hardly needs to be said that Adams's readers were well-off, beneficiaries with Adams of the economic system he decried yet considered inevitable.[7] His readership was necessarily exclusive. Even so, it included a fair portion of the country's ruling elite, which, if unified, might hold (if any group could) the national course in its hands.

Adams nowhere claims as his object the unification and direction of the ruling elite, although the readership he selected for the *Education* suggests that ambition. Perhaps it was partly to save himself from the preposterousness of such an assertion that he had established himself in the character of "failed" and, in any case, deceased elder. His statements *hors texte* are not always consistent with this characterization; some in fact openly defy the text's proclamations of its own probable futility. Diverse as were the many statements Adams prepared to accompany the *Education* on its way to the first readers, he almost always first struck an apologetic note before proceeding to reduce the book to one of its subsidiary ambitions. To Charles Milnes Gaskell he claimed that "the volume is wholly due to piety on account of my father and John Hay (the rest being thrown in to make mass)" (*LHA* 6:63). To Henry James he wrote of the *Education* as an intended preemption of the biographer, "a mere shield of protection in the grave" (*LHA* 6:136). In such statements, the book would appear to have been written in behalf of singular historical persons, Henry

Adams among them—and as the author of *John Randolph* Adams knew with what vitriol a biography could be written and so sought to give his own life its first, harsh crack. Yet he had other objects as well. In addition to Henry Adams the historical man and potential victim of biography, he cast himself also in the role of artist—a role in which much criticism to date has granted him asylum.[8] In the same letter to James, he claimed (not without self-irony) that "the intent of the literary artist—c'est moi!— [is] to make this volume a completion and mathematical conclusion from the previous volume about the thirteenth century,—the three concluding chapters of this being only a working out to Q.E.D. of the three concluding chapters of that" (*LHA* 6:136). Such an artistic motive is peculiarly scientific in its pursuit of symmetry. While working toward a revelation of what would perhaps be history's ultimate chaos, Adams, however ironically, wished to emulate Aquinas, in whom he saw artist and scientist join in the formulation of a harmonious, essentially ahistorical universe.

Again and again, in the guise of artist or scientist, he emphasized the formal aspects of the *Education*, minimizing the question of content. "Between artists," he wrote to one reader, ". . . the sole interest is that of form. Whether one builds a house, or paints a picture, or tells a story, our point of vision regards only the form—not the matter" (*LHA* 6:122). Yet Adams's view of form is one that entails the redemption as much as the deprecation of matter; his use of the term retains, albeit ironically, its old theological connotations. This may be seen in his explanation of the book's "failure" to William James, who, while he did not return the volume, offered to Adams strong if good-natured criticism, severe in its attack of the *Education*'s historical forecast as mere "retrospection projected on the future."[9] Evading James's direct thrust, Adams addresses from a distance his questionable development of historical meaning in the context of an autobiographical narrative, leaving unacknowledged the hunger for revelation that his historical forecasts always betrayed. Of all the classic autobiographical models, Adams pleaded, "St. Augustine alone has an idea of literary form,—a notion of writing a story with an end and object, not for the sake of the object, but for the form, like a romance" (*LHA* 6:119–20). Here, as in the 1916 editor's preface, Adams plays homage to Augustine the "great artist." Yet in view of *Mont Saint Michel and Chartres* and the *Education*, and the religious interest these works reveal to have awakened in this descendant of the Puritans, we must surmise that chief among what for Adams were the sources of Augustine's greatness was a belief system that beholds past, present, and future and in which "form" is God's providence and ultimately God himself. In addition to autobiographer, historian, and literary artist, Augustine was gospeler; rhetorically, object and form fuse in the *Confessions* toward didactic ends. Completion here is not a problem: Augustine's story begins praise-fully with the assumption that the chaotic moments of the protagonist's life have been already reconciled in the unity of history and that that life counts as an exemplum in a history that has been revealed as merging with God. How unlike Adams's story, which in resorting to transparent artifice (the third-person narration, the conceit of the protagonist's bygone death) draws attention to the persistent irreconciliation of its content.

Attention is drawn all the more by Adams's repeated insistence that the book "interests me chiefly as a literary experiment" (*LHA* 6:118). The implication of this claim is that the experiment has been brought to a point of failure or (not much more reassuringly) to one of definite in-conclusion. The "literary artist" only too obviously failed to transfigure Henry Adams the historical man; "my art," he wrote to Elizabeth Cam-eron, "fails of its effect" (*LHA* 6:53). Like Augustine, Adams craved the One, but unlike Augustine he could arrive at no principle of unity that did not kill off all vestige of the human in "God." To the extent that his art's intended effect was to achieve closure, symmetry, and unity, the failure confirmed that the author was alive and that his thought resisted absorp-tion in the vision of an unconscious, mechanistic omnipotence.

By minimizing the book's content and insisting that his efforts had all been an experiment in form, Adams anticipates the possibility that no audience of any magnitude can exist for such a text and that even his select readership could prove indifferent. Notwithstanding the distinct theological connotations of his use of the word "form," he largely re-sponds to William James's dismissal of his historical thesis by falling back on his purported motives as artist, citing William's brother as a fellow experimenter in literary art and doubting "whether a dozen people in America . . . would know or care" (*LHA* 6:118). He had established this line of defense well before the book had drawn James's fire. In a letter to Gaskell, he had attempted to make a virtue of what might prove the inevitable: "As my experience leads me to think that no one any longer cares or even knows what is said or printed, and that one's audience in history and literature has shrunk to a mere band of survivors, not exceed-ing a thousand people in the entire world, I am in hopes a kind of esoteric literary art may survive, the freer and happier for the sense of privacy and *abandon*" (*LHA* 6:63). Yet as "art," if by art Adams indeed means unity and economy—the seemingly effortless achievement of form that for him marked the best Romanesque and Gothic, or the transcendence of history and conflict that distinguishes Augustine's narrative—the *Education* is neither free nor happy. But then the book, as we shall see, began by renouncing a too fastidious privacy, and its author never entirely left off watching for a fit public—one that could not be so few and still fit.

In his most extreme deprecation of the *Education*, Adams characterized it as above all fit "for blame, contempt and refusal. It hobbles on its
knees, asking to be raised and educated. . . . I am ashamed of it, and send
it out into the world only to be whipped" (*LHA* 6:111). The recipient of
this characterization was "niece" Margaret Chanler, to whom Adams
could extend such remarks with the expectation of sympathy. That Mrs.
Chanler was a Roman Catholic medievalist, with what we might presume
to be a scholar's appreciation of the self-flagellatory figure, mitigates
somewhat the abject pose. In any case, even amid such language Adams
affirms that the book is meant "for revision, suggestion, correction" as
well as "general condemnation." For the two years following his initial
release of the *Education*, Adams's claim to the merely formal interest of
the artist was persistently qualified by his solicitation of advice, an attempt
to encourage his reader's participation that could not but focus on content. Even if Adams exaggerated his desire for revisionary response, his
invitation challenges his pose of detachment. And it draws our attention
to the central paradox of the initial publication: the *Education*, which
purports to close the accounts of Henry Adams, protagonist and author,
in the conceit of his foregone death, remains from 1907 through 1910 an
open text circulated "in the nature of proof-sheets" (*LHA* 6:49). No man
who was not desperate for some form of response would declare, even
facetiously, that "unless I attain my object—revision—I shall be at great
loss to know what next to do with the book—unless to throw it into the
fire like half a dozen of its predecessors" (*LHA* 6:112).

No doubt he was aware that the book, which existed at the time of
this statement in 1908 in one hundred copies, was safe from the flame. Yet
the call for revision and the recurrent insistence that the book was unfinished point to something in its substance, not so much its form, about
which Adams remained decidedly unassured. One of his motives had been
to reawaken his American neighbors to some sort of reexamination of the
past they had shared and the future that it had made possible (or impossible)—hardly the sort of motive promoted by an esoteric art. The author of
the *Education* could not, by claiming to be an artist, suppress the pedagogue; it was as teacher that he manifested concern that his lesson miscar-
ried. Could the text be written, he wondered, that would provoke (if not
command) an American readership or at least the one mind in ten that
"sensibly reacts" (A I 996)? He had counted on reaching through private
circulation none other than the superior reader. In a letter to Whitelaw
Reid he complained of the detachment that was his in consequence of his
audience's evident refusal to engage him in dialogue: "In theory, the volume is still only a proof sent out for correction. Nothing in it is supposed
to be final. As yet, no one has objected, not even the President or Cabot

Lodge,—still less their wives,—but, what troubles me most is that no one as yet has corrected. My views on education are radically revolutionary, but no one cares." This, he reflects, had been his life's lesson: "So I have always found my American audience. No one ever cares. Nothing diverts the American mind from its ruts" (*LHA* 6:177). The concluding comments drive home the degree to which the *Education* stood in its author's mind as an event more or less ironically continuous with the protagonist's life—a life given to muckraking, teaching, research, and authorship. That the *Education*'s reception should itself be the "Q.E.D." of the book's thesis had to constitute for him the last bitterness.

The *Education* was intended to serve as the basis of dialogue, not as a source of dogma or enigmas. As dialogue, it was meant to sum up a generation's, hardly one man's, peculiar experience. Hence his insistence that the text's borders remained open. "Although I have no idea of publishing, I have all the stronger idea of consulting," he wrote to his brother Charles, sounding the latter out on whether he should confer with James Ford Rhodes about those chapters dealing with Civil War diplomacy. "My notion of work is that of work among workers, that is, by comparison, correspondence and conversation" (*LHA* 6:105). Such a collaborative, dialogic notion of work had formed the basis of his labors as reformer, editor, and professor of a graduate seminar and while engaged in the writing of the *History* he had circulated draft volumes for criticism among a handful of readers. As a member of an unusually purposive and collaborative family he could only play at the contemporary forms of literary self-absorption and indeed was inclined to loath the self-consciousness that distinguished the aesthete or decadent posture. In articulating for Charles his notion of work, perhaps he was also recalling the anonymity of the Virgin's artists whose triumph, he had suggested in *Mont Saint Michel and Chartres*, had been achieved precisely because they had not become entrenched behind rival, egocentric claims. What he proposed in 1907 bore genuine resemblance to what, as we shall see, he had proposed at the beginning of his career as author: informed dialogue that could give definite shape to public policy.

"My object," he explained to the historian John Franklin Jameson, "was to suggest a reform of the whole University system, grouping all knowledge as a historical stream, to be treated by historical methods, and drawing a line between the University and technology." In sharp contrast to his claims elsewhere to a purely formalist interest in the work, he remarks in closing to Jameson, "I trust you will not let yourself be beguiled by the form."[10] That he had considered widely distributing the *Education* among his professional colleagues is evidenced by a long, unsent letter, dated January 1, 1909, which he drafted to accompany "The

Rule of Phase Applied to History" (1909). The letter begins by thanking the historians for reading the *Education*, which he had clearly intended to circulate as the foundation for further writings specifically addressing the academic and social roles of history. Abortive as this particular initiative proved to be, Adams's instrumentalist intentions make us take seriously the bantering claim that his "reminiscences . . . are meant as my closing lectures to undergraduates in the instruction abandoned and broken off in 1877" (*LHA* 6:48). For Adams, the role of teacher was at least as compelling as that of artist.

To initiate a dialogue of real public consequence was certainly among Adams's chief aims in personally dispatching the *Education*. Earl N. Harbert is right to call it the "successful experiment in two-way communication" that his essays and novels had not been and, we might add, that the *History*, written for "an audience fifty years hence," could only guardedly aspire to be.[11] But what Harbert refers to as the first readership's "staggering variety of reactions" could not have lent itself to dialogic focus—it could only have encouraged Adams to vacillate among the statements of intention that we have reviewed. Merely within his own family, that variety ranges from Charles's emotive response to the boyhood chapters—the text, for him, succeeding as a private document between them—to his brother Brooks's dissatisfaction with the book's science, which he thought must put the *Education* beyond the public whose attention Henry ought to command.[12] Henry James willingly lost himself in Adams's "ample page as in a sea of memories and visions and associations," "sticking fast" in the book's "thick evocation" "even as an indiscreet fly in amber."[13] William James congratulated Adams on the childhood and London chapters but complained that "the later diplomatic history" read obscurely and that the historical argument was pure fallacy.[14] Impatient with Adams's speculative bent, he saw as his friend's proper subsequent course the writing of Hay's biography—a task that could not have been further from Adams's agenda, which called for speculation increasingly disembodied.

Upon the writing and teaching of history, neither the *Education* nor the two essays that followed, "The Rule of Phase Applied to History" and the notorious *A Letter to American Teachers of History*, produced an appreciable effect. In 1910, evading the drift of Adams's late work, Jameson protested that he understood "philosophical reasonings as little as the estimable Wagner comprehended the remarks of Doctor Faust," preferring the more prosaic realms of the historical discipline.[15] Unwilling to engage Adams as theoretician, Jameson still could affirm to another correspondent that he ought to be regarded "as the foremost of our historical writers," but that accolade mostly attached to Adams as the profession's premier member emeritus. The dialogue the old man wished to promote did not lend itself to the working aims of his now mostly junior colleagues.[16] Nor were his writings spontaneously taken up by university administrators as the text of curricular reform.

The prospects for substantive discussion fared worse and appreciable effect was more doubtful when it came to the active public men. Henry Cabot Lodge's sole comment was "I didn't know I was as British as you make me out."[17] Against the *Education*'s presentation of Henry Adams as one whose efforts were lost, Oliver Wendell Holmes, Jr., spoke of his own indebtedness to Adams, admonishing him that "If a man has counted in the actual striving of his fellows he cannot pronounce it vain."[18] But such assurance fell short of a precise calculation of the man's effect, leaving Adams as uncertain of his present impact as he reports himself to have been of his efforts as assistant professor. "A teacher affects eternity; he can never tell where his influence stops," he had written, reflecting upon his experience as a Harvard professor (A I 994). In the years following his initial release of the *Education*, there must have been times when he wondered where his influence might start. Theodore Roosevelt promptly approved of the book, but what, if any, soul-searching it provoked concerning his own presidential position is unknown. Roosevelt thought Adams a charming man but no fit companion for the practical statesman; John Hay's "usefulness as a public man" had, in Roosevelt's view, been impaired by his friendship with Adams.[19] The judgment is consistent with Adams's characterization of Roosevelt as "pure act" (A I 1101). Roosevelt's reading of the *Education* did not measurably affect the subsequent course of his presidency.

The dialogue for which the *Education* was to serve as foundation proved intermittent and unfocused while Adams lived. Repeatedly he complained that no one cared, that the very readers "authorised" to strike out or correct had not done their job, had not returned their volumes (*LHA* 6:288). Increasingly the text became for him a private, prophetic chart of the twentieth century's course, a guide to a literal unfolding of events that appeared to be "writing" the sequel. "To me," he wrote Elizabeth Cameron from Paris in 1908, having returned from dinner and an alarmist discussion at the American embassy, "the moment looks like a supplementary chapter of my *Education*" (*LHA* 6:171). Such did not bode well for the continuation of civilized life as Adams defined it. In proving prophetic, in rightly anticipating an irruption of "forces" that must either vanquish or remake society and mind, well might the *Education* forfeit readership; in Adams's view little commonality was likely to subsist between the text and the new American. "By the bye," he wrote to Gaskell in April 1912, two days before the *Titanic* sank and two weeks before he suffered the first of two strokes that he would claim, in the editor's preface, to have "put an end to his literary activity forever," "I hardly think my 'Education' is fit for any public. It is only proof-sheets, full of errors, and I've not given it to any library here. The more I watch the coming public the more likely I think it that the public of fifty years hence will be something quite different from the past, and that we need not want to please it, for it will not want to please us. Burn up the volumes when you are done with them!" (*LHA* 6:533).

Posthumous Text

What Adams in 1912 characterized as "the coming public" has proven him wrong: the *Education* has never suffered neglect and even hostile readers have flattered it by the vehemence of their response. Upon its posthumous, trade publication in 1918 it achieved what for Adams would have surely been the vulgar distinction of becoming a best-seller and in 1919 it drew the Pulitzer Prize for a work of nonfiction. Van Wyck Brooks, T. S. Eliot, R. P. Blackmur, and other literary figures of the period between the wars made use of the *Education* as a text by which they could define their own sense of public vocation. In these and later years the *Education*'s voice made its way into the country's imaginative literature; one feels Adams's presence in works as diverse as Eliot's "Gerontion" (1920) and Ellison's *Invisible Man* (1952). It was particularly the voice of the *Education* that provoked critical response; by and against that voice Adams's whole career eventually would be reconsidered and appraised. In the late 1940s, the first book-length academic assessments began to appear; by 1962, fifty years after Adams instructed Gaskell to burn his copy of the *Education*, there were a half dozen outstanding studies of Adams, including Ernest Samuels's monumental biography, the third and final volume of which appeared in 1964.

This seminal attention and the reappraisals that have followed constitute the reception of the *Education* and the various interpretations of Adams's lifework—a singularly diverse sequence of texts to which the *Education* and the late essays lend unusual rhetorical urgency. No author exists independent of a readership, but this is particularly evident in the case of Adams, who customarily employed unusual means to summon an audience and whose work always calls attention to its public occasion. The *Education* arrives at its public occasion by way of a prolonged and studious absorption in a shared experience, a deep participation in common traditions. Insofar as the book's allusiveness requires ongoing contextualization on the part of the reader, inasmuch as the book's resonance places it as a text among texts—a "great tradition" commencing with Genesis—it fairly begs the complement of scholarly apparatus and critical commentary. Beyond that, of course, the book commends itself doubtfully to the moral and imaginative response that alone can requite the intensity of its author's concern. Given Adams's skepticism that tradition as he had known it could continue to exist as a cohesive force, given the nearly explicit despair of his late texts over the prospect of their readership, the *Education*'s diverse reception requires attention as the continuation of the book's larger story: its submission as an autobiographical text to an uncertain public on the chance that it can bring about a measure of common redemption. We shall review that reception in the final chapter, after first working back through those dimensions of Adams's thought that he essayed in the *Education* to fix in a final configuration. In the remainder of this chapter, we shall examine what in the *Education* makes for diversity of response—the various and conflicting rhetorical expectations generated by this largely disunified text. And we shall explore what is perhaps the book's one principle of unity and the source of its perennial appeal: its abiding insistence that the past be considered (even if it be rejected) as a regenerative resource and that from the past's record of violence and failure we attempt to salvage the language of "eighteenth-century" moral consciousness. That insistence constitutes the rhetorical urgency of the *Education*'s at first only artfully but afterward factually posthumous voice.

Again, Adams's two acts of publishing the *Education* reflect such different author-audience relationships that they require us to consider the 1907 and 1918 editions as two distinct books. The differences between the editions are striking: in the first publication, the author is alive and the audience is small, known, and directed in specific ways to respond, while in the second, the author is dead and the audience (a paying one) is large, diffuse, and required to sort through the author's contradictory in-text statements of intention in shaping their response. In the first, Adams's contact with his readers qualifies the text's assertion that Henry Adams is dead, silent, and henceforth withdrawn from public dialogue. Whatever else they do, the various letters by which Adams prefaced the 1907 edition affirm, against the text, that he is in life, that his text is negotiable, and that his theory is quite likely wrong. The volume awaits its last word, to be arrived at through a dialogic process. But in the second, 1918 edition, the text's closures correspond to fact. The editor's preface, signed by Henry Cabot Lodge and dated 1918, although written by Adams himself in 1916 for what he knew would be the inevitably posthumous edition, assumes two "supplementary chapters" to have ended the volume's immediate dialogic life. The first is World War I, the outbreak of which in 1914 confirmed for the author his catastrophic prognosis, leading him, as he wrote in 1916, to make his long-standing rule of silence "absolute" (A I

720). The second of course is his death, the understood condition of the trade publication that the editor's preface was written to introduce.

Given these developments, the text of 1918 is much more somber than that of 1907. For the general reader, no personally prepared preface intervenes to blunt the moral that appears after five hundred pages of dense prose—that "dispute was idle, discussion was futile, and silence, next to good-temper, was the mark of sense" (A I 1178). Having read that far, the reader must consider why, if this reflects the author's mature judgment, *The Education of Henry Adams* did not become a suppressed, closed, burned book after all. To a large degree the question remains unanswerable. Again, Adams must have known all along that to distribute close to a hundred copies of a book rendered that book virtually unsuppressible. The editor's preface may well be the concession of one who knew that he could not now do as he pleased and expunge the book—that the matter had indeed "passed beyond his control" (A I 720). Even if the posthumous publication may be said to bear Adams's deathbed blessings, the text still comes to us with built-in obstructions to our reception of it: challenges to our motivation for reading it and sabotage of our attempts to apply its lessons. If we are to succeed in opening its (closed) chapters, we must consciously reaffirm our power as readers in the face of a text that ostensibly denies our ability to read to any willful and redeeming effect.

That our readership must contend with a text uncertain of its occasion is made evident right away by the deprecation of the prefaces and by the fact that there are two of them. What from the reader's point of view is a preface, shaping expectations of what lies ahead, constitutes for the author an afterward, a consideration, perhaps treacherously ironic, of what lies behind. The 1907 preface is the fullest in-text statement of the author's intention, but our reading of that statement must take into account a context that, ironic anyway, substantially changed between 1907 and 1918. In 1907 as in 1918, the preface introduced a narrative commended to "young men, in Universities or elsewhere," the purpose of which was to fit them "to be men of the world, equipped for any emergency"; in 1907 as in 1918, the narrative culminated in "A Dynamic Theory of History" depicting historical process as absolute emergency, which the most highly developed of human minds must lack the capacity to contain. If we are to be saved, this doctrine warns us, our minds need more than to undergo education—they must evolve. Hence dispute is idle, discussion futile, and silence and good temper the mark of sense. By going out, from 1907 to 1909, under cover of various epistolary prefaces addressed to known readers and soliciting response, the *Education*'s dynamic theory of history stood as evident hypothesis, and Adams affirmed that discussion and dispute were exactly the nature of the work at hand. His junior readers could therefore credit his dispatch of the book to "young men, in Universities or elsewhere": "elsewhere" could be the White House of what to Adams was the appallingly youthful Roosevelt.[20] In contrast to the epistolary prefaces soliciting revision, the 1916 editor's preface would close off discussion and harden hypothesis into foregone certainty. Protesting that the author—silent since 1914 and now truly deceased—could not while alive "publish that which he thought unprepared and unfinished," this preface nevertheless puts the *Education*, in the company of *Mont Saint Michel and Chartres*, "within reach of students who have occasion to consult [it]." Such publication, writes Adams under the pseudonym, is "not in opposition to the author's judgment" (A I 720).

The text is not so much commended as abandoned to the coming public's readership. And our knowledge of the first readership, of the volume's former proofsheet status, reinforces our sense of its abandonment. From the 1918 editor's preface, we proceed to the preface of 1907 aware that Adams, as a source of revision and supplementation, no longer exists for this text. Unable now to dispute and discuss, he no longer serves as the living mitigation of the text's absolutist pronouncements. The book must open through the student's self-directed consultation of it—through an attention to the mitigation and revision that inheres in the text's own paradoxical life.

The 1907 preface appeals to the coming public in their capacity as students, but the aims of the book as therein stated suggest that the volume will not address conventional educational goals. No mere student is likely to understand the paradox on which the preface is built. As do most of the book's major ironies, this paradox emerges from the elder's experience, from a life for which the old man feels both affection and regret and a career that he wishes to redeem by offering as a lesson to others yet cast off, insofar as it pertains to him alone, as an intolerable weight. The paradox is that the singular story of Henry Adams may have universal value only in proportion as the willful ego is seen, in retrospect, as a tailor's dummy—the accidental recipient of so many clothes. This hardly lends itself to the student's need for examples of deliberate, self-assured action, models of self-improvement such as Franklin could provide. Yet if Franklin's entrepreneurial methods retain some practical value in the twentieth century the *Education* goes on to depict, his Newtonian universe no longer holds, and his wisdom cannot begin to address the metaphysical and social problems that are to give the new century its tone.

Interestingly, it is Rousseau, not Franklin, against whom Adams defines his intentions. As though to emphasize the *Education*'s practically didactic purpose, Adams cites Rousseau's *Confessions* as a text similarly grounded in the story of a particular life, but one that mistakenly assumed that to expose the life's unflattering particularities would be to maximize the story's universality and instructiveness. Since Rousseau's time, Adams writes, "and largely thanks to him, the *Ego* has steadily tended to efface itself, and, for purposes of model, to become a manikin on which the toilet of education is to be draped in order to show the fit or misfit of the clothes" (A I 721–22). Ironic as Adams knows his pedagogy and statements of pedagogical purpose to be, he offers them as more appropriate to his own time than the methods of either Franklin or Rousseau. Considering Adams's intense privacy, his impulse to efface himself before the prospect of a broad readership is not surprising, even though, as we shall see, he could not actually efface himself and still have a story. Like Rousseau, and unlike Franklin, Adams would seem to repent of a life of folly. He proceeds, however, not only by a more ironic but by a less settled order of old man's wisdom: one that, not genuinely given over to repentance, is yet sufficiently resigned to complicate his explicit intention to assist the young and to advise those who have just entered upon careers of worldly striving. That Adams cannot state—in the preface or anywhere else in the book—the ratio of his resignation to his belief in his possible efficacy as public mentor will keep the *Education* mystifyingly irresolute. But for that irresolution it is all the more dynamic, all the more insistently a reader's book.

Adams in fact submits two distinct although interrelated statements of didactic purpose. In the first, "Henry Adams" assumes dual identity: author-tailor, protagonist-manikin. "The tailor's object," he writes, "is to fit young men, in Universities or elsewhere, to be men of the world, equipped for any emergency; and the garment offered to them is meant to show the faults of the patchwork fitted on their fathers" (A I 722). The "garment" and not the "figure" (ego) is the purported object of study. For the old man, the manikin stands as the emblem of renounced selfhood, but for the student, it is meant as a heuristic figure, the elder's effacement serving to renew the human form's possibility. As a kind of tabula rasa, the manikin is offered to the student as an emblem of universal young manhood, one that may be fitted with a view to personal needs. Yet Adams deliberately overextends his metaphor in claiming that the tailor may adapt "the manikin as well as the clothes to his patron's wants" (A I 722). There is in his view but one basic human form, and there are limits to the wardrobe with which tradition provides us. The language by which education, particularly moral education, proceeds cannot efface all vestiges of past life without itself ceasing to exist. Besides preparing the sons "for any emergency," the new clothes are meant to expose the "patchwork" of old dogmas and irreconcilable theories by which the fathers dressed their days. But by 1907 the clothes metaphor itself was one whose cloth was old, and this points to a central tension in the text. Insofar as, generation by generation, we are creatures of education, and not evolution, we must derive new life of old. Yet how may we proceed when "education" subverts faith in the existence of common, culturally genetic purpose, when the elder's "wisdom" speaks an ironic language, one that tends toward the mature opinion that no life is renewable on the old terms? As metaphor, education-as-clothes aptly illustrates the point: it cannot but recall Carlyle, a connection hardly auspicious. For we are asked by it to think of the ego as fatally captive to illusion, to suspect that the clothes have no intrinsic truth and little durable utility, and to be caught up at all events in the web of social usage. The coat that Adams eventually offers the young man is one in which the seams remain substantially unsewn.

Significantly, in his second statement of purpose Adams sheds this old metaphor in favor of a more modern one—one that projects education less as the fit of the young man's clothes than as his fitness for the affairs of post-Victorian life. From the student's coat we pass to the student—not, however, to the student as ego, but as system: "The young man himself, the subject of education, is a certain form of energy; the object to be gained is economy of his force; the training is partly the clearing away of obstacles, partly the direct application of effort" (A I 722). Much more than education-as-clothes, education-as-economy-of-force will serve as the book's dominant pedagogical metaphor. But Adams's prefatory sequencing of the two has a darkly prefigurative logic that makes the dynamic model no more auspicious than the first. For Adams—as the book eventually makes plain—we have come to speak of "force" in consequence of having stripped absolute reality, or, alternately, the human manikin, of all its old clothes: myth, poetry, religion, an intelligible common language, a coherent history, a god-centered science. Little now remains outside the physical scientist's paradoxical and ephemeral theories to intercept the death-force of cosmic omnipotence. To the student as yet unacquainted with the theory of history in which the narrative culminates, the dynamic model may well seem a practicable approach to education, certainly more to the point than an analogy based on the appareling of the nineteenth-century student-dandy. By book's end, however, education-as-economy-of-force has positioned the student quite nakedly amid cosmic force, with no hope that Jehovah shall exist and prove merciful, and with little prospect that the best economy can assist the effort to recall and renew a now nearly spent human order.

For the author, preface constitutes afterthought: a last word that provides a kind of authorized first reading. This being so, we cannot but question Adams's intent (his seeming malice aforethought) in introducing the dynamic model as an encouragement to his student. There may be no or very little malicious intent, only an irresolvable conflict between the elder's retrospective wisdom and the student's perennial need for open prospects and operative hypotheses. We may even say Adams honors that need and that the conflict is largely internal—between what he now "knows" and his by no means spent recognition that youth, if indeed not the studious elder, needs such "illusion" as commands what he once called (apropos of the Jeffersonian democrat-frontiersman) "the energy of success" (A II 119). If the *Education* documents the lifelong disabusal of Henry Adams, it does so against the depiction of his own bygone youthful attitude that the world exists to be reformed. With youth—the young man he once was, the student-reader—he remains more or less in sympathy. Against the dynamic theory of history put forth in chapters 33 and 34, we may read the prefatory envoy to "young men" not as hoax but as statement of faith: an afterword that breaks with the overwhelmingly determinist logic of the dynamic theory, that affirms youthful effort in the face of a denuded, dehumanized, de-creating cosmos.

But this reading cannot or should not be allowed to suppress the other: that the preface mocks, has no faith in, reserves little but hostility for, the student, the "coming public." As our survey of the 1907 to 1910 correspondence has shown, Adams could profess little faith in a future readership. "In another generation," he wrote to his former student Henry Osborn Taylor, "the proportion of *us* to all, will be as unity to infinity. I am satisfied that it is immaterial whether one man or a thousand or a hundred thousand read one's books" (*LHA* 6:288). As the *Education* was until its author's death kept from the unknown but already arriving public—kept from the "new American" who "must be either the child of the new forces or a chance sport of nature" (A I 1177)—we must consider the preface as belligerent, addressing an audience that the writer is convinced could not attend his words even if it were to try. The 1907 preface, we may argue, acquires its hostility in the context of its 1918 trade publication. The editor's preface tells the paying reader just how long the book had been around before he or she was granted access; must not that reader therefore suspect that Adams's tone of public urgency comes with a measure of bad faith? For if you do have something to say, if you would redeem America, why wait eleven years (or however long it takes you to die) to say it to that public in whose behalf you pretend to speak? In the context of the 1918 trade publication, the 1907 preface inevitably raises such questions, and by doing so would appear to spurn latter-day youthful effort. And read in the light of Adams's well-known class resentment, the preface may seem the height of cynicism, the author's covert pointing of an uncommonly mean moral: that the student's fit inheritance is none other than a wasting multiverse that is his in consequence of his class's triumphant corruption of the once-youthful American possibility. The man who would go on to write *A Letter to American Teachers of History* was supremely capable of such harshness.

Although it may be tempting to exclude one reading as less persuasive than the other, both must be retained. For the drama of the *Education* lies in the possibility of both readings: the impeachment of the ostensibly affirmative preface by the dynamic theory's bleakness and the mitigation of the dynamic theory's nihilism by the author's apparent determination to provoke a live response, even among his posthumous audience. Of itself, that drama solicits the reader's, indeed a community of readers', dialogic entry. Yet as Adams's two acts of publishing the book and his persistently vacillating explanatory texts show, there is no reason to believe that the conflict of that drama is ever under the author's control. His assertion in the editor's preface that the book is "unfinished" suggests that the drama was not intended to be left up in the air. The *Education*'s irreconcilable conflicts may make for consistent drama, but it is a mistake to think of that drama as the "artful" paradox by which Adams meant to unify his text. As Adams himself protested, the text is neither artistically nor scientifically self-contained, and it comes as no surprise that commentators have had difficulties making a case for the *Education*'s unity. Yet neither is it surprising that any committed reading of the work should aspire to some purpose and unity on its own terms, along the lines of the reader's preferences.[21] On the evidence of its own engagement alone, the present reading finds the book's nihilism decidedly mitigated. That the *Education* has assumed ever since its 1918 release a place in the nation's discussion of its ultimate destiny suggests that the book possesses attributes that affirm dialogic process. Yet we cannot therefore call it a "permanent" book, one that no period can reject as of little or no use. We can hardly be certain that the book is "safe" from its own resignation—that current in the text that repeatedly threatens to withdraw the book and its public occasion from our midst. The time may come when the dominant community of readers will permit it to make good its threats. All such allegedly "permanent" texts are perhaps more or less equally imperiled; that the *Education* states and even cultivates its peril should command our particular attention.

To argue persuasively that the book does affirm youthful energy and dialogic process, we must attend to how tenuous that affirmation really is. The *Education*'s "yea" rests in its power as published text to rescue "Henry Adams" from the thesis that he has failed and died, having lived a life of inconsequence. If it is to succeed, the book in publication must reverse its own argument that Adams's lifelong efforts were futile, and for this to occur the reader must see the protagonist come alive as one who heroically managed to preserve his own high possibilities. The reader must see the protagonist as the author's sequence of antecedent selves—formation, education, perseverance of the present, vigorous (albeit posthumous) authorial voice. These antecedent selves, far from representing the pure wasteful expenditure of a futile and deceased Henry Adams, must be seen as the resource of the present voice: a voice that attempts, although without much expectation of success, to bequeath a past that may contribute to the renewal of shared possibility. In the final paragraph of the 1907 preface, Adams has no choice but to admit that the manikin, as a measure of "human condition . . . must have the air of reality; must be taken for real; must be treated as though it had life" (A I 722). Calling his own bluff, acknowledging that the volume is autobiographical, Adams ends on the question, "Who knows? Possibly it had!" The concession is major: the human form cannot (or if it can it must not) be effaced of its past; if it is to be renewed, and kept recognizably human, it will be through the office of bequeathable resources.

By admitting that the manikin must have had, and must continue to have, particular life, Adams grants what he cannot deny without suppressing his volume, grounded as it is in the narrative adventures of a particular man. Yet, in turn, the narrative reveals why Adams may have wished, in the interest of a didactic purpose, to minimize, if not efface, the self—that same self whose special history Adams as author tacitly assumes as his mandate to teach. A didactic scheme built upon the *Education*'s protagonist is bound to be problematic, and not principally because of his uncommon background, his conservative taste, his "failure" to deflect the current of his time because he remained always illiterate in mathematics. The problem with the protagonist stems from his patent superiority: Henry Adams is intelligent, energetic, and heroic in his consistent efforts to overcome obstacles and still (as of 1905) fails. Again and again through the book's first half, the aged author reductively foresees an abortive conclusion to the protagonist's youthful efforts—his various ventures in political and academic reform, his wish to renew out of the resource of his republican inheritance. In the second half, he portrays the retired author's philosophical inquiries as so much wasted, if urgent, effort. That effort is depicted as merging with the present venture, the *Education* (what he calls, in "The Abyss of Ignorance," "The Education of Henry Adams: a study of twentieth-century multiplicity"), the burden of which is to overcome not just a life but a nation and a historical era of seemingly appointed failure. The redemptive office of the highborn citizen vis-à-vis the state is felt throughout the *Education* as a fixture of Adams's thought, even as he calls into question the public relevance that up until the last decades of the nineteenth century autobiography had assumed as its social raison d'être. No individual, the book implicitly claims, is in a better position to teach than Henry Adams. Yet Adams cannot teach by his experience without progressively attenuating the book's stated didactic purpose.

That purpose is strained nearly to the breaking point halfway through. By midpoint we have followed the protagonist from his "eighteenth-century" Quincy childhood and Boston youth, through a young manhood spent on the European continent and in England, and through the first years of life's prime in Washington and Boston. We have seen him pass from a view of the world as full of reformable evil to his first strong intimations of the degree to which human affairs are governed by inertia— the tendency of society to drift in a particular direction until some impasse or violent counterthrust is met. We have seen him come up against repeated instances of the irrationality of human motivation in the public as in the private realm and even to have caught a premonitory glimpse on the occasion of his sister's death of the chaos of force that is to dominate the meditations of the book's second half. Not that at midpoint Adams the protagonist has succumbed to disillusionment. On the contrary, in those moments when the narrator refrains from depicting Henry Adams as a well-intentioned but backward mind, we see a man astute in his perceptions of contemporary problems as well as one full of unvanquished hope for the eventual redemption of post–Civil War America. Insofar as we are to applaud and not pity the young man's idealism, there is little fault to find in his "toilet of education." Its patchwork is the product of high expectations and active-mindedness: an admirable willingness to impeach inherited belief by the light of new thought and novel social reality. That it does not have the gloss of leisure, the drape of monied assertion, should be the protagonist's success.

But it is only a relative success. Measured by the old man's dynamic criterion, by the young Adams's reformist ambitions, and by his family's impossible expectations, the story is absolutely one of failure, because Henry Adams, who by rights should have redeemed America, as of 1905 had not done so. At midpoint the young man to whom the volume has been nominally commended is reminded "that education should try to lessen the obstacles, diminish the friction, invigorate the energy, and should train minds to react, not at haphazard, but by choice, on the lines of force that attract their world." But with this, the volume's stated purpose, the young man is required to balance a story whose lesson is that "barely one man in a hundred owns a mind capable of reacting to any purpose on the forces that surround him, and fully half of these react wrongly"; that "only the most energetic, the most highly fitted, and the most favored have overcome the friction or the viscosity of inertia, and these were compelled to waste three-fourths of their energy in doing it" (A I 1007). In the first half, the friction or viscosity of inertia is largely institutional. By book's end, however, such inertia as thwarts the would-be reformer of Grantism has assumed monistic, theological proportions; it is present in the atom (Adam, Adams) as in the universe ("God"). It has formed the basis of a "dynamic" theory that does succeed in imposing unity upon the multiplicity of thought and experience, but at the greatest possible expense: the consignment of the human order to such catastrophic "natural" process as tends toward the final equilibrium of death. Captive to natural force, society, according to the dynamic theory, has throughout history and with increasing peril to itself cultivated force to the point that it now (1905) has more force at its disposal than mind or morality can possibly contain—putting society on the edge of disasters no education may be able to avert. So Adams obliges himself to admit in the final chapter that the story, as the story of education, may have as much tendency "to discourage effort" as "to encourage foresight and to economise waste of mind" (A I 1178).

The conflict between Adams's prefatory avowals of didactic intent and the discouraging lesson of his life's story resists reconciliation. One may say that the conflicts resolve and the text unifies to the extent that we look upon the *Education* as a hostile and embittered gesture that mocks its readership as it flaunts its futility. But this must exaggerate Adams's capacity for cynicism to a degree that his motivation to write could have hardly withstood.[22] And it must totally disregard Adams's initial circulation of the book in which the motive to consult was clearly in play. In an effort to unify Adams's pedagogy, a number of commentators have suggested that the contradictions are intentional facets of a Socratically dialogic scheme.[23] The *Education* does function Socratically, but we should probably avoid anchoring that effectiveness in a Socratic author who has one eye on an audience and the other on an unmoving light. The closer Adams approaches to what he is willing to concede as the "truth," the less visible to him is his audience or at least his student audience: the "new man," the "child born of contact between the new and the old energies" (A I 1177). Given the distance between Adams and Theodore Roosevelt, who is comparatively a child of the old energies and traditions, how much further removed must the coming generations prove?

Adams remains ill at ease in his relation to his junior, unknown public, tentative in his claim to authority. In fact the more avowedly autobiographical the *Education* becomes, the more apt Adams is to suppress the educational motive, which particularly requires the assertion of authority, and claim a different purpose, a different order of audience. "A story of education,—seventy years of it,—the practical value remains to the end in doubt," he confesses not two pages after the preface. "Although everyone," he continues, "cannot be a Gargantua-Napoleon-Bismarck and walk off with the great bells of Notre Dame, everyone must bear his own universe, and most persons are moderately interested in learning how their neighbors have managed to carry theirs" (A I 724). Neither, as he knows only too well, can everyone be an Adams, particularly in one's failures; yet "neighbors" suggests a common ground that, excluding perhaps the university lad, may still support a fair portion of humanity. The narrative here seems directed to the seasoned student of suffering—the reader whose comparable maturity alone can absolve the private man of his failure, because such a reader too has learned to bear a universe that does not become much less tragic over time. Such a reader finds accommodation in the pronoun "one," almost as prominent in the *Education* as the famous "he," and serving at once to suggest the protagonist's isolation and essential anonymity while asserting a claim to the "universality" of his condition and response: his status as a one with whom a many may identify. Neither is this reader to be exclusively associated with the first readership: although this audience included such sympathetic contemporaries as Charles Francis Adams, Jr., Charles Milnes Gaskell, and Henry James, it also contained men like Roosevelt and Lodge, whose hubris went unchecked by tragic wisdom. Adams's neighbor is one who reads his text by the light of a comparable education in sorrow. To such a reader he may have nothing essential to teach, but in being read by him or her he would be confirmed in his common humanity.

Such a reader might be particularly well qualified to read the twenty-year hiatus that divides the *Education* in half. One needs little knowledge of Adams's life to see that that gap removes from our view the years of his prime and that what for an Adams were the expected features of life's prime—work of public consequence and the production of a family—are missing. Whatever their content, the years passed over constitute obvious loss; the moral of the hiatus is that life is bereavement, notwithstanding the fullest preparation and the keenest afterthought. With varying intimacy the first readership knew what remained unwritten: Adams's marriage to Marian Hooper, the years of their Washington residency, his massive productiveness as an author, Marian's suicide, and much of the widower's travels. The first readership, moreover, knew Adams's suppression of these years as an intimate gesture.[24] We who are familiar with Adams's life from distant perspectives may more clearly see that the twenty missing years involve the loss of opportunities that the *Education* does amply specify. Even the obvious unstated bereavement, that of Marian Adams, does not go unwritten. As R. P. Blackmur was the first to note,[25] Adams's treatment of his sister's death follows, in time, the event of his wife's and addresses an evident sequence: "For the *first time*, the stage-scenery of the senses collapsed; the human mind felt itself stripped naked, vibrating in a void of shapeless energies, with resistless mass, colliding, crushing, wasting and destroying what these same energies had created and labored from eternity to perfect" (A I 983; italics added).

In this passage we come upon what, from the perspective of the *Education*, is the recurrent crisis of the life: "the human mind stripped naked" among de-creating energies that defy the human capacity to impute to the universe a credibly rational or beneficent order, which Adams felt necessary to any open, creative view of history. Clearly the mind underwent its most radical denudations in consequence of those experiences that Adams compresses into the account of Louisa's death: her death, symbolically, constitutes the death of woman, for Adams the focus of human and cultural regeneration. But the Civil War, the Grant administration, and the course of late-century science and geopolitics all called for signal lightenings of apparel, and the chaos Adams sights when he gazes at Mont Blanc after he has come from the deathbed at Bagni di Lucca had been seen before and would be seen again—until, indeed, he would have to discipline himself repeatedly in order to see anything else. This is the crisis against which authorship (as discipline) must specifically contend; it must do so without the conviction that a community of readers and fellow workers exists and in a seemingly antiquated literary language that can but tentatively piece together a life-affirming symbology. This life crisis is manifestly a crisis of vocation, registered intimately in the *Education*'s rhetorical ambivalence. The loss that the text does specify could not be more profoundly revealing: it is none other than his career as a purposive, publishing author. "Merely in print," he writes in "Twenty Years After (1892)," "he thought altogether ridiculous the number of volumes he counted on the shelves of public libraries. He had no notion whether they served a useful purpose" (A I 1008). "As far as Adams knew," he concludes, "he had but three serious readers" and "was amply satisfied with their consideration" (A I 1019).

These spare and ironic reflections upon the prolific authorship of his middle years serve to define the *Education*'s own rhetorical occasion. If the number of volumes Adams had already completed seemed "altogether ridiculous," how much more gratuitous the present volume must seem. It is either gratuitous or the life's one necessary text, his lifelong authorship's sine qua non, the vocation's redeeming valedictory enactment. Adams concedes that he knows not which it is, only that the activity of writing goes forward irrespective of known audience, decided purpose, and the probability of a unified statement. At times he characterizes it as the compulsive habit of one who is always the benighted student: "The pen becomes a sort of blind man's dog" and "works for itself" (A I 1075). But at other times he vindicates the full vocational purpose of his writing and presents it as the one activity that stands between his readers and social chaos: "One would have been glad to stop and ask no more," he writes in "The Abyss of Ignorance (1902)," the chapter that purports to trace the *Education*'s origins, "but the anarchist bomb bade one go on, and the bomb is a powerful persuader" (A I 1114). Earlier, in summing up his experience as a teacher of history, he had revealed that even his efforts to present the past as an austere factual sequence, "in essence incoherent and immoral," had made "of his scholars either priests or atheists, plutocrats or social-ists, judges or anarchists, almost in spite of himself" (A I 994). Study of history, in short, confers moral identity; moral identity commits conduct. In Adams's case, again, study of history culminates in the *Education*: a text that would enact certain "eighteenth-century" beliefs even though it doubts the likelihood of an audience capable of possessing the resource of the past.

The 1918 editor's preface releases *The Education of Henry Adams* as "avowedly incomplete": in such terms did Adams close his career as public author. Whether Adams meant much more by this concession than that the book lacked artistic proportion cannot be said. The verdict how-ever does anticipate the reception that has kept the text dialogically alive, the writing of what from our perspective are the "supplementary chap-ters" that have productively perpetuated its incompletion. The power of Adams's vocation is to be measured finally by its capacity to call a criti-cal readership to the occasion of this skeptical authorship, a conjunction which in the end salvages his work from the aridities, closures, and si-lences of "scientific" historiography. So genuine is Adams's mistrust of his medium, and so doubtful are his late texts of the public discourse they require, that his work has the peculiar and instructive effect of making us realize that it has survived only because readers have ultimately believed more in its efficacy than could Adams. Between the 1907 and the 1918 *Education*, Adams endeavored to complete not only the life story but also all dialogue touching upon his lifelong concerns. Bearing distinct hostility to what he assumed to be his all but nonexistent audience—the void that he saw in that place where he had looked all his life for an intelligent, responsive readership—he worked to perfect a final word, the rhetorical act that would satirize and close all pretense to rational discussion of historical process. His failure to silence his own voice underscores the paradoxical, dialogic, and inventive character of his language; a character that, as this study will attempt to show, particularly distinguishes his life-long practice as an author. To the end, Adams's pleasure in dialogue was too ample for him successfully to dismiss all possibility of historical novelty or the generative resource of the past, without which discourse must unconditionally end. Yet the effort he made to do so constitutes a famous moment in his career, contributing greatly to what twentieth-century readers have found so compelling about his work; and this moment must now claim our attention.

3

The Paradoxical Spirit of
Private Conversation

A Bystander's Commentary

AFTER THE *Education* Adams completed four short works: the unsigned biographical introduction to the privately printed *Letters of John Hay* (1908), "The Rule of Phase Applied to History" (1909), *A Letter to American Teachers of History* (1910), and *The Life of George Cabot Lodge* (1911). Of the four, only the last appeared before Adams's death through the regular channels of book publication. A companion to the *Poems and Dramas* of the late "Bay" Lodge brought out by Houghton Mifflin, the *Life* was written at the Lodge family's request, and the terse prose Adams adopts to tell the poet's rather eventless life succeeded, as far as was possible, in effacing the biographer.[1] Glad to serve the Lodges, though it meant memorializing a flawed poet dead in the unpromising prime of his life, Adams would have preferred to keep his name off the volume and may even have tried to prevent the *Life* from being sent out for review with the *Poems and Dramas*.[2] Of the two short speculative works, the "Rule" received the close reading of perhaps three readers before Adams suppressed it; Brooks Adams, one of those readers, would publish it the year after his brother's death in *The Degradation of the Democratic Dogma*. Only *A Letter* (also included in *Degradation*) enjoyed its author's promotion. As many as five hundred copies were privately printed and Adams, in the role of retired historian, eagerly dispatched them to his professional colleagues.

Despite many resemblances, the "Rule" and *A Letter* are very different texts, divergent in their respective moods, conclusions, and rhetorical strategies. Together they measure the despair, confusion, and sense of incompletion that plagued Adams following the composition of *Mont Saint Michel and Chartres* and the *Education*. His own explanations of the short works vary but follow from the notion that their speculations continue a line of thought begun in "The Tendency of History" and developed in the two large works. In the draft of a letter meant to introduce the

68

ultimately suppressed "Rule," Adams speaks of it as an attempt to assign something *like* "a mathematical formula" to the law of acceleration proposed in the *Education*. Insofar as it affirms, albeit skeptically, the possibility of an unforeseen redemption in historical experience, his doubtful appropriation of Willard Gibbs's phase theory is consistent with the *Education*'s open end. The "Rule" he could plausibly represent as an extension of set themes; *A Letter* he characterized less credibly as "the connecting link between the Chartres and the Education" (*LHA* 6:320). Actually to accept *A Letter* as such requires an intense reduction of the two large works that obliges us to read them as essentially concerned only with the decline and death of instinct and art in consequence of the fatally "entropic" development of reason and science. Yet so eager was Adams to achieve "synthesis"—or, perhaps more accurately, so intent was he to find some unifying principle in the chaos of his late sequence of texts—that he repeatedly minimized what probably for him was the dangerous narrative richness of *Chartres* and the *Education* and so asserted that "the last three chapters of each make one didactic work in disguise" (*LHA* 6:238). His work's multivalence, however, was not so simply governed. Inasmuch as they count for unity, the logical consistency and recurrent paradigms of his late work are more than offset by its rhetorical discontinuity. The chaos of his texts was real.

The rhetorical discontinuity of Adams's work is evident at every stage of his career, but it becomes more pronounced from 1894 on as he feels himself increasingly pressed to court an audience—court it to the material extent of submitting texts to his select readers' hands. In proportion as he despairs of a readership he reverts to certain antiquated discursive practices: circulating his work as admonitory pamphlets among a conservative elite, he would perform the office of philosophic generalist, unifying, if only in some "convenient" formulation, the divergent paths of thought in an effort to define their moral and social significance. This "eighteenth-century" motive may be clearly discerned beneath "The Tendency of History," the "Rule," and *A Letter* and the initial publication of the *Education*. (*Mont Saint Michel and Chartres*, as I shall argue in Chapter 6, emerges from a significantly antithetical rhetoric.) Yet these works, the "Rule" and *A Letter* most particularly, labor under the suspicion that the terms and conditions of any overtly public practice (such discourse as might be conducted by pamphlets, as that of prerevolutionary America largely was)[3] are dated and testify to the writer's impotence; so much do they labor under it that the suspicion itself becomes the essential substance of these texts. Beneath the lurid, jeremiadical accounts of an accelerating humanity, a shrinking sun, and a dying social organism, the "Rule" and *A Letter* tell another, related but more specific, story: the ultimate recession of any general, informed readership; the foregone obsolescence of any common, "eighteenth-century" educated discourse. No longer to be regarded as capable of formulating ultimate, integrative truths, the "literary language" that once sufficed the callings of philosopher, historian, and statesman has been supplanted by the esoteric, more or less unintelligible languages of post-Newtonian science.

This story fills out the last chapters of Adams's aggravated suspicion that he wrote against increased odds of writing to any consequence; a suspicion articulated tacitly by the variant modes of publication his late work saw. Regular channels of publication hardly guarantee that an author's work will contribute measurably to a cohesive public discourse, but pointed withdrawal from such channels bespeaks a loss of faith in their efficacy: a conviction that through them ideas will not find the vital exchange their germination requires. In the long period of his self-styled retirement following the conventional publication of the *History*, Adams's work seldom reached print in fully public modes. "The Tendency of History," his 1894 presidential address to the American Historical Association (delivered as we have seen in absentia), appeared as a matter of course in the *Annual Report of the American Historical Association*. A short essay, "Count Edward de Crillon," was printed in the first volume of the *American Historical Review*, to which Adams, the genuinely (if narrowly) celebrated author of the *History*, had been asked to contribute. Like "The Tendency of History" (and indeed almost everything else Adams would henceforth write), "Count Edward de Crillon" was designed to challenge the historical scholar's complacence. But whereas in the "Tendency" he had delineated the political dangers amid which history's imminent scientific status must place the scholar, "Count Edward" questions whether history, at least as written by isolated scholars lacking mathematical formulations, can ever transcend the "personal error" that each historian must contribute to an already error-ridden past and whether knowledge of the historical subject is even possible given the parallax of documentary falsehood through which it must be viewed. A factual error that he had lately discovered in his own *History* supplies the example; the bulk of the essay is given to providing an allegedly corrected version of de Crillon's story. (Aptly, the count turns out to have been a thorough confidence man.) Published in a conventional manner, the "Tendency" and "Count Edward" vigorously dispute their status as regular publications in a secure professional discourse.

Beginning with *Memoirs of Marau Taaroa, Last Queen of Tahiti* in 1893, Adams committed himself more and more to the practice of privately printing and personally circulating his work. In draft-stage the *History* had likewise circulated, but Adams had been soliciting criticism to aid him in preparing what he never doubted would be the commercial, definitive publication of that work in his lifetime. *Memoirs of Marau Taaroa* was meant to be definitively esoteric: about ten copies came of the first edition; the revised edition of 1901, with the emended title *Memoirs of Arii Taimai*, came out to between fifteen and twenty-five copies.[4] Presumably most of these were distributed among the book's very particularly intended readership, the Teva clan, while the remaining copies were sent quietly to university libraries. *Mont Saint Michel and Chartres* would follow in 1904 in an initial edition of one hundred copies. Few as they were, they generated an interest over the years that went beyond Adams's private circles; admittedly flattered by the attention the book drew from younger medievalists, he printed a revised edition of five hundred copies in 1912 and later that year gave the copyright to the American Institute of Architects, which published a trade edition in 1913. The private printing and circulation of the *Education* and its later preparation for posthumous publication have already been described. *A Letter*, as we shall soon see, would define a final extreme to which self-publication could be taken. If the continued authorship and the printing, revision, and reprinting of texts prove that an audience existed in spite of Adams's remonstrances, his restrictive and tentative distributions indicate the tenuous hold Adams felt that he exercised over his readership. Consisting of small, isolated readerships, his audience remained fragmented. The Tahitian memoirs, later to prove a valuable source for historians of the islands, were written primarily for the Tevas; *Chartres*'s primary audience consisted of the nieces, along with whatever "nephews" it might attract in the university libraries across the land to which this book too was quietly sent. Although the readership of the *Education* sometimes overlapped with that of *Chartres*, the two did not always coincide, and few readers of *A Letter* had read anything by Henry Adams since "Count Edward de Crillon" fifteen years before. If, with the possible exception of the Tahitian memoirs, he wished to regard his late works as a continuum, he vitiated whatever cumulative force they may have possessed at the time of their writing by distributing them all to no one cohesive community of readers.

Adams's failure to command such a readership may have been as much the inadvertence of a distracted writer as the result of any determination on his part to exclude readers. The point is best seen in his troubled relations with the American Historical Association, the one cohesive larger audience Adams might well have been able to engage constructively. A few privileged members received *Chartres* and the *Education* (more members would receive *Chartres* after its 1912 reprinting), but most of his colleagues read nothing of his after the 1895 "Count Edward de Crillon" until *A Letter* was dispatched in 1910, and *A Letter* could hardly be meant to encourage a genial renewal of relations. Yet Adams certainly did have ambitions to develop a continuous line of inquiry with the association serving as principle readership and respondent; this is made clear by his short-lived intentions with regard to the "Rule." He set such high stakes upon what he at one point believed to be the essay's power to focus discussion that in 1908 he considered distributing the *Education* to the membership-at-large as the necessary (if lamentably "garrulous") prelude to the theoretical and didactic points made in the "Rule." And this we know because he went so far as to draft a lengthy letter introducing the "Rule" in the light of what would be his colleagues' familiarity with the *Education*. Yet he suppressed the "Rule," and with it any idea of further distributing the *Education*, sometime after reworking it in view of Professor Henry Andrew Bumstead's critical reading of an earlier (now lost) version of the text.[5] Bumstead, a Columbia University physicist whom association president, J. F. Jameson, lined up at Adams's request to critique the "Rule," praised the ingenuity of Adams's analogical applications but left no doubt in the historian's mind that he possessed no knowledge, let alone mastery, of the language of scientific thought—what Adams in the text refers to as the "higher mathematics."

The first paragraph of the version of the "Rule" that had been revised in the light of Bumstead's remarks admits as much; it almost appears to anticipate the essay's ultimate suppression. "Although the name of Willard Gibbs is probably to-day the highest in scientific fame of all Americans since Benjamin Franklin," begins the second sentence, "his Rule of Phases defies translation into literary language" (*D* 267). Defiance of *translation* (one of the most pivotal terms in Adams's vocabulary, as our discussion of *Mont Saint Michel and Chartres* will show) is the key: such effectively disenfranchises Henry Adams as one whose "literary language" is his stock-in-trade and the fabric of his "eighteenth-century" inheritance. The obsolescence of eighteenth-century modes of understanding is one of the few coherent strands in the essay's tangled exposition; for this reason the reference to Franklin is crucial. Statesman, scientist, and, as Adams reminded us in the 1907 preface to the *Education*, writer of didactic autobiography, Franklin was a generalist in an era when knowledge had not yet dispersed along a multitude of increasingly esoteric lines. Confident of the ultimate intelligibility of human experience, Franklin could at once contribute to the period's knowledge of electricity and command a highly adaptable literary language: one by which he could attract a popular following, help shape the polity of the nascent Republic, and win the greatest prizes of early American diplomacy.[6] The problems of translation were minimal. Franklin's fame was never a specialized one; Willard Gibbs, for all of his scientific renown, is a comparatively obscure figure, as we know from Adams's own confusion of the Yale physicist with Wolcott Gibbs, the Harvard chemist, in the 1907 *Education*, a confusion corrected in a revised edition.

In Franklin's age, scientist and man of letters were occasionally the same man; in the case of Franklin and Jefferson, that same man happened also to be a statesman. Between Henry Adams and Willard Gibbs stretch distances mitigated by no apparent common medium. Science, Adams suggests, has become willfully esoteric and untranslatable; Gibbs's rule, by Enlightenment standards, so much *mystery*: "The mathematical formulas in which he hid it [that is, the theory] were with difficulty intelligible to the chemists themselves, and are *quite unintelligible to an unmathematical public*, while the sense in which the word Phase was used, confused its meaning to a degree that alters its values, and reduces it to a chemical relation. Willard Gibbs helped to change the face of science, but his Phase was not the Phase of History" (*D* 267; italics added). This passage is remarkable for its general depiction of a discourse lost to unintelligibility and for its specific characterization of language usage that confuses, alters, and reduces a once commonly understood term to a concept that is untranslatable but that appears to approach more nearly some ultimate "truth." By the end of the first paragraph of the "Rule," Adams speaks from a position of displaced authority. Somewhere between the "unmathematical public" and the priestcraft of the new science, the author identifies himself as the practitioner of a literary language more or less incapable of rendering intelligible a new class of truths. The essay appears stillborn, and it has not yet formally set the problem before the reader.

The problem in fact is set before the reader only fragmentarily over the course of fifteen pages. No link to the *Education*'s last three chapters is made; no introductory statement addresses why one should apply the rule of phase to history and what one might stand to gain from such an application. Launching into an extended discussion of phase as it had come to be redefined chemically and thermodynamically, Adams neglects the regular forms of argumentative discourse (statement of premise and thesis and some anticipation of the demonstration to follow and the conclusions to be drawn therefrom) and yet clearly seems to be arguing, or desiring to argue, a particular point. As in the *Education*, "one" is the pronoun used to denote the human inquirer; "we," although more appropriate here than in the life narrative, is suppressed as though the writer is indeed skeptical that his inquiry can find sharers. Yet, by the third page, there are suggestions that the issue concerns reforming the university so as to equip the "young man" for an unprecedented future order. Increased knowledge of physicochemical process, asserts Adams, has "made a new world that is slowly taking the place of the world as it existed fifty years ago; though as yet the old curriculum of thought has been hardly touched by the change." This "new world" or (alternately) "new field can be entered only by timid groping for its limits, and with certainty of constant error" (D 269); but, as Adams clearly implies, it is imperative that "one" enter it, and to "begin by following the lines given by physical science."

As in the *Education*, the lines given by physical science are for Adams increasingly metaphysical, but the basic analogy he would derive from phase theory is simple enough. Phase transformation occurs when a substance passes from one state of equilibrium to another—solid to fluid, fluid to gas, and the reverse—under variable conditions of temperature, volume, and pressure. With the major difference that historical process so far appears to be irreversible, human society, from Adams's perspective, presents the spectacle of likewise progressing though distinct phases of stepped-up activity. Human thought, from phase to phase, becomes an ever more powerful instrument, developing at an exponential rate its capacity to unlock, dissolve, and assimilate to its own purposes the energies of the natural world. The phases of history are distinguished by their respective dominant modes of thought: society passes from a long "religious" phase, in which its gradually less torpid movements are governed by fetish objects and sacred iconography, to a "mechanical" phase, in which the mind rapidly develops systematic, instrumental knowledge of the material nonhuman world, to an "electric" phase, in which thought (by means of post-Newtonian "higher mathematics") learns to extend its domain into the natural world's plexus of intangible energies. To view history as a succession of phases or states of equilibrium was, as Adams wrote, hardly new; in the "Rule" he makes pointed reference to Turgot, Comte, and Mill, who like Herbert Spencer had speculated on the subject of historical phases and had been seminal influences upon Adams the young social thinker. What he would specifically derive from Gibbs's phase theory is not always clear, but from the scientific example he does try to construct a provisionally predictive model of historical transformation. Converting the physical variables of temperature and pressure into the historical variables of "attraction" and "acceleration," he suggests that the future historian-physicist may "assign mathematical values in order to fix the critical point of change" (D 287). For his part he is willing to propose, on the basis of the inverse law of squares, the approximate moments of past and future changes of historical phase. Thus from a religious phase of 90,000 years, society passes, in 1600, to a mechanical phase of 300 years, to an electric phase of 17.5 years, and finally to an ethereal phase of 4.18 years, bringing "Thought to the limit of its possibilities in the year 1921" (D 308).

Thus far, phase theory affords Adams only one more model for social acceleration, a further pretense to mathematical formulation, and an additional mode of depicting society at the edge of known forms. What is distinctive about the "Rule" lies in the suppositions Adams makes along the way, the awe-inspired considerations these suppositions lead him into, and the daring conflation of post-Newtonian mathematical physics with something resembling Thomist theology and Emersonian idealism. And what lends the "Rule" supreme interest, as well as pathos and expository difficulty, is the author's insecurity as he refines his suppositions: the embarrassment of a man unable to speak the language of the new and possibly marvelous world into which he has irresistibly strayed.

It is by what he calls the "law of solutions" that Adams follows "the lines given by physical science" into the metaphysical realm. This law, built on the premise that a "solvent has been suggested or found for every form of matter," invites from Adams's perspective the speculation that "every solid is soluble into a liquid, and every liquid into a gas, and every gas into corpuscles which vanish in an ocean of ether," which in its turn evaporates to mere "potential motion in absolute space" (*D* 270). In the hierarchy of phases, the first three—solid, fluid, vapor—alone fall "within the range of human sense" (*D* 274); those phases that follow—electron, ether, space, and hyperspace—are increasingly immaterial. Throughout the latter half of the nineteenth century, chemists and physicists "had been dragged into regions where supersensual forces alone had play"; and "where they refused to go as experimenters, they had to go as mathematicians. Without the higher mathematics they could no longer move, but with the higher mathematics, metaphysics began" (*D* 272–73). What, inspired by the law of solutions, Adams more nearly proposes is that metaphysics at this juncture resumes an old ambition, that the "higher mathematics" may allow it to realize: the merging of human intelligence with a realm of ideality—the divine, creative intelligence at the heart of things, the fountainhead of vital energy.

In its highest—or most extended—reaches, Adams concedes, human thought may simply subside "into an ocean of potential thought" (*D* 309), losing most of its motive energy until it posseses merely "the capacity for self-disturbance." Such would constitute an entropic equilibrium but still one that "cannot be absolutely dead" (*D* 276). But thought, becoming in its passage from the electron to the ethereal phase and beyond, increasingly thought in terms of itself, may have another destiny that Adams is content to express as a marvelling and inconclusive *if*: "If, in the prodigiously rapid vibration of its last phases, Thought should continue to act as the universal solvent which it is, and should reduce the forces of the molecule, the atom, and the electron to that costless servitude to which it has reduced the old elements of earth and air, fire and water; if man should continue to set free the infinite forces of nature, and attain the control of cosmic forces on a cosmic scale, the consequences may be as surprising as the change of water to vapor, of the worm to the butterfly, of radium to electrons" (D 309). The consequences, in short, are potentially miraculous and unforeseeable by the light of any known law.

"At a given volume and velocity," Adams states at the end of the paragraph quoted above, "the forces that are concentrated on [man's] head must act" (D 309). The tone of admonition, the jeremiadical note sounded by the forecast of an ultimate, historical threshold (since for Adams the possibility of extinction never disappears), is tempered by his admission that life and thought may yet be possible beyond that threshold. More than once in the "Rule" Adams turns aside to register, indeed celebrate, the mysteries of phase transformation, as when "a bulb bursts into a tulip, or a worm turns into a butterfly" (D 282).[7] On these terms, phase theory appears remotely intelligible after all: Emerson and Thoreau had turned to such examples to image an ongoing culmination, an ecstasy that releases the human inquirer from the predictable stultifications of historical process. Although Adams's study of Saint Thomas Aquinas left its stamp upon his later metaphysical speculations, a memory of New England transcendentalism is vividly suggested by Adams's projection of a world of phenomena from a realm of pure thought and by his preparation for the miraculous, as in his affirmation that "nothing whatever is beyond the range of possibility" (D 308). More importantly, however, he sustains in the "Rule" his own appreciation of the historical miracle, the unforeseen outburst of human genius, such as distinguished eighteenth- and early nineteenth-century America and twelfth- and thirteenth-century France. In the "Rule" as in the *Education*, twentieth-century society is depicted as requiring a new outburst of genius simply in order to survive. Yet despite the catastrophic mood, Adams displays reverence for the mysterious processes that surround and indeed constitute human life, the most mysterious, that of its own thought, being also the most familiar.

But if he turns aside to celebrate mystery, the task at hand remains onerous—the construction of a quasi-mathematical model out of materials that derive from inquiries conducted in what for Adams is always an alien discourse. His ignorance of the "higher mathematics" exists in the "Rule" as a strong but unreckoned undertow, baffling the inquirer in his efforts to (re)take an authoritative position. Such "ignorance" had baffled the inquirer in the *Education*, but the narrative dimensions of that work permitted him to lay claim to a moral authority that the largely disembodied discussion of the "Rule" cannot afford. ("A mathematical paradise of endless displacement promised eternal bliss to the mathematician," he had reason to declare in the *Education*, "but turned the historian green with horror" [A I 1135].) His ignorance in the "Rule" is not Socratic; Adams freely acknowledges that there are authorities who know more than he, who make of him a "by-stander" (D 270). Without the higher mathematics, he knows that he may contribute to the new synthesis only by rather intuitive means, yet he resists ceding intellectual leadership to the mathematical physicist. Properly trained, the historian in Adams's judgment is still the best candidate for the office of synthesizing generalist— the one best able to meet what he vaguely suggests must be the grave social consequences of the current epistemological crisis.

To the physicist as possessor of the higher mathematics Adams bears an intense and yet semiconscious ambivalence compounded of submission, fear, jealousy, and condescension. Early in the "Rule" he assures the reader that "the future of Thought, and therefore of History, lies in the hands of the physicists, and that the future historian must seek his education in the world of mathematical physics" (D 283). Yet he would have the future historian hold somewhat aloof from the physicist; the historian after all has his own scientific tradition, and the mathematical physicist comes to the notion of phase as a comparative novice. "Nearly a hundred and fifty years before Willard Gibbs announced his mathematical formulas of phase to the physicists and chemists," Adams reminds us, "Turgot stated the Rule of historical Phase as clearly as Franklin stated the law of electricity" (D 285). In his reverential invocations of Turgot, Franklin, and Comte—his celebration of the old curriculum's clear verbal and mathematical statement—Adams appears to express a suspicion that the physicist's current practice is impotent and obscurantist. Yet the suspicion exists only as the shadow of his conviction that the higher mathematics do represent the closest human approximation so far to absolute truth. If he recalls the heritage of a specifically scientific historiography, it is to spur the present-day historian from the lethargy that came of the late nineteenth century's problematizing of positivist knowledge. The general "failure to penetrate the ultimate synthesis of nature," Adams declares, "is no excuse for professors of history to abandon the field which is theirs by prior right, and still less can they plead their ignorance of the training in mathematics and physics which it was their duty to seek. The theory of history," he adds epigrammatically (but falsely in view of his own intellectual requirements), "is a much easier study than the theory of light" (D 285).[8]

Yet so far is Adams himself from the eighteenth-century ideal of the clear statement that nowhere in the "Rule" does he manage to enlighten his reader as to why historians should mount a campaign to retake "the field which is theirs by prior right." The specific tasks of the newly educated historian are never defined; indeed Adams seems fundamentally confused as to where the future historian's tasks begin and those of his collaborator and rival, the mathematical physicist, end. The development of a formula by which the successive phases of history may be fixed is alternately the work of the "mathematical historian" (*D* 293) and the "physicist historian," who from one paragraph to the next can become simply "physicist." Inexplicably, Adams at one point requires that the physicist work to the exclusion of the historian (*D* 310). Only by inference can the reader gather that the historian's task is more integrative than the physicist's, and more social in its consequence, and that it consists in the main of nearly impossible feats of translation. Yet Adams makes no attempt to define the historian's social role.

The best clue to Adams's purpose in the "Rule" comes not in the text itself but in the draft of the letter by which he had thought to introduce it to his colleagues in the American Historical Association. His application of the rule of phase, he hoped, might "serve as a universal formula for reconstructing and rearranging the whole scheme of university instruction so that it shall occupy a field of definite limits, distinct from the technical." How it might so serve is not further clarified, but Adams's explanation here suggests that he is as jealous of the technical exploitation of knowledge—the conversion of knowledge to brute power—as he is of the physicist's philosophical authority. Against the university's current ideological and theoretical "chaos" he would submit the "Rule" as a motion toward an integrative, generalized, and disinterested discourse, built upon a conception "of the University as a system of education grouped about History; a main current of thought branching out, like a tree, into endless forms of activity, in regular development, according to the laws of physics; and to be studied . . . not as now by a multiversal, but by a universal law; not as a scientific but as a historical unity" (*LHA* 6:207). The trouble with such an explanation lies in Adams's inability to identify the historical field except as the one realm where, paradoxically, a unity modeled after the old Newtonian synthesis still seems possible. The "history" he desires is the old "scientific" historiography of the eighteenth and early nineteenth centuries. As ever, the specific social consequences of a reformed academic discourse are not spelled out. After several pages of explanation his meaning remains unclear; this must have been obvious to Adams himself who remarked in the letter's closing paragraph, "I am inclined to think that only the defects of my old University training prevent my success in making myself intelligible" (*LHA* 6:208).

Unintelligibility, whether of the new science or the "by-stander" who dabbles in it, emerges in the "Rule" as a major if involuntary motif. About the nature and scope of the higher mathematics Adams can never decide: he alternates between viewing it as the latest projection of human ignorance and a possible reading of the mind of God. Although he affirms that "always and everywhere the mind creates its own universe," he reasserts, theologically enough, that "the force behind the image is always a reality" (D 310).[9] In any case, he must position himself outside the new science. A casualty of the old curriculum's dissolution, he becomes the historian of a shattered discourse: "The average man, in 1850, could understand what Davy or Darwin had to say; he could not understand what Clerk Maxwell meant" (D 306). "The older ideas, though hostile, were intelligible; the idea of electro-magnetic-ether is not" (D 307). For what he says of the "average man" Adams draws on his own experience. As self-confessed "ignorant student" (D 304) he stands, in 1908, much closer to the "unmathematical public" than to what he conceives as the future elite.

Unlike either the *Education* or *A Letter*, the "Rule" is disarmingly free of literary conceit: there is little authorial posture to lend moral drama to intellectual inquiry and no irony sufficient to contain the chaos of thought and allow Adams to make use of the theme of unintelligibility. For this reason, the "Rule" is easily the most difficult text Adams ever produced: it has nothing consistently to say to any clearly envisioned audience. Still, in its metaphysical indecisiveness, its reaffirmation that "nothing whatever is beyond the range of possibility," the "Rule" resists closure, in spite of rhetorical problems so grave that the essay can scarcely inform itself of its occasion and purpose, making it a most unpromising motion toward coherent dialogue. Adams's seriousness with respect to the essay is measured by his repeated schemes for publishing it. When Jameson rejected it for the *American Historical Review*, Adams, confessing his ignorance, sought the scrutiny of a mathematical physicist before revising it for a contemplated resubmission to the review or for a fresh submission to his own former organ of generalized discourse, the *North American Review*. And after he had laid aside those possibilities, he briefly prepared, as we have seen, to publish the essay himself.

Yet as Adams suppressed the fundamentally open "Rule," he saw fit to publish *A Letter to American Teachers of History*, a text that seems determined to close its subject, not least by satirizing the dialogic process Adams had sought as recently as the "Rule" to foster and engage. "About a hundred pages of no consequence, announcing the end of the Universe" was the way he described it to Gaskell (*LHA* 6:289). *A Letter* poses few of the difficulties of the "Rule": its title names its audience, the text defines an intelligible, if extravagant, problem, and although the discussion is more abandoned than concluded, we may easily see the terms of its inconclusiveness. But the comparative clarity of *A Letter*'s argumentative lines is due to a signal reduction in Adams's application of thermodynamics to history. Whereas in the "Rule" he had been willing to regard thought as a mysterious and vital energy, in *A Letter* he stacks the evidence against an exemption of thought from the second law of thermodynamics.[10]

According to the first law of thermodynamics, within a closed system energy can neither be created nor destroyed. According to the second law, although energy cannot be destroyed, its tendency is to dissipate as heat until the unequal intensities of energy necessary for the existence of form, motion, and life at last dissolve; "the ultimate destiny of the celestial universe," in Adams's fancifully precise extrapolation, is "to become atomic dust at $-270°C$" (*D* 246). All energy, animate and inanimate, astronomical and social, unites in the tendency to dissipate. The argument that there exists a separate and exempt energy, an élan vital that has built up intensities through the process of evolution, is not tenable. Rather than develop intensities of energy, evolutionary process has in fact hastened their dissipation; human intellect, the highest achievement of that process, serves to check instinctual reflex action in reflection. Thought must accordingly be regarded as a "degraded Act" (*D* 203), Will in the scorpion being stronger "than in Monkey or Man, where it is conscious" (*D* 224). Even where human will has been exerted with efficiency and rational purpose, the object has commonly been wasteful, as in the development of "armies and armaments which are made avowedly for no other purpose than to dissipate or degrade energy"; characteristically, humanity is given to an "unintelligent passion" for the waste of riotous amusement (*D* 217). The process of dissipation is irreversible; the effort to restore a former intensity must dissipate more energy than could thereby be retrieved. The sun must eventually darken.[11]

Such constitutes the cosmic dilemma behind the more specifically academic "problem" that *A Letter* ostensibly treats. Given what Adams alleges to be the physicist's establishment of the second law of thermodynamics as the law of life, the historian can no longer in good faith represent human experience as a progressive and ameliorative process, yet that is what the university as an intitution subserving the ruling social interests requires that he do. To broach this conflict—between the historian's intellectual honesty and what society wishes to be told—is what Adams submits as his official pretext for writing. The difficulty of *A Letter* consists not in the logic of the problem as much as in the artificiality of the pretext and in what for Adams himself remains the uncertain object of submitting such a matter for consideration. In the prefatory letter to the short, privately printed book, Adams seeks to establish the discussion as a sequel to "The Tendency of History." (He seems very deliberately to address his association readership: as though to invoke the context of works previously submitted to the association's perusal, he even refers in the preface to his "personal error" as a limiting factor upon the "truth" of his remarks, clearly alluding to the opening paragraph of "Count Edward de Crillon.") Rather than declare that his book announced the end of the world, he speaks of it as "a Report, unofficial and personal," which follows the 1894 presidential address ("on the relations of the Historical Department to society") by examining the question of "hierarchy in the sciences"; in so doing, he would consider the probability that some day "one department, or another, is to impose on the University a final law of instruction" (D 137). In understated anticipation of the book's calculated extravagance he concedes that it "has too much the air of provoking controversy"; to the degree that the controversy is real, he wishes at present to confine it to the ranks of historians and other interested academicians. The book will therefore "not be published, or offered for sale, or sent to the press for notice" (D 138).

"For the same reason," he begins his next paragraph, "the volume needs no acknowledgement." Not so much apologizing for as doubting the usefulness of the book's "air of controversy," he spends the rest of the preface discouraging response, as though returning to the verdict that had closed the *Education*—that "discussion was futile" (A I 1178). "Unless the questions which it raises or suggests seem to you so personal as to need action," he explains, "you have probably no other personal interest than that of avoiding the discussion altogether" (D 138). Such a remark is typical of the aging Henry Adams but genuinely problematic inasmuch as it occurs in a text that the author felt sufficient urgency to write, print, and dispatch to his readers at his own expense. Doubtless he expresses scorn for what he considered the paltry (nonmetaphysical) pursuits of his colleagues, but perhaps too he registers a fleeting suspicion that he suffers from monomania. The rhetorical conflicts that subsist between the prefaces and narrative of the *Education* reappear on a smaller scale in *A Letter*, and again the reader is left at an impasse: "action" is absurd in a world morally dominated by the second law of thermodynamics, and unless one is prepared to spend one's life meditating on the dying social organism, the discussion certainly is better avoided.

That Adams had knowingly written an all-but-unnegotiable text seems particularly clear in the preface's final paragraph-length sentence, in which he "explains" his book's literary form. The statement merits attention clause by clause. "If I call this volume a letter," it begins, "it is only because that literary form affects to be more colloquial or more familiar than the usual scientific treatise" (D 138). "Colloquial" (etymologically, speaking together) and "familiar" are both adjectives expressive of shared enterprise, yet it is not these qualities so much as their affectation that Adams specifies as preferable to the tone of the "usual scientific treatise." By implication the usual scientific treatise is noncolloquial, nonfamiliar— resistant, insofar as it has abandoned "literary language," to the dialogic entrance of the general reader.[12] A lifelong reader of scientific treatises increasingly frustrated by the growing unfamiliarity of scientific thought,

Adams draws here on his own experience. But the question remains: By affecting the colloquial and familiar does Adams mean to achieve those qualities, or merely mimic what he believes to be outmoded forms of address? The statement continues: "But such letters never require a response, even when they invite one" (D 138)—leaving rather delicately in doubt the question of whether this particular letter does invite a response, whether its affectation of the colloquial is meant to initiate colloquy. The last part of the statement suggests that it does not: "And in the present case, the subject of the letter involves a problem which will certainly exceed the limits of a life already far advanced, so that its solution, if a solution is possible, will have to be reached by a new generation" (D 139). Response here must contend with irony as bitter as Adams could make it. Nearing the end, he would bequeath a discussion concerning his posterity's certain death, the gradual cessation of all generation, and the eventual absence of all readership—hardly a subject that lends itself to extended dialogue! The *Education* too bequeathed on the assumption of the author's death, but even the genuinely posthumous 1918 edition, with the particularly bleak 1916 preface, did not foreclose to this extent. Adams in fact appears to have regarded *A Letter* as a text that did invite a response; at least he affected disappointment at what he considered its neglect. This book, as we shall see, did draw a response, and Adams's complaints that it had met with indifference suggest that he meant all along to see it fail.

The story that *A Letter* tells almost requires that the book dialogically fail—that it be, as Adams described it to Gaskell, a book of no consequence. Chapter 1, "The Problem," recounts the dissolution of the old curriculum, the breakdown of the Newtonian universe that, with its grand affirmation of regularity and recurrence, preserved the older theological notions of cosmic unity. The second law of thermodynamics replaces the image of an eternally harmonious order with one of cosmic decrepitude: dying suns, cooling planets, and a universe sustained by no divine will. Once classical mechanics and its assumption of a perpetual order have been condemned, the more specific ambitions of midnineteenth-century science are fatally undercut. Here the story, not overtly autobiographical, concerned Adams personally as one who had come of age just after midcentury. Uniformitarian geology and evolutionary biology had been built on the premise that energy is conserved, if not created, over time. Upon the work of Lyell and Darwin arose a "new creed" embraced by "the generation which began life in 1850" (D 160): that human society, with all other "natural" processes, evolved under stable (uniformitarian) conditions toward states of perfection. His writings of the 1860s confirm what we are told in the *Education*: that Adams was hesitant when it came to many articles of this creed, but in his turn he too had found the prospect of human improvement ravishing, particularly "the differentiation" in the New World "of a higher variety of the human race" (A II 125). His early literary efforts, although trained militantly upon a foreground of political corruption, were able to conceive just such a differentiation, a matter of the free but dialogically concerted effort of the human will. The Adams heritage and Unitarian Boston were more important to Henry Adams's progressive view of history than Charles Darwin. "Social perfection," he had been reared to believe, was assured "because human nature worked for Good, and three instruments were all she asked:—Suffrage, Common Schools and Press" (A I 750). Yet the "violent contradiction between Kelvin's degradation and Darwin's Elevation" (D 162) upset Bostonian beliefs as well as specifically Darwinian views of upward differentiation. As energy is lost, as the various doctrines of progress become discredited, democracy, universal education, and public discussion become instruments without an object; worse still, they become agents of dissipation.

Part of Adams's point is that the object has been long gone, that the doctrine of progress has long stood exposed, but that it has taken society, historians, and scientists themselves over half a century to catch on. Kelvin published "On a Universal Tendency in Nature to the Dissipation of Mechanical Energy" in 1852; "to the vulgar and ignorant historian" of the day, the law of entropy "meant only that the ash-heap was constantly increasing in size; while the public understood little and cared less about Entropy, and the literary class knew only that the Newtonian universe, in which they had been cradled, admitted no loss of energy in the solar system" (D 142). As in the *Education*, the tendency of public discourse to cling to old illusions receives harsh treatment, but Adams's promotion of the second law of thermodynamics to the status of an "absolute Truth" (D 261) makes Victorian inquiry with its strained and self-conscious optimism appear as a particularly bitter delusion. His (evident) acceptance of entropy as law absolutizes his own failure as nothing in the *Education* could do. In 1852 he was just beginning to identify himself as a member of the literary class; he was ten years away from residence in a London alive with scientific ferment, and ten years more would pass before he would begin to apply, in literary language, evolutionist thought to the writing of history. The historical review of "The Problem" requires that Adams's lifework through the "Rule" be seen as having rested on a fundamental misconception—namely, that the universe remains open—that was cleared up before Adams had turned fifteen.

As "The Problem" progresses, most semblance of argumentative method vanishes; it is as though Adams, freed from the constraints of a text that aimed at producing discursive consequence, felt that he could compose from a stream of unexamined association. The text coheres inasmuch as Adams's observations flow from and return to the one inexorable law. Once again the physicist appears in the role of lawgiver, but although he presides over a realm of forbidding abstraction his singular gospel, the law of entropy, is highly intelligible. In the "Rule" he was commonly referred to as the *mathematical* physicist; in *A Letter*, he is the *degradationist* physicist. Specialized as his researches must be, his conclusion, Adams claims, finds support across the curriculum, old and new, and the first chapter is filled with lengthy quotations from a remarkably mixed company—Jean-Jacques Rousseau, Henri-Louis Bergson, and Emile Durkheim in addition to Lord Kelvin (William Thomson) and a host of recent "authorities." Much of the so-called evidence that vital energies are in decline is rather preposterously impressionistic: for example, incidence, in the more intellectual "races," of early tooth and hair loss, inability to bear or suckle children, and suicide. If we recognize a startling variety of autobiographical reference in such particulars, so too may we read autobiographically Adams's asseveration that "the poets are pessimists to a man—and to a woman" (*D* 188).[13] This reflects not only Adams's reading of the French decadents and his companionship with the doomed young American poets Bay Lodge and Trumbull Stickney, but also his own overwhelming intuitive apprehension of decline. In *A Letter* Adams expresses that apprehension more in images than in arguments, and does so as it were on his own authority as poet—for what that authority may be worth. Although he appoints the degradationist physicist as lawgiver, he assembles an odd consensus among the scientific and artistic communities, the various specialized discourses uniting in the apprehension of decline. The lunatic in the asylum and the mood of the popular press are cited as additional proofs of the degradationist view.

Nevertheless, Adams insists that the more common and healthy response to so inclusive an application of the second law is resistance, however futile. As far as it can go, the species' survival requires it: "Though science should prove twenty times over, by every method of demonstration known to it, that man is a thermodynamic mechanism, instinct would reject the proof, and whenever it should be convinced, it would have to die" (*D* 230–31). As instinct is a function of vital energy, this is the same as saying that the organism must die. Chapter 2, "The Solution," goes through the form of surveying possible ways out, although it is clear all along that the author cannot stir from his degradationist stance. The central feature of this chapter is an imaginary dialogue between an evolutionist biologist and degradationist physicist conducted as though it were a diplomatic exchange intended to produce a treaty between warring academic factions. Although the dialogue fills over forty pages, all that emerges is the irreconcilability of the two positions, and this had been sufficiently clear from the start. As an assistant professor at Harvard, Adams had advocated instruction by the ancient heuristic of dialogue: he wished to expose his students to the more or less irreconcilable positions of "rival" professors and actually proposed that he and his then protégé, Henry Cabot Lodge, together teach the course in early American history, Lodge from the Federalist, he from the Democratic perspective. In *Mont Saint Michel and Chartres,* his presentation of the intellectual life of twelfth-century France focused on the dialogical combat of Abélard and William of Champeaux. But the debate between Adams's evolutionist and degradationist is a patently rigged contest, the satire of open inquiry. After pages of circular colloquy the physicist grants a single empty concession— that (and here Adams quotes Bernhard Brunhes) "the appearance on earth of living beings more and more elevated, and . . . the development of civilization in human society, undoubtedly give the impression of a prog- ress and a gain" (*D* 256). But the impression is of course false. "The reality behind the illusion" of an elevated human order comes down to an "absence of the power to do useful work,—or what man knows in his finite sensibilities as death" (*D* 257). On this point *A Letter* remains perfectly intransigent.

As its full title suggests, *A Letter to American Teachers of History* spe- cifically addresses the historian's role in the telling of a heretical and un- popular truth. Importantly, it is a distinctly subordinate role. Whereas in the "Rule" the historian still had a hand in determining the application of physics to history, in *A Letter* the reader is simply referred to the sec- ond law of thermodynamics—as Kelvin himself phrased it in literary lan- guage—for the ultimate truth about historical process. The truth arises in the physicist's discourse, not the historian's, and throughout the short book the historian is presented as having diminished authority and dig- nity. He is "vulgar and ignorant" (*D* 142); he prefers to linger "in the pleasant meadows of antiquarianism" (*D* 169) and must look on help- lessly as the physicist "invades his territory and takes the teaching of history out of his hands" (*D* 191). In the *Education,* the historian was similarly depicted as ignorant and helpless, scrupulously indifferent to the moral effect of his teachings. But, as we have seen, the historian, as Henry Adams, broke from this character and on the basis of his admittedly error- prone readings attempted to translate the new science and its social conse- quences into moral terms. In practice he had not actually renounced the ideologies of the Puritan and eighteenth-century heritage that compelled his lifelong philosophic exertions and fostered his finalizing moral authority. In contrast, the historian whom Adams depicts and ostensibly exemplifies in *A Letter* has little to advocate and nothing to secure but the law of entropy from obscurantism. His role (inasmuch as he is vulgar) amounts to providing a vulgate rendering of the second law, delineating in literary language its social consequences. But because the historian is expected to affirm the doctrine of progress, and because his teachings directly affect the morale of the young man, his advocacy of degradation must expose him to attacks from which the physicist, aloof in a predominantly mathematical discourse, remains free.

The hapless historian is thus cast politically in the role of Galileo. The university, Adams reminds us, had traditionally one "proper function": "to teach that the flower of vital energy is Thought, and that not Instinct but Intellect is the highest power of a supernatural Will"; that as the "incorruptible solvent of all earlier or lower energies" thought was "incapable of degradation or dissolution" (*D* 206). This remains Adams's own premise in the "Rule." In *A Letter* Adams presents the incorruptible historian as having to uphold an opposite doctrine and at great professional risk: "The American professor who should begin his annual course by announcing to his class that their year's work would be devoted to showing in American history 'a universal tendency to the dissipation of energy' and degradation of thought, which would soon end in making America 'improper for the habitation of man as he is now constituted' " would preserve his conscience at his position's expense. "The University," Adams affirms, "would have to protect itself by dismissing him" (*D* 189–90).

He cannot but acknowledge the absurdities to which his arguments lead. To adopt degradation as the principle of the new curriculum is to dismiss all human initiative and all creative occasion, thus eliminating all motive for education. It must cause both the universities and the technical schools to "close their doors without waiting for the sun to grow cold" (*D* 237). But Adams never openly concedes that such absurdities paralyze his inquiry; to the end of *A Letter* he maintains his deadpan aspect, holding to the line that he broaches the subject as a prolegomenon of some future "common understanding about the first principle of instruction" (*D* 262). The final paragraphs, totally inconsistent with the entire argument of *A Letter*, are yet congruent with Adams's abiding pretense that the text is a call for curricular reform. For in the face of his argument that the second law remains absolute and that thought, as degraded act, is but a symptom of an already far-advanced cosmic entropy, Adams closes the discussion by suggesting that the physicist and historian may yet arrive at "an arrangement" that would save the university, even though such would seem "to call for the aid of another Newton" (*D* 263).

By so doing, he appeals to the very doctrine that he had repeatedly decried as a delusion—that thought is exempt from the second law, that hope can lie in "the loophole called Mind" (*D* 191). Adams perhaps never parted with the notion that "another Newton" might appear in the world, a messiah of prodigious intellect reestablishing a vital and unified epistemology in defiance of the mere unity-in-death of the second law of thermodynamics. But given his context, his closing statement appears willfully disingenuous, intended to register as a mockery of the appeal to further discussion that is customary in learned treatises. What he would accomplish specifically by such argument remains ill-defined by that argument: for his text's manifest absurdities he seems fundamentally unable to establish rhetorical purport, so that readers seem called upon only to witness the inadvertent, if consistent, satire of the dialogical process that Adams could no longer believe in sufficiently to engage. His problem indeed was that he had lost command over a language by which he could define public purpose in his continued authorship. As the "Rule" and *A Letter* both show, discourse in practice led to impasse. By the time he was finishing *A Letter*, that impasse had become his central demonstration.[14]

At a more symbolic level we may of course read *A Letter* as a moral or political allegory, but such readings do little to relieve the absurdities the text accumulates as a call for curricular reform. Those absurdities are fundamentally rhetorical and stem, as we have seen, from Adams's suspicion of the very process by which dilemmas and truths are defined publicly. That the language of *A Letter* does in fact encourage readers to translate the argument into terms and conclusions that have not been made fully explicit is itself problematic and another dimension of the rhetorical crisis *A Letter* enacts. Granting that Adams has adopted a vocabulary of physical science to address fundamentally moral and political dilemmas, one must question the motive for such indirect discourse.

Certainly, to speak of "man" as a "thermodynamic mechanism" obedient to the law of entropy is reductive, but reductive to what effect is far from clear, especially since Adams's withdrawal of an overtly moral causality from the story of human decline may serve conflicting purposes. One object may be the purgation derived from publishing a hypocrisy. Refusing to pay lip service to the familiar moral explanations of human experience, Adams keenly hones the proposition that, far from securely inhabiting an ethical realm, humanity has all but irrevocably subjected itself to the rule of natural law—through its will-to-power, pride, stupidity, and headlong and reckless democratizations. The intense bleakness of the prognosis may yet, at a further remove, be aimed at provoking a reexamination of the moral and political sources of social vitality. The correspondence of the period shows Adams to have vacillated between vague avowals of such purpose. But the vacillation itself suggests that the most decided purpose of *A Letter* was to allow Adams to vent griefs and frustrations in a self-amusing, satiric virtuoso performance. His authority in *A Letter* may indeed be chiefly that of a poet but that does not make the text less problematic. Despite the cultural promotion of the necessary "isolation" of the modern poet, poetic authority in practice can hardly transcend dialogical process: the poet too must exist purposively for a body of readers. Even if we grant that the text succeeds best as a poem, we still have the problem of identifying the coherent readership for whom it has so existed or could exist.

Although to read *A Letter* as either moral or political allegory does not free its author from his late discursive impasse, Adams has made it impossible for us not to consider the second law of thermodynamics as the ultimate figuration of humanity's moral decline. The degradationist physicist, Adams suggests, is the rightful heir to the perennial Judeo-Christian sermon against pride. Were it not that the physicist himself is degraded and so has "lost the high literary potential of Swift and Voltaire, he would . . . handle the unfortunate creature called Man in a temper such as any one may renew who cares to go back to Bunyan or Dante or the Bible, not to mention the prophets in particular; but he would convince no one" (*D* 230). Yet far easier is it to renew their temper than their office, which existed by virtue of a faith in human redeemability; it is exactly redeemability (of a physical *and* metaphysical kind) that Adams represents the degradationist physicist to have dismissed. The moral is that a theologically based moral causality is no longer tenable. The physicist's jeramiad adverts to no God, covenant, or promise of future glory; it searches out no sin, pausing only to comment upon humanity's unintelligent wastefulness, and makes no call to repent. It simply speaks of "man" as a "thermodynamic mechanism" that must die along with the whole dying cosmos, humanity and "God" sunk together in the final entropic equilibrium. Still, Adams points out, the physicist would "convince no one. Man refuses to be degraded in self-esteem" and, as we have seen, Adams maintains that as long as there is instinct (or vital intensity) in the human, that instinct must remain unconvinced that life is governed by thermodynamic law. Although the degradationist physicist is the creature of Adams's ventriloquy, the author of *A Letter* always speaks in the character of "by-stander," and this allows him to complicate (though he refuses to invalidate) the physicist's alleged gospel with his accustomed moral paradox.

As bystander, he suggests that whereas humankind may be quite simply "condemned," its moral predicament is anything but simple. Humanity has experienced God in two ways: as indwelling creative force known through instinct and as an external and largely destructive force, nature, as known through reason, science. Quite apart from its depravities, suggests Adams, humanity has always been torn by its divided nature; only now, late in its history, can one see the convergence of its "instinctive" insistence on unity and its rational insistence that it arrive "scientifically" at an absolute truth. "Man had always flattered himself that he knew—or was about to know—something that would make his own energy intelligible to itself, but he invariably found, on further inquiry, that the more he knew, the less he understood" (*D* 149). The second law of thermodynamics sets a term to that inquiry by making human energy intelligible as the process of its own dissipation. Its "attraction on the mind" must prove irresistible. "The idea of unity survives the idea of God or of Universe; it is innate and intuitive" (*D* 242). The synthesis offered by the second law thus commends itself equally to reason and intuition (in Adams's usage more or less interchangeable with "instinct"); but the vital instinct on such terms would seem almost to betray a death-wish. Again, there seems to be no comprehensible moral causality in this complex moral condition: for all of his unattractiveness "man" remains a mystifyingly "unfortunate creature."

If *A Letter* read as moral allegory concludes thus ambiguously, any narrowly political reading finds little with which to mark even an ambiguous beginning. Indeed the strongest argument for the attempt is that Adams, in the correspondence of 1909 and 1910, encouraged such a reading when he was not writing the book off as a belligerent and inconsequent joke. "Whether our energy is really declining," he wrote Gaskell, "I do not know; but I send you herewith my small volume discussing the subject as concisely as I can state it" (*LHA* 6:323). The larger subject here alluded to is socialism. Adams's most consistent explanation of *A Letter* outside of the text is that it was meant to sound an alarm against collectivizing trends. Derisive references to Darwin's "popular following" (*D* 161) do occur in *A Letter*, and the specter of mass society appears a number of times in the discussion. Late in the book there is mention of the "State Organism" (*D* 260) that, in the view of the recent European historians Adams had been reading, dominates and dissipates the individual's energy, but at no point is socialism formally identified as the ideological expression of the second law of thermodynamics. Nevertheless, adopting a vocabulary alien to that of *A Letter*, he claimed to have written it "hoping to prove that the Universities are already extinct, and incapable of facing the socialist phase of mind" that must sink the high human intensity in the low. He wished to awaken the historians to the perils of the welfare state ("old-age pensions,—universal education,—trades-unionism,—and the rest") as well as amuse himself by "poking fun at mathematicians, who are truly the bottom of all possible depths of imbecility" (*LHA*

6:323). (With the term "imbecility" a resonant note with distinct political overtones is struck. Adams had used this word in *A Letter* to name the condition that "man and beast" after "a diversified agony of twenty million years" [*D* 185] cannot hope to escape; years before he had employed it in the *History* to characterize the moral and intellectual paralysis of the popularly elected Congress during Madison's second administration.) But what exists in his texts as the more or less focused association between popular government and a universal decline of intensities of energy hardly makes *A Letter* a polemic against socialism. The book becomes an anti-socialist tract only through such generalized reading—or, to cite a practice traditionally deplored by the Adamses, such loose construction—as must render unimportant the terms and argumentative lines that Adams did adopt.

If it amused Adams to speak thus freely of *A Letter*, it was not the first time he had described past work as something other, or less, than what it was. In the *Education*, as we have seen, he dismissed his previous work in a few forcedly facetious comments, blurring his large accomplishment's wealth of specific occasion and argument; it was as though his lengthy bibliography, failing to enter what he thought a vital national dialogue, had had no social existence. This ritual dismissiveness takes on added significance in the correspondence of 1909 and 1910 insofar as Adams similarly reduced the whole American dialogue, its vast lexicon of types and instances, to the "meanings" he had loosely assigned to *A Letter*. The book, he wrote Barrett Wendell, "is a scientific demonstration that Socialism, Collectivism, Humanitarianism, Universalism, Philanthropism, and every other ism, has come, and is the End." As the final step in his satire of the American dialogic process that he had set out in youth to raise to a higher power, he asserted that the great experiment, in all its (discursive) diversity, collapsed in one lesson whose moral is the law of entropy: "The Declaration of Independence, Jeffersonian Democracy, the Principles of 1789, the Trades Unions, the Old Age Pensions, Death Duties, Andrew Carnegie and John D. Rockefeller all preach it, and why not I?" (*LHA* 6:337).

He had become thus indifferent to whether the book said anything in particular as long as it registered a sneer at progressive views of history and beat its dirge of general decline. Given his despair of precise meanings—a despair that perhaps too easily led to an impatience with his own production of them—well might he characterize the text at last as a physical act, which the argument subserves by being not so much meaningful as sensational: "When I flung my little volume in professorial faces last winter, and—so to speak—kicked my American Universities in the stomach as violently and insultingly as I could, I calculated on getting one sharp

reaction and protest for every hundred copies of the 'Letter' I sent out."
He did in fact draw objection that was at times quite sharp, alternatingly
stern and genial rejections of the second law's relevance to historiography.[15] But such was not the reaction he had in mind, and what he pretended to be the failure of his readers to respond led him to exclaim that
"society is ready for collectivism" (*LHA* 6:355). As a corollary to his
hypergeneralization of discourse, he collectivized his readers out of existence. Out of touch with his professional colleagues, unable to arrive at a
unitary explanation of what he had been about in authoring *A Letter*, he
drew whatever conclusion suited his convenience. Hence the "fun" of the
book was that none of his colleagues would "understand the fun." Calcu-
latingly disingenuous, he was able even to admit that he probably would
not "see the joke myself if I were not its author" (*LHA* 6:301). When
necessary, *A Letter* could shrink to the dimensions of a private jest.

Correspondence

One respondent did offer what Adams was willing to acknowledge as an
opposite if unequal reaction. "My poor dear old friend and fellow William
James," he wrote Gaskell, "alone has put up some sort of fight" (*LHA*
6:355). In a letter and two postcards from Bad Nauheim full of his wonted
grace and incision, James dismissed the second law of thermodynamics as
"wholly irrelevant" to the study of history. Citing such activities as the
authorship of books and the contemplation of cathedrals, he argued in his
letter of June 17, 1910, that human intelligence is able to "guide the energies of the shrinking sun into channels which would never have been
entered otherwise" and thereby "*make* history."[16] It was the vigorous and
genial fight of a dying man whose search for health in the waters of Bad
Nauheim would prove as futile as John Hay's five summers before, and if
A Letter has accomplished little else it at least gave James an opportunity
to exhibit his peculiar powers of resistance as he took to his deathbed.

In response Adams claimed, as was his wont, never to have "held an
opinion of my own" but merely to have read and quoted the reigning
authorities "till my pages weep with repetition" (*LHA* 6:347). Although
he justly appreciated his friend's "energy" and "wisdom on the sandy
wastes of time," neither James's words nor his example deflected Adams's
own current of reflection, and his letters of the period persist in embroi-
dering the world's "rot" and "decay." In his final, brief letter to James,
responding to James's last postcard (memorable for the philosopher's recollection of a student who on an examination gave the answer "hydraulic
goat" for "hydraulic ram"), Adams abandons the terms of the argument
in favor of reminiscence, recalling the common past when William was

"the light and joy of Beverly Farms and Harvard College. Ah, but I never let myself think of that!" (*LHA* 6:350). Such recollection, so quickly suppressed, led him to profess indifference to how soon his own "brook dries up altogether." Subtly, tentatively, the life story appears once again as a text behind a "scientific" argument. Beverly Farms had been the summer place of Henry, Marian, and the Hooper family, and the Jameses had been Marian's friends in youth. In his condolence letter to Henry James, Adams would mourn William's death as one more step in the demise of their generation's gifted set, whose lives made "about the only unity that American society in our time had to show" (*LHA* 6:406–7).

If in this instance *A Letter* did lead to something like genuine correspondence, it was largely because the old friends had argued similar points before and so were effectively revisiting established positions vis-à-vis one another. In James's impending death Adams no doubt felt the generational correspondence of their lives: the unifying finality that awaited himself and their epoch's other aging holdouts. With younger men in general and teachers of history in particular, he was little disposed to engage in argument. Like James, they commonly responded by rejecting Adams's terms, and hence his authority, more or less bluntly; they could hardly do otherwise. But in the absence of generational commonality there remained for Adams scant ground for discussion, and objection carried little credit. The younger man was expected to react but defer; in the abstract he was held to be a nonentity. At times it seemed "strange" to Adams that there were "young people yet";[17] he had grown accustomed to regarding the successors of his "already forgotten" generation as "dead before us." Measured by his own experience, "they have never lived" (*LHA* 6:315).

Yet neither his writing, his historical interests, nor his contact with his successors terminated with *A Letter to American Teachers of History*. Putting aside his more arrogant claim to being "the Doyen" of an American "historical school" (*LHA* 6:323), he was drawn into a correspondence with three Yale medievalists: Frederick Bliss Luquiens, Albert Stanburrough Cook, and Raymond Weeks. Their common interest was antiquarian—old French texts; encouraged by the attention of the younger men Adams revised and reprinted *Mont Saint Michel and Chartres* in 1912. In his role of elder he offered to subsidize Professor Weeks's research in Barcelona into the origin of the chansons de geste, explaining that he wished patriotically to see his country claim scholarly distinction in that field. As correspondent, Adams always returned to the theme of the imminent "end," in tones ranging from the bitter and nearly obscene to the lightly ironic, and with a fund of lurid portents that included the wreck of the *Titanic*, his own stroke and temporary paralysis, and the long-expected outbreak of the Great War. But this strain nearly always coexisted with an ongoing, lively registry of observations and reflections, gossip, condolence, and moral wisdom. When his stroke in 1912 deprived him of the service of his right hand and failing eyesight rendered the page invisible, he dictated his letters. The correspondence went on with the life. In *A Letter* Adams had come as close as he could to asserting an unanswerable argument, built as it was upon an unnegotiable sentiment. If we understand the letter as a form of writing that addresses particular readers in a way that obliges or encourages response, Adams's book, from its title and preface to its redundancies of exposition, must strike us as thoroughly ironic. But the motive articulated by the title is not merely ironic. With avowed malice Adams wished to write the unanswerable and watch his select readership rise to the challenge of answering it, but he probably could not have foreseen the extent to which he would reject the response that did not confirm his drift. As much as he could mean anything, Adams did intend the book as a letter, and although it took the form of a book addressed to a plural readership, we must not lose sight of *A Letter* as the product of a practice by which Adams preserved social contact, resisted closure, and affirmed (though not often explicitly) the unforeseen possibility against his iteration of all that had been, or was about to be, lost.

Nearly all of Adams's work from "The Tendency of History" (1894) on grows out of his practice as a writer of letters, the genre in which he first mastered "the paradoxical spirit of private conversation" (*D* 133). His abandonment of the regular modes of commercial publication in favor of private printing and circulation by hand blurred the distinction between book and letter. As we saw in the preceding chapter, the 1907 *Education* was accompanied by a variety of prefaces on its way to its first readers; the letters by which Adams introduced and later reconsidered the book in its "proof-sheet" phase constitute with that book an intertext without firm boundaries. In the letter drafted to introduce the "Rule" to his American Historical Association colleagues, he even refers to the *Education*, which he had thought to reprint and distribute among his colleagues as the necessary preface to the "Rule," as a letter. The term was liberally extended to designate texts that were dispatched directly from author to reader on the basis of a more or less personal relation.

The first paragraph of the letter drafted to introduce the "Rule" tells us so much about what Adams saw as the social practice of letter writing that it is worth considering nearly in full:

My dear Sir

Many thanks for the favor you have done me by reading the *Education*. It is ponderous and it is private; two qualities which enhance the favor; but it has a certain excuse for both.

Especially the privacy is vital to it. Every ward politician teaches us the first lesson of politics, that only direct, personal contact exerts influence; and since the distances which separate us make personal contact impossible, we can only fall back on the archaic resource of letter-writing. . . . The volume sent you was meant as a letter; garrulous, intimate, confidential, as is permitted in order to serve a social purpose, but would sound a false note for the public ear. In truth, for the occasion, I am frankly a conspirator; I want to invite private confidence, and the public is my worst enemy. (*LHA* 6:205)

Although archaic, the letter is that form of writing that most nearly approaches direct, personal contact; to the degree that it is discriminating in the contact that it makes, it remains the one form of writing that can exert palpable influence. These notions fit with Adams's long-standing belief that democratic society, inasmuch as its movement is not purely mechanical, may be guided only by an elite whose effectiveness is grounded in close personal relation. (Mathematicians and their unintelligible discourse seem to have represented for Adams the parody of such an elite.) The reference to "ward politician"—a phrase redolent of the machine politics the Adamses so vociferously despised—is in part autobiographical: growing up in the bosom of the Free-Soil party Adams knew his statehouse politics and throughout the late sixties and early seventies had even acted the part of ward politician in his epistolary efforts to organize a coalition "junto" behind the cause of civil service reform.

As he carried out such work amid degrees of confidentiality, he was publishing articles that spelled out the reform party's platform in the *North American Review*. If a certain element of privacy was thought vital to a shared "social purpose," the public was hardly perceived as the "worst enemy." To Adams the reformer (and self-styled conspirator against Grantism) the public was more purely problematic: the seemingly indifferent and unreachable, unknown but indispensable quantity in reform-movement calculus. In the first paragraph of the prefatory letter to the "Rule," Adams writes as though under condition of civil war and abrogation of duly constituted government. Certainly he believed that the U.S. Constitution as drafted by the Founders had long been extinct and that American politics had been corrupted by European socialist ideology, but he scarcely writes as though convinced that his efforts engage anything real or represent an initiative to fill the moral and intellectual vacuum at the center of American public life. In what by 1909 was his routine and perhaps no longer controllable extravagance of expression we may sense that Adams himself remained puzzled as to his rhetoric's dimensions of facetiousness. Falling back on "the archaic resource of letter-writing," he would conspire with the association membership-at-large to exert an influence, which he never defines, against what he persists in only vaguely invoking as the drift of a debased democratic society. Writing as it were in memory of former occasions when letter writing served a distinct political purpose, he at once fantasizes a present occasion and more or less deliberately parodies (by calling his means archaic and by keeping his purport vague) the notion of actual engagement. What Adams wrote about his early education applies to the diction of the paragraph: its atmosphere is "colonial, revolutionary, almost Cromwellian" and it seems "steeped . . . in the odor of political crime" (A I 726). Yet despite the suggestion of a somewhat playfully fantasized conspiracy, the projected tandem circulation of the *Education* and the "Rule" must have answered a serious, if hazy, intent.

Adams's most revealing explanation of what he saw as the social practice as opposed to the aesthetic discipline of letter writing is thus formulated in the retrospective light of that practice's perceived defeat. Upon further reflection, the publication of the "Rule" and the *Education* as companion texts must have appeared to carry too much risk; the prefatory letter remained unsent, the "Rule" was suppressed, and the *Education* never went out to the association membership-at-large. Perhaps Adams came to regard that membership as too amorphous and too hard to distinguish from his worst enemy, the socialist public. In any case the "private confidence" that the *Education* and the "Rule" invite "in order to serve a social purpose" was not to be sought in the association, and the text sent to measure the character of that readership would be the comparatively disingenuous (if also avowedly confidential and hazily intended) work, *A Letter*.

Beyond *A Letter* Adams never again overtly sought to address a plural readership in the supposed interest of marshaling social influence, and except for *The Life of George Cabot Lodge* and the biographical introduction to Hay's letters he wrote as a private correspondent. Depending upon his correspondent he varied his tone of private confidence: to Luquiens and Weeks he wrote as the decorously submissive retiree, whereas in his communications with the indulgent J. F. Jameson he rather freely asserted his elder statesman's prerogatives. Niece Mabel Hooper La Farge was audience to a light sardonic gossip that, if on occasion harsh, tended to observe the constraints proper to an old man's genteel affection for his junior kinswoman. With his brother Charles his tone assumed a gravely laconic character that reflected shared disappointment and estrangement of temper. With Brooks Adams, the perennial younger brother, or with his longtime intimates Elizabeth Cameron and Charles Milnes Gaskell, familiarity was such that he felt free to express himself with inactive censor. To these he could speak complacently of kicking his American universities in the stomach or refer with scorn to an "Irish maggot, rather lower than the Jew, but more or less the same in appetite for cheese" (*LHA* 6:301). This audience was insufficiently critical to discourage Adams from repeatedly confirming old judgments and prejudices.

But if he never again aspired as letter writer to exert a contemporary public influence, his correspondence must still have gone forward in the consciousness that his recipients preserved his letters and that the letters would almost certainly one day be edited and see public light. The likelihood was at times troubling, for much of the routine correspondence directed to Gaskell, Hay, and Mrs. Cameron came out of what for Adams was the necessarily unrestrained exercise of his pen, which permitted candid avowal and purgative phrase, and which moreover kept Adams the author actively immersed in language, his medium of daily (if embittered) renewal. In 1900 he asked Elizabeth Cameron (with characteristic unrestraint) to destroy his letters to her lest she "leave them knocking about, as a mash for the female pigs who feed out of the magazine-troughs at five dollars a page, to root in, for scandal and gossip" (*LHA* 5:103). Yet fifteen years later he proposed that she edit and publish the Adams-Cameron letters along with their correspondence with the old Lafayette Square set as a memorial to a bygone episode in the social life of Washington and as an encouragement to others who might wish to rescue the capital from its narrowly political concern. A lifelong reader of the letters of statesmen, authors, and other celebrated figures, he was well aware of the tendency of a distinguished private correspondence to become public text. Of this his own house provided ample evidence in the letters of John and Abigail Adams; Henry Adams once referred Gaskell to Abigail's letters for examples of the best American writing in the genre. Conscious as he was of his own distinction, at no point could he have written letters in the absolute conviction that the text would go no further than its recipient, even though there were occasions (as in Japan and the South Seas) when he undoubtedly wrote with little thought of a large and anonymous future readership.

As private correspondent he would continue after *A Letter* to engage public questions, although in his isolation often treating them as important only insofar as they constituted his own private agonies. Such had been his practice since 1890 when, with the *History* behind him, he was able to devote his whole energy to cultivating the posthumous life, retired authorship, and the spectator's pose of detachment. As we have seen already in his letters from the South Seas (where he felt "devoured by curiosity" with respect to the reemergence of Jay Gould), his detachment was actually an aloof but more than merely spectatorial involvement; still, from the early nineties on Adams increasingly writes in a language vexed by what it takes to be its powerlessness to intervene in the events it so steadily observes. To the degree that he felt this powerlessness as the result of America's submission to the craft of international capitalism (the banker, "gold-bug," "Jew") it appears on his page as a highly impressionistic and irresponsible moral analysis. It is such that glares at us in those passages documenting his brief career as a spontaneous and virulent anti-Dreyfusard in which his anti-Semitism totally abrogates his sense of justice: germane to the discussion of the convicted officer's exculpation is the fact that he "is a howling Jew as you see from his portraits" (*LHA* 5:26). Such discourse wells from a revulsion that Adams, far from resisting by means of critical naming, generalizes through a process of easy metaphorization, a coining of false equivalents: "So I don't talk Dreifuss and don't read it; but there is little else to talk about, and South Africa, which is the British Dreifuss, being a Jew interest, we are not allowed to talk of, for we all know that too much money is in it to permit of any result but one in any case" (*LHA* 5:9). Adopting the attitude of one persecuted, he would portray himself as the lone, plain-speaking man in a world of repressed discourse, a clear-sighted Yankee in a Europe given over to obscurantists.

Speaking magisterially in the exclusive, permissive hearing of men and women amused by extravagant talk was a lifelong pleasure for Adams, which he could indulge within limits in early letters to his brother Charles but only cultivate after he had begun his correspondence with Charles Milnes Gaskell. It was a pleasure realized supremely among the Lafayette Square set of the late seventies and early eighties, particularly in the company of men like John Hay and Clarence King but also in the mixed group that included Marian Adams and Clara Hay, the "five of hearts" whose exclusivities included a correspondence conducted on special stationery. Whether conversation took place on the page or in the well-fitted rooms of their Washington residences, it was free to take hypothetical, facetious, and paradoxical turns. Attracted to bold ideas, Adams's thought is always more deeply distinguished by its capacity to suspend conviction and its impatience with definitive conclusions that eliminated the play of paradox; such conversation was no doubt congenial to the writer of the self-consciously experimental *Democracy*, *Esther*, and *History*. Beyond its broad intellectual latitude, however, and in a way that probably compensated for what he felt to be his narrowed field of influence, his inner-circle discourse released itself from any obligation to tolerate the views and enterprises of other social interests. The dismaying spectacle of brilliant language expended upon racist perception and hateful sentiment intensified in the midnineties but was an established dimension of his correspondence long before.

As he grew old in solitude, a self-consciously neglected author, his letters became an increasingly insular discourse with stock generalizations and set motifs: "corners" to be turned in the dangerous world of geopolitics, crises that made him "turn green," indictments of "Jew" influence, and announcements of the world's end. Brooks Adams's writing and rewriting of *The Law of Civilization and Decay* engaged the retired author from afar; drawn into the current of Brooks's humorless pessimism, he compiled statistics, framed aphorisms, and criticized drafts for the younger brother's benefit. John Hay's reemergence in the nineties as ambassador to Great Britain and then secretary of state brought Adams new sensations of power and powerlessness. In a position to advise, he made suggestions in a circumspectly extravagant language that manifested his conviction that Hay's judgment, if not the surest, was his own to exert, and that although the secretary could on occasion accomplish apparent miracles (as the saving of the foreign legations during the Boxer Rebellion), he was a man whose health was delicate. In colloquy Adams and Hay may have "killed and buried, in advance, half the world and the neighboring solar systems" (*LHA* 5:128), but such talk did little to mitigate a deepening mutual sense of their own fragility.

The tall talk, the unrestraint that flirts with obscenity, and the suggestion of one entrapped in ranting monologue make all the more impressive the major efforts to reengage broad public dialogue that *Mont Saint Michel and Chartres* and especially the *Education* represent. As a chapter of engineered cruelty, the genocidal programs that would come in consequence of the nineteenth century's discourse of hate far exceeded Adams's worst expectations of the twentieth century; he could not have imagined the experiments that the language he sometimes spoke (and that indeed was spoken commonly in American upper-class conservative circles) would invite. "Only in history as a fairy tale," he wrote as the stories of the *Titanic*'s sinking were learned, "does one like to see civilisations founder, and to hear the cries of the drowning" (*LHA* 6:538). The line between the fairy tale and the realm of public consequence has been narrowed by twentieth-century events and our consequent sense of language as constituting the real, yet Adams himself was deeply troubled by the distinction—the sensation that language for him had become so much egoistic, demoralized play. Inured as he grew to it, he recognized the degradation if not always the public dangers of a discourse that was cut off—language proceeding in the conviction of its own inconsequence. "I have grown so used to playing the spider," he wrote Sir Robert Cunliff in 1899, "and squatting in silence in the middle of this Washington web, and I have seen so many flies and other insects caught and devoured in its meshes, that I have now a little the sense of being a sort of ugly, bloated, purplish-blue, and highly venomous, hairy tarantula which catches and devours Presidents, senators, diplomates, congressmen and cabinet-officers, and knows the flavor of every generation and every country in the civilised world. Just now my poor friend Hay is caught in the trap, and, to my infinite regret, I have to make a meal of him as of the rest" (*LHA* 4:667).

Kill and consume as his language did, it submitted to the requirements of sustainable dialogue within the variable if generally lax constraints of Adams's correspondence partnerships. Granted that Adams did not perpetuate exchanges with those who vigorously challenged his views, the monologic dimension of his letters never expended his avid inquiry into his regular correspondents' personal circumstances. He was at times painfully aware of his reader's indulgence on his behalf. "Forgive all this egotism," he wrote Elizabeth Cameron from Beirut. "I am perfectly aware that I talk of nothing but myself, but it is consciously done" (*LHA* 4:553). The marvel of Adams's letters, particularly those in which the obsessive lucubrations of Washington and Paris are abandoned for a season of travel, is how much of the world—geographically, ethnologically, politically—he was always able to register without ceasing very long to talk about himself. If the range of the sedentary Brahmin's ideology was narrow and given to contraction, the traveler's range of sensuous susceptibility and spontaneous sympathy remained elastic. Hence it was as traveler that he suffered most the burden of ego, the sorrows of bereavement. " 'Bleibe doch,' " he might say to the passing hour as the beauty of the world returned for him in one of many exotic scenes, " 'du bist so schön!' Three days in any place on earth is all it will bear. The pleasure is in the movement, as Faust knew when he let the devil in to the preposterous contract" (*LHA* 4:248). Travel, as we have already seen, made him aware of others in the world bereaved of their means of personal and cultural renewal and enriched his capacity for what as years passed became an abiding dimension of his continuous dialogues, the expression of condolence. That at least remained within the province of literary language, and, from his own discovery in 1885 through the condolence letters addressed to him that the "whole of society" secretly groaned "with the same anguish" (*LHA* 2:644), personal suffering existed for him as an experience that at once isolated individuals and established the deepest human bonds.

In explaining the character of his egotism he nearly always returned to the public nature of what he steadfastly perceived as his defeat. "We leave no followers, no school, no tradition," he wrote Charles in 1911. "My correspondence and literary connection is fairly large, but it is as passive-minded and childlike in attitude as so much jelly-fish" (*LHA* 6:480). Still, to his death he kept up his end of a dialogue diminished by the deaths of friends and haunted by public nightmares and in doing so resisted as he could the catastrophic closures that his every letter projected. He thus continued to record the never entirely closed chapter of his generation's historical experience. Although he remained horrified by the fundamental indeterminacy of the post-Newtonian scientific concept, and although his historiography's tendency to generate contradiction had long ago confirmed for him the inadequacy of literary language, his insistence upon conversational paradox was a means finally of affirming a measure of historical openness. It was his practical way of demonstrating that, to the degree that history does consist in what we say of it, he was a participant in as well as the spectator of its processes. "I am in a new society and a new world which is more wild and madder by far than the old one," he wrote in his last letter to Gaskell a few weeks before his death in 1918, "and yet I seem to myself to be a part of it—and even, almost to take share in it. I speculate on what is to happen as actively as I did at your table fifty years ago, and the only difference is that I terribly miss your father's conversation and his dry champagne" (*LHA* 6:786). It is telling that conversation here provides the focus for deepest memory.

The steady blurring after 1890 of the line between Adams's correspondence and his more publicly directed work acquires further interest given the odd beginning of his career, for his debut as a public author emerged from the twenty-two-year-old man's already inveterate practice as a writer of letters. His first published work documented his journey in April 1860 to Austria and revolutionary Italy undertaken during his post-baccalaureate year abroad. About to leave Dresden, Henry wrote to his brother Charles that "this trip may perhaps furnish material for a pleasant series of letters, not written to be published but publishable in case they were worth it" (*LHA* 1:106). Out of such studied inadvertence came a sequence of nine letters that began as a rather garrulous travelogue but culminated in the correspondent's passage to a freshly revolutionized Sicily and a meeting with Garibaldi. The sequence is interesting for its exposure of Adams's ambivalence toward popular movements: his paradoxical position as an American aristocrat appears in his sympathy for displaced monarchy while his enthusiasm for the Italian liberals is tempered by what he characterizes as the repulsiveness of the Sicilian insurgents. Editing the letters for concision, Charles arranged for publication of all but one of them in the *Boston Courier*.

Later that same year, after moving to the nation's capital to serve as private secretary to Charles Francis Adams, newly elected to the House, he would write in a more strictly political vein as the anonymous Washington correspondent of the *Boston Advertiser*. Such newspaper correspondence was directed at promoting his father's actions in the Committee of Thirty-Three in the early days of the secession crisis prior to Abraham Lincoln's formation of the new government. Removing to London when his father was named minister to Great Britain, he would play a similar role the next year as the correspondent of the *New York Times*, explaining for the benefit of the American people and (as Edward Chalfant has argued) Lincoln's cabinet the perils of American diplomacy from the legation's near perspective.[18]

Although liking the sense of contest that lively political journalism brought, he was impatient from the start with its constraints. He complained to his brother Charles that Charles Hale, the *Advertiser*'s editor, "does not encourage brilliancy. Chaff seems to be his horror and he promptly expunges all that I write of an unfavorable personal character. The consequence is that I lose all interest in what I'm saying" (*LHA* 1:227). His more serious literary pursuit of the winter would be another kind of correspondence: one written for a less immediate public. "I propose to write you this winter a series of private letters to show how things look," he wrote to Charles soon after his arrival in the tense capital. "I fairly confess that I want to have a record of this winter on file, and though I have no ambition nor hope to become a Horace Walpole, I still would like to think that a century or two hence when everything else about us is forgotten, my letters might still be read and quoted as a memorial of manners and habits at the time of the great secession of 1860" (*LHA* 1:204). One dimension of Adams's early ambition as a letter writer is given by the phrase (echoed throughout his career) "a century or two hence": he wanted his language to possess the intrinsic interest and power to generalize that would make it permanent in the way that even the best journalism seldom was. Two motives at this time seem to have governed his practice as private and public correspondent. He wished to write about manners and habits, scenes, and personages in the brilliant language of a semidetached yet gravely serious sensibility; at the same time he was irresistibly drawn to political analysis, framing exhortations as to the citizen's imperatives and writing with the sensation that he wrote to an immediate and calculable public consequence.

Behind Adams's emergence as a correspondent are various letter-writing practices. The Walpolean example (the Whig outlook rounded out by social observation and a detached aestheticism) is certainly one, but more indigenous models lay in the high-toned correspondence of John, Abigail, and John Quincy Adams and their contemporaries. From his family's papers alone Henry Adams would have formed a large idea of the letter, for it existed in the Quincy archives in a number of capacities: as an instrument of private and public philosophical inquiry and concerted political action, as the record of history in the making (such as Henry would aspire to assemble during the secession winter), as the principal text of diplomacy, and as part of the daily machinery of statecraft. Understandably, when Adams turned to the writing of political biography and history, he made correspondence, official and private, more than just his central documentary source; conspicuously, Adams's protagonists appear as letter writers, discussants behind the spectacle of public life. The more immediate background of Adams's emergence, however, is a dialogue conducted through the mails between himself and his older brother Charles, which commenced with Henry's ill-fated journey to Berlin to study the civil law and continued through his lengthy residence in London as his father's private secretary, and which turned upon a question that for an Adams could not long remain casual: the choice of profession.

On opposite sides of the Atlantic Charles and Henry deliberated the career paths open to them. The discussion assumed weight from the circumstance that their father, aligned with the new Republican party, was elected in 1858 to the House, a possible first step toward the presidency (or treasury) and restoration of the family to active national eminence. Charles himself had chosen law and would complete his legal apprenticeship in 1860; having secured for himself a profession, the question for the older brother now mostly concerned how he should advance toward a public career, and political journalism seemed to offer the best means of advancement. In its early phases the discussion focused more on Henry whose plan to study civil law at the University of Berlin had foundered on his nonfluency in German; his new plan, to study the German jurists on his own in Dresden, a city more congenial than Berlin, appeared hardly more auspicious. Charles, suspicious (as was their father) of the effect of Europe on American youth, disapproved of Henry's pursuit of a legal education abroad; more than that, he felt that Henry was particularly unsuited to practice law and that rather than waste energy in legal training the obviously gifted younger brother should turn immediately to literary work.

Even as Henry admitted that he looked upon law as little more than a foundation for other pursuits, he resisted his brother's objections to his course and especially resented Charles's suggestion that he become a professional man of letters. The older brother, he complained, would make him "a writer of popular sketches in Magazines; a lecturer before Lyceums and College societies; a dabbler in metaphysics, poetry and art; than which I would rather die, for if it has come to that . . . mediocrity has fallen on the name of Adams" (*LHA* 1:22). Yet having accused Charles of trivializing his ambitions, Henry in the same letter turns around and objects to his brother's exaltation of his powers, particularly the assumption that he was "capable of teaching the people and of becoming a light to the nations" (*LHA* 1:24). What he may really have reacted against is his brother's insistence that he become a type of provincial New England culture.[19] Even so, he proceeded to work up a minor disquisition entitled "Two Letters on a Prussian Gymnasium" with intentions of placing it in the recently established *Atlantic*, a magazine for which he not only affected, but no doubt genuinely felt, contempt.[20] Yet even before finishing it, Adams determined to suppress the article. From Rome the next year, "very" struck by the experience of reading Gibbon in the eternal city, he wrote presciently that "perhaps some day I too might come to anchor like that. Our house needs a historian in this generation and I feel strongly tempted by the quiet and sunny prospect, while my ambition for political life dwindles as I get older" (*LHA* 1:149). His ambition for political life would in fact wax and wane, and he was soon to enter upon his brief career as a newspaper polemicist with genuine if superficial gusto. Thrown by secession and the Civil War into the currents of diplomacy and political journalism, Adams never had to abandon formally the legal profession to which he was so clearly disinclined. And beyond the cataclysm of war, Reconstruction, and Grantism, the "quiet and sunny prospect" of the grand historical narrative would indeed be his to claim.

In urging his brother to adopt writing as his profession, Charles was picking up on an alternate gravitation that Henry himself had long since recognized. Of his future plans and prospects he had written the following in the Harvard class of 1858 "Life-Book": "Ultimately it is most probable that I shall study and practice law, but where and to what extent is as yet undecided. My wishes are for a quiet and a literary life, as I believe that to be the happiest and in this country not the least useful."[21] His indecision as to a law career is here plainly forecast as well as what would prove to be the confusing amalgam of gratification and social purpose that accompanied his pursuit of the literary life. The "literary life" in Adams's 1858 usage was already one of various paths: belles lettres, reportage, and essays on a wide range of public issues aimed at a literate general readership. Perhaps too at this early date he had in mind scholarly monographs, biography, history, fiction, and even autobiography. Before leaving Harvard he had explored a number of literary forms, from the evocative sketches and personal essays printed in *Harvard Magazine* and the satire he produced as Hasty Pudding Alligator to his stern Class Day oration in which he called upon his classmates and the university community to examine the narrowness of their objects in the light of their professed New England ideals. Whatever he had principally in mind when he referred to the literary life, there was nothing problematic about "literary language": he might fail as a writer but not through any inherent incapacity in the common medium of discourse. Nor was he troubled at this point by any suspicions that an intelligent and responsive readership might cease to exist.

But given the circumstances of his two years' travel and study in Europe and his seven-year residence in London, his first mastery as a literary man was as a correspondent, his genre, the letter, fertile in its comparative indeterminacy. In his first serious essays published after the war in the *North American Review*, he often wrote in what we might call the New England Ciceronian mode: a style that was never far from oratory, in which the writer argued and exhorted as though he and the review's readership together constituted a Roman forum of American questions. While such a mode may have answered his conception of how an Adams of literary inclination must (on occasion) sound, he had long before established through his correspondence a conversational mode of remarkable range—as remarkable as the range of correspondents with whom by his midtwenties he had conversed. In addition to the shades of familiarity adopted in exchanges with parents and brothers, his early letters exhibit gradations of formality in his communications with distinguished friends such as Charles Sumner and John Gorham Palfrey, forcefulness in his contact with newspaper editors, and command in the legation correspondence that fell to him as his father's private secretary in London. By his midtwenties he could speak with self-possession to anyone, at least on paper; in his hand the letter had become a highly adaptable and confident instrument.

The most telling letters of Adams's first decade of serious authorship remain those to Charles Francis Adams, Jr.[22] The series of 162 letters commencing with Henry's residence in Berlin and concluding on the eve of his departure in May 1868 from London comprehends a wealth of expression and documents a rapidly growing command over the written word. They were a conscious exercise in craft; on a couple of occasions he even composed (emulating perhaps the bilingual Walpole as well as his fluent ancestors) in French. If in his London isolation he gives himself over to the dark metaphysics of youthful soul searching, he is able to rescue his spirit and sharpen his phrase in satiric treatment of British life and manners; anxious analysis of the short diplomatic term finds relief in long, picturesque, and comic accounts of travel. Constantly he exercises his powers of observation, but more than that he strives to depict dramatic (or novelistic) scene—of family life, social encounters, or decisive moments in affairs of state. From a variety of angles he returns to the perennial question of the brothers' respective paths; he gives and takes advice and spars with his brother as the discussion turns to their respective strengths and weaknesses. Increasingly he establishes himself as a writer of set tones and authoritative pronouncements. His position as a foreigner in London and unofficial employee in the legation no doubt encouraged him to cultivate the stance of often-magisterial spectatorship that we find him taking in the letters; yet, in correspondence with Charles, he submits himself always to the give-and-take of their transatlantic dialogue, and he is always candid about their common vulnerability to the freaks of historical process. Still, he reserves the right to say anything on an experimental basis.

Early in his correspondence with Charles, Henry half-consciously formulated for himself an aesthetic of letter writing that is striking in view of what he would later cultivate in his public texts as "the paradoxical spirit of private conversation." In response to his brother's objection to certain remarks he had made about Boston young women, Henry, readily acknowledging Charles to be "in the right," insisted on the conditional rightness of his own remarks: "What one writes [in a letter] is considerably influenced by the accidental state of his mind at the instant of writing, and it is not strange if, among so many letters, when I am hurrying to put down the first thing that comes into my head ... I say many silly things" (*LHA* 1:18). Adams excuses the silly things he says as so much dross produced by what is understood as the essential activity of letter writing, but he seems also to reveal an interest in and affection for the "accidental" state of mind. This interest and affection would have to contend with his lifelong desire for the semblance of absolute truth. In time he would propose that the mind, unable to arrive at truth, could only know itself and then only as a sequence of accidental states; the subject of an overwhelmingly accidental education, the mind was itself but an accident. He would write of the historian's "personal error" and, in the closing paragraph of *Mont Saint Michel and Chartres*, despair over "the irregularities of the mental mirror" (A I 695). Thus disabused, he could sincerely affect to be little more than the detached observer of his own intellectual life: someone who cut and pasted ideas until, as he remarked to William James, his pages wept with repetition. Yet from first to last he insisted on the (potential) authority of that accidental state, in spite of the fact that he looked upon discourse as in practice conditional—in play amid relatively unfixed meanings. For Adams, one's mind was the first if not an ultimate reality and the language of private conversation was the prime medium of experience. The aesthetic of his early correspondence anticipates the solemn relativism of the *Education*—his conviction that, "reduced to his last resources," the value of historical forces "could have no measure but that of their attraction on his own mind" (A I 1069). What he early assumed as his privilege to contradict himself may later have diminished to the rhetorical device of *A Letter*; still we should not lose sight of the fact that, in the *Education,* Adams proposed the socially conscious self-education of the accidental mind as a bulwark against epistemological, moral, and political chaos.

If he indulgently transcribed the conceit of the passing moment, his letters to Charles consistently resist the merely accidental development of their careers; the unforeseeable course of secession and the Civil War had given both men sufficient taste of that. From 1858 to 1868 Charles passed from the sedate activities of an apprenticing lawyer to a commission in the Union army and thence, through a series of hard-fought campaigns and flattering promotions, to a state of restless retirement in Quincy. There, as the head of his own young family, he worked to fulfill his end of the brothers' joint plan to enter public life as writers on public issues. In the same decade Henry progressed through as many transitions, but his situation at any moment was more anomalous than Charles's, more in need of self-definition. He had not been admitted to the bar and served the Union cause as his father's factotum—while Charles mounted his charger Henry tutored the younger siblings and escorted his sister and mother about. His one early claim to independence in London had been his secret employment as the *New York Times* correspondent (only Charles and Henry Raymond, the *Times* editor, were privy to this), but the *London Times'* humiliating exposure of him as the author of "Two Letters from Manchester," which was published in the *Boston Courier,* lead him to cut short his association with the *New York Times* for fear of more serious embarrassment. Only as the Union army and the American legation gained ground, and as his own self-education progressed in the speculative atmosphere of intellectual London (and, aided by champagne, at the hospitable table of James Milnes Gaskell), did he reemerge in his own eyes as a man with definite tasks. Alarmed in 1863 by the fact that at ages twenty-five and twenty-eight neither man could see his future (with of course the constant fear that Charles would be maimed or killed in battle), Henry asked, "Have we both wholly lost our reckonings and are we driven at random by fate, or have we still a course that we are steering though it is not quite the same as our old one?" (*LHA* 1:347–48). By 1866, with two articles accepted for the *North American Review* and about to complete and submit a third, he could report to Charles that he had "never varied my course at all" and that "the accidents of life have fallen in with the bent of my disposition and the previous course of my training" (*LHA* 1:515).

After the war the roles at one point reversed and Henry, whose despairing meditations previously had been scorned by the vigorous cavalry officer, now admonished the sometimes depressed and directionless veteran. A harsh critic of his brother's—and his own—verbose style, he was even harsher with Charles's complaint that he (Charles) "had not cleverness enough to interest readers unless" he made himself "vulgar." Conceding that Charles might be right, Henry asserted that he had "no business to say it without first trying the better way—and the trial ought to last your life." So in 1867 Henry Adams conferred the benefit of the doubt respecting their American readership. "Give the public a chance. So it is vulgar!" That did not excuse the brothers' common stylistic defects. "Just read a page of Macaulay or Balzac or who you please," Henry advised, "and then take up a sheet of your or my stuff, and you'll see quickly enough why we still want an audience" (*LHA* 1:555).

While Henry broadened his resources as a writer and gave himself, in his isolation, to the pleasing indeterminacies of correspondence-discourse, he plotted his brother's and his own emergence as major influences in their country's public discussion. The brothers' correspondence bore fruit as a series of essays all but one of which first appeared in the *North American Review* and collected thereafter in the single-volume *Chapters of Erie and Other Essays* published in 1871. In view of the terrible insularity and self-suspicion of his late work, it is significant that Henry's first book should be a collaborative venture devoted (in the words of Charles Francis Adams, Jr.) to "that healthy public opinion . . . which is the life's breath of our whole political system."[23]

4

The Romance and Tragedy
of Statesmanship

Reform Author

DESPITE THE Union victory at Antietam two months earlier, the war in
November 1862 remained undecided, and legation business daily went
forward on treacherous diplomatic ground. At a loss on the question of
his long-term career, Henry Adams did his best to reconcile himself to its
necessary deferral. "The future is a blank to me as I suppose it is also to
you," he wrote Charles. By calling it a "blank" he doubtless meant that
the future is unforeseeable, but the text of the letter encourages another
reading—that the future is to be seen as a blank page, inviting inscription.
Restricted as his London activities were "to a careful observation of events
here and assistance in the manual labor of the place," he had committed
himself in his free hours to no less than "a study of history and politics
which seem to me most necessary to our country *for the next century*"
(italics added). Having thus unaffectedly named his curriculum's purview,
he proceeded to register his fear that such studies, given his Hamlet-like
temperament, must miscarry before they could translate into action. The
good of the world appeared too inseparable from its evil, the evil too
inseparable from the good; confusion and disenchantment clouded for
him what the brothers had been brought up to regard as life's higher
objects. He admitted that the fault lay in his mind: insufficiently "positive
and absolute," it was ill-equipped for "action, which requires quickness
and perseverance. I have steadily lost faith in myself ever since I left college," he wrote, and he worried that he was headed for "a truncated life"
(*LHA* 1:315).

Nevertheless he went on to outline a program that he would pursue
with perseverance over several decades, clinging to its aspiration even in
what recurrently appeared to be its defeat. The particular career paths of
the Adams brothers were not the essential questions; "What we want," he
lectured Charles, "is a *school*. We want a national set of young men like
ourselves or better, to start new influences not only in politics, but in

literature, in law, in society, and throughout the whole social organism of the country. A national school of our own generation." This call for renovation is made poignant by the fact that in 1862 the nation stood divided and his own generation was killing itself in a conflict inherited from the Founders. No wonder he added, "And that is what America has no power to create." Lamenting the dispersion in his country of genius and leadership, he seems almost less mindful of the Civil War than clairvoyant of the decades to come. "It's all random, insulated work," he complained, "for special and temporary and personal purposes, and we have no means, power or hope of combined action for any unselfish end" (*LHA* 1:315). Of Adams's vast correspondence this is one of the most famous passages. In it the broadly national and aspiringly disinterested nature of Henry Adams's vocation finds its best early statement. The object of that vocation is a renovated, if not perfected, republic, but Adams would enlist more than the obvious methods of statecraft. Impatient with the political emphasis of American culture and family experience, he would have his generation treat the country's basic curriculum, its moral and imaginative constitution broadly conceived. Given what was then the wreck of the *United* States, it was perhaps the only way he could envision his generation effectively preparing "for the next century."

In calling for a concerted shaping of the social organism he no doubt wished to see the emergence of a more refined national character, one comparable in self-assurance (if not yet in cultural resource) to the educated Europeans with whom he had become well acquainted. Ideologically the passage reflects several currents in the young Adams's thought. Probably at that moment Tocqueville and John Stuart Mill were making their first serious impact upon his thinking, both confirming his Brahmin view that democracy offered to redeem humanity from the evils of Old World class structure, but it could do so only under the leadership of able and virtuous men. To the extent that the letter of November 21, 1862, addresses statecraft, it focuses (with the evident encouragement of Adams's advanced studies) upon a classically republican moral ideal; the key phrases are "combined action" and "unselfish end."[1] From other writings of the period we can see how Adams's moral formulation translated into specific policy: a republican belief in hard currency, a liberal subscription to the tenets of laissez-faire economics, and above all a desire to return at war's end to the scrupulous balance of powers as set forth in the Constitution.

Such politics were conservative if not nostalgic. And yet this makes all the more remarkable the desire Adams expresses to move out of the past: the young man speaks emphatically if vaguely of "new influences," "a national school of our own generation." Beyond what we know to have been his wish to see the constitutional system (sabotaged through its own weaknesses) restored and perfected, he invokes a progressive course responsive to fresh energies and yearns for what he sees as the obscure but needful national transformation that must come of his generation's initiative. If his wish for a national life that did more than favor commercial aptitudes took a tone different from Emerson's, he would nonetheless likewise write for many years to come "in the optative mood."

Three years after Adams's death in 1918, the lines he had written to Charles in the shadow of the Civil War met with the impatience of the young Van Wyck Brooks, tried sorely in his attempt to piece together a usable past for the benefit of his own generation, his own postwar America. Approving of Adams's clear-sighted diagnosis of the American problem and taken with his call for a corrective and revitalizing school, the critic fixed upon Adams's reservation, "And that is what America has no power to create." This, wrote Brooks, was "the perfect illustration of that mass fatalism" of American writers from the Civil War on, "and Henry Adams himself, in his passivity, is the type of it."[2] But Adams himself had been the first to detect the element of fatalism in his temperament. From London in 1861, on the basis of what he called his "profound conviction of the littleness of our kind," he spoke of his attraction to determinist philosophy; from Samoa in 1891, as we have seen, he described himself as "cursed with the misfortune of thinking that I know beforehand what the result must be, and of feeling sure that it is one which I do not care to pursue; one with which I have little or no sympathy, except in a coldly scientific way" (*LHA* 1:395–96; 3:382). Yet his fatalism coexisted with a decidedly interventionist impulse, one sufficiently strong and original to diverge from family precedent. The letter of November 21, 1862, illustrates one paradox of his temperament: complaining of his lack of "quickness and perseverance," he nonetheless proceeds to imagine a course that requires a sanguine outlook. Again and again, his faith that the future (as indeed the past) remained unwritten rescued the author Adams from any actual passivity. In fixing on Adams's doubt, in hastening to the conclusion that by not signing his novels he failed to "become the founder of the school that he desired," Brooks misses the extent to which Adams overcame the fatalism that not only existed as an element of private temperament but increasingly dominated the discourse of the period.[3] In one way or another, through his various phases of public and retired authorship, his more or less successful experiments, his life would be given to establishing the school that a vast democracy would require—an object that (as we have already seen) Adams would continue to pursue even as he recoiled in disgust from democracy's evident failure.

Although Adams would continue to write for newspaper publication, by the end of his English residence he had moved on to the generally lengthier and more philosophical discourse of the quarterly article; he would never realize his ambition of commanding a New York daily, a hope that in London he still held for "some indistinct future" (A I 934). In 1866 and 1867 he dispatched from London three essays to the *North American Review*: "Captain John Smith," "British Finance in 1816," and "The Bank of England Restriction." All three reveal a partisan perspective and possess polemical thrust. Written with a view to the economic follies the United States was already embracing in its emergence from a wartime economy, the financial articles examine tariff and currency measures adopted by Great Britain during the Napoleonic Wars and so constitute an early statement of Adams's hard-money, free-trade stance. They are notable for their statistical detail, their interest in portraiture, their treatment of economics as morality, and their tone of long-suffering scorn and self-righteousness. "Captain John Smith," the first to be published, is more discursively problematic. This essay grew over the course of several years from a suggestion made to Adams by John Gorham Palfrey. In his debut as a historian he took as his remarkably destructive purpose "the entire erasure of one of the most attractive portions of American history," the Pocahontas legend (*NAR* 104:2). The article takes the innocuous form of a review of two primary texts that had been recently edited by Charles Deane: *A Discourse of Virginia* by the colony's first president, Edward Wingfield, and Smith's own *A True Relation of Virginia*, an early account in which Pocahontas makes none of the famous appearances that she makes in Smith's later *Generall Historie*. Aimed rather dryly at discrediting Smith, the article applied the northern author's animus to the substance of Virginia's chivalric myth. It was taken, much as Adams meant it to be, as an affront to the Virginia aristocracy.

By 1868 he was on his own as a free lance in Washington, where he naturally acquired a more urgent sense that his readership constituted a potential electorate. Setting up in the capital with the expectation of siding with the newly elected Ulysses S. Grant against a Senate dominated by the Radical Republicans, he soon found his energies motivated against a pervasive corruption that would worsen in the next years until it became known as Grantism. Paper currency, protective tariffs, haphazard revenue collection, the intricate workings of lobby and party politics by which laws were shaped and votes bought: such "fields," wrote Henry to his fellow reformer Charles, "are gloriously rich and stink like hell if we were only of the force to distil their flowers" (*LHA* 2:14). The distillation took the form of a series of combative essays: "American Finance, 1865–1869," "Civil Service Reform," "The Legal-Tender Act," "The New York Gold Conspiracy," reviews of two congressional years entitled "The Session," and various shorter pieces. Most often finding outlet in the *North American Review*, Adams's work also appeared in E. L. Godkin's *Nation*, the *New York Post*, and two British quarterly reviews, the *Edinburgh* and *Westminster*. The letters of 1868 and 1869 depict Adams as throwing himself into the reform movement with youthful ardor and hectic glee, "a regular conspirator" aligning himself with likewise forceful, reform-minded men of his own or a slightly older generation. Beneath the fine sensation of righteous opposition Adams remained skeptical of progress in the near future; confronting the "new school" in whose ranks he now stood was what he described to John Bright as "our outrageous political corruption," one which an intelligent coterie alone could not dissolve. "The reform we need," he acknowledged, "must come from the people and the people show no signs of asking it" (*LHA* 2:18).

The disgust that Adams initially felt after Grant's appointment of George S. Boutwell as treasury secretary rapidly enlarged to a simmering contempt for the new president's evident indifference to restoring the power of the executive branch. The free lance quickly determined that he would become the administration's leading antagonist and make his unpopularity with government a public force, and he was willing to court the publicity of general opprobrium by publishing American scandal in British quarterlies. As he would in *Democracy* and again in *A Letter*, he wrote to create a sensation, although in these early writings his provocational rhetoric served nameable political goals. Yet even in the late sixties, Adams's work betrays confusion as to how his polemic might work to actual consequence. The public always represented to him a doubtful moral force, but without popular support he knew that his ambition must miscarry: "The true policy of reformers," he wrote in "Civil Service Reform," "is to trust neither to Presidents nor to Senators, but appeal directly to the people" (*NAR* 109:474). Occurring as it does in the pages of the *North American Review*, the most important American quarterly of the day but hardly a publication with a popular following,[4] the statement suggests that direct appeal might prove difficult; rather noticeably it stops short of affirming that the people, unlike presidents and senators, can be trusted. Yet if he had doubts, he silenced them by proceeding to the easy assertion that "the public must be convinced that reform is a vital question" before progress can be made and then by concluding his article's penultimate paragraph with the rather astonishingly unguarded fantasy of an audience response. As for awakening popular outrage, "there is no way but to attack corruption in all its holes, to drag it before the public eye, to dissect it and hold the diseased members up to popular disgust, to give the nation's conscience no rest nor peace until mere vehemence of passion overcomes the sluggish self-complacency of the public mind" (*NAR* 109:

474–75). This evidently is how he wished to envision his efforts as a reform movement writer. Yet his letters suggest that "vehemence of passion" was usually the last thing he realistically expected from the public.

Where the writing is overbearing the young Adams betrays his lack of rhetorical self-confidence. Strong verbs, heavy adjectives, scenes suggestive of theatrical confrontation: such would be lifelong features of Henry Adams's style, and although he would learn to restrain his penchant for the lurid phrase and create a language of scalpel-wielding dexterity, metaphors calculated to impress by their violence recur in the depictions of what he always felt to be the drama of political and intellectual history. Such writing often achieved the finesse of stylistic (if not strictly rhetorical) self-confidence. But if the old man who spoke of kicking his American universities in the stomach did so in the more or less conscious conviction that his writings could have little consequence, the young man who spoke of holding "diseased members up to popular disgust" lived out in language those triumphs which he already must have suspected were not to be his in any such dramatic or decided form. To be sure, protracted abuse of the public trust legitimately gave to Adams's work a purgative motive and denunciatory tone; densely argumentative in support of a lush militance, his articles at once served the reform cause and his private need for the sensation of enlistment. In the writings of this period the compensatory function of language is consistently evident. He had not yet reached the stage at which defense mechanism could be dropped and language, if it compensated for a sorry present, could at the same time come into a more lyrical life and be put to the genuinely creative task of invoking a possible future order.

Other characteristics of Adams's early public style are more conventional: the double negative of cautious affirmation, the learned citation of historical precedent, the embellishment of mythic parallel, the epigram, the epithet, the lengthy periodic sentence that invested public discussion with the drama of the Roman Senate or what nineteenth-century Americans might imagine as that drama from the orations of Cicero. Oratory was of course a part of the contemporary curriculum and contributed to the larger fiction that the American Republic renewed—with the hope of perfecting—the democratic examples of Greece and Rome. As the grandson would later note, John Quincy Adams himself, in his brief tenure as professor of rhetoric and oratory at Harvard, "created the school of oratory to which Edward Everett's generation adhered" (A III 1322). The grandfather's lectures took as their premise the inseparability of oratory and political freedom: as "liberty" was "the parent of eloquence," so eloquence was "the last stay and support of liberty," and he invoked the shades of Demosthenes and Cicero to be his witnesses![5] For his part,

Henry Adams worked to suppress the grand oratorical gestures of Edward Everett, whose Faneuil Hall eulogy delivered over the bier of his former teacher, the deceased president, would be remembered in the *Education* as a striking instance of attitudinization. "Our oratory is a falsehood which degrades the nation," he wrote to Charles in 1867 (*LHA* 1:544). Between the early "The Great Secession Winter of 1860–61" (written and suppressed before he left with his father for London) and "The New York Gold Conspiracy" (1870) Adams does not renounce the stock device, but he does begin to master a style less stiffly artificial, which employs simple as well as complex clausal structures, and which can maintain clean argumentative and narrative lines in spite of a bristling satire. Although accused in 1869 of Burkean excess and given as late as the *Gallatin* to oratorical flourishes reminiscent of Gibbon and Burke, his early public style often reveals a remarkable suppleness and restraint and frequently succeeds in bearing the rhetorical strains of satire and jeremiadical reproach.[6]

With "The Session" articles in particular Adams had reason to believe that his literary efforts might have a measurable political effect. Modeled on Lord Robert Cecil's unsparing critiques of the parliamentary sessions, these ascerbic reviews of the annual congressional sessions won wide and decided notice; in 1872 the Democrats issued the second as a campaign pamphlet in their bid to turn Grant out of office. Exultant over a flattering review of the first "Session" written by Franklin Benjamin Sanborne for the *Springfield Republican*, Adams observed to Charles that "Republics are *not* ungrateful"; as he continued to savor his success he resolved to "make my annual 'Session' an institution and a power in the land" (*LHA* 2:29, 30). To Gaskell he wrote as though his iconoclast musings had emerged at last as a palpable force: "For once I have smashed things generally and really exercised a distinct influence on public opinion by acting on the limited number of cultivated minds" (*LHA* 2:31–32). This was not the same as a direct appeal to the democratic public, however, and while he remained uncertain as to the relationship between readership and electorate, corruption burgeoned under Grant, who won a second term despite the assiduous muckraking of the reform movement writers. Following the tumultuous summer of 1870, during which he placed "The New York Gold Conspiracy" in the *Westminster Review*, attended his sister's deathbed at Bagni di Lucca, and first refused and then accepted Charles William Eliot's offer of an assistant professorship, he found himself teaching medieval history at Harvard and editing the *North American Review*.

No single explanation can account for his suddenly agreeing to suspend his Washington experiment. The family pressure that was applied in favor of his acceptance of Eliot's offer no doubt weighed on a man com-plexly fatigued by the excitements of a prolific, polemical authorship, the dismaying difficulties he had had in finding a British editor willing to publish his exposé of Jay Gould and John Fiske, and of course the meta-physically horrifying spectacle of his sister's death by lockjaw. Yet the move to Cambridge must have come too of a conviction that he had worked as long as he could in the persistent uncertainty of his rhetorical relation to the general public, an uncertainty that could probably find little relief in the finally ambiguous "limited number of cultivated minds." Despite many inducements to continue "The Session," he did not.

The final paragraphs of the second "Session," written just before his trip to Europe, suggest why. Under Grant, actual political power had gravitated away from the electorate and away from the sphere of influence belonging to the *North American Review*'s writers and readership. Gov-ernment by special interest had grown so subtle and pervasive that it could evade the reform opposition's thrust. "While the reformers in Congress rejoice at their victory in carrying a small reduction on pig-iron," Adams observed, ". . . they turn about in their seats and create by a single stroke of legislation a new Pacific railway, an imperishable corporation, within its own territory, an empire within a republic . . . inconsistent with the purity of Republican institutions, or with the safety of any government, whether democratic or autocratic." The "fault" Adams hastened to add was not the reformers'; the imperium of corporate power existed because "the people require it," and even if they were opposed, "with the prodi-gious development of corporate and private wealth, resistance must be vain" (*NAR* 111:61). Against such ironic reversals and the apparently irresistible erosions of republican purity that they bespoke, well might Adams regard his efforts as random and insulated.

At issue were the U.S. Constitution (especially concerning balanced and independent powers) and constitutional government generally and beyond that the larger directions of democratic society: Could its tendency to give individuals over to their native initiative survive the tyrannies to which the corruption of republican institutions gave rise? Could a mere text constrain the largely selfish and irrational movements of human so-ciety? "The discussion of so large a subject," Adams wrote, as though in reference to the career ahead of him, "is matter for a lifetime, and will occupy generations." Focusing on "the next century," in concluding "The Session" he signally revises his rhetorical position. "The American states-man or philosopher who would enter upon this great debate must make his appeal, not to the public opinion of a day or of a nation, however large or intelligent, but to the minds of the few persons who, in every age and in all countries, attach their chief interest to the working out of the great problems of human society" (*NAR* 111:62). In thus altering his sense of readership he admitted defeat; yet it would be in the shaping of such an appeal that Adams's enduring powers would emerge.[7]

Scholar, Editor

Although uncertainty over his public effect may have done much to prompt Adams's early withdrawal from a career in political journalism, he had in three years developed far as a writer and made crucial discoveries pertaining to the power and poesis of literary discourse. Beneath the militant idealism of these early writings Adams often reveals interests that look away from matters of immediate prosecution to fix on the mysteries of the discourse he has engaged, those particularly that suggest the degree to which language invents reality. In his early correspondence he had, as we have seen, been fascinated with the process by which things are named and thereby take on existence. At times it was an existence that remained for him quite consciously textual (as he protested when Charles rebuked him for the aspersions he had cast on the young women of Boston), but text and world must have blurred frequently for the young man who spent so much of his life at the writing desk and whose consciously variant sense of self was created and revised in the texts of the letters. Yet while he refined a pose or sketched a scene, many acts of naming were for Adams clearly noninventive, serving rather to confirm old and established truths —the "truth" about paper currency, or civic virtue, or corporate power that a people will not restrain. When it came to the promulgation of such truths in published essays, the writer's duty was chiefly rhetorical. To convince the public that "the evils and dangers are real, and not mere inventions of a lively fancy" (*NAR* 109:475), he had to create a lively fancy of the breach of public trust. For the young Adams, abstract truths existed absolutely, but to bring the popular imagination into relation with a truth was another matter.

The issue was complicated by the popular imagination's power to bring "truths," particularly of a historical nature, into relation with itself, beyond recovery of *wie es eigentlich gewesen ist*.[8] It is this problem that Adams addresses in "Captain John Smith," and he could not have devised for himself a better introduction to the problematic dimensions of historiography than in this his first serious work as a historian. Proposing, in his deliberately extreme phraseology, the erasure of a much-cherished vignette from the American past, he begins his career by tracing the fabrication of what for three centuries had passed as historical truth and by inquiring into the conditions that had kept its counterfeit from detection. In the course of the essay he proceeds from the pose of detached interest in the probable untruth of Pocahontas's celebrated rescue of Smith to the vigorous pursuit of its falsehood; in so doing he makes clear to the reader that he understands that rough handling of a tradition (however apocryphal) must embitter those for whom it exists as a source of shared identity. Yet as hostile to the South and contemptuous of John Smith as Adams of course proves to be, he displays the sophisticated awareness that the story possesses a mythic power and social reality apart from the question of its truth.

That awareness is kept subordinate, however, to the enmity of conscious impulse, at least in the initial version of the essay published in the January 1867 *North American Review*. Assuming the air of an impartial reviewer of Charles Deane's editions of *A Discourse of Virginia* and *A True Relation of Virginia*, he balances his opening suggestion that the Pocahontas stories are false by stating (too categorically perhaps to be convincing) that "no object whatever can be gained by their discredit, except the establishment of bald historical truth" (*NAR* 104:2). Twelve pages later, having joined the fray, he asserts solemnly that the inventions of the *Generall Historie* (made with a view to Smith's self-promotion) constituted "falsehoods of an effrontery seldom equalled in modern times" (*NAR* 104:14). Bald historical truth, in such an impassioned utterance, would seem to involve more than academic interest, especially as Adams has become intent on correcting what he calls "the tyrannical sway still exercised by Smith over the intelligence of the country" (*NAR* 104:14). Yet besides the matter of John Smith's fraud, there existed the mystifying datum of his "tyrannical sway," the discursive curiosity that "one after another, all American historians have contented themselves with repeating the words of the Generall Historie" (*NAR* 104:12). Nor was it a question merely of the historian's competence. George Bancroft, whose work commanded Adams's passing respect (though certainly it did not excite his reverence),[9] had succumbed with the others to the "spirit of Smith." As Adams speculates, before Bancroft had set himself to reading *A True Relation of Virginia*, "the brilliant popular reputation of Smith had already created a degree of illusion in his mind"; seduced by his materials, the historian "saw something which was not there, the exaggerated image of a figure beyond" (*NAR* 104:13) and so committed the blunder of attributing to *A True Relation of Virginia* the fabricated episodes of the later *Generall Historie*. Although a "microscopic error," Bancroft's lapse alerted the future author of "Count Edward de Crillon" to the perils of historical research, the unreckonable illusiveness of the historical record.

The durability of Smith's fictions alerted Adams to something larger than the isolated historian's susceptibility to error: the force of an idea, a story, a personality that possessed great public appeal. Impressed by the volume of Pocahontas lore, he observes that "romantic incidents in her life would be created, if they did not already exist, by the mere exercise of the popular imagination" (*NAR* 104:29). Thirty-five years later he would similarly depict the miracle-literature of Mary, a creation of the popular imagination that had built Chartres. "Tradition exaggerates everything it touches," he would affectionately observe, "but shows, at the same time, what is passing in the mind of the society which *tradites*" (A I 525). Still sooner than that—in "American Ideals," the culminating chapter of the *History*'s prologue—he would write of the popular imagination of Jeffersonian America as an inventive force, one which allowed the democrat to inhabit that world of illusion necessary to the fostering of what for Adams was the early Republic's popular ambition and accomplishment. What in 1867 was an attitude of qualified condescension to the "popular imagination" would become one of increasingly scientific interest and, on occasion, of informed respect; he had been perhaps partly in earnest when he had declared that no object but bald truth could be gained by discrediting the Pocahontas legends—"one of the most attractive portions of American history" (*NAR* 104:2). In the first as in the two subsequent versions of "Captain John Smith," he would conclude by observing that the "readiness" with which the mendacious *Generall Historie* "was received is scarcely so remarkable as the credulity which has left it unquestioned almost to the present day" (*NAR* 104:30), but this, by the time he revised the text for his *Historical Essays* (1891), had become almost a subordinate point. Having made extensive cuts ("falsehoods of an effrontery seldom equalled in modern times" among them), he added a remark that makes explicit what the essay had always said—that "the growth of a legend is as interesting as the question of its truth" (*GSW* 49).

We learn more about Adams's early sense of the dynamics of discourse from his October 1868 review of Sir Charles Lyell's *Principles of Geology* (tenth edition), an essay that suggests much about what was for the young Adams the nature of satisfactory truths and the imagination's role in scientific inquiry. An amateur in the field of geology, Adams came to this task after Lyell, a longtime friend of the American legation, consulted with him about arranging for an American notice of the new edition. Impulsively Adams volunteered his own services and then spent over a year reading geology and writing the review. This assignment was more serious than the previous articles, for he was required not only to master the vocabulary of a discipline with which he had little more than undergraduate acquaintance, but also to steer his discussion among the shoals of what was still a religious controversy. The *North American Review* had begun to move away from the anonymous printing of articles; for the first time in his professional writing his literary performance would be signed.

As Adams reported to Charles Eliot Norton, one of the current editors of the review, he did not himself "wish to be controversial," aiming rather to represent the "more valuable opinions" (*LHA* 1:569) of the rival geological schools: the uniformitarianism of Lyell, which worked from the premise that geological change occurred under uniform conditions over long periods of time, and the catastrophism of Louis Agassiz, which held that the earth's crust bore witness to abrupt change, a theory more compatible with theological accounts of the earth's history. The essay particularly focused on the schools' respective handling of the question of glaciation, a stumbling block for the uniformitarian explanation of terrestrial change. As Earl N. Harbert suggests, Adams worked to attain a balanced view of the debate, using "information from his research to point out deficiencies in the evidence offered by both parties."[10] Throughout his elaborate balancings, Adams clearly aspires to the rhetorical position of the informed man, fostering such educated, open discussion as John Stuart Mill encouraged in *On Liberty*. But the essay's language is one of manifestly strained impartiality, vacillating in a play of unreckoned ambivalence.

In 1868 Lyell's basic assumptions were hardly new. Considering them however in the larger context of scientific inquiry, Adams treats the scrupulously secular explanations of Lyell and his school as the recent and revolutionary ideas that they still were for a conservative public hoping to see a reconciliation of traditional religion with scientific advance.[11] In his review of the new *Principles*, Adams chose to discuss what he called (with overstatement) "some of the most striking changes of view, which make the tenth edition almost a new book" (*NAR* 107:470); these were Lyell's account of Pleistocene glaciation and his adoption of Darwin's theory of progressive evolution, points on which the elderly geologist might again appear as a radical. Given what we know to have been Adams's desire "to start new influences," we should expect him to promote a wider acceptance of Lyell's project, which nearly always exemplified the scientific methodology that Adams already looked upon as the type of future inquiry. In the ongoing war of ideas that for Adams always constituted intellectual history, Lyell figures as the recently established insurgent, appreciated rightly only as the successor of James Hutton, the first to propose the uniformitarian theory and deny biblical time. Rather theatrically, Adams depicts Hutton as a casualty of an earlier and more repressive dialogic condition: "Against a combination of scientific and religious intolerance," he writes, "no power on earth could prevail. Dr. Hutton was suppressed. His theory was dropped" (*NAR* 107:466). If it was too early to predict that Lyell's theories would prevail, it was clear that they had withstood an intolerance that had weakened since Hutton's day and had won a period of fair consideration. It is consideration, rather than decided advocacy, that the reviewer seems determined to give Lyell's thought; yet by implication he seems repeatedly to cast doubt upon the adequacy of Lyell's methods in the discovery of truth.

The austerity of scientific method and formulation already exerted a powerful attraction on Adams's mind; as early as 1863 he had recorded a conviction "that the laws which govern animated beings will be ultimately found to be at bottom the same with those which rule inanimate nature" (*LHA* 1:395). The attraction would develop into the emulation of his scientific history; and in what he wished, some forty years later, to represent as his steadfast pursuit of such laws, he spoke of his having aimed at "the severest process of stating, with the least possible comment, such facts as seemed sure, in such order as seemed rigorously consequent" in order to "fix for a familiar moment a necessary sequence of human movement" (A I 1069). Adams clearly admired Lyell the methodologist, the economist of thought, the severe truth-seeker who took "pleasure in lopping away fanciful excrescences which other men foster, and in treating the earth's marvellous history in that coldly scientific spirit which admits only what is enough, and no more than enough, to produce the result observed" (*NAR* 107:467). In such language we hear Henry Adams the hereditary economist, the soon-to-be champion of the laconic Albert Gallatin, even the future admirer of the Norman temperament, which "states the facts, and stops" (A I 392); we hear too Henry Adams the iconoclast, whose pleasure it was to erase the sentimental deceptions of the popular and unproductively conservative mind. Yet what is remarkable in view of his persistent desire to emulate the methods Lyell exemplified is the degree to which the review protests against the economy of scientific inquiry—its tendency to discourage speculation, reject "imagination," and otherwise constrain the resources of literary language.

Adams can hardly speak of "the earth's marvellous history" without an intimation of regret that marvels should be placed under ban, while the phrase "coldly scientific," though it is meant chiefly to suggest the virtues of tough-mindedness and argumentative tenacity, may also imply rigidity, absence of sympathy, lifelessness: meanings that are uppermost when the phrase recurs in Adams's 1891 New Year's letter to Elizabeth Cameron from Samoa. Repeatedly Adams describes uniformitarian theories as lacking imaginative appeal: he speaks of their "bald and prosaic stamp" (*NAR* 107:466), declares that Lyell's "great principle" is "bold," "but scarcely to be called fanciful or paradoxical" (*NAR* 107:468). He specifically suggests the improbability of arriving at the truth of an event as large and marvelous as the Ice Age by way of cautious method. Although he concedes that "Sir Charles's books, if they have not the charm of a lively imagination" possess "a certain solidity which gives them high authority"

(*NAR* 107:469), he calls Agassiz's theory of glaciation "certainly the most brilliant geological discovery of the last half-century" (*NAR* 107:468) and speaks favorably of the Swiss geologist Heer, whose catastrophic hypotheses were tested "by an experiment so bold that the imagination cannot fail to be impressed by it" (*NAR* 107:472). Whether or not the imagination has been persuaded emerges, in the review, as a supreme if ill-defined criterion of satisfactory theory.

Adams's effort to transmute his active ambivalence into the tone of assured impartiality is further complicated by his own occasional flights of extravagant statement, one of which strikingly anticipates the paradoxical rhetoric of the *Education*. "We cannot," affirms Adams, "say that the 'Principles' . . . would amuse persons who look for a vivid series of pictures reproducing the mysterious and poetical outlines of a dead world. Sir Charles," he continues, casting the geologist as a prosaic knight-errant, "wanders among the monotonous and flowerless forests of the coal-measures without saddening our spirits, and describes the enormous reptiles of the lias in language as calm and little sensational as though ichthyosauri were still gambolling in shoals along the banks of the Thames" (*NAR* 107:467). In the passage's studied facetiousness we may detect a number of serious yet rhetorically inconclusive considerations that leave in doubt the message Adams means to transmit to his *North American Review* readers. Given what other passages suggest is his admiration of Lyell's rigor, Adams appears to satirize the popular taste for vivid pictures reproducing a dead world's "mysterious and poetical outlines." Yet he calls more sustained attention to the geologist's comic phlegm, focusing tellingly on his language—"as calm and as little sensational as though ichthyosauri were still gambolling in shoals along the banks of the Thames." The calculated sensationality of Adams's final clause (so prescient of his manner of figuring anachronism in the *Education*) affirms a language use that diverges pointedly from Lyell's model, even as it proclaims a sophistication (the capacity for satire) that holds itself aloof from more naive leanings toward mysterious and poetical outlines. The issues, in such a passage, become subordinated to the writer's assertion of his capacity to give a virtuoso performance. As the urbane reviewer he claims the prerogative of having the last (ironic) word, which is contingent upon his ability to name it in the turning of a memorable phrase.

Self-consciously performative as the prose occasionally becomes, Adams's official position is one of submission to the experimental and dialogical process by which he believed ideas were properly matured. With regard to the rival theories of species transformation developed by Lamarck and Darwin, for instance, he proposes a critically aware suspension of judgment: "When the leading authority in any branch of science announces that the basis upon which one half . . . of his science rested, is insecure . . . the public cannot be too cautious in avoiding to take sides in the dispute, nor can it be too rigorous in exacting an explanation of the reasons which have caused such a revolution in opinion" (*NAR* 107:483). If Adams's skepticism tends to serve a conservative outlook, he is not in principle unyielding to new ideas; in discouraging the premature espousal of one side he may well have in mind the doctrinaire suppression of Hutton. Whereas the scientific community "cannot prevent the mass of imaginative human beings from wild speculations" (*NAR* 107:475), the critic can attempt to control such speculation as a factor of public opinion, as well as to suggest the occasional usefulness of the speculative mind to scientific inquiry. Above all, Adams would encourage a level of lay scrutiny that would make scientific inquiry publicly answerable. The triumph in fact of Adams's review is that as a nonexpert's treatment of controversies in a specialized field, it induced Lyell to reconsider and refine his theory of glaciation. No wonder Adams was later outraged with scientific inquiry that had become a closed door to all but the specialist and that therefore could not be made answerable to social or ethical inquiry.

Whether Adams in 1868 really favored Agassiz's views over those of Lyell (or vice versa) is impossible to determine.[12] Strictly refraining from explicit endorsements, the review on many points seems to shore up the Harvard professor's credibility and to mark out the lines of an agnostic's acceptance of the doctrine of special creation. But we must remember that Adams was writing as a young man, Harvard graduate, and former student of Agassiz, for the *North American Review*, a conservative quarterly edited at Harvard and circulated among a readership composed largely of Harvard graduates. Even the most contentious temperament might without conscious recognition yield to such pressures. In any case, it is well to recall that in these years Adams was just beginning to rationalize his pursuits as a writer and that beneath a fairly conventional repertoire of rhetorical attitudes his thought was in a state of flux. To be sure, family doctrines informed his early writings, which duly reflect the Adamses' devotion to constitutional government, hard currency, cautious democratization, and "the old Ciceronian idea of government by *the best*" (A I 749) with its complement of rhetorical forms and its ideal of public discussion that Adams naturally assumed as his own. Beyond his inheritance he wished, rather vaguely, "to start new influences" and to pursue knowledge scientifically with a view to absolute laws, activities consistent with family ideals but allowing wide latitude for original work. Although that latitude remained undefined, by the early seventies Adams's work—his public essays and private correspondence—already exhibited distinct traits. It demonstrated acute awareness that it existed, and desire that it should exist, in dialogic relation to other work and a conviction that the bearings of public dialogue determine social life. It manifested a fascination with the prospect of establishing the truth of reality "scientifically," in the form of necessary law, but also an impatience with the prosaic aspects that the postulated "truths" of the physical or social world often wore. Almost in spite of itself, as we have seen, it demonstrated an appreciation of popular myth, while betraying a desire for truths capable of exercising mythic command over the imagination. And it exhibited an already strategic recourse to ironic perspective and paradoxical reflection—resources by which he could consign prosaic truth, commonplace opinion, and sordid reality to a mere corner of what existed for him then as the great universe of untried experiment. His energies required immediate harness and a far-reaching social vision, but as long as that vision remained centered in ideals of statesmanship it would prove less than fully sustaining.

Except for one year spent mostly in Europe, from 1870 to 1877 Henry Adams taught history at Harvard and edited the *North American Review* while continuing to participate in the reform cause, which consolidated after Grant's reelection as a movement of disaffected independents. At no period in his life would he have less leisure or undertake such a diversity of tasks, and the story of his development must be traced in a fecund variety of concurrent and short-lived pursuits. Yet even his arcane research as a historian of medieval jurisprudence forms an item on an interestingly cohesive agenda, one given to intensive scrutiny of popular government, past, present, and future, as well as to the starting of those new influences capable of raising the moral and intellectual tone of American society.

"Anglo-Saxon Courts of Law," Adams's longest single text of these years, represents the culmination of his efforts to recover the European (Teutonic) genealogy of constitutional democracy, a subject requiring treatment in a scholarly monograph for a necessarily restricted readership. The essay examines the workings of the district law court of England from around 600 to the reign of Edward the Confessor, whom the argument represents as having inaugurated the English feudal era when he granted a royal charter of legal jurisdiction to the church of Saint Austin, a private manorial entity, breaking with Anglo-Saxon tradition in which law had existed as a public trust. Taking the form of the critical monograph, the principle mode of "scientific" history as it had developed in Germany, "Anglo-Saxon Courts of Law" proceeds according to the "German" method of philological analysis. Why Adams should have been interested in such specialized study is explained by the fact that at this stage in his career as a historian he looked upon legal history as that branch of the discipline that stood the best chance of detecting necessary sequences; his learned exposition of sac and soc counted as detail work in the larger enterprise of describing the evolution of constitutional government. Accompanied by three other monographs, the theses of the first candidates in the doctoral program he himself had set up, "Anglo-Saxon Courts of Law" appeared as the lead entry in *Essays in Anglo-Saxon Law*, a volume meant to signal a coming-of-age of American professional historical scholarship. Although the texts belonged to a narrowly learned discourse, the collection was intended as a public example of the excellence of American research. As "the fruit of his administration," the book was dedicated to Charles William Eliot, Harvard's young reform-minded president.

The collaborative undertaking of the *Essays* reflects the nature of Adams's work in these years and his conviction that any worthwhile purpose must have the support of a community and the theory and practice of a school. Throughout Adams's work, early and late, we come upon the idea that learned inquiry, art, technology, and social policy develop in the context of schools, and although the term never acquires strict meaning, it refers to what for Adams always remained the dialogic condition of the life of the mind. *School* indeed admitted of a fluid definition that discouraged parochial thought. The graduate course in medieval institutions created a school within the Department of History and within the larger school of serious inquiry that Eliot was attempting to make of Harvard; at the same time, Adams's seminar had associations with the school(s) of historiography established by German and, following their lead, British academic historians. Constitutional history, medieval and modern, had furthermore a place in the school of public inquiry that Adams intended to foster as the editor of that ongoing collaborative text, the *North American Review*; the same quarterly that printed his brother's exposés of railroad mismanagement also carried his own reviews of Henry Maine's *Village Communities* and Rudolph Sohn's *Procedure de la lex salica*. In 1871 the brothers had of course represented themselves as a school of two in *Chapters of Erie and Other Essays* (to which Henry contributed "Captain John Smith" in addition to his early financial articles), a volume intended as a kind of manifesto for what they hoped would cohere as the school of their own generation. To the considerable extent that *school* for Adams is associated with idealism and experiment, it appears as a generational, renovating force.

Although a school might be international in character, common purpose for Adams always required an intellectually intimate community, a relatively small number of persons in regular contact unified in moral consensus. In his experience family had provided the model for such community, the adult males of the Adams name serving often as a nucleus for particular public purposes. The networks of criticism and scholarship that centered in Adams's seminar and office as editor of the *North American Review* must have preserved for him the atmosphere of intellectual exchange and continuing experiment that distinguished his conception of participatory democracy. Although he wearied of Harvard and Boston, as long as Grant remained in office the intellectual community alone could approach an ideal that the political state clearly repelled: what in his characterization of pure primitive democracy he had called the "body of free men in healthy and active cooperation. From the moment the small state became merged in a great nation," he continued, writing of the Anglo-Saxon confederation from his own American experience, "the personal activity of the mass of free men in politics became impossible, if for no other reason than for the mere difficulties of distance" (ASCL 4). In the United States there had developed other reasons than the difficulties of distance; as he would demonstrate in the first chapter of the *History*, obstructions to intercommunication gravely beset the representative democracy of what in 1800 was still a mostly seaboard republic, yet these would check neither the country's active popular intelligence nor the capacity of the federal administration to govern. In an expanding, urbanizing postwar America, the preponderance of the party machine more effectively discouraged "the personal activity of the mass of free men."

For the time being at least, "healthy and active cooperation" was to be sought in other realms, and it was no doubt with real satisfaction that Adams and Lodge claimed (in their 1876 "Von Holst's History of the United States") that "however bad an institution Tammany Hall may be, it at least did not corrupt our American universities, nor pervert the moral sense of our historians" (*GSW* 282). Although Adams was required to center his activities in the sphere of overlapping schools, his continued participation in the reform movement demonstrates his belief that school, in America, could ultimately affect state, without the academy having to stoop to the vindication of national polity, as Adams and Lodge claimed had happened in a Germany where federation had come partly in consequence of a vigorously nationalistic historiography. Henry Cabot Lodge, Adams's graduate student, rival instructor in American history, and coeditor of the *North American Review*, of couse would himself pass from the academy to the world of state, where he would become more and more the exemplar of a school of politics obnoxious to his former teacher.

Adams's editorship of the *North American Review* is the story of ambition sustained against recurrent frustration. With the majority of his attention turned first to medieval and later American history, the review, as he wrote to fellow reformer David A. Wells, permitted him to maintain his "old connections," and with the 1872 (and later the 1876) election in sight he endeavored to make his journal "a regular organ" of Liberal Republican opinions (*LHA* 2:85). To do so required little innovation of editorial policy since under Norton, Lowell, and Gurney the review had already published most of Adams's political writings thus far as well as his brother Charles's "A Chapter of Erie." Under Adams, vigorous muck-raking articles would appear, as in April 1871, when he celebrated the notoriety (in the form of a libel suit) won for him by "The New York Gold Conspiracy," published the previous October in the *Westminster Review*, by printing two further exposures of the Erie scandal: his brother Charles's "An Erie Raid" and Albert Stickney's "Lawyer and Client." But participants in the Liberal Republican movement appear to have been less eager than Adams to make the *North American Review* the central organ of their opinions. Over a period of six years Wells came through with two articles; Jacob D. Cox, Grant's onetime interior secretary, submitted one. The editor often had to plead for contributions. "I *must* have a man to write me a political article for the North American for April," Adams wrote Congressman James A. Garfield late in 1873. "I wrote to Cox, but of course he can't. I suppose you won't and it is no use to ask you . . . I want a horoscope cast; a birds-eye view of the situation; a vigorous state-ment to our friends of what they can hope to do . . . and whether their wisest policy is to organise inside the party or out of it. Tell me whom I could apply to. Schurz himself is the right man, but I fear he cannot do it" (*LHA* 2:185). Garfield declined the invitation and never wrote for the review; Senator Carl Schurz of Missouri, emerging leader of the Liberal Republicans, repeatedly disappointed Adams's attempts to put the review at his disposal.

So eager was Adams to print an article bearing Schurz's signature that he was willing to ghostwrite under the senator's supervision from "notes and general directions" (*LHA* 2:108). To engage the nationally prominent westerner in an account of his defeat of the Grant Stalwarts in Missouri or in a review of the congressional session would have been a considerable editorial triumph that would have promoted Adams's design to move the quarterly, a staid New England institution, out of the confines of region and increase its appeal to the cultivated audience of a nation. Exasperated by Schurz's failure to contribute, Adams saw fit to lecture him on the precise merits of appearing in the *North American Review*. The senator's speeches and newspaper leaders, Adams averred, could have "little or no effect upon the class of readers who can only be reached by more perma-nent influences than the daily press, while through the daily press any-thing you say to a small and cultivated audience would at once be spread everywhere over the country" and hence diluted among the ephemera of newspaper discourse. "The object I have at heart is to obtain from you a bit of political diagnosis that will last, and to which all our friends can appeal as applicable to the condition of the country now and at all times" (*LHA* 2:108). These comments do much to define the sort of discussion, at once idealist and pragmatic, to which he hoped to give national currency through the *North American Review*; as editor he wanted to believe that the philosophical pursuit of "the great problems of human society" could be made to have direct bearing on the public opinion of the day.[13] In urging Schurz, the practical if uncommonly thoughtful politician, to make his appeal to "a small and cultivated audience," he voiced again his distrust of the public at large when it came to effecting needed purgations of the public life. It was a distrust that did not however discount the power of the daily press and its audience: in 1874, Adams tried to engage friends in the purchase of the *Boston Advertiser*, of which Schurz was to serve as editor. But in Adams's view only the personal activity of a high-toned elite could break down the machine politics to which the public had grown effectively indifferent; if the caucus system of the party regulars was to be thwarted, it would be through the quiet efforts of an ad hoc "junto" (*LHA* 2:250). So Adams advised Schurz in 1876, several months before the Republican National Convention at which the Liberals were to hold aloof, reserving the right to endorse a presidential candidate of either party on the basis of reform criteria. Schurz's early decision to support Rutherford B. Hayes eliminated the independents' threat and aborted the specific political aim of the *North American Review* under Adams.

Samuel J. Tilden, the Democratic candidate for whom Adams voted rather than for Hayes even with Schurz in his camp, was pursued in vain for an article on the successful prosecution of the Tweed Ring, which he had directed as governor of New York. Although, as Ernest Samuels observes, Adams "wanted articles that would carry out his favorite intellectual maneuver of smashing things generally," such articles were often not forthcoming.[14] Assuming broad editorial powers over the texts he had agreed to publish, Adams's own iconoclasm as a writer was confined to the twenty-three unsigned critical notices that he himself contributed to the *North American Review*; in these he was particularly harsh with his rival British historians of medieval institutions, his first specialty as an academic historian.

Perhaps the finest realization of the discussion he had aimed at— contemporaneous but farseeing, of practical application but also philosophical permanence—came in his January 1876 centennial issue. In it he sought "to measure the progress of our country by the only standard which I know of, worth applying to mankind, its thought," and to do so through the contributions of six specialists "who belong rather to the younger school of our time" (*LHA* 2:243). The areas surveyed were science, religion, economics, politics, law, and education, and Adams's contributors were advised that, in ascertaining "whether and to what degree Americans should feel satisfaction or disappointment," the "moral should be tolerably sharp-pointed" (*LHA* 2:231). From writer to writer the moral was consistent as well as sharp-pointed: that the country's thought, the one real measure of achievement, lagged behind its headlong material and social development; that this held true in science, economics, and theology and was not likely to find remedy in the educational system of the day, the emphasis of which was narrowly practical. In the less abstract field of law more unqualified success had been achieved; but the issue as a whole suggested that, in proportion to its vast energies, the United States lacked the intellectual discipline and moral self-consciousness it would need not merely to rival the great civilizations of the Old World, but to keep from destroying itself—a theme to which Adams would return often and of course most memorably in the *Education*. The January issue markedly diverged from the tone of the usual centennial blandishment; E. L. Godkin, editor of the *Nation*, a reform man ever in sympathy with Adams's ambitions for the *North American Review*, worried in his highly favorable review that the practical men who governed the country would be put off by the issue's harshness of outlook.[15]

Throughout his tenure as editor Adams had run excoriating political articles whenever he could find them, but the aesthetic of unrelenting militance was best achieved in the October 1876 number, Adams's last, which appeared after the conventions but before the election. Spearheaded by Charles's "The 'Independents' in the Canvass," the issue pursued the graft of the retiring administration and attacked the policies of the party regulars with such fury that James R. Osgood, the publisher, repudiated the opinions expressed in the issue as those of the editors only, forcing Adams into what by then was the desirable position of having to depart at once from the editor's chair. The October issue rapidly sold out, but such had not been the rule during Adams's editorship. Able to increase the regularity of forceful political writing, he had not proportionally increased its sales, and the journal had become a financial liability to the conservative Osgood's already failing house, which had been recently acquired by Henry O. Houghton who was no more sympathetic with the editors' opinions than Osgood. Unwilling to buy the *North American Review* himself, Adams was suppressed by the interests that retained the journal as a property, and at the end of his tenure it for the most part remained the conservative New England periodical with a small circulation and undersubscribed advertising space that he had inherited from Lowell and Gurney.[16]

Adams, of course, never meant to alter the review's essential charac-

ter. Rather he had aimed to give national currency to the regional tendencies that it embodied: the intellectual breadth of Boston and Harvard and
the high moral tone that New England inquiry tended to assume in time of
crisis. If Adams's review proved often harsh, it was also true that jeremiadical denunciation was a traditional New England mode. From its
inception in 1815 the *North American Review* had been a regular organ of
family views; publication in its pages was almost as much an Adams
tradition as graduation from Harvard. Certain aspects of the review encouraged the still-youthful editor to outgrow the regional forms and constraints that it inevitably perpetuated. In particular, its commitment to
keep abreast of scientific and philosophical advance productively engaged
Adams's wide range of interests, and the substantial articles on economics,
history, evolution, geology, geography, and ethnology allow us to trace
Adams's continuing education. Yet committed as it was to liberal learning,
the *North American Review* of Henry Adams exhibits what even at the
time may have been recognizable expressions of Brahmin narrowness and
commonplaces of conservative thought. In the first article of the four-part
series entitled "An Episode of Municipal Government" (October 1874),
Charles F. Wingate and C. F. Adams, Jr., introduce the principals of the
Tammany scandal with searching attention to their ethnic derivations,
extending to racial characteristics of physiognomy in the cases of the
Irishman and the Jew, so that the mix of distinct peoples, the various Old
and New World types, comes to exist as a subtextual explanation of New
York City corruption. In "Pauperism" (April 1875) Charles L. Brace re-
peats the conventional wisdom of the propertied class when he observes
that the "English Poor Law, from which our own has been derived, fell
into the mistake . . . of giving the English working classes the feeling that
they had 'a right to relief,'" a "communistic impression" of which the
"natural effect" was a diminished "habit of self-support" and eroding
"dignity of independence" (*NAR* 120:316). The new influences that Adams had longed to start as reform writer, editor, and scholar thus far left
untouched the core of postwar capitalist ideology. Much of his work of
the period was directed at cleansing the body politic by retrieving a classically republican vision of moral leadership, but he was not yet able
to recognize the basic incompatibility of those ideals with laissez-faire
capitalism.

Perhaps the best measure of Adams's conservatism relative to the
growth of his thought is to be found in "Primitive Rights of Women," his
1876 Lowell Institute lecture, in which he set out as he had in "Captain
John Smith" to correct the historical record. The main purpose of this
essay, presented first as a lyceum address, was to refute learned and popular perceptions that woman's lot until recently had been one of degrada-

tion and enslavement. Rather, Adams argues, the woman possessed an original social dignity supported not merely by legal rights but (far more importantly) by an apotheosizing notion of her sexual identity. The argument represents a new stage in Adams's continuing discovery that societies live by their symbologies as much as by their self-consciously rational discourse—their science, philosophy, polity. In making his case Adams draws upon a broad array of sources, gleaning evidence from American Indian ethnology, from the *Odyssey* and the *Njalsaga*, and perhaps most importantly in view of his long-term development, from ancient Egypt: the family trinity of Osiris, Isis, and Horus supplies the contrast with the womanless and intellectualized Christian Trinity upon which Adams would later build his denunciation of Western, commercial, patriarchal culture. Yet even this early, Adams recognizes that the Christian philosophers' alteration of the Trinity as they had found it in Egypt constituted an act of violence against a central popular myth, one that articulated the timeless relations of popular experience: "The irresistible spread of Mariolatry, the worship of the Virgin Mother, proved how strongly human nature revolted against the change" (*GSW* 343). Some thirty years later he would employ the same emphatic verb (if in a different, even ironic, usage) to depict the patent falsehood of the church fathers' assertion that the woman is frail: "The idea that she was weak *revolted* all history" (A I 1127; italics added). As early as 1876 he recognizes that her weakness is but a doctrine of Christian ideology, the instrument of her subjugation. And appreciating her singular energies, he is able to speak almost religiously of "the insoluble mystery of generation, insoluble then as now," in which the man and the woman meet "on the same plane" (*GSW* 343).

Nevertheless the essay ends in strong affirmation of the patriarchal family, on the grounds that it is the natural social unit for the "Aryan" peoples whose males are given instinctively to the pursuit of property and who therefore require a patrilineal succession of wealth. Adams argues that given the genius of Roman and British law, which developed from the race's acquisitive aptitude, women enjoy full legal recognition; equipped as they are with formidable rights, their political equality is unnecessary. Moreover, as Roman history has shown, women's independence leads to the disintegration of the family and civil anarchy. Although it challenges received opinions regarding the subjugation of women, "Primitive Rights of Women" lends itself decidedly to the status quo. In the *Boston Telegraph* of December 11, 1876, a synopsis of the address appeared below the synopsis of a speech given the following evening by Susan B. Anthony, placing Adams's pronouncements in admonitory juxtaposition to Anthony's advocacy of women's suffrage.[17]

Adams might never favor the political recognition of women, but he would not again categorically describe the patriarchal family as "the strongest and healthiest of all human fabrics," destined, in the curious bellicosity of his Darwinian phrase, to "trample every rival system under its feet" (*GSW* 360). Although some time would pass before Adams could turn his attention to the absence of a contemporary apotheosis of female or male sexual identity, the symbology of *Democracy*, written two years later, registers his at least half-conscious recognition that the American family was in trouble. Yet even as he read it in December 1876, the peroration of "Primitive Rights of Women" might have already existed as a point of departure. In his own experience the family had unquestionably proven to be a strong fabric: economically supportive and psychologically stabilizing, it bound its male members to abstract ideals and educated them in the moral force of personality. Yet such a rigidly doctrinaire and unrelentingly ambitious identity as that of the Adamses burdened as much as it supported. As a tradition of philosophical statesmanship, a school that was also a public force, this family had suffered unmistakable eclipse. After 1872, Charles Francis Adams could no longer be considered a presidential candidate; following the dissolution in 1876 of the independent movement, Henry withdrew from most direct forms of political involvement. The fourth generation sons found it particularly difficult to cut the figures of patriarchs in the political, and for Henry and Brooks even in the domestic, realm. With the other sons of Charles Francis Adams, Henry would labor henceforth to meet the crisis of the family's impossible renewal.

If the country's centenary occasioned a somber recognition of his family's continued absence from high public office, Henry Adams did not dwell on it. At the end of his never very satisfying career as a political reformer he seems deliberately to have renewed his idea of an American future worthy of his best energies. His disgust with the fate of the independent movement, in which he had invested more time and effort perhaps than actual hope, was offset by his now long-term engagement as a scholar of social evolution, who had passed from the study of Anglo-Saxon law to the American experiment in democracy. As he absorbed himself in the comparatively timeless modes of social and philosophical inquiry, he met his contemporary imperfect America with a patience that mitigated invective. As scathingly as he and his brother Charles reported the abuses of constituted government, they concurred in the belief that "the struggle is to be one, not of our own day, but for an indefinite future, and the utmost that can now be hoped is not to destroy, but only to make head against, the political disease" (*GSW* 331).

So wrote Charles in "The 'Independents' in the Canvass." Another

article in the October 1876 farewell issue also took the long view but with
what by contrast is a sanguine emphasis. In "Von Holst's History of the
United States," Henry Adams and Henry Cabot Lodge begin by commending the German scholar's severe treatment of American federalism as
"a far better centennial oration than any which the centenary has produced" (*GSW* 256), but end by deflecting his charges that the U.S. Constitution is defective and that American popular veneration of the document
is unfounded. The review's central assertion that, defects notwithstanding,
"the Constitution vindicted its energy in its working" (*GSW* 279) represents a shift in Adams's thinking: where formerly he had perceived the text
of the federal republic as icon, the ideality of which contrasted with the
sorry reality of government, he now appreciated it as the instrument of
realized if imperfect nationhood. To be sure, the Constitution would ultimately come to symbolize for Adams the failure of reason to constrain
history, but his more pragmatic view of the document is in keeping with
his increasing tendency to regard language in discrete texts not only as the
repository of a content that may be deemed true or false, honored or
violated, but also as a rhetoric productive of distinct social effects. Perhaps, as Edward Chalfant has suggested, the thesis that the Constitution
"has made a nation" (*GSW* 286) is more properly Lodge's contribution,
but the editor-in-chief who cosigned the review could not have been far
out of sympathy.[18] In the final paragraph, which Adams claimed as "*my*
centennial oration," we find the expression of what for Adams persisted as
the long view's power to inspire. "If the historian will only consent to shut
his eyes for a moment to the microscopic analysis of personal motives and
idiosyncrasies, he cannot but become conscious of a silent pulsation that
commands his respect, a steady movement that resembles in its mode of
operation the mechanical action of Nature herself" (*GSW* 287). At such
moments Adams's denunciation falls away to reveal, quite in the manner
of the American jeremiad, affirmable faith in the active promise of future
glory. As historian, he must now establish the nature and strength of the
forces that sustained the republic's promise against those that thwarted it.

Biographer, Novelist

The promise lay in what for the Henry Adams of this period remained
the astounding historical phenomenon of American nationalism—the tendency toward political unity that had produced the Constitution, resisted
the secessionist movements of New England and the South, and survived
armed rebellion and the chaos and poisoned relation engendered by civil
war. For Adams, the immediate question of the postwar decade had been
whether the nation as created by the Constitution could survive unwar-

ranted assumptions of power—the tyranny of party managers over elected representatives, of the Senate over the executive branch and the vanquished South, of the great corporation over republican government, whose resistance must entail suicidally autocratic concentrations of power. Behind that question lay the suspicion that the Constitution had expired in the moral laxity and public indifference that permitted such corruptions, but there was no denying that an America of wealth and power, of expanding settlement and swelling population, existed and grew with a necessary life of its own, a natural pulsation that commanded the historian's respect even though it provoked his moral alarm. By the end of 1876, Adams was prepared to speculate beyond the constitutional impasses that had proliferated under Johnson and Grant. Although the nomination of Rutherford B. Hayes confirmed the strength of the party caucus, his election brought into government a number of reform movement men, a consolation that had its use. For the transition came at a time when Adams clearly wished to refrain from the microscopic analysis of political corruption, suspend somewhat his inherited view that the country was but the brittle creature of its constitution, and begin to approach American democracy as an evolving organism.

In the spring of 1877, Adams was asked by Albert Gallatin's son to edit his father's papers, a task that would likely lead to the writing of a biography. The project fell to him at a time when he had begun to focus his historical interest upon the Jeffersonian period, and it gave him a reason to resign from Harvard, leave Boston, and return to Washington, where much of the research would have to be conducted. The move promised to be restorative. Increasingly Adams had become aware that as long as he lived in Boston he would be unable to resist the hereditary role of the Adams-in-exile, in his case the journalist who had had to suspend operations in the Washington of Grant, the reform editor become odd man out in the compromises of the 1876 Republican National Convention. He wished to return to an early ambition—to study, with as much hope as the subject warranted, the future course of democratic society, and Washington held for him the prospect of escaping his own set tones of denunciation. He could not look for relief in continued professorship, for despite Eliot's reforms and his own innovations Harvard seemed deeply to resist American currents, to grow vapid amid "an atmosphere of 'culture'" that hankered after "the very latest European fashions." So Adams described the university to Sir Robert Cunliffe in August 1875; characterizing the ennui of his confinement to New England, he may have been more in earnest than he was willing to admit when he facetiously claimed that "the only disastrous consequence of my stagnation is that when I write letters I find that I really have nothing under the sun to say" (*LHA* 2:235). As a

Harvard academic historian he could no more say what he wished than as a politically active editor. His engagement of the larger questions of human society required a new setting to accommodate what would be his invention for himself of a public role. Seeking power in the form of influence over the minds of future generations, Adams merged his political and academic fortunes and took office in Washington as the self-appointed founder of an American school of historiography, one that might ultimately speak to and shape political and popular life.

Probably he did not often see his own ambition on so grand a scale, but undoubtedly there were moments when he reeled with the conceptions of his own and his country's opportunities. Such moments are particularly suggested by his letter of November 25, 1877, to Gaskell posted from his new Lafayette Square address. Quoted as a matter of course by nearly every commentator on Adams's work, the letter is important because in it Adams describes the authorial role that would make possible the work of his prime. As an invention that could only be espoused and sustained as a matter of conscious illusion or faith, this role provides one measure of his originality as an Adams and as an American man of letters. "As for me and my wife," he writes his British friend, "we have made a great leap in the world; cut loose at once from all that has occupied us . . . and caught new ties and occupations here." Ever doubtful of uniformitarian theories whether applied to geological, national, or personal history, Adams characterizes his and Marian's move as a happy cataclysm, one that yet seems to conform to a predictable tendency: "I gravitate to a capital by a primary law of nature." Here he would find variety and amusement, and he and Marian could "distinctly occupy niches which ought to be filled." "Literary and non-partisan" by avowal, he could make of Washington the permanent residence that it had failed to become for him ten years earlier and that it had never been for any of his male Adams forbears. Consciously giving a "rather poetical or imaginative description" of his new situation, he nevertheless formulated the authorial identity, the enabling assumptions of his long-contemplated literary ambition. "As I belong to the class of people who have great faith in this country and who believe that in another century it will be saying in its turn the last word of civilisation, I enjoy the expectation of the coming day, and try to imagine that I am myself, with my fellow *gelehrte* here, the first faint rays of that great light which is to dazzle and set the world on fire hereafter" (*LHA* 2:326). Perhaps the poetry of the description may be attributed to the fact that he is addressing, as an American, his rival contemporary Englishman. Yet how hard and how consistently he tried to imagine himself as a first faint ray is finally to be measured by the monumentality of his literary achievement over the next twelve years.

The first in the series of volumes that Adams dispatched from Washington was one that had been in progress before the move. *Documents Relating to New-England Federalism, 1800–1815* brought for the first time to public light papers that clarified the isolated and much maligned stand of John Quincy Adams, whose desertion of the New England Federalists and support of Jefferson's embargo clouded his regional reputation during his life and long afterward. The volume comes out of both joint and rival ventures of Adams and Henry Cabot Lodge to excavate primary source materials and begin the critical narrative treatment of the men and events of the early national period. More specifically, *Documents* was prepared as an answer to *George Cabot*, Lodge's biography of his grandfather who had been a central player in the Hartford Convention. The centerpiece of *Documents* is John Quincy Adams's "Reply to the Appeal of the Massachusetts Federalists." Written after his unhappy presidency, the "Reply" defends assertions he had made during the 1828 campaign that the Federalists had conspired throughout the Jefferson and Madison years to sever the Union. John Quincy Adams himself suppressed the "Reply" as excessively vituperative; his grandson's publication of it in the context of documents that lent credence to its main points was aimed at concluding, in the better temper of fifty year's distance, a heated exchange that bore on what to the grandson was the still vital issue of allegiance to the national cause.

Although Henry Adams took extrascholarly interest in clearing his ancestor's name (to the extent of suppressing "a few passages of a personal nature, relating to Mr. H. G. Otis"), he wished genuinely to pursue the larger issue of regional versus national loyalty beyond the heat of partisanship. In the preface to *Documents* he pleads his impartiality in comparatively good faith. "So far as the editor is concerned," he writes in a mildly ironic third person, "his object has been, not to join in an argument, but to stimulate, if possible, a new generation in our universities and elsewhere, by giving them a new interest in their work and new material to digest" (*DNEF* viii). Only later, in the *Education* and *A Letter*, would he push the art of prefatory disingenuity to its rhetorical limits. The preface of *Documents*, though anticipating the posture and even the exact phrasings of the future prefaces, names Adams's lifelong pedagogical aspiration with little of the later ironic reservation. He offers old documents as new material to feed new interest in a new generation. His grand implied object is the mature reconsideration of the American past, an enlarged and steadying sense of the national identity.

Adams spent most of 1877 editing the Gallatin papers for publication and applying to state historical societies and the descendants of Gallatin's colleagues for letters and other documents from which he would write the

Gallatin. In his search for primary materials he unearthed ever larger contexts and found himself drawn into the dialogic exchanges that determined the course of the Jefferson and Madison presidencies. At what precise stage of the Gallatin project he fixed upon the scope of his *History* it is impossible to say, but as early as June 1879 he had begun to pursue the misadventures of Jeffersonian diplomacy in European archives and in September was able to refer, in a letter to the Virginia historian Hugh Blair Grigsby, to his "intended 'History of the United States from 1801 to 1815' " (*LHA* 2:371). *The Life of Albert Gallatin* had gone to press early that year; *Democracy*, his first novel, written in secrecy for the experiment of anonymous publication, had been dispatched to Henry Holt in May. His first two years as an independent scholar and author had been prolific, but his initial productions do not take the tone of his sanguine letter to Gaskell. Only very ambiguously do they suggest the faith requisite to a long-term project that had as its object the narration of the emergence of "a new race."

The Life of Albert Gallatin and *Democracy* represent two distinct reconsiderations of the national past. As biographer, Adams examines crucial phases of pre–Civil War experience in a narrative that patiently steers its way through a scholarly assemblage of documents. The novelist, on the other hand, treats postwar Washington in a satiric roman à clef, a fiction that might well have taken form as its author's firsthand testimony and that becomes in its profounder reaches a somewhat inadvertent allegory addressing the decline of the patriarchal family and America's prospects of renewal. The two works are a study in contrasting unassimilated styles. The *Gallatin*, a work of historical scholarship yet also a somewhat uncertain attempt at tragic narrative, sacrifices narrative pull to inclusiveness of detail, and the densely clausal expository prose becomes oratorical, for want of subtler resources, when the author wishes to point a moral. *Democracy*, an unconscious pastiche of conflicting modes, eventually loses its satiric thrust in sententious, sentimental, and horrific effect.[19] Intended for different (if overlapping) readerships and aimed at producing distinct responses, the books feature statesmen as central figures and leave equally in doubt the questions of whether the public man of high character can redeem democratic society and whether the public man of low character must degrade it. Although neither work can be reduced to its numerous expressions of political despair, expressions of confidence in the democratic future are infrequent, and at few points do the particulars of the American past support the faith in his country that Adams professed to Gaskell. Yet both the *Gallatin* and *Democracy* explore the past with an eye to the future, seeking confirmation of the country's prospects in a fresh, if harshly critical, retrospect of national experience.

The Life of Albert Gallatin represents Adams's first sustained treatment of "the great problems of human society" apart from the heat and smoke of a day's debate. As the first full-length work of his new career it was bound to show the influence of old attitudes and practices that Adams had only begun to modify and reveal that his "great leap" had not yet carried him far. Indeed, compared to the review of Von Holst's *History of the United States*, the *Gallatin* suggests retreat. Its tone is compounded of moral elegy and political reaction, as though this first book, despite what would prove to be its author's expanding sympathies, had to take shape inevitably as a record of his ancestors' as well as his own disaffection. In narrating the life of Jefferson's Geneva-born treasury secretary and later John Quincy Adams's colleague in the negotiations at Ghent, Henry Adams was afforded the opportunity to vindicate family doctrine and ideals, particularly the fiscal policies of hard currency and central banking that Gallatin, when unobstructed, had implemented to great effect as well as the commitment to American nationhood that the Genevan had made as a naturalized citizen without sectional roots. In Gallatin, moreover, he had the rare public figure free of moral blame, whom even the captious grandfather had pronounced "an honest and honorable man" (G 676). Without engaging directly in ancestor-worship, Adams could eulogize one who exhibited an Adams-like integrity and who not only offered the advantage of being outside the family and region but also possessed qualities that had made him a more successful statesman and diplomat within the bounds of the familiar tragic fate. And as Gallatin, like John Quincy Adams, had been caught between reluctant loyalty to Jefferson's foreign policy and vindictive party opposition, and as he later likewise came to deplore the character and policies of Andrew Jackson, the biographer was given ample opportunity to go over the ground of ancestral disgusts and betrayals.

Henry Adams however could hardly forget that it was on the occasion of the first serious blow to the House of Adams that Gallatin attained national preferment as Jefferson's secretary of treasury. In the eyes of John and Abigail Adams, Gallatin figured as a member of the enemy camp, and reviewing the tumult of the second president's administration from the Genevan's perspective must have given the great-grandson some unpleasant moments. Even as one who made it a rule to refrain from personal abuse, Gallatin shared the general antipathy for John Adams; in 1797, as a Pennsylvania congressman, Gallatin related to his wife an anecdote unflattering to "*her* majesty" Abigail Adams (G 185), and the day after Jefferson's first inauguration he spoke of "the meanness, indecency, almost insanity" of John Adams's conduct at his term's end (G 265). The biographer quotes such aspersions without contesting them, just as later in the book he lets stand Gallatin's assessment of John Quincy Adams as "a virtuous man" whose deplorable lack of judgment could, if left unchecked, prove "fatal to the country" (G 599). If in the *Gallatin*, as much later in the *Education*, Adams concedes that such strictures were not unfounded, it is partly because he locates the true battleline of American politics elsewhere and positions Gallatin and the Adamses on the same side. For Henry Adams the underlying conflict of the Washington and Adams presidencies consisted in the ideological struggle between the democratic school of Jefferson and the monarchical school of Hamilton. These "brilliant men who led the two great divisions of national thought" appear in the *Gallatin* as morally flawed, on a plane below that of Gallatin and the Adamses; in fact John Adams did owe his downfall more to the treachery of Hamilton and the extreme Federalists than to the forthright opposition of Jefferson. For Henry Adams writing in 1878, "it was easy to see" that the party of Jefferson "must triumph in the end" (G 159), and although the triumph ruined John Adams he cannot but cast Gallatin in a heroic light, "waging active war" against "the theoretical doctrines and ulterior aims" of the extreme Federalist school (G 199).

If by such mitigations Adams sought to minimize the differences between Gallatin and John Adams, his ultimate strategy was to suspend all conflict with the suggestion that John Adams and Albert Gallatin converge in a common tragic fate.[20] Seeing his party triumph in the election of 1800, even the sober Gallatin "felt the power of the strong wine, success," and believed with Jefferson "that human nature was to show itself in new aspects, and that the failures of the past were due to the faults of the past." In the devastatingly ironic perspective Adams takes of the treasury secretary-to-be at the close of book 2, Gallatin appears suddenly callow, as yet undereducated by experience to judge correctly the shortcomings of an Adams. "He had yet to pass through his twelve years of struggle and disappointment in order to learn how his own followers and his own President were to answer his ideal, when the same insolence of foreign dictation and the same violence of a recalcitrant party presented to their and to his own lips the cup of which John Adams was now draining the dregs" (G 266). As the result of the best-intended public career, the martyrdom of the second president foreshadows the moral Adams will develop in the remainder of the text—that the power of circumstance is greater than even the most broadly conceived and ably managed enterprise of republican government and that human littleness lies eternally in wait to sabotage what human greatness can do.

The final bitterness of Gallatin's disappointed tenure as treasury secretary would come in 1811, when congressional rejection of a bill to recharter the U.S. Bank deprived him of his chief financial instrument just as the country was going to war. The destruction of the bank culminated a long-maturing intrigue to break his power, one originating in his own party and nurtured in the very cabinet on which he served. This was practically a chapter out of the biographer's family experience, and he wrote of Gallatin's defeat at the hands of Duane, Giles, Leib, and the Smiths with an outrage that was an ingrained response. Yet the turning point in Gallatin's fortunes, as in the fortunes of Jefferson's experimental republic, came toward the end of the second administration when "the insolence of foreign dictation" put Jefferson's pacific theories to a test that undid his presidency's accomplishment and forced the abandonment of its increasingly visionary agenda, its bold scheme of moral and economic improvement.

For Adams the Jeffersonian accomplishment was a very real one. Under the financial direction of Gallatin, government had extended the country's territory to the Rocky Mountains (constitutional questions being, at Gallatin's bidding, subordinated to perceived national imperatives), while it had steadily increased revenues and put the national debt in sight of full discharge. Seldom losing an opportunity to impugn Jefferson's probity and courage, Adams had to admire the vision of a man whose ambitious program of improvements, deferred and largely forgotten, would be later taken up by John Quincy Adams in his turn as president. "To make one comprehensive, permanent provision for the moral and economical development of the people," wrote Henry Adams, ". . . was the highest statesmanship, the broadest practical philanthropy" (G 355). The first steps toward making that provision were the enhancement of interregional communication and the establishment of a national university, and these Gallatin planned in 1807 as presently realizable objects. For the long term Gallatin hoped to commit the country to steady progress free of the strife of local interests in annual competition for funds. Both this agenda and its example ("Few persons have now any conception of the magnitude of the scheme" [G 350], wrote Adams pointedly) would become permanent casualties of the 1808 embargo, adopted in response to British and French depredations of American shipping and aimed at proving that American commerce was so valuable to Europe that the threat of nonintercourse alone would assure respect for American property and privileges. Rather than bear out Jefferson's theory that America existed in a political isolation that gave it moral superiority and economic command over the Old World, the embargo, as Adams argued in the *Gallatin* and would illustrate painstakingly in the *History*, had no coercive effect on England and France, while it opened American susceptibilities to corruption. For implementation the embargo required the Enforcement Act, an antirepublican assumption of powers that yet proved insufficient to effect nonintercourse, while it encouraged contempt for the law and bred the factionalism that culminated in the Hartford Convention. In the biography's most tragic moment, Gallatin is depicted as authoring this act in full consciousness that it abrogated his republican principles. These agonies were undergone to forestall a war that took place anyway.

In both the *Gallatin* and the *History* Adams defends Gallatin's judgment that the country should have gone to war long before 1812. Still, he concedes that Jefferson's experiment in pacifism had to be made if only to confirm, once and for all, that America could not exempt itself from the common experience of nations. Adams very carefully absolves Jefferson and Gallatin of blame for the "disaster" brought on by European aggression: "it was the result of forces" that neither the eminently practical Gallatin "nor any other man or combination of men, neither his policy nor any other policy or resource of human wisdom, could control" (G 355). In the *Gallatin* the nature of these forces is never precisely defined; invoked most often by the term "circumstance" they are opposed to the terms "principle" or "theory"—the a priori assumptions and "sanguine" outlook of the Jeffersonian statesman. The occasional Spencerian phrase or explanation suggests that "forces" and "circumstance" amount to environmental pressures that "inevitably" favor what Adams's period conceived as the instinctive, egoistic self-interest that equipped individuals and nations for success in "the struggle for existence."[21] But the nature of the forces is kept shrouded, as if they were unknowable beyond their tendency to thwart the best human intentions. Nevertheless Adams does argue that the Jeffersonian response to circumstance was handicapped by the ideological disposition to "put too high an estimate upon human nature" (G 492). Such was the lesson of the embargo, and an epoch was marked by the country's recognition that "the failures of the past were not due to the faults of the past only, and that circumstances must by their nature by stronger and more permanent than men" (G 379). The recognition had been costly, and Adams, characterizing the national mood at Jefferson's departure, sounds an elegiac note prophetic of *Mont Saint Michel and Chartres* when he speaks of "a sincere popular faith that could never be revived" (G 391).

The catastrophe of Jefferson's presidency came in 1808; the biographer was faced with the problem that his subject led a life of comparative anticlimax from that point until 1849. This was complicated by the fact that Adams could never decide whether Gallatin emerged from his crisis of faith as a greater or a lesser man—whether he was preferable as the example of a statesman who was at once visionary and practical or as the example of one who, in defeat, was able to preserve his dignity and interests if not his passions. The indecision no doubt reflects Adams's unsorted sensations in the late seventies of despair over his family's political eclipse and of faith in the value of his own "scientific" ambitions, but the predominant mood of the *Gallatin* remains that of uncompensated defeat. When his statecraft went to pieces, we are told that Gallatin had known better than Jefferson "how to accept defeat and adapt himself to circumstances, how to abandon theory and to move with his generation" (G 379), which for the young Adams was a formula for the rediscovery of the creative occasion in the often catastrophic flux of history; but the biographer never assigns a distinct coherence to that generation's movement and seldom depicts Gallatin as a man whose qualities were magnified in disillusion. After skillfully managing the course of the Treaty of Ghent, Gallatin's epoch as a vigorous public servant had closed; in 1816 he had to decline Madison's request that he resume his old post as treasury secretary. "Riper, wiser, and infinitely more experienced than in 1800, Gallatin had still lost qualities which, to a politician, were more important than either experience, wisdom, or maturity. He had outgrown the convictions which had made his strength." His mind and character retained their wonted tone, but he no longer possessed "that sublime confidence in human nature which had given to Mr. Jefferson and his party their single irresistible claim to popular devotion." Gallatin's "statesmanship had become, what practical statesmanship always has and must become, a mere struggle to deal with concrete facts at the cost of philosophic and *a priori* principles." With his generation, he had outgrown the old dogmas: "There was no longer any great unrealized conviction on which to build enthusiasm" (G 559–60).

Adams focused on Gallatin what increasingly had become his despair over the opportunities for statesmanship in American experience. Whereas the country had been to an exceptional degree a political creation, the brilliance of which had led to the popular exaltation of the man of state, its political life had commonly negated the vision and ideals of the Founders and the younger men (such as Gallatin and John Quincy Adams) who approached their stature. As Adams would argue in *Democracy*, the politician who succeeded tended to be one without genuine public aspiration. Undistinguished men might govern successfully and even improve the country's moral tone, but to the brilliant redemptive personality the field of statecraft per se appeared closed. "The inevitable isolation and disillusionment of a really strong mind—one that combines force with elevation—is to me the romance and tragedy of statesmanship" (*LHA* 2:376). So Adams wrote with regard to the moral of the *Gallatin* in a letter to Lodge several months after the book's publication, and the statement reveals the extent to which statesmanship had become, for the author, a predetermined text, which followed an inevitable course to a tragic conclusion and so conformed to classical (Old World) paradigms. Besides Gallatin he no doubt had in mind the statesmen John and John Quincy Adams, who at a symbolic level join with Gallatin to form a party of three; but in speaking of "the inevitable isolation and disillusionment" of the strong mind he referred to a family experience that had also been his own. Disillusioned with statesmanship, Henry Adams still felt the romance of American possibility—the sense that in the New World the problems of human society were destined to be worked out. He therefore sought in the *Gallatin* not only to portray the end of a heroic American statesmanship but also, if less convincingly, to affirm the opening of new fields of activity through which the romance of America could still be pursued.

Unlike the average politician—an "animal" who went "to his grave without suspecting his own limitations"—Gallatin "could and did refuse power when he found out what vanity it was, and yet became neither a cynic nor a transcendental philosopher" (*LHA* 2:376). So Adams filled out for Lodge's benefit Gallatin's moral example.[22] Yet what he did become is addressed with some ambiguity by the *Gallatin*: if in his political disillusionment Gallatin took up the scholarly work to which his "scientific" cast of mind most inclined him, the incidents of the later years that attract the biographer's notice have more to do with Gallatin's inability to put the public life behind him. In characterizing Gallatin's retirement, his transition from statesman to scholar, Adams draws upon what he had already established for himself as an apologia, a rhetoric, of repudiation: the notion that by disengaging his energies from the present corrupt realm of politics he could undertake tasks that accrued directly to the future glorious order—what he would call, early in the *History*, "the America of thought and art." As scholar (economist, ethnographer) Gallatin is portrayed as moving with his own and the younger generation away from the realm of politics toward "the study of social and economical principles, to purely scientific methods and objects, to practical commerce and the means of obtaining wealth. Old though Mr. Gallatin might think himself, it was to this new society that he and his mental processes belonged, and he found it a pleasure . . . to turn away from that political life which no longer represented a single great political conception, and to grapple with the ideas and methods of the coming generation" (*G* 635). So Adams had characterized his own movement in becoming a Washington-based independent scholar. Yet he overburdens his rhetoric in applying it to the past condition of Albert Gallatin. To the terms "new society" and "coming generation" he can assign no historical specification, and they become little more than invocations of a redeeming futurity that the actual (political) present appears powerless to support. In practice Adams would never succeed in disengaging his vision of the country's cultural possibilities from the tone of its political life; he could not turn to an exposition of the "coming generation" and ignore the fact that "the politics of the United States from 1830 to 1849 offered as melancholy a spectacle as satirists ever held up to derision" (G 635). Although Adams claims that Gallatin achieved lasting greatness as a scholar, he never devotes more than cursory attention to Gallatin's pioneering work as an ethnographer. Instead he focuses on the retired statesman's continued if unofficial attachment to public affairs and his participation, as pamphleteer, in the public controversies of the time. He thereby demonstrates that Gallatin could not turn away from public life and abandon his conviction that its errors must be judged by a great political conception.

In presenting the aged Gallatin in this character, Adams begins to construct the role he himself ultimately assumes as the Henry Adams (author and character) of the *Education*; indeed the *Gallatin* in this regard constitutes a remarkable, if entirely blind, anticipation of certain key rhetorical features of the later work. The aging Gallatin, like the aging Adams, registers numerous notices to quit. "I think that we have discharged our duties honestly," Gallatin is quoted as writing to an old friend, "and the next generation must provide for itself" (G 631). Or as Adams narrates: "In the frightful chaos which followed the inauguration of General Jackson the old servants of the government instantly saw that new principles and new practices left no place for them in the national service" (G 632). As Gallatin nears death during the war with Mexico, the world about him is portrayed as dissolving in universal chaos, much as the world of the aging Adams and the dying Hay would be portrayed, and yet his sense of public responsibility remains excruciatingly intact. Certain public tasks still required his specific attention. "The warnings to be quick came thick and fast. . . . His old associate, J. Q. Adams, breathed his last on the floor of Congress. . . . In Europe society itself seemed about to break in pieces, and everything old was passing away with a rapidity that recalled the days of the first French Revolution." Drawn out of retirement to protest the Mexican War, Gallatin, besides addressing a potentially dangerous New York crowd, wrote and published "Peace with Mexico" and "War Expenses," pamphlets Adams contends to have "had their share in leading the government to accept" an early peace (G 677).

The final moral of the life thus underscores the fact that Gallatin could not after all "abandon his faith in human nature" and that he saw himself as having no choice but "to make an appeal to the moral sense of the American public, and to scatter this appeal broadcast by the hundred thousand copies over the country" (G 676–77). In Gallatin's return we have an anticipation of Adams's depiction, in "The Abyss of Ignorance

(1902)," of his own response to the emergency of his time—his attempt, at the bidding of the anarchist's bomb, to establish a sequence of history in the light of which redemptive action might be taken. The parallel is instructive inasmuch as Adams cannot as an old man claim a faith in human nature comparable to that which, as a scholar of forty, he could categorically ascribe to Gallatin on the basis of that old man's eleventh-hour publications. Adams's "appeal" (from "The Tendency of History" through *A Letter*) remained rhetorically unassured, its urgency unable to lend itself to "broadcast by the hundred thousand copies over the country." Yet although *A Letter* approaches the satire of Gallatin's gesture, certainly Adams's late efforts preserve something of the motive of the statesman he modeled in his first book.

The Life of Albert Gallatin establishes the tension between retrospect and prospect that informs all of Adams's subsequent work. It records the painful experience that began the demolition of the dogma of American exceptionalism, laments the passing of "a sincere popular faith" (G 391), and bears witness to a phase of financial speculation "during which the public morality was permanently lowered" (G 657). Especially discouraging for someone who still hoped to introduce new influences, it sets in the past the period in which "government was still plastic and capable of receiving a new impulse" (G 268). The measure of this decline was none other than the vision of Gallatin, Jefferson, and Madison, "broad as society itself, and aimed at providing for and guiding the moral and material development of a new era,—a fresh race of men" (G 491). Yet this vision is also the legacy of the American retrospect, the source of the redemptive prospect, the measure of a new generation's achievement. "Since the day when foreign violence and domestic faction prostrated Mr. Gallatin and his two friends, no statesman has ever appeared with the strength to bend their bow,—to finish their uncompleted task" (G 492). Although the *Gallatin* largely discourages the expectation that the long-absent Odysseus of American statesmanship will appear, future possibility is affirmed (however vaguely) by the phrase "uncompleted task." The example of Albert Gallatin, a man of physical and moral courage who is loyal to his convictions and to his lofty conception of public life, is offered finally in support of that affirmation.

The Life of Albert Gallatin was not designed to be taken up vigorously by a national readership. Less specialized in method and materials than "Anglo-Saxon Courts of Law," it can still hardly be said to court a general audience. Adams's format is that of the well-established life and letters, a mode that had achieved popular success in George Trevelyan's *Life and Letters of Lord Macaulay* but that also lent itself to Adams's interest in primary documents and to his fascination with the dialogues that reflected and shaped public life. In his one-page preface Adams explicitly commends the book to colleagues in the profession: "A large part of the following biography relates to a period of American history as yet unwritten, and is intended to supply historians with material which, except in such a form, would be little likely to see the light" (G iii). Considering that the *Gallatin* so frequently engages a rhetoric of closure, it is profoundly significant that Adams should speak of "a period of American history as yet unwritten": the paradox preserves what for the historian in 1879 was the prospective *History of the United States during the Administrations of Jefferson and Madison*, a work that diverges from the "romance and tragedy" of the *Gallatin*. To the degree that the national experience remained unwritten, it beckoned to the brilliant redemptive personality who had found the field of statesmanship closed; to the historian, necessarily scientist and poet, fell the task of constructing the narrative by which the high American prospect could be preserved.

Whereas he would come to have firm notions as to the intended readership of the *History*, he seems never to have settled upon who among nonhistorians should read the *Gallatin* or to what effect. By 1879 he affected not to concern himself with the question and described himself as only "rejoiced to throw it off and forget it, in my pursuit of the larger subject," the *Gallatin* having served as "a preliminary study" for the magnum opus by which he would more purposively work to impress "a moral on the national mind" (*LHA* 2:371). The biography had never been intended for a popular audience; early in the writing he had decided not to translate the letters in French from Gallatin's youth, explaining that such would not be required by the book's "class of readers" (*LHA* 2:330). Schurz and Tilden were among those who received copies of the book published by Lippincott of Philadelphia, a house that had printed the papers and lives of other American statesmen, but it can hardly be said that Adams's readership constituted a school. The *Gallatin* drew mixed reviews, the harshest by far written by Charles Francis Adams, Jr., for anonymous publication in the *Nation*. While praising the book's moral treatment of its subject, the older brother attacked the clumsiness and ponderosity of the volume in order, as he himself explained to E. L. Godkin, "to induce Henry not to treat any audience at all as a thing beneath an author's consideration."[23] As we have seen, Henry had sought twelve years earlier to teach Charles a similar lesson. Although its bulk and slow pace have nothing to do with contempt for "any audience," the *Gallatin* does betray its author's sense that it would command at best a specialized readership. Anticipating his characterization of the *History*'s reception in the *Education*—that he had had "but three serious readers" yet "was amply satisfied with their consideration" (A I 1019)—he wrote Mary

Dwight Parkman shortly before the *Gallatin* had come out that his "two readers are you and Mrs George Bancroft. I shall have no more, but these two are enough to satisfy my ambition—if they approve" (*LHA* 2:360). His defense mechanisms as an alternately hopeful and despairing public author had become thus early a matter of reflex.

Adams's avowal that Mrs. Parkman and Mrs. Bancroft (respectively the in-law and the wife of the historians of those names) could constitute a satisfactory readership is interesting not only because they are an audience of two but because they are women. We can interpret this as a further (if unconscious) admission of defeat insofar as the portrait of the ideal states-man should preferably circulate among present and future statesmen, a term that for Adams was of course rigidly states*men*, politics in his view being an exclusively male realm. Yet his statement also reflects his growing conviction that a higher judgment than can be found among men resides in the sensibility of the cultivated woman. The brilliant women of his family and acquaintance—Marian Hooper Adams, his wife since 1872, preeminent among them—provided the basis for this conviction. Follow-ing his abandonment of the intensely male sphere of politics, Adams steadily developed the superiority of the woman as a conceit in the corre-spondence and as a serious literary theme, first in the novels and later in *Memoirs of Arii Taimai, Mont Saint Michel and Chartres,* and the *Educa-tion.* For the historian of the Jeffersonian period history would remain strictly male—male in its typically political dominant personalities and male in its voice, the patriarchal authority of the grand historical narra-tive. "The study of history," he would later admit, "is useful to the histo-rian by teaching him his ignorance of women" (A I 1042), but although in 1879 his operative notion of historical sequence was one that condoned that ignorance, Adams clearly felt his historiography's failure to account for the woman's part in historical process and so turned to the novel as a means to consider the great questions of human society from the perspec-tive of female protagonists. Moreover, in publishing *Democracy: An American Novel* anonymously and *Esther* pseudonymously under the name Frances Snow Compton, he was able to put in public play a voice of uncertain gender in the first novel and, in the second, one that pretended to be female.[24] The experiment of both novels consisted partly in seeing what response such voices could draw.

Adams closed the letter to Mary Dwight Parkman with the line "D——y is d——d," most likely "*Democracy* is despatched," the manu-script of the novel having just been sent to Henry Holt.[25] The message's cryptic form reflected Adams's utter determination to keep his authorship secret, for to be linked with *Democracy* not only would have prevented the directness with which he could watch his victims squirm, but also would have nullified his pose as nonpartisan scholar, which was crucial perhaps to preserving his privileged access to State Department archives. As he rightly foresaw that the *Gallatin* would attract little notice, he was also correct in supposing that his relentless satire of Washington personalities and democratic clichés would create a sensation. The book's sale required nine printings alone in 1880; not until the posthumous publication of the *Education* would he again achieve such commercial success.[26] If he suspected that being the known author of *Democracy* would make it difficult for him to cultivate a reputation as the great historian of the nation's formative years, he must also have seen that anonymity must encourage numerous attributions, increasing the degree of discomfort the book was capable of producing. And certainly it was intended to produce discomfort, particularly to Senator James G. Blaine, whose checkered past reappears thinly disguised in the story of Silas P. Ratcliffe. By publishing the book unsigned Adams may have tacitly proposed that a book of this kind was particularly apt to be rewritten by its readers. But he suggested more profoundly that the novel was ultimately collaborative, hardly the production of a single author, written rather by the tarnished, yet possibly regenerable, society in which it appeared—its true authorship named by its title.

The world of *Democracy* is post–Civil War Washington as it is reflected in the fascination, seduction, and horror of Madeleine Lee, an outsider who flirts dangerously with the opportunity of becoming an insider. A New York widow of independent means and ambitious energies, Madeleine at thirty has exhausted the world's resources of distraction in an effort to ease her sorrow and sense of lost purpose after the double loss of her husband and baby. She has traveled abroad and returned with fashionable plunder, read German philosophy and become "serious," and involved herself in the social work of upper-class philanthropies. Avowedly "American to the tips of her fingers" (A I 4), she has formed no deep attachment to European life and standards yet has found her desire to endorse her country frustrated by the spectacle that it makes of aimless wealth and stunted growth. "You are just like the rest of us," she remarks to her intellectual Boston friends. "You grow six inches high, and then you stop. Why will not somebody grow to be a tree and cast a shadow?" (A I 6). Wishing to study the nature and extent of the apparent national failure, and subliminally seeking an explanation for her own loss and stunted growth, she decides to spend a winter in Washington and get "to the heart of the great American mystery of democracy and government." Her interest is at once scientific and erotic. "She wanted to see with her own eyes the action of primary forces; to touch with her own hand the massive machinery of society; to measure with her own mind the capacity of the motive power." Student that she is, her ulterior aim does not lie in detachment: "What she wanted, was POWER" (A I 7, 8). A part of her wishes passionately to retrieve the elusive promise of democratic life, but for her that promise seems to reside in the prominent man of state: "She was aware that the President, the Speaker, and the Chief Justice were important personages, and instinctively she wondered whether they might not solve her problem; whether they were the shade trees which she saw in her dreams" (A I 7). Yet consciously Madeleine has no thought of going to Washington in search of a husband.

Accompanied by her younger sister Sybil, Madeleine takes a house on Lafayette Square and rapidly establishes a distinguished salon, the gathering place of a group of Washington specimens: a New York senator, a defeated Connecticut reform congressman, a Boston historian desiring diplomatic reappointment, the British and Bulgarian ministers, a protective tariff lobbyist, and a female reporter. Madeleine's two most frequent and attentive visitors are John Carrington, a Virginia lawyer, and Silas P. Ratcliffe, senator from Illinois, who emerge as the disappointed rivals for her hand. A kinsman of her late husband (a member of the Virginia Lee family), Carrington takes the newly settled Madeleine under his wing, and, bearing in dignified silence his experience as a ruined and marginalized southerner, educates her in the day's personalities and power struggles. It is Carrington who directs Madeleine's attention to Ratcliffe, the archetypal Grant Stalwart and party manager who has put himself in the position to dictate terms to the newly elected president and who, as Carrington observes, covets the post of treasury secretary on what he hopes is his path to the presidency.

The most powerful politician in Washington, Ratcliffe becomes the focus of Madeleine's quest, and by artful means she makes her way into his confidence. "Through him she hoped to sound the depths of statesmanship and to bring up from its oozy bed that pearl of which she was in search"; rather coldly, she meant "to experiment on him and use him as young physiologists use frogs and kittens." Although in their initial meeting Madeleine recognizes his coarseness and is able at once to manipulate his vanity, Ratcliffe's physical impressiveness and enormous vitality discourage any hasty taking of his measure and prevent her from gaining the upper hand. Provincial as the senator is, "Madeleine Lee had fully her match in Mr. Silas P. Ratcliffe" (A I 20). Because, seeking distraction, she has (we are later told) kept herself ignorant of her deepest motives in coming to Washington, Madeleine cannot know her own susceptibility to manipulation by this man whose power lends him a fascination that for a time confounds her science. The plot thus turns upon her deepening attraction to, but never love for, the senator, the fluctuations of her sense of duty that Ratcliffe masterfully exploits, her increasing willingness to join him in the rationalization of his corruption, and finally the restoration of her moral sense and her belated recognition of the baseness of her motives for desiring ties with him. Following Carrington's last-minute epistolary revelation of a particularly flagrant bit of jobbery involving the senator, the novel culminates in Madeleine's dismissal of Ratcliffe's marriage proposal and her flight from Washington and America.

The action takes place in the interregnum between the retirement of the old administration and the installation of the new—always, for Adams, a fascinating interval in American politics, during which the cohesiveness of the nation had more than once been in doubt. The arrival of a new president marks, in *Democracy*, the natural occasion for various reflections on the status of the American experiment, and the eclectic company in Madeleine's drawing room allows Adams to orchestrate a range of conflicting views and construct a dialogue that abounds in upmanship and dramatic silencings. In form *Democracy* reflects its author's fondness for theater; not only is the action essentially dialogic but the dialogue is sometimes set against a significant backdrop, as when the company picnics and philosophizes at Mount Vernon, or when Carrington and Sybil converse at an Arlington cemetery that the Virginian first knew as the vanquished Lees' ancestral home. Although the plot is meager and the characterization thin, the novel often achieves brilliance in the play of voices in particular scenes. And the colloquy is the more interesting, engaging of the reader's participation, inasmuch as Adams—the strategically anonymous, *absent* author—assigns to no one voice unimpeachable authority.[27]

As the group is international, there are predictable discussions of the comparative virtues of the Old and New Worlds, and Madeleine's unreconstructed national pieties are first revealed when she speaks out peremptorily in behalf of the New World. Overhearing Sybil help the Italian secretary of legation with an epigram disparaging of American society, she hastens to supply her sister and Count Orsini with the correct view. " 'Society,' " asserts Madeleine, "in America means all the honest, kindly-mannered, pleasant-voiced women, and all the good, brave, unassuming men, between the Atlantic and the Pacific. Each of these has a free pass in every city and village, 'good for this generation only,' and it depends on each to make use of this pass or not as it may happen to suit his or her fancy. To this rule there are *no* exceptions, and those who say 'Abraham is our father' will surely furnish food for that humour which is the staple product of our country" (A I 25). These words are enough to silence the young attachés who stand perplexed as Madeleine brandishes "her sugar-tongs in the act of transferring a lump of sugar to her cup, quite unconscious of the slight absurdity of the gesture." But it will take much more to appease her own growing doubts about her country's virtue or to meet the more than slight absurdities of her position as an affluent, gifted citizen for whom America has little use. Significantly, Madeleine never directly takes on the novel's dangerous spokesman for the European view, the Bulgarian minister, Baron Jacobi, "a witty, cynical, broken-down Parisian *roué*" (A I 21), a man who does not deal in mere slights. Disdainful of America's presumption that it should be "excepted from the operation of general laws" (A I 37), Jacobi delivers a ferocious speech early in the book on the impurity of American politics and society that ends in the prophecy that, in a hundred years, the United States will surpass the worst examples of corruption that European history has to offer. To Jacobi's remarks the novelist opposes no direct response, and his prophecy hangs over the company, and the novel, with the authority of an unanswered challenge.

As the principal addressee of Jacobi's remarks, Ratcliffe is the character positioned to refute the Baron's argument, but he can only look stern and say "with some curtness" that he sees "no reason to accept such conclusions" (A I 38)—a response so weak that it merits only the narrator's indirect quotation. He is morally incapable of answering the Baron, whose fury particularly fastens upon the senator's willful naivety with regard to the ultimate consequence of his practices—a state indeed "more corrupt than Rome under Caligula." What galls the European of course is not the American's corruption but his air of moral superiority, his routine and unacknowledged hypocrisy. For Ratcliffe and his brother senators what Jacobi and Congressman French call corruption is simply political business, "a mere struggle to deal with concrete facts at the cost of philosophic and *a priori* principles," as Adams defined "practical statesmanship" in the *Gallatin* (G 560), but without much pretense that anything beyond a senator's narrow ambition is ever served. In depicting Ratcliffe's pre-Inauguration intrigues, his shadowy and skillful consolidation of power and eventual checkmate of the president-elect, Adams portrays a man guided only by the criterion of self-promotion. "If he were always to wait until he could afford to tell the precise truth, business would very soon be at a standstill, and his career at an end" (A I 79). Such typifies his moral reasoning, which observes no distinction between private ambition and public good. His answer to reformers is that representative government simply reflects the morality of the society it represents. "Purify society and you purify the government." Adams himself, though always subscribing to "the old Ciceronian idea of government by *the best*," had conceded in "Civil Service Reform" and the "Session" articles that little could be done to check corruption without a popular impulse. But Ratcliffe's real conviction is that reform as French "wants is utterly hopeless, and not even desirable" (A I 37). Purification of government or society is his last thought.

It is interesting that Adams should portray Congressman French, his specimen reformer, as a lightweight in the novel's dialogue, easily silenced by the muscular assertion, though not the argument, of the elder senators. The novelist's profile of the outgoing representative, "who aspired to act the part of the educated gentleman in politics, and to purify the public tone," approaches satire of Adams's former self, especially as, "in a solemn mood, he talked as though he were practising for the ear of a college debating society" (A I 21–22). Had not Adams, in his early political writings, sounded such a tone, underestimating the grizzled incumbent's tenacity? Obvious as Ratcliffe's moral idiocy becomes, the novelist makes it quite clear that there is as yet no *political* solution to the senator, and Madeleine and Nathan Gore, the two would-be defenders of the democratic faith, must maintain that faith willfully in the face of evidence that overwhelmingly supports the position of Jacobi—an argument that takes Ratcliffe as its chief example.

Nathan Gore, whose Tocquevillian acceptance of democracy approaches what Adams had thus far established as his own, is a curious portrait of literary success and political preferment shadowed by disappointment and compromise. His story is drawn from the careers of James Russell Lowell and John Lothrop Motley: a writer of satiric verses in his youth, he goes on to become a "deep student in Europe" and to write a "History of Spain in America" (A I 23), an accomplishment that leads to his appointment as minister to Spain. Relieved of his duties by the retiring administration, he has come to Washington to press for reappointment. Ernest Samuels is doubtless correct in writing that, through Gore, Adams voices his own deepest convictions, "the irreducible dogmas of his proud inheritance."[28] "I believe in democracy," Gore confides.

> I accept it. I will faithfully serve and defend it. I believe in it because it appears to me the inevitable consequence of what has gone before it. Democracy asserts the fact that the masses are now raised to a higher intelligence than formerly. All our civilisation aims at this mark. We want to do what we can to help it. I myself want to see the result. I grant it is an experiment, but it is the only direction society can take that is worth its taking; the only conception of its duty large enough to satisfy its instincts; the only result that is worth an effort or a risk. Every other possible step is backward, and I do not care to re-

peat the past. I am glad to see society grapple with issues in
which no one can afford to be neutral. (A I 40)

The experiment, Gore affirms, is worth what Madeleine suggests (and
Adams believed) was the risk that society might destroy "itself with universal suffrage, corruption, and communism." As we shall see, Gore's
views receive resounding reaffirmation in "American Ideals," the key early
chapter of the *History*.

How intriguing, then, that Adams should express visionary sentiments through the lips of one who, like French, nurses an impaired dignity. A Brahmin historian cast in the role of office-seeker, pursuing
through Ratcliffe a post that will allow him to take leave of America, is an
ambiguous spokesman of the democratic faith. So much does Gore desire
the restoration of his diplomatic mission that he becomes, temporarily, the
defender of Ratcliffe, his tepid champion in the quest for spoil. And he is
rendered pathetic in his disappointment, which stems in part from the
president-elect's dislike of the cut of his coat, "which is unfortunately an
English one" (A I 99) (a variation on the story, which Adams and E. L.
Godkin had maliciously spread ten years earlier, that Grant took a dislike
to the part in Motley's hair and that this had cost Motley the British
mission). It is as though Adams meant to create in Gore a personally
monitory figure, the casualty he still could become should his old wish for
promotion tie his fortune to the wheel of democratic politics. Gore's uncertain standing is further reflected in the confidentiality with which he
speaks his democratic "catechism": Carrington and Madeleine alone are
permitted to hear his affirmation of democracy, "never," he warns, "to be
repeated or quoted as mine" (A I 40). In this he presents his most intimate
resemblance to Henry Adams, who similarly shrank from public recita-
tions of anything that might simply be construed as his creed and who
similarly longed with troubled conscience for a position of neutrality that
he knew he could ill afford.[29] Like Adams, Gore maintains his faith (or
perhaps more precisely the renewability of his faith) beneath a paradoxical
discourse that makes possible various conflicting and experimental avowals, shielding his rather vulnerable beliefs from the rough-and-tumble of
open discussion. Adams's anonymous publication of *Democracy* in its
own way makes the proclamation, "not to be quoted as mine," the condition under which in 1879 he could break his self-imposed silence with
regard to recent American life.

Although Gore's pronouncements convey the authority of large and
redemptive views, it is through Madeleine that the novelist has chosen to
explore "whether America is right or wrong" (A I 39), as Madeleine
phrases the object of her query after listening to Jacobi's harangue. More

precisely it is through the circumstances of Madeleine's past life and her marriageability to Ratcliffe (and his marriageability to her) that the question is addressed, apart from the ever-inconclusive dialectics of Madeleine's entourage. If America is right, it is in spite of its long decline into political corruption, the squandered opportunity for electoral renewal represented by the incoming president. In her answer to Count Orsini Madeleine had touched upon the traditional vindication of America: the unassuming dignity of the average citizen and the essential purity of the American character, of which George Washington emerges during the group's trip to Mount Vernon as the supreme type in the remarks of the Virginian Carrington and the New Englander Gore. Madeleine herself embodies some of the traits she would like to think her people embody: she "was sober in her tastes. She wasted no money. She made no display." But the novelist must admit that "the general impression she made was nevertheless one of luxury" (A I 11). In contrast to Sybil, the younger sister who "had her dresses from Paris" and whose privileged life in Newport and New York has kept her oblivious to tragic conceptions prior to her visit to Arlington cemetery, Madeleine is the portrait of republican virtue, yet although she "always paid the bills" (discharged the debt) of Sybil's ostentation, it cannot be insignificant that she underwrites an existence that contradicts her own professed democratic values.

 We enter here an area of notorious ambivalence for Henry Adams, who despised the display of the newly rich yet always wished to make his own impression of luxury (one that did not exclude his wife's Worth dresses). But we enter more profoundly what for Adams in this period was an inchoate and perhaps mostly unconscious meditation on the imperiled virtue and fecundity of the American family, the matrix of public morality to an Adams. What the novelist represents as Madeleine's comparatively chaste affluence is a condition that she has reached after a life of departures of a decidedly symbolic cast. Half-Bostonian by family connection, she is the daughter of a Philadelphia clergyman yet spends her youth as "a rather fast New York girl before she married" (A I 126). In marriage she takes for her husband the stockbroker Lighthorse Lee, whose name and occupation, all we ever know about him, tell us that he was a defeated aristocratic southerner who moved north after the war to learn the money-making ways of the victors. His story contrasts sharply with that of Carrington, who ventures just north of the Potomac to eke out a subsistence for his mother and sisters down on the farm. New York had long been in Adams's view a city that stood for wealth, power, corruption, and recent arrival as suggested by his resonant title, "The New York Gold Conspiracy." Although Madeleine and the fictional Lee scion prosper for a while materially, they cannot in New York found a new family on the old (heroic) stock that each represents. Curiously, the novelist offers the deaths, one week apart, of Madeleine's husband and baby as pure contingency, probably because he was uncertain of the novel's allegorical drift and had failed, in his rapid composition of what he considered a topical burlesque, to become fully cognizant of the symbolic force of such details. In any case, the debacle of Madeleine's private life punctuates with biblical simplicity the motif of wandering that the novelist has put at the center of his secular national fable.

Given this motif, with its vestigial suggestion of a progressively fractionalized covenant, the sudden death of Madeleine's family cannot but appear as a judgment, a warning to quit the ways of error, an injunction to begin anew. But the novelist writes in a tradition that had long since absorbed the sacred millennium of Puritan rhetoric in the secular millennium of the American Republic, and Madeleine's dilemma is posed as national, sexual, and at most quasi-religious. Her personal tragedy at once serves as instance and metaphor of the general blighting of the American promise; for this reason she becomes in her sorrow conscious of a national tendency toward arrested growth, and in her search for modes of self-renewal she has come to question America's essential rightness. Insofar as Madeleine's and her country's problem is secular, renewal must be sought in the human initiative of the gifted individual sustained by the virtue and resource of the people, but it is here that Madeleine and her novelist arrive at an impasse. Although Madeleine is inclined sentimentally toward the egalitarian society whose merits she has brought to the attention of Sybil and Count Orsini, her experience as a cultivated, agnostic, upper-class woman has borne her irresistibly away from it, and what she knows first-hand of the "people" she has learned from the outcasts with whom she has come in contact through philanthropic activities she has undertaken in her widowhood to satisfy a vague expiatory impulse. Through Ratcliffe, the public man of common origin whose westernness proposes a renewed covenant, she wishes to establish a regenerative contact with democratic society that will confirm her optative theories. If the statesman stands up to her scrutiny she is willing to join her refinement, artistic tendencies, and sympathy—qualities Adams looked upon already as the culturally procreative energies of the brilliant woman—to his male political power. Such a marriage offers to confirm the American character in its traditional virtues and provide for its steady elevation.

John Carrington and Nathan Gore meet Madeleine at her level of refinement but neither receives encouragement as a suitor. Distinctly regional and recessive types, they possess none of the western senator's force. As a westerner, Ratcliffe is much more the representative American; having begun life in New Hampshire, his development has been transregional—he has grown up, and westward, with the country. Yet, to the ruin of Mrs. Lee's theories and aspirations, this exemplar of "robust American-ism" (A I 51) can only confirm moral decline, disproving the hypothesis that the West purifies. His case suggests that popular virtues have not held out against the corruptions accompanying the wealth and power that con-tinental development has placed in the hands of the people—a people (as Baron Jacobi pointed out) with an ideological reluctance to learn from experience. Ratcliffe's career seems particularly to illustrate the erosion of a once-lofty national character. Entering politics as a supporter of the abolitionist cause, he has come to serve no greater purpose than the ag-grandizement of his own power; having memorized as a boy Washington's "Farewell Address," in his postwar senatorial hubris he speaks of the first president's comparatively "inferior powers" (A I 69) and asserts that, if Washington were president now, "he would have to learn our ways or lose his next election" (A I 71). The fact that Ratcliffe represents not only the degradation of past ideals but also a trend in public life that leads away from renewal of the American opportunity is reflected in his widower status: the female, in his company, has perished, and he has established no family to give public purpose an object beyond the sterile conservation of a single generation's status quo. While bereavement is a condition that Mrs. Lee and Ratcliffe have in common, it is also one by which we come to see the irreconcilable differences that confirm them in their respective widow(er)hoods.

Like Gore, Madeleine is induced by a combination of idealism and ambition to give temporarily the senator the benefit of the doubt, but although she nearly accepts Ratcliffe's Mephistophelean proposal that she help him purify American politics, it is clear throughout that marriage will prove impossible. Their failure to join in marriage emerges as the novel's central metaphor, articulating its ulterior thesis: the improbability of na-tional renewal given the repulsiveness of America's highest expression of masculine vigor to its highest expression of feminine refinement. The theme of nonmarriage was clearly important to Adams, expressing sym-bolically what Adams felt was not right about his country; it would emerge as the central metaphor of his other, more intimate novel, *Esther*. The one engagement that transpires in *Democracy* is distinctly satiric: that of a lisping and aggressive Washington gossip columnist to a passive Irish count—hardly a match calculated to renew the social order of the Old or New World! Reeling from her near misstep and renouncing all claim to a genuinely creative existence, Madeleine takes herself to task over her dis-loyalty to her dead husband—she had forgotten that "second marriages were her abhorrence" (A I 165). Having discovered that "democratic gov-ernment . . . was nothing more than government of any other kind," she decides "to return to the true democracy of life, her paupers and her prisons, her schools and her hospitals" (A I 168–69), becoming a kind of Mater Dolorosa and consoling those who, like herself, have abandoned hope of an American redemption. But in the initial violence of her flight she travels to Egypt in order to be out of the sphere of America absolutely. It is from the Nile that Madeleine delivers her final and bleakest judgment on the democratic faith. This occurs in her postscript to a letter Sybil writes to Carrington to encourage him to resume his pursuit of Madeleine when they return to New York. Referring to her rejection of the senator, Madeleine declares that "the bitterest part of all this horrid story is that nine out of ten of our countrymen would say I had made a mistake" (A I 184). So much for glowing estimates of the national character.

In his 1891 New Year's letter to Elizabeth Cameron from Samoa, Adams would write that "a man cannot with decency or chance of success take a part in a stage-play when he cannot help showing the audience that he thinks the whole thing a devilish poor piece of work" (*LHA* 3:382). Yet he had portrayed his country as a devilish poor piece of work not two years after he had embarked on his second Washington experiment. His sequel to what he had wanted to be the still-ennobling tragedy of statesmanship that Gallatin exemplified had become the bitter satire of statesmanship that the composition of the novel had (perhaps quite unexpectedly) summoned—a satire that, as J. C. Levenson has pointed out, ends in sheer horror.[30] In her experiment, Madeleine "had only to go quietly on among the supernumeraries and see how the play was acted and the stage effects were produced" (A I 8) to satisfy herself that she was witnessing something like "the end of American society" (A I 45) and to wish herself as far from it as possible. The decline of the American character that Adams portrays is made to appear irrevocable in what he also portrays as the country's inability to renew itself. The malaise *Democracy* probes in its symbology is beyond the reach of the surgery Adams would have the book's satiric rhetoric perform. For his own purposes, however, Adams chose to suspend the novel's bleakest message, if indeed he ever allowed himself to be conscious of it, and to set to work on Nathan Gore's perhaps unfounded affirmative tenets to construct a symbology and rhetoric of renewal.

5

The Democratic Ocean

Text and Drift

BETWEEN JUNE 1877, when he left Harvard to undertake the Gallatin project and August 1890, when he quit Washington for the South Seas, Henry Adams sustained a remarkable phase of productivity that saw the composition of three biographies and two novels as well as the nine-volume *History*. Such a prolific authorship may not have required close relations with an audience, but it does suggest a settled notion as to the objects authorship serves. Except for *Esther*, the second novel that Adams published under extremely restrictive "experimental" conditions, his work cannot really be said to have suffered neglect. While *Democracy* and *John Randolph* won popular and, in the case of the novel, international reader-ship, the *History* in "proofsheet" form enjoyed the scrutiny of an elite circle, and the long labors of the magnum opus steadied Adams in what outwardly resembled the venerable role of patrician historian.[1] From the first, Adams meant his narrative to describe, and on occasion even to celebrate, the emergence of a uniquely American character as the latter should appear in the comparatively dry light of a "scientific" method-ology, and in concluding the *History* he could see his volumes coincide with that intention. In passing he ventured to frame for his generation a large conception of its historical task, which could set the terms of a national affirmation and renewal. Yet beneath these evidences of industri-ous repose, Adams played host to doubts that regularly jostled the founda-tions of his enterprise, impeaching his motive conviction as to the ultimate bearing of his work.

The very first mention of the *History* in the correspondence is in fact accompanied by the expression of decided despair. "To make it readable," he wrote to Hugh Blair Grigsby, "is the great hope of my life. To get it read, however, is beyond my most sanguine expectations." By the time he was ready to "come to anchor" in a work that might rival the accomplish-ment of Gibbon, he had developed a rather forbidding measure of success. "America is increasing so rapidly, and her future is so vast," continued

Adams in the letter to Grigsby, "that one man may reasonably devote his life to the effort at impressing a moral on the national mind, which is now almost a void" (*LHA* 2:371). Still in formative stage, Adams suggests, America may yet prove receptive to historical lessons, and the historian can do no better than to seize what may well be his chance to affect the course of a vast human movement. Unequivocally, Adams designates the "national mind" as the object he would impress, the aims of his greatest work-to-be emphatically requiring a general readership. Yet here, again, the ambition is conceived in desperate terms. Although the winning of a popular audience transcends his "most sanguine expectations," he remains convinced of the imperative of impressing "a moral on the national mind," characterized darkly in his afterthought as "now almost a void." As the writing of the *History* was all before him, he could perhaps look upon this near mental void as the tabula rasa of a young people—part of the manikin of national character that the historian would dress to advantage as he could. Yet his phrasing rather suggests a deterioration, proportionate to the country's growth, of the national mind's ability to retain a sense of history, and the clause ends with the intimation that, worthy as it is to make the attempt to impress a perhaps saving moral on the national mind—and thus reclaim it from its tendency to become a void—there may yet prove too little mind to impress.

So Adams in 1879 figured his ultimate nightmare of an absent readership. Having attenuated even as he magnified his expectations for the *History*, he closed the letter to Grigsby with a last deprecation that yet reaffirms the grand ambition. "The America of the next century will be one of the greatest problems of all history. To reach one's arm over into it, and give it a shove, is at least an amusement" (*LHA* 2:371). The conceit that he was laboring in behalf of a future America had nearly always surfaced when he sought to define his life's work: in the depths of the secession winter he had set himself to writing letters that would memorialize that time for a distant age, while in the Civil War's darkest moments he had begun to address problems that he identified as those of the "next century." As we have just seen, for the frustrated reform writer the future constituted the saving myth to which his rhetoric could safely incline. As American sacred and secular millennialism had always asserted, and as Tocqueville had recently confirmed, the New World presented an unexampled dimension of futurity, which had emerged since the late eighteenth century as the great theater for the democratic experiment. Its failure, if it should come to that, would rank among history's greatest, and whether it be ill or well its destiny must prove inherently, millennially meaningful.

Therefore, insofar as it appeared to hold ultimate meaning for human history, the future guaranteed a measure of redemption to a present vexed by civil war, political corruption, and rapid, extravagant growth. On arriving in Washington in 1877, Adams had observed to Gaskell that "in another century" America would "be saying in its turn *the last word* of civilisation" (*LHA* 2:326; italics added). From the perspective of the reform writer become historian, whether that word condemned or approved the people through whom it was reached, it did promise to redeem the country from its state of apparent drift, its progress among indeterminant meanings, its development in the virtual absence of a central, consensual text. Since the great constitutional crises of midcentury, if not before, the country in its strict political development had been without such a document. Adams's coming-of-age as a political thinker lay in his recognition that the work of the Founders had not succeeded, and was not likely to succeed, in constraining the national experience: toward the end of the second "Session" he had conceded that "the great political problems of all ages cannot, at least in a community like that of the future America, be solved by the theory of the American Constitution," and that "discussion of so large a subject [problems that the Constitution in its strict construction had failed to solve] is matter for a lifetime, and will occupy generations" (*NAR* 111:61–62). He had discovered early that the historian must join with others in the open-ended, dialogic (re)constitution of the country whose fate would be that of humankind, a task far more difficult than the Founding Fathers, in their profoundest skepticism, could have supposed.

Writing "for a continent of a hundred million people fifty years hence" (*LHA* 2:535), Adams intended the *History* as a contribution to a grander text of American and democratic evolution, the "last word" to be arrived at by another generation than his. Guardedly confident at the outset of this period that the American experiment would be pronounced a success, he worked in the conviction that his writing (should the national mind prove receptive) could contribute valuably to the country's self-awareness. In any case, such moratoria as he was wont to impose on the drawing of final conclusions gave his authorship ample space in which to work. The rhetoric of deferral is not less characteristic of Adams's writing than the rhetoric of closure; as we have seen in our discussions of the *Education*, the *Gallatin*, and *Democracy*, the two are inseparable, the paradox that keeps his discourse open. Although as he aged Adams steadily foreshortened the period between the present moment and the crisis that should supply the "last word"—until in *A Letter* he argued that the word had been long since proclaimed by Lord Kelvin—even his late works go through the motions of submitting to future judgment.

More secure in the resource of hope, the works of his early middle years proceed in the conviction that the word of another century may yet confirm the United States as a successful and ongoing experiment: it is on this assumption that he speaks of having undertaken in the *Gallatin* "the heavy and unpopular task of hewing wood and drawing water for the history that is to be" (*LHA* 2:456) or that he designates *John Randolph* as, like the *Gallatin,* "only a preliminary essay" (*LHA* 2:477). Each book thus becomes in turn a preparation not so much for the "last word" as for another precursor text in a continuous unfolding of chapters that address the story of American democracy. Although his aspiration in the *History* had been all along to produce a definitive account of the national character's formation, Adams had not wished to project that character's destiny as absolutely, "scientifically" foreseeable. Yet such foreseeability is what his final pages announce is at hand: "the coming of an epoch when man should study his own history in the same spirit and by the same methods with which he studied the formation of a crystal" (A III 1334). Such an epoch seemed closer at the conclusion than it could possibly have seemed at the commencement of the *History*'s composition; more and more he had come to reconceive his magnum opus as not so much appealing to the future as being superseded practically as it was written. "The more I write," he remarked to Francis Parkman, "the more confident I feel that before long a new school of history will rise which will leave us antiquated": a school that would have the last word to the degree that, joining psychology and physiology, it would prove "man to have as fixed and necessary a development as that of a tree; and almost as unconscious" (*LHA* 2:563). This projected closure would confirm after all that the national mind, viewed as a historical development, must be a void, with little use for historical morals; but Adams's own practice goes forward on rhetorical assumptions that hold that conclusion in abeyance.

The premise that a historical moral can be impressed on the national mind undergirds the 1882 *John Randolph.* Less problematic than the *Gallatin* with regard to what can be learned from the past, the often libelous biography at least superficially proposes that certain forms of statesmanship determined particular courses of national development and can therefore be brought to moral account. If in Albert Gallatin Adams had a pure character whose tragedy lay in circumstances that prevented his powers of invention from having their deserved historical effect, in Randolph he had a troubled character whose obvious flaws produced evident and lasting mischief. Moreover, unlike Gallatin who was by temperament laconic and knew when to hold his tongue, Randolph was maniacally if brilliantly loquacious, and his aberrations could be directly traced in the many examples of his public language. For Adams the author, Randolph's astonishing verbal powers, vented repeatedly in a public display of insane but also poetic expression, lent to the Virginian a fascination that Gallatin, for all his vast moral superiority, probably could not equal. Whatever Adams's intentions were, *John Randolph* became a study of the effect of an undisciplined, unstable, at times insane personality upon public life at a time when certain precedents were being established in constitutional interpretation—a time when the ideals of rationality, disinterest, and verbal decorum were in Adams's view most in need of consensual realization. The spectacle of John Randolph in Adams's rendering is that of a speaker who follows his brilliant, if also vicious, flights at the expense of his principles and to the disruption of rational public dialogue. The lesson was finally greater than the book itself could comprehend; Adams's dismay over Randolph's harangues no doubt reflects his own experience and fear of the subversive elements of language.

In the *History* Adams continues his close study of the language of public dialogue and is particularly intent upon measuring Jefferson's explicit statements as a centralizing president against his states' rights republican principles, against his obvious enmities and ulterior motives, and against what Adams regards as a range of thought that Jefferson himself could never fully articulate. The statesman's participation in political discourse is approached as more necessarily self-deceptive than in *John Randolph*. The Constitution as a text admitting of strict constructions is held to have perforce expired in 1803—in Jefferson's own phrasing to have become "blank paper"—and the broadening of power on the part of John Adams's successors is treated as a historical irony, which benefited the country and promoted the formation of a strong national character, rather than as a crime. The country, in Adams's narrative, develops according to a text that remains mostly closed to the historical actors' scrutiny and that the *History* itself can only partly read and formulate in retrospect. The accountability of the historical actors, as well as the capacity for moral response on the part of the "national mind" that must read this history as its own, is problematized by Adams's avowedly transitional historiography: a practice that hovers between portraying past human action as at least partially conscious, free, and hence morally responsible and representing that action as conforming without consciousness to laws that may be ascertained only retrospectively. Rhetorically, again, the *History* ever hovers, ostensibly for lack of the perfected science that could reach and refine the last word. Yet that science, Adams suggests by the work's end, will come eventually, if only to demonstrate the necessary sequences that must render historical consciousness irrelevant to the course that society must take. The text of American development thus threatened to become, by the light of "a new school of history," only too prewritten, the ultimate drift of American democracy too deadly obvious.

The Impulse to Contradict

Although *John Randolph* was not part of the agenda that he had shaped for himself over the past twenty years, Adams threw himself into the project with an intensity that belied the fact that the book was a commissioned work. In 1881 John T. Morse, Jr., asked Adams to contribute a life of the Virginia congressman to the American Statesman Series that Morse edited for Houghton Mifflin. Consenting to write the book in April, Adams went promptly to work and by July had established a first draft, his subject engrossing for three months his unusual capacity for horrified fascination. As subject, the mercurial John Randolph naturally commended himself to a sensibility that responded to paradox; given the feuds that subsisted between the Virginia Quixote and the second and sixth presidents there was the added relish of vented ancestral animus. To write for the American Statesman Series in itself made for a congenial engagement of Adams's energies: Morse's project proposed a sequence of critical political biographies written for a popular audience by a generation educated by the Civil War and the crusades to retake government from the manifold abuse of Grant-era politics. Not only did Adams agree to do Randolph but volunteered for Burr—indeed proceeded to write a life of Burr that Morse never intended to accept.[2] In the hope perhaps of making the series an expression of his old, loose "school" of reformers, Adams nominated a number of his former colleagues to write the lives of other statesmen.[3]

Why the opportunity to write popular biographies of Randolph and Burr drew Adams into passionate if short-lived digressions from the larger pursuit of the *History* is a question of considerable interest. Because Adams ultimately destroyed the Burr manuscript, probably after assimilating much of it into the *History*,[4] *John Randolph* alone can be summoned to explain the path of his pen. It is clear, however, that certain motives that produced the one book produced both. "Randolph," wrote Adams to Morse, "is the type of a political charlatan who had something in him. Burr is the type of a political charlaton pure and simple, a very Jim Crow of melodramatic wind-bags. I have something to say of both varieties" (*LHA* 2:424). He could have his say with immediate satisfaction as he worked up his portraits of (respectively) the failed and false statesman from materials already at hand, and he could contemplate the possibility of winning for himself a broad readership for whom he would wish to exist as named author. The near prospect of publication must have offered to mitigate the isolation peculiar to the historian of the grand narrative, who reported to Gaskell that he was obliged to "grind on, slowly covering vast piles of paper with legible writing, but without even thinking of a day when it will be read by others" (*LHA* 2:461).

To be sure, Adams's adherence to such ideals of statesmanship as he had figured in the *Gallatin* stands behind his wish to produce an anatomy of political charlatanism—a hobby begun in his correspondence and re-form essays and resumed under cover in *Democracy*. But his desire to point the moral of Randolph and Burr could not have proceeded from a simple intent to foster in the public loftier expectations of its officials. In the *Gallatin*, as we have seen, he had conceded that the statesmanship of Gallatin and the Adamses was mostly antiquated by 1825. It would be far easier for Henry Adams to frame the known, negative examples of the past than to model the effective yet virtuous magistrate of a new era. In any event, the solution to that problem may have seemed to him less urgent in the spring of 1881 than it had been for the past fifteen years. Grantism at least was a thing of the past: "Our fight," he wrote to Henry Cabot Lodge a month into *John Randolph*'s composition, "is now pretty well won," and although confirmed in an inveterate mediocrity of leadership, American government had grown "free from organised corruption" (*LHA* 2:427). In these brief respites from the writing of the *History* Adams sought to sketch what he presumed to be the discards of an American political evolution, but he was hardly confident that that process would breed types equal to the best representatives of the old American statesmanship. Nevertheless, by focusing on individual careers and, in the case of Randolph, judging the man as a willful and potentially valuable historical actor, Adams affirmed some measure of individual responsibility for the course of the nation's development, a responsibility that the broader perspectives of the *History* tended to dismiss.

John Randolph reveals additional and more complicated motives. Given his obstruction of most aims of the John Quincy Adams presidency, Randolph held a central place in that family's demonology, and Henry's opportunity to write the Virginian's life afforded him a chance to have the last word in the vituperative exchange that had always characterized relations between Randolph and the Adamses. No doubt Henry drew satisfaction from the fact that here, as elsewhere, the author gave definitive, literary shape to conflicts arising in the political realm, and that memory of the statesman became the charge of a historian who did not have to be merciful. The historian in the "fourth" Adams generation qualified little of his political forebears' moral assessment of Randolph. Yet the harshness of Adams's treatment lies perhaps less in any filial obligation he may have felt to avenge his grandfather, against whose opposition Randolph allegedly consolidated the slave power, than in his fellowship in the generation that eventually bled to overcome the slave power. If in *John Randolph* Adams assumes the role of family spokesman, it is to establish the degree to which the family's doctrines were vindicated by the generation for whom he more ultimately presumes to speak.

By a rhetoric that consists more of imagery than argument, Adams characterizes Randolph as the one man most responsible for the southern secession and, hence, the Civil War that broke out twenty-eight years after his death. The biographer creates the tone for such a thesis as a first order of business and with an amazingly heavy hand. Tracing in the opening paragraphs the genealogy of the American Randolphs to their foothold in the lower Appomattox, he writes of the region's early associations with violent disturbance—Bacon's Rebellion and Benedict Arnold's raid. Cited as vague, premonitory correlatives of John Randolph's violent temper, such episodes, Adams tells us, could not make "the region nearly so famous as it became on June 30, 1862, when fifty thousand northern troops, beaten, weary, and disorganized, converged at Malvern Hill and Turkey Island bridge, and the next day fought a battle which saved their army, and perhaps their cause, without a thought or a care for the dust of forgotten Randolphs on which two armies were trampling in the cradle of their race" (R 2). In this one sentence, which concludes the book's second paragraph, Adams has condensed his indignation with his subject: long before he comes to argue that Randolph coined the sophistry that led to civil war by "prostituting" the honorable doctrine of states' rights "to the base uses of the slave power" (R 271), he has proposed that a certain just vengeance was wreaked in the inadvertent dishonor done to the remains of Randolph's ancestors in the course of a battle that saved ("perhaps") the righteous Union cause.[5] In contrast to its own suggestion, Adams's rhetoric very deliberately dishonors the Randolph dead, and the insult to this lineage is magnified by the implication that (as of 1863) the family had left little memory of itself and that the ruin brought to the region by John Randolph must at all events consign it to oblivion. We also seem encouraged to believe that John Randolph is only worth remembering in that it was the mischief of his regional eccentricities that brought on the great national tragedy.

This strain of imagery and suggestion extends through the opening chapters. Following a brief and remarkably savage account of Randolph's boyhood, which fixes upon the young man's failure to acquire "self-control or mental discipline" (R 6), Adams depicts Randolph's entrance into national politics as motivated by a strong disunionist sentiment. Randolph, the biographer reminds us, politically came of age in the atmosphere of the Kentucky and Virginia Resolutions, and his first important appearance as an orator occurred in 1799—the year before he was elected to Congress at the age of twenty-eight—when he spoke before a public gathering to uphold "the establishment of the armory for the purpose of opposing Mr. Adams's administration" (R 30). The sensation he created was in large part due to the fact that he had to face the objections of no less a personage than the aged Patrick Henry. Although the speech was not preserved, Adams speculates that it "could have been only a solemn defense of states' rights; an appeal to state pride and fear; an *ad hominem* attack on Patrick Henry's consistency, and more or less effective denunciation of federalists in general" (R 30–31). Patrick Henry pronounced such militance as Randolph expressed "parricidal" (R 29), and although Randolph and his doctrines were then (as Adams points out) beginning to assume popularity, our attention is directed at the vignette's close to "the awe that surrounds a dying prophet threatening a new doom deserved." Unable to heed the old man's private words to him after the debate—that he "keep justice, keep truth," and so "live to think differently"—Randolph is portrayed as never living to think differently but ending "as he began, trying to set bounds against the power of the national government, and to protect those bounds, if need be, by force" (R 31).

Judged by the *History*'s masterly refinements—the keen sense of the paradoxical course an idea can take in application, the nice appreciation of the interplay of personality, ideology, and political process—the rhetoric of *John Randolph*, particularly in the first chapter, is decidedly crude, giving the impression of an undisguised attempt at a potboiler. Midway through the second chapter, Adams himself visibly draws back from his eager conflation of states' rights, rebellion, and John Randolph's unmanageable temper. "For a generation like our own," he writes, excusing the inexact face he or anyone else may have put on the matter, "in whose ears the term of states' rights has become hateful, owing to its perversion in the interests of negro slavery, and in whose eyes the comfortable doctrines of unlimited sovereignty shine with the glory of a moral principle sanctified by the blood of innumerable martyrs, these narrow and jealous prejudices of Randolph and his friends sound like systematized treason" (R 38). Yet the states' rights doctrine, as the biographer is obliged to explain, figured centrally in "the honest convictions of that generation which framed and adopted the Constitution" (R 38), and in an exceptionally lucid exposition of classical republican ideology (R 31–37) Adams justly places states' rights within a theory of government that dreaded above all the despotic, self-defining power of a central authority. States' rights, Adams reaffirms later in the book, "was in itself a sound and true doctrine; as a starting point of American history and constitutional law, there is no other which will bear a moment's examination; it was as dear to New England as to Virginia" (R 271). Indeed the slave power, Adams argues, "when in control, was a centralizing influence, and all the most considerable encroachments on states' rights were its acts" (*R* 270). Randolph's defense of slavery in the name of states' rights therefore entailed a contradiction that betrayed the pure republican principles that he claimed were his. The only affirmation of Randolph's participation in the vast causality of secession and civil war lies here, in what Adams claims to have been Randolph's seminal "identification of slavery with states' rights"; which was, Adams reflects, "one of those unfortunate entanglements which so often perturb and mislead history" (*R* 270, 271).

To establish Randolph as the evil, if nevertheless lightweight, genius of southern secession—the man who charted "the whole course on which the slave power was to sail to its destruction" (*R* 299)—may be the guiding as well as the least subtle purpose of this hastily written biography. But contemptuous and dismissive of his subject as the biographer proves, Randolph, as Adams pointed out to Morse, "is the type of a political charlatan who had something in him," and by the least flattering light of Adams's presentation Randolph emerges as one who has a great deal in him indeed: audacity, courage, a puritanical streak that revolted on occasion against the realpolitik of Jefferson, Madison, and Monroe, and a character that, for all of its vices, remained "free from the meaner ambitions of political life" (*R* 190). Above all, Randolph possessed an astonishing verbal facility, the distinction Adams no doubt had most in mind when, in the more balanced assessment of the *History*, he referred to Randolph as "in many respects the most gifted man produced by the South in his generation" (A II 855). But Randolph had something else in him that provided the ultimate focus of Adams's attention as well as the grounds for a certain horrific and secret affinity: a temper given to unpredictable and contradictory affirmations. Adams's troubled yet irrepressible fascination with this aspect of Randolph complicates the fury of his northern partisanship and retrieves the text from its strong current of vilification and dismissal. It allows the book to become, if only inadvertently, something more: a committed if inconclusive meditation on the influence an irrational personality can exert over the course of a government ostensibly devoted to orderly processes and rational ideals.

In what must seem to us a remarkable instance of self-disclosure, Adams early in the book names the peculiar and unsettling condition of Randolph's personality: "His mind was always controlled by his feelings; its antipathies were stronger than its sympathy; it was restless and uneasy, prone to contradiction and attached to paradox. In such a character," continues Adams, very close to an open admission that he reads by the mirror of his own experience, "there is nothing very new, for at least nine men out of ten, whose intelligence is above the average, have felt the same instincts: the impulse to contradict is as familiar as dyspepsia or nervous excitability; the passion for referring every comparison to one's self is a primitive quality of mind by no means confined to women and children" (R 14). Such traits, Adams suggests, are as universal as they are danger-ous, and in a florid conclusion to this utterance he insinuates that the disruptiveness of John Randolph lay in conditions that discouraged him from cultivating a common, rational self-restraint: "What was to be ex-pected when such a temperament, exaggerated and unrestrained, full of self-contradictions and stimulated by acute reasoning powers . . . was planted in a Virginian, a slave-owner, a Randolph, just when the world was bursting into fire and flame?" (R 14–15). In addressing the common "impulse to contradict," Adams had begun to formulate the biography's most important, if never more than half-posed, question: How may we govern rationally and morally when the aspiring unity of our intellectual life and the fragile consistency of our moral sense are subject to the disrup-tion of personality with its inexplicably "wayward impulses" (R 222)? His easy attribution of Randolph's waywardness to the fact that he was a "Virginian, a slave-owner, a Randolph" merely suspends the larger prob-lem in a tautological explanation of Randolph as a specific case.

In view of what we know to have been Henry Adams's onerous life-long effort to run "order through chaos, direction through space, disci-pline through freedom, unity through multiplicity" (A I 731)—an effort beset, if also relieved, by his persistent love of paradox and his need to subvert the authoritative pronouncement (his own included)—the fascina-tion with Randolph's unruliness appears acutely personal.[6] Beneath the crude, if largely implied, thesis that John Randolph caused the Civil War through acts of regional narrowness and intellectual irresponsibility lies a subtler intelligence intent on tracing the formation and progress of one who never acquired the artifices by which his gifted mind might have been controlled. In Randolph, Adams creates a kind of distant, nightmarish double, an extreme version of the free-speaking, contrary self he had long projected in his letters.[7] The propinquity that he must have felt for Ran-dolph focused ever on Randolph's language, which Adams felt was admi-rable in its terse statement and brilliant illustration and its mordant analy-sis of his partisans' inconsistencies, astonishing in its fluency, and capti-vating even in its digression and error. And, accordingly, the peculiar monstrosity of Adams's Randolph is above all linguistic. Attributing to Randolph the full complement of "Virginia vices"—an appetite for bru-tality and a passion for drink—Adams reserves for particular emphasis the fact that his subject early acquired habits "of talking as freely as the utmost license of the English language would allow" (R 7).

In Adams's judgment, the Virginian's specifically literary education could not curb such habits, acquired as part of a plantation heritage in which coarse pleasure flourished beneath a squirarchical veneer of high breeding. As hedonist in his boyhood consumption of books as Adams would one day portray himself to have been, John Randolph is presented as morbidly stimulated by a library that favored the marvelous and profane over the pietistic. Pursuing a course of recriminating speculation, Adams tries Randolph by New England standards that had survived as only vague constraints upon his own intellectual development: "It is quite safe to say," writes Adams sententiously, "that . . . Randolph never learned to love two books which made the library of every New England farmhouse, where the freer literature would have been thought sinful and heathenish. If he ever read, he must have disliked the Pilgrim's Progress or the Saint's Rest" (*R* 9–10). The contrast Adams had in mind here was no doubt with the home curriculum of John and John Quincy Adams, whose exemplary, if largely mannered, Puritanism had dated before Henry's own boyhood, three generations removed from the farmhouse. Adams's own tastes likewise inclined toward the "freer literature"; he too preferred Shakespeare and kept a vivid memory of *Tom Jones*.[8] Like Randolph, Adams "read his Gibbon, Hume, and Burke" (*R* 10); criticizing the bombast of the "young Virginia school" that Randolph headed Adams could not have entirely forgotten his own and his older brother's stylistic vices, the "stilted and pseudo-Ciceronian sentences" (*R* 46) that marred the reformers' journeywork. The mortification that the young Congressman Randolph suffered after complaining indecorously to President John Adams of being jostled by two marine officers (who were offended by Randolph's public characterization of servicemen as "ragamuffins") must have touched some memory of Adams's own mortification at being lampooned in the *London Times* following the disclosure of his authorship of "A Visit to Manchester." Perhaps the parallels did not vanish entirely even with Randolph's always shocking absence of self-restraint and logical consistency, the egotism that would lead to much more than merely youthful breaches of rhetorical decorum.

The absurdity of John Randolph more fully emerges in the account of his congressional career. As a national politician, Randolph began as the fervently ideological partisan of the Jeffersonian revolution—the movement to rid the executive of "monarchical" powers, open the judiciary to processes of democratic review, and generally return the definition of federal powers to the states. In *John Randolph* as in the *History*, Adams constantly reminds his reader that the Virginia presidents, contrary to their principles, strengthened the executive and made the federal government more vigorously self-defining than it had been in the most "monarchical" moments of the first Adams presidency. Devoted abstractly to strict construction, the Republicans almost instantly made (in a phrase of Jefferson's that Adams loved to quote) "blank paper" of the Constitution in the broad assumption of powers that was necessary for the acquisition of Louisiana. Although Adams endorses the Republicans' centralization as requisite to the successful emergence of an American nationhood, he remains the acutely ironic, and often satiric, observer of the public and private language by which they reconciled themselves to policies that their doctrine defined as unconstitutional exercises of power. Caught with his colleagues in this glaring contradiction, Randolph's position was further destabilized by a tyrannical temperament and an irredeemably regional point of view—traits that caused him alternately to champion and condemn Jefferson's centralizing initiatives. For Adams, Randolph the statesman deserves study insofar as he counted as the Jeffersonian party's legislative leader and its only spellbinding orator, as well as the partisan who most maintained the regional bias of Virginia republicanism. Yet the treatment of Randolph's career returns always to the spectacle that career presents of a rational and honorable if antiquated ideology betrayed by a discourse abounding in personality and digression.

Although upon assuming the presidency Jefferson himself quickly abandoned his principles of strict construction, his actions would always be treated with comparative leniency. The executive, in Adams's view, labored under the extenuating circumstance that his office constrained him to rule, and the historian took Jefferson more seriously to task for evading the semblance of what he perforce had become—a centralizing energy in national politics. No such extenuation could exist for Randolph. Rapidly rising in congressional rank, Randolph became in 1801 chairman of the Ways and Means Committee and, with his influence over Speaker Nathaniel Macon, effective leader of the House. As House leader, his specific task was to enact legislation that reflected the principle of strict construction, a duty for which Randolph, with his bad temper and undisciplined language, was pathetically ill-suited. By Adams's account, personal animosity nearly always undid Randolph's adhesion to principle and subverted his powers of argument. Speaking in behalf of the bill to repeal the Judiciary Act of 1800, a key initial reform of the new Jeffersonian majority, Randolph squandered his "moment for laying down those broad and permanent principles which the national legislature ought in future to observe in dealing with extensions of the central power" (*R* 68) for a mere display of temper—the much easier ad hominem attack on the Federalist "pretension of rendering the Judiciary an hospital for decayed politicians" (*R* 69). Now that his party was in power, suggests Adams, Randolph shrank from the vigorous espousal "of that really great argument which alone justifies his existence or perpetuates his memory as a statesman" (*R* 68): the doctrine of limited powers, which Jefferson laid aside as chief executive and Randolph violated as a congressman attempting to diminish the powers of the judiciary.

The crowning inconsistency of the partisan who early and late proved

so violent an exponent of states' rights, limited powers, and strict construction came in 1803 with the Louisiana Purchase. As Adams shows,
Jefferson himself authorized the transaction with a troubled conscience
and urged an amendment to the Constitution to legitimize it. "Shocked to
find that his party, perverted by the possession of power," resisted this
course, "he supplicated them to listen to him: 'Our peculiar security is in
the possession of a written Constitution. Let us not make it a blank paper
by construction'" (*R* 89). Randolph, "probably the most thorough-going
states'-rights man in the republican party" (*R* 89), figures as the implied
center of this perversion. Far from objecting to the purchase on the
grounds that it gave the federal government lordship over a vast territory
and that such sovereignty must threaten the autonomy of the original
states, Randolph "advanced an astonishing argument" (*R* 90) that the
Constitution not only provided for the acquisition of territory but that the
government might acquire western lands insofar as the boundaries drawn
by the 1783 treaty were unclear. Capable on this occasion of the most
liberal rendering of the Constitution, on other occasions he could return
to the text with vengeful and bombastic literalism. Opposing the exemption from duties of imported books to be used in colleges, he spoke of the
Constitution as "a grant of limited powers," the "leading feature" of
which "was an abhorrence of exclusive privileges"; this meant that "all
duties, imposts, and excises shall be uniform throughout the United
States" (*R* 122–23). Such, Adams writes, "was strict construction run
riot," and the oxymoron justly sums up what he everywhere seeks to
establish as the intractability, the essential irrationality, of Randolph's
discourse.[9]

In reviling Randolph for the inconsistency he demonstrated in arguing the constitutionality of the Louisiana Purchase, Adams remains true to
the biography's tone. Yet a comparison of his handling of the purchase in
John Randolph with the treatment it receives in the *Gallatin* and the
History reveals that Adams was willing to sacrifice a broader and, as
concerned Randolph, more extenuating perspective to preserve his text's
rhetorical cast. In the *Gallatin*, the treasury secretary himself is identified
as the original proponent of the theory that the United States' right to
acquire territory proceeded from its treaty-making power. Although in
most cases he was a strict constructionist, we are reminded that Gallatin
was not of the "Virginia school." His Hamiltonian recommendations regarding Louisiana clearly clashed with his Republican ideology, but Adams tacitly dismisses such inconsistency in arguing his central thesis that
Gallatin's highest commitments attached to national ideals, in pursuit of
which he was always admirably willing to abandon abstract theory. Neither in the *Gallatin* nor in the *History* does Adams develop the sugges-

tion that Jefferson's party was deeply "perverted by the possession of power." Although in the *History* Randolph's Louisiana arguments are again treated with contempt, we meet them there in the larger context of congressional debate and observe his fellow Virginians rival his feats of casuistry. What matters most, in the larger text, is that the national government proved that it did have the vigor to acquire territory—a necessary step if the United States were to metamorphose into a true nation. "Whether the government at Washington could possess Louisiana as a colony or admit it as a State," Adams writes in concluding "The Louisiana Debate 1803," "was a difference of no great matter if the cession were to hold good; the essential point was that for the first time in the national history all parties agreed in admitting that the government could govern" (A II 379).

From the biographer's perspective, Randolph's easy accommodation of the Louisiana Purchase suggested the perversion, if not the bankruptcy, of his intellect as a tool of rational discourse. Not until the impeachment of Judge Samuel Chase, however, did Randolph find himself "compelled to follow a long and consecutive train of thought within the narrow bounds of logical method," and his mismanagement of the prosecution therefore exists as "the only exact test of his reasoning powers" (R 142). Randolph's failure was decided, but the Republican case in Adams's view was never very strong. Chase, an old and bitter Federalist, had attacked the doctrines of the new administration in remarks made before a grand jury, and an offended Jefferson moved House lieutenants to impeach the Maryland judge. The task, motivated politically and requiring the nicest handling of an always infirm legal substance, fell to Randolph, who proceeded to draw up an ill-considered theory of impeachment accompanied by a set of unwieldy articles. The arguments of the prosecution were easily met by Luther Martin, attorney for the defense, whom Adams portrays as a figure of "rugged and sustained force" and "elemental vigor" (R 146), qualities that he tended to attribute to intensely masculine types and expressions—Gallatin, Norman architecture, Saint Thomas Aquinas. Answering a comparatively impotent Randolph, Martin indicated "the distance between show and strength, between intellectual brightness and intellectual power" (R 145–46).[10] Routed argumentatively, Randolph's closing remarks revealed his personal discomfiture, and Adams quotes his grandfather (who would be named professor of rhetoric and oratory the next year) at length to illustrate the disintegration of Randolph's discourse: "He began a speech of about two hours and a half, with as little relation to the subject-matter as possible . . . the most hackneyed commonplaces of popular declamation, mingled up with panegyrics and invectives upon persons, with a few well-expressed ideas, a few striking figures, much distortion of face and contortion of body, tears, groans, and sobs" (*R* 148–49). A Senate dominated by Republicans proceeded to acquit Chase in the first major check of Randolph's influence.

As pathetic a figure as he is made to cut in this biography, Adams cannot deprive Randolph of his fascination, his unusual gifts, his occasional rightness, and his capacity for honor. In his opposition to the Yazoo settlement, for example, Randolph acted forthrightly upon principles Jefferson and Madison had deserted, and a regard for private ambition did not discourage him from attempting to recall the party to its doctrines. "Madman" in this as in many instances "he may have been, but his madness had a strong element of reason and truth" (*R* 110). If Randolph "raged like a maniac because his party had gone off after false leaders," it was to his credit that he "had the courage" to proclaim the hypocrisy of his colleagues and followers (*R* 126, 127). Yet the absence in Randolph's moral offensives of intelligent self-restraint induces Adams nearly always to qualify or withdraw his praise. Against Madison's promotion of legislation favoring the Yazoo claimants Randolph fought "with a courage fairly to be called heroic, had it not been to so great an extent the irrational outcome of an undisciplined and tyrannical temper" (*R* 129). Again, Adams sympathizes with Randolph's opposition to Jefferson's so-called two million policy, by which the president and secretary of state sought in closed session to procure from Congress money to purchase Florida, then a Spanish possession, from a France that held Spain at its mercy. No answer, Adams concedes, could ever be made to Randolph's objection that it was "a base prostration of the national character to excite one nation by money to bully another nation out of its property" (*R* 181), but in the biographer's view Randolph forfeited his moral advantage by his public betrayal of the secret negotiations and by his attempt to assassinate Madison politically. "His deepest passions," Adams concludes, were roused not by indignation over the "two million job," but by jealousy of Madison's influence over executive policy.

Despite the invidious character of his motives, Randolph ever remains for Adams the most fascinating of American political rhetoricians. "His method of attack," the biographer marvels, "was always the same: to spring suddenly, violently, straight at the face of his opponent"; manifesting the instinct of the frontier ruffian, "in the white heat of passionate rhetoric he could gouge and kick, bite off an ear or a nose, or hit below the waist; and he did it with astonishing quickness and persistence." A sickly man, he could nevertheless "stand on the floor of the House two or three hours at a time, day after day" and "pour out a continuous stream of vituperation in well-chosen language and with sparkling illustration" (*R* 170–71). In these and many other passages, as well as in the lengthy quotations from Randolph's speeches that make their way into *John Randolph* and the *History*, Adams fully concedes the genius of Randolph's language. Yet his fascination always returns to the paradox that Randolph's astounding oratory could embrace a multiplicity of irreconcilable assertions, and that while on occasion he could give commanding utterance to a high moral stand, his ability to impress hearers bore no necessary relation to true morality or constancy of conviction. Indeed, as Randolph grew older and ever more ravaged by alcohol, chronic jealousy of Madison and Monroe, and his unlimited capacity for malice, he became "a worse man than in his youth, but a better rhetorician" (R 290).

Of the many examples quoted, the speech that Adams in fact singles out as "Randolph's masterpiece" was one that the biographer deems "wicked and mischievous beyond all precedent even in his own mischievous career," and that he alleges to have done much "to create the dangers which it foretold" (R 276). Speaking before the House on January 31, 1824, Randolph, in the name of states' rights, rejected the latest internal improvements bill on the grounds that the power to regulate domestic trade that the measure gave to the federal government augured a steady broadening of powers that might lead to such acts as the general emancipation of slaves. In view of the usurpations that the bill must encourage, Randolph recalled his colleagues to a strict reading of the Constitution, which specifically affirmed "the power of the States to extinguish" the federal government "at a blow" (R 273). By such oratory Randolph prostituted the states' rights doctrine "to the base uses of the slave power" (R 271); but to the extent that the past assumes a literary and dramatic value with reference to the spectatorship of the historian and his partisan audience, Adams openly admires this speech that "flashes through the dull atmosphere of the time, until it leaps at last across a gap of forty years and seems to linger for a moment on the distant horizon, as though consciously to reveal the dark cloud of smoke and night in which slavery was to be suffocated" (R 272).[11] Pernicious in its motive, reasoning, and effects, the speech remained for Adams "wonderfully striking" (R 276). Randolph's rhetoric was hardly less formidable in its manipulation of the "slave-owning oligarchy." "Where," asks Adams, "among the most venomous whispers of Iago can be found an appeal to jealousy more infernal than some of those which Randolph made to his southern colleagues in the Senate?" (R 280).

Adams's likening of Randolph's gift for insinuation to that of Iago furthers the book's most important subthesis—that Randolph was our most resourceful, if also most malicious, political rhetorician. But the suggestion that he be comprehended as a type of past literature can only be meant to discourage any consideration of him as a fit participant in the orderly dialogue of a rational polity. Randolph appears not only as Iago, but also as a Virginia Quixote, Squire Western, Milton's Satan, and (in a quotation of John Quincy Adams) Ovid's picture of Envy. The proliferation of likenesses suggests how difficult it was for Adams to contain Randolph, whose monstrosity lay in the instability and contradiction of the language he employed as an absurd, but nevertheless consequent, participant in the American political dialogue. Still, Adams does succeed in reducing Randolph to one stock type, as familiar to the ancients as to the moderns but incongruous in a man who in later life masqueraded as the last true Virginia republican: that of the tyrant, whose intemperate wish is "to rule or ruin" (R 209). In the portrait of the John Randolph who "organized the South" on the doctrine that equated states' rights and slavery, and who gained a disastrous leverage at the expense of Clay and John Quincy Adams, the biographer presents what he meant to be seen as a dangerous anomaly in American politics: the demagogue who in his intoxication with power misleads a region into an exaggerated and militant sense of self-interest. The nobler example lay in the coalition of Clay and Adams, whose great regional differences were mitigated by a shared national vision. But as *Democracy* had already suggested, and as the *Education* would later confirm, the nobler example had not become the norm. If his eccentricity proved to be as singular as his eloquence, Randolph's pursuit of power for the intoxication of possessing it had become the rule.

As if to affirm the eighteenth-century assumption that humanity has the capacity for rational self-government, Adams resists, in the end, explaining Randolph's irrationality as necessarily the operation of an insane mind. Strictly abstaining from pronouncing Randolph sane or insane, Adams suggests that his subject's morbid "condition of mind" lay principally in "over-indulgence of temper and appetite," and that Randolph's peculiar hardships provided no "excuse for habitual want of self-restraint" (R 304). As though to strengthen his argument that Randolph may be held morally accountable, Adams quotes in his last sentence a rational, self-critical John Randolph who "never in his candid moments pretended to defend his errors: 'Time misspent, and faculties misemployed, and senses jaded by labor or impaired by excess, cannot be recalled'" (R 304). This core of reason supposedly subsists even in Randolph's instable and digressive utterance, a source of forced consolation, perhaps, for one who wished to affirm the purposiveness and essential rationality of literary language.

In certain regards, however, Adams, had begun to doubt seriously whether the dialogue of statesmen, rational or otherwise, much determined the direction that America had begun to take. As he explained early in *John Randolph*, "The resistless force of northern democracy lay not in its leaders or its political organization, but in its social and industrial momentum, and this was a force against which mere individuality strove in vain" (*R* 39). Here it is not impossible to detect an expression of regret; scoundrel that he was, Randolph conformed to an antiquated imaginative type. In any case, the observation looks ahead to the *History*, in which the imminent disappearance of the individual seems more and more sure, the democratic momentum counting increasingly as an ultimate and nonrational force.

Published in October 1882, *John Randolph* drew mixed reviews, its reception predictably hostile in the South.[12] But even before the book produced a critical response it had become for Adams an object of revulsion, his disgust with it far surpassing his usual ambivalence for the recently completed works of his hand. "Do you know," he wrote John Hay, "a book to me always seems a part of myself, a kind of intellectual brat . . . and I never bring one into the world without a sense of shame." Yet *John Randolph*'s difference was marked: "This particular brat is the first I ever detested" (*LHA* 2:475). Whereas he characteristically spoke of his books with a proud if deprecating advocacy, his remarks on *John Randolph* only varied with respect to the source of its repulsiveness. "To me," he wrote John T. Morse, Jr., who was evidently pleased to have *John Randolph* in his series, "it is an unpleasant book, which sins against all my art-canons. The acidity is much too decided." Perhaps Adams himself remained unconvinced that "the tone was really decided by the subject, and the excess of acid is his" (*LHA* 2:479). The dismissal, in any case, suggests how difficult it must have been for Adams to reconcile the book as "a part of myself."

John Randolph's motive enmity is in keeping with the determination to assault and provoke that characterizes much of what Adams wrote, early and late, for a contemporary audience. On a smaller scale, "Captain John Smith" was as calculated to offend as *John Randolph*. The muckraking articles aimed at deadly engagement. *Democracy* was issued as a general challenge to the complacent assumption that America had solved the problem of government and as an irritant to particular Washington personalities. Returning from the South Seas, Adams, as we have seen, proposed a collaborative, anonymous "Travels" that included among its objects the grilling of certain literary and political gentlemen; in *A Letter* he would seek to deliver a kick to the stomach of the American university. The *Education*, profoundly consensus-seeking as it is, betrays animosities and settles old scores. At no point in his long career did Adams abandon the strategy of engaging readers with a rhetoric that bullied them into choosing, or worried them into attempting to choose, sides. Yet of his many aversions none surpassed his distaste for the protracted literary furor that required an author to answer publicly for the sensation he had wrought, and few characteristics of Adams's authorship are more remarkable than his determination to create sensations and then to hold aloof from their more public consequences—through anonymous publication, private printing and circulation, or the conceit of his imminent posthumous status. His name could hardly have appeared as the biographer of John Randolph without suggesting the settling of accounts that the book indeed pursues. Adams's detestation of the book therefore must have stemmed from what he knew to be its betrayal of personality—his own in confrontation with the always personal Randolph—fusing the antagonists in the perilous discourse of the ad hominem mode. From Henry Adams the long-departed John Randolph had exacted an ironic exercise in emulation.

The Severest Process of Stating

Probably Adams had equal ambition for the contemporary as for the future reception of *The History of the United States during the Administrations of Jefferson and Madison*. Although he claimed to write "for a continent of a hundred million people fifty years hence," he also deeply desired that his achievement be recognized upon publication and that that recognition be reflected in sales. Given its nationalist thesis, Adams legitimately hoped that his magnum opus would prove acceptable as a national legacy. That the work should instantly draw a furious review entitled "A Case of Hereditary Bias" was no doubt inevitable: an Adams could hardly tell the story of the Hartford Convention without prompting critics to search for evidence of family partisanship.[13] Readers determined to detect such partisanship could find satisfaction: it may be seen in the tarnishings of Hamilton and Pickering as in the ever-present if implicit argument that Jefferson and Madison governed best when they acted from a comprehension of national imperatives that approached what Adams always represented as the genuine federalism of his presidential forebears. Yet the historian's extenuating if captious treatment of Jefferson, as well as his sympathetic, if mostly speculative, recovery of the democratic populace who chose Jefferson for their leader in 1800, gave him the right to regard his work as a triumph of what would later be called consensus history. Adams not only argued that a distinct national character had evolved, but he also implicitly appealed beyond ephemeral partisanships to that character in his readers.

No project could have been better suited to the ripening of Adams's peculiar powers. *John Randolph*, the lost *Burr*, the second novel *Esther*—all written concurrently with the *History*—demonstrate his need to maintain contact with a live readership. Yet the lengthy composition of the *History* put Adams at a healthy remove from his intense ambivalence toward questions that centered on the character and scope of his contemporary audience. As may be particularly seen in the *History*'s final pages, isolation from a responsive public eventually took its toll on Adams's authorship, but his working hypothesis of a future, receptive readership made it possible for him to shed at once what remained of his pseudo-Ciceronian, debate-society rhetoric, the luridly vindictive phrasings that belied a nervous compulsion to score points. In the *History* Adams was not distracted by the impulse to name the ills of a contemporary America, and his broad and comparatively impersonal consideration of the national past permitted him at least to dilute the hereditary feud. He struck, and largely sustained for nine volumes, a tone of serenity neither approached nor much sought after in the writings that preceded and followed. Featuring notable if innumerous dramatic moments and comprehending passages of lyric power, trenchant analysis, and satiric reduction, the *History* scrupulously abstains from a sensationalism of mere commentary, which is a gain in art that was instrumental to Adams's realization of the scientific aesthetic that lends the work much of its rhetorical distinction.

As much as its scope, length, and Olympian perspective, the ostensible science of its aim sets the *History* apart from the biographies.[14] Always more an aesthetic mode than a method with a particular object, this science in time would radically complicate what existed for Adams as the rhetorical considerations of historical writing, but by eliminating (in theory) the question of the historian's personality it simplified matters more immediately bearing on style. In the *Education*, Adams would arrive at an illuminating if exaggerated formulation of the challenge he assumed in undertaking the *History*: "Whether, by the severest process of stating, with the least possible comment, such facts as seemed sure, in such order as seemed rigorously consequent, he could fix for a familiar moment a necessary sequence of human movement" (A I 1069). Even here, where he wished particularly to emphasize the science of the task, the repetition of the verb "seem" confirms the essentially aesthetic nature of his enterprise. Ever believing that exact science sought truths that transcended the aesthetics of human discourse, he composed the *History* in the conviction that the art of what he knew to be his limited effort to emulate science could still manage to grasp "a necessary sequence." Its rhetorical objective as historiography was thus in part a function of an aesthetic of lawful relations and foreordained denouements. Suspending until nearly the last page the question of what an American readership should do with a science that "brought mankind within sight of its own end" (A III 1334), the historian strove to create the impression that he obtruded "the least possible comment" on the facts in sequence—that the recovered historical materials told their own tale with an impartiality and authority that the scientific historian modestly subserved.

"Scientific" has various meanings in its nineteenth-century application to historiography, and Adams's *History* qualified as such in at least two prevalent constructions of the term.[15] It was scientific first in its commitment to evidence: its critical assimilation of documents into a historical narrative, extracting from them "such facts as seemed sure" and arranging them in "such order as seemed rigorously consequent." This commitment had been the distinguishing feature of the "German" school associated with Leopold von Ranke, whose cautious objective had been to recover *wie es eigentlich gewesen ist*—what had actually happened—and (supposedly) no more. In his earliest work as a historian Adams had adopted the documentary method and demonstrated an attraction to Ranke's ideal; "Captain John Smith" precisely offers "what actually happened" by means of a critical evaluation of texts. The document exists as the irreducible stuff of history in "Anglo-Saxon Courts of Law" and the *Life of Albert Gallatin*, while *Documents Relating to New-England Federalism*, printed as material for a new school, counts perhaps as Adams's most extreme experiment in stating facts with the least possible comment. Although *John Randolph* sinned in particular against Adams's sense of economy—for him an art canon as well as a historiographic principle—the popularly written biography in its turn incorporated a wealth of documents. In the *History*, Adams more strictly assimilated German method to a nonacademic historical narrative. Citing statistics and immersing his readers in the striking as well as in the more routinely mediocre or "imbecile" moments of public discourse, Adams no doubt was himself convinced that the documents of themselves indicated decided sequences and that the historian's arrangements simply followed the linearities of historical process that the documents permitted the student to see.[16]

In proposing that history be understood as "a necessary sequence of human movement," however, Adams's historiography was scientific in a way that went beyond German method. Ranke and the German historians of his school wrote lengthy nationalist narratives, but in America German method was more commonly seen in the monograph or book-length study of a specific problem—the historiography of the academic historian who had been groomed in such post–Civil War graduate seminars as Adams established at Harvard in the early seventies and as Herbert Baxter Adams presided over at Johns Hopkins. Pursuing his long-standing desire to write a grand historical narrative, Adams chose to stake his reputation on the continued serviceability of a mode that he knew was past its prime. Yet in so doing he was willing to hazard an ambitious proposition: that an exhaustively documented narrative, prepared in response to a carefully framed interrogation of a brief but momentous period, could provide an illustration of historical law to which the historian could give a provisional formulation. Committing his attention to the knotty course of trial and error that characterized the "familiar moment" of the Jefferson and Madison administrations, the experiment would allow him to address the larger questions of democratic nationhood that Tocqueville and Mill had so indelibly imprinted upon his pages-to-be while the United States was dissolved in civil war. Comte and Spencer offered the conceptual strategy and particular nomenclature by which Adams could simulate and so (perhaps) actually anticipate what was for him the inevitably scientific treatment of democratic social history.[17]

The result, for author and reader, might well fall short of science; but the effort could nevertheless be scientific if, by a signal clarification of the procedures and matter of the history-to-be, it credibly projected "an epoch when man should study his own history in the same spirit and by the same methods with which he studied the formation of a crystal" (A III 1334). Submitting the *History* as part of the larger, collaborative enterprise of ascertaining the tendencies of national, and ultimately international, democratic development, Adams could acknowledge that a predictive science of history did not yet exist without really running the risk that his authority would be called into question. To be sure, his rhetoric often obscures the difference between *does not yet* and *shall presently* exist. The voice of the *History* confidently intimates not only that forces playing at the periphery of our comprehension determine human affairs and that those forces abide by laws that have only thus far resisted Newtonian statement, but also that historical prediction is in certain instances possible before the exact science has been formulated. The country's belated declaration of war in 1812 evidenced, we are told, an upsurge in popular energy that marked the beginning of a new twelve-year cycle of national vigor and centralization; on the basis of such apparent regularity "a child could calculate the result of a few more such returns" (A III 381). "With *almost* the certainty of a mathematical formula," writes Adams of the Americans in 1817, ". . . they could read in advance their economical history for at least a hundred years" (A III 1300; italics added). William Jordy suggests that Adams dangles "the proposition of large-scale prediction before his readers" only, at the end, "to snatch away the prize"; but it is probably more accurate to say that the historian was engaged in the more complicated project of preparing himself and his readers for a history that he believed in good faith would one day proceed with genuine mathematical certainty.[18] Unlike Herbert Spencer and his followers, Adams remained always aware of the provisionality of his work's claim to represent historical and metaphysical truth.

In the late nineteenth century, inquiry that represented itself as in whole or in part scientific could actually be quite unmathematical, even unempirical, and still lay claim to the prestige that attached to science. Adams's vast compilations of primary evidence, his frequent if primitive use of statistics, his insistence that his conclusions cannot be definitive until tested by the experience of a larger frame of time, sincerely mimic exact scientific method even if they do not conform to it. Behind his effort to mark distinct epochs and perceive long-term developmental trends, we may perceive the examples of Darwin and (more particularly) Lyell, whose sciences called for generalization that no more lent itself to experimental verification than did propositions concerning social development. Still, the *History* derives much of what at the time would have passed for scientific authority from its partial alignment with the tenets of force determinism, a discourse that exerted considerable hegemony over the social thought of the post–Civil War era.[19] Throughout the long narrative expressions such as "struggle for survival," "bred a new type," "energy," "inertia," and "collision of forces" invoke biology and mechanics less than Herbert Spencer's synthesis of scientific metaphor, a "philosophy" that had acquired a secure place in the curriculum of the educated American reader. Although Adams never referred to Spencer without some measure of scorn, many of his key explanatory terms may be traced to the Englishman's texts. Probably he bore some grudging half-consciousness of his debt: as Ernest Samuels has shown, Adams employs water as a metaphor for social development in ways and phrasings that are essentially plagiaristic.[20]

The self-confidence of Herbert Spencer and his followers (in America such men as John Fiske and William Graham Sumner) tended to erase the distinction between the sensation of awaiting an imminent synthesis and the conviction that it had already been achieved. Not until *A Letter*, and then mostly as a troubled rhetorical experiment, would Adams himself seriously blur that line. Far from resting complacent in the authority of his magnum opus-in-progress, Adams worried over its adequacy: his determination to innovate sharpened his awareness of his genre's conservative nature and the literary rather than mathematical character of his medium. To the degree that he seriously entertained Spencerian models of mechanistic evolution, he expressed impatience with anything falling short of an exact expression of social dynamics. "The more I write," he confessed to Francis Parkman in December 1884, his task approximately half completed, "the more confident I feel that before long a new school of history will rise which will leave us antiquated" (*LHA* 2:563). Such demoralization was the price he paid "to grapple," as the lonely Gallatin was said to have done, "with the ideas and methods of the coming generation" (*G* 635). "Democracy," he continued to Parkman, "is the only subject for scientific history. I am satisfied that the purely mechanical development of the human mind in society must appear in a great democracy so clearly, for want of disturbing elements, that in another generation psychology, physiology and history will join in proving man to have as fixed and necessary development as that of a tree; and almost as unconscious" (*LHA* 2:563).

His remarks to Parkman genuinely reflect the fear that his own efforts might become dated before they should be of much use, the fate of many an ambitious but ill-starred experimenter; yet he must have thought his own practice considerably advanced beyond the objects and methods of his older colleague. In his generous 1875 review of *The Old Regime in Canada*, Adams characterized Parkman as primarily a raconteur who "prefers to follow action rather than to meditate upon it, to relate rather than to analyze, to describe the adventures of individuals rather than the slow and complicated movements of society" (*Sk* 134). While it was the distinction of *The Old Regime in Canada* to illustrate "great and permanent principles in political science," Adams could feel no real affinity with the historian of the American forest. The burden of his own, transitional historiography was to follow *and* meditate upon, relate and analyze, a course of action; above all it was to comprehend in the adventures of conspicuous individuals clues to the increasingly rapid and complicated movements of society. Although by focusing on the shadowy formation of national character Adams quite knowingly asks his scientific historiography to elucidate what always remains a poetic construct, he rejects the romance that borders on parable by which Parkman explores the European personality's adaptation to the New World. As for Bancroft, who likewise preceded Adams in the treatment of national character, Adams's strongest wish could only have been that his own work stand in sharp contrast to the naively heroic portraiture, the effusive faith in the divine appointment of American progress that characterizes to some degree all ten volumes of the elder's *History of the United States from the Discovery of the Continent*—the first volume of which was published four years before Adams's birth, the last (concluding with the close of the War of Independence) in 1875. In a generally fault-finding notice in the *North American Review*, Adams weakly commended the last volume as manifesting "a more searching spirit of criticism than was fashionable in the days of President Jackson" (*Sk* 151).

If the *History* was never intended as a definitive model for the coming generation, its structure manifests the good faith of Adams's scientific aesthetic. Taking as his hypothesis the proposition that between 1800 and 1815 American character evolved as a distinctly national type, Adams fashions an expository framework by which to establish and pursue distinct lines of transformation. A six-chapter prologue delineates the physical, intellectual, and spiritual conditions of the country in 1800. Drawing upon census figures, travelers' reports, and the newspaper and literature of the day, the historian samples the diverse circumstances, folkways, types of mind, and inarticulate but active idealism from which the experience of the next fifteen years would breed a "new man." A four-chapter epilogue measures progress along these preestablished lines and suggests probable future developments. Between the first six and last four chapters, which comprise Adams's treatment of the complicated movements of American society as a whole, stretch 143 chapters of what is essentially political, diplomatic, and military history, with special attention to the details of constitutional and economic development. The representatives of a sanguine people, Jefferson, Madison, and Gallatin are brought before the reader, and the ironic course of their republican experiment unfolds: the centralization of power in the interest of territorial acquisition; the economic success of the first term, which inspired visionary, further centralizing schemes for internal improvement; the failure to hold aloof from European conflict and the fiasco of pacific resistance; and the war ineptly waged but effectively won by the ability of individual Americans to rally at the few critical military and diplomatic moments when the nation's fate hung in the balance.

In telling this story Adams continues to tread the paths of traditional narrative historiography, treating such men as Jefferson and Napoléon not merely as the types of a larger, "racial" character—a feature of the scientific aesthetic—but as individual personalities whose actions admit of moral analysis. What scientific knowledge the reader stands to gain from the moral analysis of history is one of the major unresolved problems of Adams's magnum opus: Adams seems to wish us to infer that although a people cannot prosper long if its ways are corrupt, it does not necessarily follow that a high individual moral example is a source of power. Here paradox flourished. Morally weak, Jefferson is depicted as disingenuous but not dishonest: his character remains always pure. Napoléon, the epitome of the evil tyrant, for a time forces Old and New World alike to accommodate his whims. Both are portrayed as indifferently "borne away by the stream" in the company of all other men of state, the whole cast of subalterns on either side during the great revolutionary period of the West, "each blind to everything but a selfish interest, and all helping more or less unconsciously to reach the new level which society was obliged to seek" (A II 1135). In the *History*, Adams's irrepressible moral analysis is kept subordinate to what with increasing insistence becomes the work's official interest: the comprehension of American and democratic history as a mechanical evolution. Initially through the triumphs of their leaders and afterward through their leaders' reverses, ignominy, and exhaustion, the American people in the *History* take on character as a commercially resiliant, patriotic, and scientific, if not particularly thoughtful, race, whose economic destiny is for the time being overwhelmingly favored by their youthful vigor and rich continent.

Affirming the American national character as a successfully evolved type, Adams in the end generally avoids celebratory rhetoric. In his final realization of the *History*'s scientific aesthetic, he strives to achieve a nearly absolute detachment that places his historiographic mode no less than his argument in abeyance. As the story of a democratic society's evolution, American history must become the exclusive domain of a scientific historical inquiry, which is itself evolving. Such science must make what it can of the practical aptitudes and moral ambiguities of the national character. In concluding, Adams defers to the coming generation not only the question of where American development must lead materially and morally, but also the question of how the historian should plot its movements and whether the deciding of that question will abrogate or affirm a moral comprehension of the subject. It is thus that Adams suspends what has been his problem all along: his practical inability to treat human history as the amoral, dehumanized force field it is required to be by the inquiry he prophesies but never practices.

"The scientific interest of American history," Adams writes in the concluding chapter, "centred in national character, and in the workings of a society destined to become vast, in which individuals were important chiefly as types" (A III 1332). It was the evident homogeneity of this character and its prospect of "undisturbed growth" in America that gave history its scientific chance. From the standpoint of historians and their readers, Adams acknowledges, this chance could have none of the traditional aesthetic enticements that had given Old World historiography its brilliance and had earned for such writers as Gibbon and Macaulay—and such patrician American historians as had written in the old heroic tradition—a general and at times popular readership. If "the complicated story of rival European nationalities" must always prove intractable to science, it had "movement and color" that commended it nevertheless to poetic and dramatic treatment. The cynosure of Old World historiography had been the hero, the great man who typically emerged from military conflict and who "deserved more to be studied than the community to which he belonged; in truth, he was the society, which existed only to produce him and to perish with him" (A III 1333). The new subject of historical study, "the economical evolution of a great democracy," must prove far more answerable to scientific inquiry but seemed unlikely to inspire a historiography of high artistic merit; work in this field must very soon fall outside the established standards of historians and their audiences. This development was not necessarily unhappy. Despite their great stock of action and pageantry, few Old World historians had "succeeded in enlivening or dignifying the lack of motive, intelligence, and morality, the helplessness characteristic of many long periods in the face of crushing problems, and the futility of human efforts to escape from difficulties religious, political, and social" (A III 1333). The scientific historian might possess none of the aesthetic and (hence) rhetorical advantages of his nonscientific precursors, but he was not likely to share their embarrassment over a history that took few if any redemptive turns.

Adams of course had not himself achieved that scientific freedom from embarrassment, and although he had just completed a long chapter in the history of a people who had escaped from Old World difficulties precisely of a religious, political, and social nature, he could hardly be sure that some larger futility did not await the American people in the midst of their material contentment. It remained doubtful whether he had "succeeded in enlivening or dignifying the lack of motive, intelligence, and morality" that he portrayed as besetting the Jeffersonian experiment beyond its initial success, and he had felt his efforts stultified in particular by the "helplessness" ("inertia," "imbecility") characteristic of government during almost the entire Madison administration. The truly scientific historian, availing himself of "the severest process of stating," might hope perhaps to absolve himself of such considerations, but as one who had aimed to impress a moral on the public mind (skeptical as he had been of that mind's receptivity) Adams had been required to accommodate a condition at once moral and rhetorical. "To scientific treatment only one great obstacle existed," he affirms, and it is significant that this obstacle has nothing to do with what for Adams was the problematic threshold that divided a literary from a mathematical historiography. The problem was that "Americans, like Europeans, were not disposed to make of their history a mechanical evolution." Indeed their need as readers for the "heroic element" surpassed that of readers in the Old World inasmuch as Americans "breathed an atmosphere of peace and industry where heroism could seldom be displayed." Rarely did their leaders achieve true heroism or possess any merit beyond the "faculty of reflecting a popular trait"; but the people could hardly be expected to espouse a history of the commonplace that science offered to reduce to laws and processes scarcely recognizable as human. "Instinctively they clung to ancient history as though conscious that of all misfortunes that could befall the national character,

the greatest would be the loss of the established ideals which alone enno-
bled human weakness. Without heroes, the national character of the
United States had few charms of imagination even to Americans" (A III
1334).

Protoscientific as he had hoped the *History* to be, Adams had undertaken the work not merely to enliven and dignify such perennial human
weakness as had taken distinctive American shape, but to argue if possible
that motive, intelligence, even morality had been reborn in the character
of the typical American. Only the ghost of this argument appears in the
History's concluding pages: compared to his European rival the American
is pronounced the superior economist as well as more skilled in the arts of
war; average American intelligence and morality are said to surpass Old
World standards, although a higher morality than had been attained as of
1815 was not to be expected. The American was a "new variety" and
could not possibly revert to European social and political models; indeed,
an irresistibly democratizing Europe must ultimately adopt American
ways. America offered a contrast to Europe, but instead of presenting that
contrast as a sharp exception to European experience, Adams requires
that we think of it as an evolution from a common past leading to a
common future. Beneath its often brilliant surface, Old World history may
have principally concerned an absence of motive, intelligence, and morality, but what Adams identifies as the scientific, industrious, homoge-
nous, uncritical, and materialist nature of the American character scarcely
projects a redemptive outcome to the democratic phase of human society.
Insofar as the history of the American people offered itself (although
against that people's preference) as a mechanical evolution, the worst misfortune, "the loss of established ideals," had perhaps befallen the national
character; if not lost to isolated memory, those ideals had proven irrelevant to the overwhelmingly unconscious course of American social development—a development that had failed more egregiously to bring forth
high and uniquely American ideals from the national mind's unusual and
enabling capacity for illusion.

The historian of the epilogue thus speaks as a detached and almost
apathetic observer of a mass and minimally self-conscious social movement, the question of national character subordinated to questions pertaining to the social mechanics of "mankind" brought "within sight of its
own end" (A III 1334). Without the insistence that is to characterize the
Education, the concluding paragraphs nonetheless register what has been
called the nineteenth-century "crisis of historicism"—the recognition that
history entails change without necessary progress, that it is not self-evidently, much less optimistically, teleological. Although the stylistic constraints that govern all nine volumes of the *History* tend to disguise the

historian's change of heart in the course of its ten-year composition, at the end the tone differs markedly from that with which Adams had opened his inquiry into national character.

In his initial treatment of the subject of national character, the idea that society evolves in a manner comparable to the growth of a crystal is remote indeed. At the outset the historian approaches the nation's mental life as at best inchoate and only partially self-conscious, but nevertheless as a force to be considered formidable and mysterious. "The growth of character, social and national,—the formation of men's minds,—more interesting than any territorial or industrial growth, defied the tests of censuses and surveys" (A II 31). So Adams writes at the commencement of his second chapter, "Popular Characteristics," which follows the first, "Physical and Economical Conditions," by examining the diet, conversation, amusements, incentives, and aptitudes of the common people, the human presence that was the true source of the astonishing fifteen-year national transformation. Far from depicting American society as a mechanical system, the historian works in these opening chapters to recover the distinctly human expressions of an obscure populace, drawing (for lack of other evidence) on the comic anecdotes that enliven the generally dour and dismissive reports that European and New England travelers filed of American life.

Incorporating throughout the first six chapters the accounts of hostile and conservative witness, Adams assumes with increasing vigor the role of advocate, speaking in behalf of a people who were supposedly unable to speak for themselves, positing an ideal that he can represent as the reality belied by appearances. Against allegations that Americans volubly and impertinently questioned strangers, the historian avers that they "were never loquacious, but inclined to be somewhat reserved" (A II 41); against reports of widespread idleness he counters that "the *true* American was active and industrious" (A II 42; italics added). Adams's advocacy does not minimize those attributes of the people that endangered the success of their political experiment, which involved no less than "embracing half a continent in one republican system" (A II 52); clearly his strategy is to insist upon the backward elements over which the progressive, nationalizing spirit must triumph. Although the country stood in need of technologies to facilitate interregional communication, a "popular inertia" of conservative suspicion resisted the value of science. Higher education must languish until the mass of Americans became "satisfied that knowledge was money" (A II 53). The peculiarities and jealousies of regional thought did the most to obstruct national progress. Neither the southern slaveholding planter class, which preserved as it could the oligarchy of its colonial phase, nor the New England conservative elite with its residuum of theocratic preference exhibited what Adams calls the tendency "to become American in thought or feeling" (A II 62). The thought and feeling of America was emphatically democratic, and with the understatement that is to characterize his moral analysis throughout the nine volumes, Adams encourages a proper contempt of the conservative reaction—the self-appointed "wise and good" who "urged the use of force as the protection of wisdom and virtue" (A II 60), or the able man who bounded his influence by mere prejudice, as exemplified by an Alexander Hamilton who wasted his brilliance in shaping a memorable slur: "Your people, sir,—your people is a great *beast*!" (A II 61).

Skeptical of democratic government as Adams had always been and would continue to be and dismissive as his narrative would often prove when it came to the details of Jefferson's experiment, Adams opens the *History* with explicit affirmation of the American's divergence from the past, a divergence that his rhetoric presents as a human evolution much more than a mechanical one. Alternately comic and heroic, the human image dominates. In "American Ideals," the last and most affirmative of the prologue chapters, the historian endows his "true American" with an ideality that would seem to reproach pointedly the common, conservative virulence that Hamilton compressed into his famous epigram. "Stripped for the hardest work, every muscle firm and elastic, every ounce of brain ready for use, and not a trace of superfluous flesh on his nervous and supple body, the American stood in the world a new order of man" (A II 109). The image is emphatically physical, the portrait clearly meant to convey a notion of the American's animal virtue. So Adams commends to his reader a figure who not only has a wilderness to clear but who stands "in the world" prepared to compete in the international struggle for survival. The American must prove himself physically as a species. But although "every ounce of brain" be harnessed to outwardly material tasks, the historian in these early chapters develops the idea that the "energy" for such tasks was generated by the least material realms of the popular mind.

Again and again Adams insists that the obstacles to be overcome were of a moral and intellectual rather than of a physical nature, and that while the population divided more or less consciously into ideological camps, a conservative "inertia" remained common to all, limiting the range of even the most active-minded. "Radicals as extreme as Thomas Jefferson and Albert Gallatin," writes Adams, "were contented with avowing no higher aim than that America should reproduce the simpler forms of European republican society without European vices, and even this their opponents thought visionary" (A II 52). Yet the change in direction that American society already manifested (at least to the retrospection of the 1880s) was fabulous beyond the democratic prophets' telling. The New England Federalist and South Carolina planter naturally resisted the innovative trends, but the "true American" claimed by the enterprise of the rich land was himself scarcely prepared to appreciate their full force. Even in the waning hours of the eighteenth century, for most of the population "conservatism possessed the world by right. Experience forced on men's minds the conviction that what had ever been must ever be" (A II 52). The force of experience could be broken only by a force proceeding from the contrary conviction that the past need not be repeated; and in the first six chapters Adams suggests the slow but certain course by which this conviction possessed the American mind—a mind that often clung needlessly to conservative expectations.

National character, in short, was to be traced to the *re*formation "of men's minds" in the conviction that average citizens could direct the course of their lives and make that course answer to personal and public desires. Such reformation had required an act of the imagination, some deep recognition on the immigrant's part that in the New World he met a novel and necessary phase of human experience. For the mass of American democrats, Adams suggests, an imaginative if imperfect grasp of the New World's possibilities was intuitive and instantaneous upon first contact; even conservative observers confirmed that something in America effectively "turned the European peasant into a new man within half an hour after landing at New York" (A II 115). According to individual capacity, such recognition led to specific perceptions of material and moral opportunities; but the apparent nature of the citizenry's immediate objects of desire counts less for Adams than the mentality by which they were pursued. Yet evidence of that mentality—that deeply transformative state of mind—did not offer itself to direct scrutiny. In a three-chapter survey of the American intellect ("Intellect of New England," "The Middle States," "The Southern States"), the historian succeeds only in assembling expressions of a colonial nature—which if not British were only regionally American—and so proves unable to account for what he is determined to read as a renovating consensus activity. Having established from the first that ultimate interest must attach to the American democrat's mind—a mind that had not yet left its stamp on the regional literary intellect—Adams reserves for "American Ideals," the sixth and culminating prologue chapter, sustained inquiry into this central datum of America's growth into actual nationhood.

He had good reason for postponing sustained inquiry into the democrat's mind, for when it came to this subject the historian had found little but circumstantial evidence. Evidence for Adams consisted preeminently in the primary text, the language of direct participation in an event; scrupulous to avoid the appearance of a merely invented history, he advances his narrative by means of a critical assimilation of documents, ever attentive to the disingenuities of private and public discourse.[21] The attempt to arrive at the animated germ of national character met therefore with a serious difficulty. "The American democrat possessed little art of expression, and did not watch his own emotions with a view of uttering them either in prose or verse; he never told more of himself than the world might have assumed without listening to him." The writing of history out of the language of primary texts is a hermeneutic, poetic, rhetorical activity in which invention plays a large if concealable role; but for Adams, the document certifies that his practice is scientific, and its absence here gives him pause. "Only with diffidence could history attribute to such a class of men a wider range of thought or feeling than they themselves cared to proclaim. Yet the difficulty of denying or even ignoring the wider range was still greater, for no one questioned the force or the scope of an emotion which caused the poorest peasant in Europe to see what was invisible to poet and philosopher,—the dim outline of a mountain-summit across the ocean, rising high above the mist and mud of American democracy" (A II 116). History, Adams tells us, must in this case proceed with its attributions—"national character" after all is his key object of inquiry; but there is nothing diffident in his assertion of what the poorest peasant saw or in his pronouncement that "no one questioned the force or the scope" of the emotion that gave rise to such a sight. Although he hedges his intuitions with cautions and expresses them in ventriloquy, Adams commits himself in "American Ideals" to inventing the inner life and language of the typical American democrat.

The reader, moreover, can hardly fail to perceive the extent to which Adams invents that life and language against the rhetoric of conservative opposition—the travelers' reports and satiric verse, the Federalist jeremiad and European ridicule that insisted upon the democrat's meanness even as they betrayed fear of his social force. The most articulate language of the day, Adams argues, was anything but sympathetic to the program and poetry of the American democrat. And Adams discovered no more forceful illustration of his argument than a passage from *The Excursion* in which Wordsworth, "although then at his prime" according to Adams, utterly misprizes the excitements of the American immigrant; the poet in many respects most equipped to understand the transformative experience of landing in the New World "could do no better, when he stood in the face of American democracy, than 'keep the secret of a poignant scorn'" (A II 116). Affirming that American idealism amounted to no more than "high pretentions"—"big passions strutting on a petty stage"—Wordsworth joined Adams's company of conservative critics who could see in the American only an example of avarice compounded by anarchism. "With equal reason," Adams writes, the poet "might have taken the opposite view,—that the hard, practical, money-getting American democrat, who had neither generosity nor honor nor imagination, and who inhabited cold shades where fancy sickened and where genius died, was in truth living in a world of dream, and acting a drama more instinct with poetry than all the avatars of the East, walking in gardens of emerald and rubies, in ambition already ruling the world and guiding Nature with a kinder and wiser hand than had ever yet been felt in human history" (A II 117–18). What begins in "American Ideals" as the historian's lack of textual evidence with respect to the democrat's mental life becomes through Adams's interpolations a great poet's missed opportunity.

Making strategic use of contrast, a well-established convention of (to quote Madeleine Lee) "that humour which is the staple product of our country" (A I 25), Adams finally lets his fictive democrat speak for himself; the context is the traditionally comic colloquy between John and Jonathan, Old and New Worlds. " 'Look at my wealth!' cried the American to his foreign visitor. 'See these solid mountains of salt and iron, of lead, copper, silver, and gold! See these magnificent cities scattered broadcast to the Pacific! See my cornfields rustling and waving in the summer breeze from ocean to ocean. . . . Look at this continent of mine, fairest of created worlds, as she lies turning up to the sun's never-failing caress her broad and exuberant breasts, overflowing with milk for her hundred million children! See how she glows with youth, health, and love!' " It was the boast of a mind that lived wholly in the future, and the foreigner, Adams concedes, could hardly be blamed if he persisted in seeing only primitive conditions and rude signs of life and so dismissed the American democrat as "a liar and swindler" (A II 118). Yet with the rapid progress of the intervening years solidly in view, the historian fairly exalts the creative power of that illusion which he takes to have been the people's accustomed mental atmosphere. "Whether imagination or greed led them to describe more than actually existed, they still saw no more than any inventor or discoverer must have seen in order to give him the energy of success" (A II 119). Here, as later in *Mont Saint Michel and Chartres*, Adams shows that he understands the material consequences of certain forms of idealism as deeply as William James.

In no other instance, without or within the *History*, would Adams so affirm the national character, so celebrate an American people. The squatter with his continental utopian vision spoke from what the historian presents as consensual if inarticulate ideals. Adams asserts on the unsentimental authority of the European traveler that nearly "every American, from Jefferson and Gallatin down to the poorest squatter, seemed to nourish an idea that he was doing what he could to overthrow the tyranny which the past had fastened on the human mind" (A II 119–20). Much of the power—one might even call it the grandeur—of Adams's affirmation stems from his depiction of the essential reasonableness and cogency of the disbelieving conservative perspective. If the European and the Federalist dismissed the democrat in slurs and satire, human experience, which is to say *history*, justified their resistance to the protestations of democratic ideology; yet mere knowledge of precedent left them blind to what Adams represents as the heroic energy of the democrat's faith. "Nothing was easier than to laugh at the ludicrous expressions of this simple-minded conviction, or to cry out against its coarseness, or grow angry with its prejudices; to see its nobler side, to feel the beatings of a heart underneath the sordid surface of a gross humanity, was not so easy" (A II 120). The author of the *Gallatin* and *Democracy* had himself demonstrated the difficulties of that task; by registering the ways in which "American Ideals" attempts at least to suspend the skepticism of the earlier texts we see far into the *History*'s ambition and rhetorical life.

The historian who would have us feel the beating of the Jeffersonian democrat's heart had in the *Gallatin* expressed horror at the "frightful chaos" (G 632) of Jacksonian democracy and scorn for the attitude that little could be learned from Old World experience. That scorn reappears in *Democracy* through the interchange between Ratcliffe and Baron Jacobi, while through Madeleine the novelist proposes that "nine out of ten" (A I 184) of his Grant-era countrymen should fail to perceive the scruple by which his heroine refused celebrity and power. Common to both the *Gallatin* and *Democracy* is the elegiac suggestion that honor and virtue once characterized the American people, and that the democratic leader and his populace once united in the good faith of their republican ideals. While both works leave open the possibility that America will recover its moral opportunity and realign government with the "healthy ocean current of honest purpose" (A I 98) that ideally animated democratic society, the spectacle of a government corrupted by the tyranny of party managers, whose actions remained on the whole too invisible to call to public account, makes such renewal doubtful. The virtue of a people who cannot make their virtue felt becomes the central object of doubt: Adams, in *Democracy*, projects the contemporary citizenry as cowed into a "droll aping of monarchical forms" before the "mechanical action" (A I 4–5, 44) of a presidential reception and offers Ratcliffe as the product of popular social conditions. Beneath Ratcliffe's mouthing of democratic ideals we can see little more than the sordid depths of a gross humanity. The historian Gore may commend democracy as the only experiment currently worth making, but the society that the novelist portrays is one that, from an idealist's point of view, has lost its generative capacities. Sincerely baffled as to the moral tone of contemporary American society, Adams had hoped to learn something decisive about that tone from the response his accusations might draw.

The Adams of "American Ideals," on the other hand, suspends his concern with the always ongoing battle between corruption and reform in order to argue that (in the long view) a peculiarly American character founded in a powerful if (again) inarticulate idealism had sprung to vigorous life despite the efforts of conservatives—the best-informed and most literarily resourceful among them—to gainsay it. The fact that in many respects the United States stood as a fait accompli as he wrote in the 1880s, a prosperous nation that had survived civil war to embrace a continental empire, momentarily freed his affirmation from the more routine cautions of scientific assertion, allowing it to assume the tone of magisterial eloquence required to answer the doubt, past and present, of his anti-American Federalist and European interlocutors that the American democrat had made a great nation. Never again would Adams project so magnificent an image of American society: a people united "from Jefferson and Gallatin down to the poorest squatter" in a common purpose—the liberation of human energy, preeminently inventive in nature, from artificial barriers. Adams represents this purpose as so consensual, and he is so intent to establish American society as a unity beyond the multitude of differences of party and region, that he even cites John Adams (although not by name) as part of the movement that expressed itself above all in the election of Jefferson over the Federalist incumbent: in 1800, "the actual President of the United States, who signed with Franklin the treaty of peace with Great Britain, was the son of a small farmer, and had himself kept a school in his youth" (A II 123). The nation's advent was to be traced to the signature of men of obscure origin, and the historian enlists his own genealogy in arguing that national character derived from a people's emancipated potential.[22]

Again and again Adams observes that nothing in the historical record entirely articulates the mentality that conservatives so obviously feared, no single source comes close to verbalizing the genius proclaimed by the nation's material achievement. From the standpoint of the historian scrupulous of documentation, "nothing was more elusive than the spirit of American democracy. Jefferson, the literary representative of the class, spoke chiefly for Virginians, and dreaded so greatly his own reputation as a visionary that he seldom or never uttered his whole thought. Gallatin and Madison were still more cautious. The press in no country could give shape to a mental condition so shadowy. The people themselves, although millions in number, could not have expressed their finer instincts had they tried, and might not have recognized them if expressed by others" (A II 120–21). With a sympathy of statement that never completely relinquishes the hypothetical tone, and with a concern for representing the conservative reaction in its reasoned assessment as well as in its hysterical flight, Adams works in "American Ideals" to give that mental condition shape and to express as he can the people's finer instincts. Given Adams's belief in the supreme importance of national character, he would certainly have thought himself justified in inventing the text that could otherwise not exist, availing himself of the poesis of historical discourse to fill the lacunae in the documents. No doubt Adams was convinced that such lacunae did exist, yet we are bound to note that the inadequacy of the democrat's expression is an assertion (an invention) rather than a fact and of strategic importance to Adams's authorial ambition. By claiming that the elusive spirit of American democracy has never arrived at its proper statement, Adams reserves for himself the opportunity to create its text. And in so doing, he proceeds to formulate its ideals in terms of his own generation's need and make good his wish to enliven and dignify past and present in a generative vision of history—one that retains the American future as guarantor of the millennial meaningfulness that Adams (in good company) assumed to inhere in American experience.

From the post–Civil War historian's perspective, the Jeffersonian democrat could exist only as a remote and comparatively alien creature. Adams can dress that abstraction and make it speak; he can sincerely celebrate what he reads as the popular idealism that motivated a people to fight a war for little besides national dignity and marvel over the technological genius of Americans in common circumstances—men like John Fitch, Oliver Evans, and Robert Fulton, who labored without the advantage of education or capital. Yet Adams more precisely approaches those activities with sympathy as they reflect the sanguine expectations of Jefferson and Gallatin. The rhetoric of Adams's peroration to "American Ideals" fuses enterprising democrat and visionary philosopher in one common progressive purpose; with an eye to the raw activities of 1800 the historian asks (as it were) of the anxiously skeptical conservative of the day questions that could well serve to recall the resource of the American past to present (1880s) and future readerships. "Who would undertake to say that there was a limit to the fecundity of this teeming source? Who that saw only the narrow, practical, money-getting nature" of the American democrat's inventions—the steamboats, wooden clocks, and miscellaneous industrial processes—"could venture to assert that as they wrought their end and raised the standard of millions, they would not also raise the creative power of those millions to a higher plane?" (A II 124).

Adams's attempt to name the features of that higher plane marks a major moment in his career as a self-conscious and indeed programmatic American author. In the *Gallatin* he had written with clear admiration of the democratic intelligentsia's vision and had lauded in particular the effort of Jefferson and Gallatin to secure for the United States the economical progress and internal improvements that could support a philosophic national aspiration. The "insolence of foreign dictation" (*G* 266) had figured in the *Gallatin* as the catastrophic end to all but a remote possibility of a high American civilization. In the penultimate paragraph of "American Ideals," however, Adams asserts with much greater decision the supposed content of that vision—he writes, in fact, as though he can read their vision more clearly than Jefferson and Gallatin ever could. And in the process of essentially creating the text of the democratic intelligentsia's ultimate ambitions, he formulates what he thought to be the proper agenda of his own, and indeed many succeeding, generations. "The American democrat," writes Adams,

> knew so little of art that among his popular illusions he could
> not then nourish artistic ambition; but leaders like Jefferson,
> Gallatin, and Barlow might without extravagance count upon a
> coming time when diffused ease and education should bring the
> masses into familiar contact with higher forms of human
> achievement, and their vast creative power, turned toward a no-
> bler culture, might rise to the level of that democratic genius
> which found expression in the Parthenon; might revel in the de-
> lights of a new Buonarotti [*sic*] and a richer Titian; might create
> for five hundred million people the America of thought and art
> which alone could satisfy their omnivorous ambition. (A II 125)

Certainly no work of the *History*'s theme and magnitude could mention an "America of thought and art" without offering itself as a contribution to that order's realization.

Yet the chapter does not end before the actual prospective attainment of that order has become subject to doubt. The historian tells us that whether or not the "illusions" that animated democratic society took the forms he has represented them as having taken, certain problems "lay before American society," the solution of which "was necessary for its complete success." Success in some areas seemed reasonably assured. Adams's first readers could feel confident that the country had taken "permanent political shape," and that in America one already met in the mass of citizens "those habits of mind which had hitherto belonged to men of science alone." Such accomplishments figured among those with which Adams would credit the seventeen years of his purview. Other problems were more obviously open-ended, and Adams lay them before the contemporary and future society that he meant the *History* to address: Could that society "transmute its social power into the higher forms of thought? Could it provide for the moral and intellectual needs of mankind?" More ambitious still: "Could it physically develop the convolutions of the human brain? Could it produce, or was it compatible with, the differentiation of a higher variety of the human race?" (A II 125). The relentless idealism of such phrasings seems directed at measuring the degrees of America's probable lack of success, if not indeed its complete failure. If, in "American Ideals," the historian allows his poesis to uphold the Jeffersonian prophecy, he draws back in the final paragraph to suggest the tragic limitations to such ambition as he too would espouse.

The grandly affirmative, sympathetic rhetoric of "American Ideals" concludes thus in studied ambiguity—its prophetic (re)statement of the American ambition complicated by a memorandum of requisite accomplishments that sets as high as possible the measure of national attainment. To the degree that we read that measure as impossibly high, Adams's affirmation of the democrat's cause reappears in a distinctly ironic light, less as prophecy than as prelude to elegy, an establishment of the scale by which an inevitable disappointment may be gauged. Did Adams, at the very threshold of his narrative proper, mean to suggest that Jefferson's experiment and the "omnivorous ambition" that he gladly attributed to the democratic intelligentsia must inevitably fail? He had of course been over the ground of the Jefferson and Madison administrations twice before and in the *Gallatin* specifically argued that the treasury secretary's realization that the country could not hold aloof from international conflict had set a boundary to the period of republican idealism. But the *History* is a much different work, not simply more indulgent of Jefferson but proceeding from a determination to regard the people who had expressed themselves in his election as the ultimate moral focus of American development. To be sure, in writing the *History* Adams discovered qualities in Jefferson that even an exhaustive account of his failings supposedly could not tarnish, and it was always through Jefferson and Gallatin (if also the likewise philosophic John Adams) that Adams approached the anonymous American democrat. His official subject, however, is the people—more abstractly, the national character: a "force" that sustained no necessary or lasting injury in the mortifications of the federal government and that in the final pages is reaffirmed as "a new variety of man" (A III 1332).

Compared to the warmth of "American Ideals," the tone of the last pages is apathetic, the human image of the American democrat displaced by the mechanical image of a democratic ocean. The narrative of the Jefferson and Madison administrations consists of a brief, brilliant success followed by a sequence of political blunders and military misadventures from which the nation emerged intact mostly because the new social inertia worked in its favor. The visionary aura of 1800 has evidently dissipated in the overwhelmingly commercial project of early nineteenth-century America, and Adams plainly suggests the degradation of the American possibility; still, we should resist readings of the *History* that would make it a "final" demonstration of the necessary failure of American idealism.[23] Certainly by the last volume there is so little in the assembled record to support the prospect of an "America of thought and art" that Adams makes no mention of it and indeed would appear to suppress, in the final chapter, any possible resonance of the phrase; but we fail to perceive the *History*'s complicated and contradictory rhetorical life by asking it to conform to a unitary intention. The portents of its final paragraph notwithstanding, "American Ideals" projected cultural goals that, as Adams claimed in his November 25, 1877, letter to Gaskell, he had moved to Washington a second time to promote; at least in the early stages of composition he could only hope that the *History* would sustain progress toward "the coming day" when America would "be saying in its turn the last word of civilisation" (*LHA* 2:326). Yet in its writing the text took difficult if not wholly unanticipated turns, and Adams would never be able to reduce a difficulty that he perhaps only partially recognized: the problematic nature of a history that proposed to speak meaningfully (though hardly definitively) to a future society that would itself be the test of whether American experience was inherently redeeming.

For Adams, the one American history worth writing began with the transformation of the European commoner into an enterprising American, a transformation that he explains as having come of an imaginative response to the material fecundity of the New World. Recovery of the shadowy genesis of national identity required an act of imagination on the part of the historian, an exercise of what in *Mont Saint Michel and Chartres* he would call *sympathy*; in "American Ideals," Adams participates in what he takes to have been the democrat's imagination to the remarkable extent of inventing the text of its illusions and dreams. The science of the ensuing narrative purports to measure progress toward the realization of the moral and material potential whose formulation the historian had been constrained to arrive at imaginatively; but inasmuch as Adams, unlike the Lyell of his 1868 review, regarded the imagination as an instrument necessary to scientific inquiry (or at least inquiry of a nonmathematical nature), his method harbored no serious contradiction and he remained free to draw upon the pure poesis of his discourse. What is problematic in the

History has another source. In "American Ideals" Adams participates in the rhetoric of the American prospect, offering a text that sought to account for the future not only as it may have appeared in 1800 to a sanguine democratic intelligentsia, but also as it still appeared, circa 1882, to one who belonged (quoting again from the November 1877 letter to Gaskell) "to the class of people who have great faith in this country" (*LHA* 2:326). Such rhetoric was integral to the idea of national identity that Adams undertook to test and accordingly reappraise in his magnum opus and that served in the first place as the rationale for undertaking a grand narrative with a view to instructing present and future national readerships. But the common rhetoric of historical writing resisted acknowledging the radical novelty, the breadth of cultural invention, that Adams read into Jeffersonian democracy in the work's opening. Beyond "American Ideals," he was almost bound by the rigors of his discourse to assume a methodological hostility toward the claims of the Jeffersonian democrat, which meant courting a troubled relation with the very rhetorical premise on which the work was based—that the *History* has something essential to contribute to the moral consciousness of an emerging civilization.

To some degree Adams embraced this problem knowingly. In "American Ideals" he had established with decided relish the embarrassing limitations of mere historical wisdom. Again and again the inarticulate, prospective vision of the American democrat is represented as having been erroneously set at naught by the murderously articulate, retrospective knowledge of the Federalist and the European observer. But although the *History*'s superior retrospection vindicates much of the democrat's claim at more than half a century's remove, its voice, like those of the Federalists and Europeans it scorns, remains nonetheless a voice of experience, conservative in the expectations it will actually warrant if not on principle opposed to prophecy. Adams's interest in approximating scientific prediction reinforces the caution that he required, at least at this point, of historical discourse. Although in later life he would forecast on the premise that history moves catastrophically from phase to phase, in the *History* his predictive gestures rest on the assumption that, beyond the national character's initial coming-of-age in 1815, the United States conforms to patterns of uniformitarian evolution, the future to be read by a past that science is learning to illuminate. The Civil War, in this view, counts as a period of violent adjustment; likewise the uprisings of the Dos de Maio, the revolutions of 1848, and the convulsions that followed mark the progress of European society toward that state of equilibrium that the society of the New World is to reach first.

Nowhere in the *History* does Adams explicitly face up to what his narrative suggests to have been the catastrophic if invisible moral diminution of the American populace. No doubt this change has much more to do with the text's growing skepticism of the democratic subject than with any historical mutation of the subject per se, but it nevertheless leads by the work's end to a significant lowering of expectations regarding democratic civilization in America. Yet what possible confirmation of a prospective America of thought and art could Adams have in any case hoped to win from the era of Jefferson and Madison? No one knew better than he the paradox and failure, the incompetence and cowardice, that characterized that era's political history. Ideals of strict statecraft fared badly from the start. Most of Jefferson's first-term domestic success could be traced to his party's centralization of power in flagrant contradiction of its avowed principles. Internationally, although the third president stood as a symbol of hope in the reactionary climate of the Napoleonic epoch, his foreign policy colluded in the realpolitik of the Old World and opposed the republican movements in Haiti, Latin America, and Spain. Ironically, it was the point on which Jefferson would not compromise his principles that proved, in Adams's estimate, the source of his administration's worst fate, and the historian pursues in massive detail the economic and moral cost of the embargo that served to refute the president's pacific theories. Under Madison, government operated in Adams's view always in a state of greater or lesser incapacity that reached its nadir in the abandonment of the capital to the torches of Ross and Cockburn. The politics of the period invited increasingly savage satire. Only on the military and diplomatic fronts, hardly free from mortifications themselves, were skilled and gifted individuals able to preserve the national dignity.

Still, what mitigates much of the *History*'s satiric reduction of its materials is Adams's consistently high regard for the vision and refinement of Jefferson the man, who of all historical personages that ever drew Adams's interest exerted the closest approximation of a charismatic effect on his scrutiny. The fascination was in part aesthetic: without the comic horror of John Randolph, Jefferson possessed the charm of paradox and offered the pleasing spectacle of multiple significations. "A few broad strokes of the brush would paint the portraits of all the early Presidents," we are told, "but Jefferson could be painted only touch by touch, with a fine pencil, and the perfection of the likeness depended upon the shifting and uncertain flicker of its semi-transparent shadows" (A II 188). No doubt a great part of Adams's fascination for Jefferson lay in the Virginian's duplication of what Adams regarded as his own traits; his initial portrait of Jefferson in the *History* has been commonly recognized as a striking instance of self-portraiture.[24] Jefferson, Adams writes,

> led a life of his own, and allowed few persons to share it. His tastes were for that day excessively refined. His instincts were

those of a liberal European nobleman, like the Duc de Lian-
court, and he built for himself at Monticello a château above
contact with man. The rawness of political life was an incessant
torture to him, and personal attacks made him keenly unhappy.
His true delight was in an intellectual life of science and art. To
read, write, speculate in new lines of thought, to keep abreast of
the intellect of Europe, and to feed upon Homer and Horace,
were pleasures more to his mind than any to be found in a public assembly. He had some knowledge of mathematics, and a little acquaintance with classical art; but he fairly revelled in what
he believed to be beautiful, and his writings often betrayed
subtile feeling for artistic form,—a sure mark of intellectual sen-
suousness. He shrank from whatever was rough or coarse, and
his yearning for sympathy was almost feminine. That such a
man should have ventured upon the stormy ocean of politics
was surprising, the more because he was no orator, and owed
nothing to any magnetic influence of voice or person.
(A II 99–100)

Aloof as this man was, he could also appear as the apotheosis of popular
sympathies; "every one admitted," the historian reports, "that Jefferson's
opinions, in one form or another, were shared by a majority of the American people" (A II 117). A man of such qualities, freely chosen by a young
democracy, merited the closest attention, as he claimed in the world "the
place of an equal between Pit and Bonaparte" (A II 126).

In corduroy smallclothes Jefferson cut the apparently ill-equipped,
typically comic figure of the stage American, but as much as any historical
actor he counted as a force to be reckoned with. He counted, moreover, as
a force of more than comparative personal honesty, and although the
value of moral examples becomes exceedingly problematic in the course of
the *History*, in "The Inauguration" Adams pronounces almost as an article of faith that Jefferson was ethically sound. Susceptible to the "self-
deception inherent in every struggle for personal power," Jefferson, avers
Adams, "might occasionally make misstatements of fact; yet he was true
to the faith of his life, and would rather have abdicated his office and
foregone his honors than have compassed even an imaginary wrong
against the principles he professed" (A II 133). The importance of this
statement becomes obvious at once as Adams proceeds to open his inquiry
into republican government by inviting readers to marvel over the lengths
to which Jefferson's Inaugural Address misstated the militance of his true
sentiments in a rhetorically inept show at conciliation. Again and again
the historian offers to our scrutiny the inveterate misstatement and the
vague, slippery, and downright disingenuous qualities of Jefferson's lan-

guage—implicitly encouraging the reader to ponder whether such qualities are to be explained and excused by what has been praised as his writing's exhibition of a "subtle feeling for artistic form." Whatever the verdict, it remains for Adams important to credit the purity of Jefferson's character and intentions, since the assumption of that purity serves as the basis of his portrayal of Jefferson as a figure whose genuine idealism provided the starting point of the one national history that he cared to write. In the last analysis, Adams finds in Jefferson a compelling mystery: no text could ever be cited as evidence of Jefferson's full appeal as an idealist or of his considerable skill as a practical politician. Such evidence remained enveloped in the enigma of the man's "rambling and often brilliant conversation" (A II 127). "The influence he exerted," the historian would conclude, "could rarely be seen in his official and public language; it took shape in private, in the incessant talk that went on, *without witnesses*, at the White House" (A II 1033; italics added). The country is depicted as having been directed by an unbounded and now irrecoverable language.

Few traces remain of the undoubtedly paradoxical spirit of Jefferson's private conversation, but in his correspondence and public addresses Adams has ample evidence that this language must have been a fabric of contradictory impulses and intentions. In the end Jefferson could guide the course of American progress no more than John Randolph by a unitary formulation, a consistent principle. The object lesson of Jefferson's first term concerned precisely the difficulties of aligning principle with power: taking office with the express purpose of retrieving, by a policy of strict construction, the consensuality of the U.S. Constitution, Jefferson and his party broadened power far beyond that consensus text. Their centralizing actions, crowned by the Louisiana Purchase, were for Adams positive "signs of reaction toward nationality and energy in government" (A II 397). Yet in rightly obeying the impulse to secure the country's geographical future by a bold if unconstituted action, Jefferson, virtually alone in his party, also expressed a proper constitutional scruple and correctly observed that the acquisition of Louisiana without an amendment permitting it made "blank paper" of the Constitution. Disinclined to resist his party's will, Jefferson chose not to press his conviction, an illustration for Adams of the lack of command that vitiated his leadership; but the passing of Virginia strict-construction theories and Jefferson's particular authority as their spokesman was in any case not to be detained by an amendment. The Constitution of 1787 could hardly stand as the closed, master text of a present and future polity if the party of Jefferson responded (albeit necessarily) to the exigencies of rule by at once relaxing its constraints.

Thus three years into Jefferson's presidency the country had practically laid aside its principles of limited and state-defined powers. By its most zealous keepers the fixed, consensual, written Constitution, chief bulwark of republicanism, had been subjected to revision, construction, and neglect; "No century," concludes Adams, "of slow and half-understood experience could be needed to prove that the hopes of humanity lay thenceforward, not in attempting to restrain the government from doing whatever the majority should think necessary, but in raising the people themselves till they should think nothing necessary but what was good" (A II 389). The majority would rewrite the Constitution as often as suited its convenience; only a popular morality could restrain government from the tyrannical exercise of majoritarian power. Yet the people had to be raised before they could serve in this highest of democratic capacities, and Adams's phrasing suggests that that task, far from being one that the people could undertake by themselves, must devolve upon an elite, in whose superior virtue alone lay the hopes of humanity.

Insofar as he regards Jefferson as compelled by the nature of the executive office, Adams cannot condemn him for those precedent-setting departures from the Constitution that required of the people a more perfect morality. It is rather for Jefferson's failure to raise the people that Adams betrays a greater bitterness, but even this could not be strictly regarded as Jefferson's fault. Among the working propositions of his republican experiment was the belief that the people must be entrusted with their own moral improvement, and Adams, quoting a remark that the ex-president made in 1815, allows Jefferson to detect his own miscalculation: "I fear from the experience of the last twenty-five years that morals do not of necessity advance hand in hand with the sciences" (A II 122). On this particular count, Adams partly vindicates the Federalist critique of Jefferson's "sanguine" assumption that the people required no direct moral instruction; yet here too his deeper sympathies remained with Jefferson, and the bitterness was more truly reserved for a human nature that by all appearances resisted the highest stimulants. The historian who had begun work with the ambition of impressing a moral on the popular mind had sought particularly to do so by recovering, (re)writing, reaffirming what he took to be the essential Jeffersonian vision—the America of thought and art that the country, by combined material and moral right, should become. Success would involve redeeming Jefferson from his specifically political failure. But more importantly it would require affirmation of the people's ability to author their own history, which would be above all moral in its advancement, and this (still) would depend on their being raised "till they should think nothing necessary but what was good."

As passionate in his reaffirmation of the Jeffersonian vision as Adams proves, his deepest sympathy—and affinity—for Jefferson comes out perhaps most in his account of the beleaguered and mortified president's retirement, his retreat from office after the spectacular failure of his second-term aspirations. Taking to task the lame-duck president for his premature abdication of the burdens of government, and demonstrating contempt for what he viewed as Jefferson's unmanly concern for his personal popularity, the historian in the end essentially absolves the outgoing statesman of these and the other, more serious tarnishings that he has received in the course of the narrative. The "fallen leader," anguished by the disasters brought on by the failed embargo and the prospect of certain war, and wounded by the discourtesies of a hostile Senate, endured his mortifications "with dignity and in silence" (A II 1249). The historian whose ancestors had returned home in defeat, and who himself possessed some experience of withdrawing dejectedly from the field of public striving, takes an acute if understated interest in the return home of the statesman stung by the collapse of his utopian visions. Reprinting Jefferson's remarks to his Albemarle County neighbors, Adams registers the pathos of the gifted man's retirement and honors Jefferson by permitting him to offer his own "challenge to the judgment of mankind." "Of you, then, my neighbors," Adams quotes Jefferson, "I may ask in the face of the world, 'Whose ox have I taken, or whom have I defrauded? Whom have I oppressed, or of whose hand have I received a bribe to blind mine eyes therewith?' On your verdict I rest with conscious security" (A I 1252). Rhetorically, these questions (marking the *History*'s midpoint) echo those that conclude "American Ideals" and "American Character," with the ironic difference that a lone, defeated individual—a visionary who in his final isolation appears pathetically unequal to the task of bringing on the millennium—exists as the subject of the inquiry.

Thus Jefferson in the end falls out of unity with his democratic populace; the historian likewise draws back from his own warm projections of an American people. An elevated citizenry's conscious, consensual authorship of history finally cannot be affirmed by a retrospective knowledge of 1800 to 1815 and indeed is increasingly denied by the "science" of Adams's analysis, aligned as it is with the metaphorics of force determinism. The more or less conscious thought of society provided important clues to the development of a national character, but the international movement toward a uniform human condition—which must consume any merely national character—was ultimately to be explained in terms of an essentially unknowable gravitational attraction. In a famous passage in "American Character" (all but its eloquence derived from Spencer), Adams likens that movement to the watershed of the Rhine: as water that trickled from the Alpine glacier in a topography of sublime and heroic cast, so the human energies set free by the successive decay of European social order gather and descend, relinquishing the drama of movement as they meet the rising ocean of democratic society. By such a view it was absurd to think that the text of American development could ever have admitted of a statesman's, a historian's, or a people's invention. In the end they are to be displaced by a severer knowledge, a rhetoric of finalities. "In a democratic ocean science could see something ultimate. Man could go no further. The atom might move, but the general equilibrium could not change" (A III 1335).

Adams's disgust with what increasingly appeared to be the inevitable miscarriage of the *History*'s moral purpose seldom broke through the pliant restraint of his prose but was permitted furious statement in the correspondence. Of Jefferson and his successors, Adams wrote Tilden in January 1883, "I am at times almost sorry that I ever undertook to write their history, for they appear like mere grass-hoppers, kicking and gesticulating, on the middle of the Mississippi river." "My own conclusion," he went on to pronounce some five years before he would write the *History*'s last chapter, "is that history is simply social development along the lines of weakest resistance, and that in most cases the line of weakened resistance is found as unconsciously by society as by water" (*LHA* 2:491). No conclusion for Adams was ever quite final or ever closed a subject to future reconsideration. In the *Education*, indirectly vindicating his efforts as a historian, he would write that his onetime student Henry Cabot Lodge "betrayed the consciousness that he and his people had a past, if they dared but avow it, and might have a future, if they could but divine it" (A I 1104). Even in 1907 Adams forbore entirely writing off the national mind as a void, yet the contemplated difficulties of prompting an avowal of the past and encouraging constructive divination of the future had caused the *History* to veer from the generative view of American evolution projected in "American Ideals," which took as its central image the immense fecundity of a female continent.

American society betrayed an absence that remained ever unnamed in the *History* but that Adams had detected in the writing and experimental publication of *Esther*; an absence that the widower, by the light of his various bereavements, began to confront in his Polynesian letters and *Memoirs of Arii Taimai* and that he would pursue with increasing directness and lucidity in *Mont Saint Michel and Chartres* and the *Education*. Always the "eighteenth-century" rationalist in his approach to "the great problems of human society," he had long realized that the emergence, growth, and flowering of a culture did not proceed exclusively by rational processes. And he had begun to understand that the assured national self-consciousness that he long had hoped to foster depended on partly unconscious stimulants, a symbology that could focus the nation's generative capacity without excessive self-consciousness and confirm a people in the conviction that they can create the historical exception. The absence Adams would come to define concerns above all the failed materialization of such a symbology.

6

The Eternal Woman

Authorship without Advertisement

BY THE SUMMER OF 1883, the chapters on Jefferson's first administration were in the proofsheets of a private printing, and Adams, taking a brief respite, turned a second time to the novel. If speed of composition has anything to do with an expression's urgency, it was clear that *Esther* was not a mere vacation hobby pursued in the seclusion of the Adamses' Beverly Farms retreat. A comparatively short work, the novel was itself in proofsheets by early November; in March 1884, under the pseudonym Frances Snow Compton, it appeared as the third selection in the American Novel Series published by Henry Holt.

Satisfied as Adams may have been with the progress he had made on the *History*, his materials had already proved disenchanting; we have seen that in his January 1883 letter to Tilden he admitted to being "at times almost sorry" that he had undertaken the project, having become disheartened at the spectacle of compulsion by which American society and its leaders unconsciously moved. With three-quarters of the writing ahead of him, he had begun to perceive that discipline more than enthusiasm would have to see him through the task. He affected and perhaps genuinely felt a certain indifference to appearing ultimately as the author of the completed *History* and characterized himself as inured to isolation to the point of desiring nothing else. Formulating a rhetorical motive that he later would partly realize with the posthumous *Education*, Adams wrote Gaskell in September 1883 that he "would rather let the stuff lie till I'm dead. There is a sort of pleasure and triumph in proving to oneself that one does not care a nickel cent for the opinion of one's fellow-men. At all events," he added, somewhat conceding the bluff, "I am not yet in a hurry to say: Plaudite!" (*LHA* 2:511).[1]

Strong as his troubled desire for a contemporary celebrity remained, his publication of *Esther* the following spring shows that his more immediate concern lay in verifying the existence of a responsive readership, since any public success could only have been claimed by the phantom of the pseudonym. In offering the book to the public, Henry Holt had been directed simply to place it on the market without circulating copies for review or other advertisement; the author, sufficiently well off to dictate terms, guaranteed the publisher's indemnity. By this experiment, Adams sought to determine whether a certain kind of book could find and identify a specific public, and whether that book, by the force of intrinsic appeal, could become the focus of a shared if inchoate sympathy. In the first months after *Esther*'s March 1884 release Adams expressed a willingness to give the experiment at least five years to produce results of any meaning. "Don't get impatient," he counseled Holt. "Remember that authors, if not publishers, have to look many years ahead and yet sometimes miss their mark" (*LHA* 2:543). Such had been and would continue to be the condition and risk of the in-progress *History*. However, Adams agonized over the novel's slow sales (514 of the 1,000 copies printed would sell in the first year), troubled more than he let on by its failure to draw an unprompted recognition.[2] By January 1885, before *Esther* had even been out a year, Adams had begun to draw conclusions. "My experiment has failed," he declared to Holt. Although the failure left "the matter" of whether an audience could exist for him "as undecided as ever," his suspicions concerning the contemporary American readership had been gravely confirmed. "So far as I know," he continued, "not a man, woman or child has ever read or heard of *Esther*"—or, for that matter, any other of Holt's series. "My inference," he concluded, "is that America reads nothing—advertised or not—except magazines" (*LHA* 2:567).

Having established that "authorship without advertisement" (*LHA* 2:568) was not possible in the United States, Adams devised a scheme to test the perspicacity of English criticism. *Esther* was to be republished in England along with another book in Holt's series, *Among the Chosen* by Mary S. Emerson, the two books circulated and advertised together simply as new, female-authored novels from America. The circumstances of *Esther*'s British release only partially conformed to Adams's specifications; but whatever the second publication's value as experiment, the mixed reviews that greeted it did nothing to alter the novel's sluggish and silent American reception. In any case, before the term of this second experiment had closed, Marian Adams had died by her own hand, and Adams had become, as he reported to Holt in March 1886, "almost amused at the idea of my caring now for anything that so-called critics could say" (*LHA* 3:5).

Esther holds a place of singular interest in Adams's oeuvre not just in that its experimental publication reflects the author's growing fear of an absent general readership. Adams's restlessness with a project that committed most of his attention to the bygone acts of public men is confirmed by his turning a second time from the Jeffersonian past to contemplate the crisis of his contemporary America through the romantic misadventures of a fictional young woman. If the historical record as Adams recovered it bore little trace of the woman's active influence, he nevertheless deeply felt her presence in the life he knew, and several generations of family experience had produced ample evidence of the woman's command over the domestic sphere that formed the man of state.[3] Although in "Primitive Rights of Women" Adams had elevated the woman to the status of historical subject (and had done so in fact with a certain insistence meant perhaps to mitigate the essay's reactionary strain), the domestic sphere that the woman ruled scarcely figured in the explanation of national character that he was in the process of framing. His historiography remained ill-equipped to recover that sphere as a dimension of national evolution. Yet the woman's influence as Adams experienced it in the forms of contemporary upper-class life merited consideration as a potential historical force, and such shadowy existence as could not yet impress on the historical record offered itself for study once again in the more freely speculative poesis of the novel.

In *Democracy* Adams had made a preliminary study of an American woman's agonized interaction with the grossly political form of (male) historical life. By the time he had begun to write *Esther*, he had both reaffirmed (in "American Ideals") his capacity to envision a high American civilization and refined his skepticism as to whether it could be attained. His second heroine is accordingly more complex, deserving study not only as another gifted female whose failure to marry corresponds to her conservative and unimaginative society's inability to make use of her, but also as something like the unespoused soul of an America of thought and art. In *Esther* we observe Adams at work imagining a desired future order and see him strain for the most part unsuccessfully against the social, intellectual, and sexual impasses he and his society put in the way.

Like *Democracy*, *Esther* draws upon the life and intimates of its author, but the biographical interest of the second novel is intensified by the heroine's exact resemblances to Marian Adams and by the author's intimate and speculative probing of the heroine's emotional and spiritual states. It can hardly surprise us that Adams the widower withdrew the book from publication. Read biographically, *Esther* suggests the ideal light by which Henry wished to contemplate Marian Adams, but it also offers disconcerting glimpses into a marriage soon to be dissolved by Marian's willful death; a marriage that, for all of its evident companionability, must have given the Adamses reason to know what the novelist gave Esther emphatically to declare: that "of all things on earth, to be half-married must be the worst torture" (A I 331). The parallels between Esther Dudley and Marian Hooper Adams are striking: not only are the circumstances of Marian Adams's upbringing mirrored in Esther's upbringing, but early in the novel Esther is described in terms that resemble, and even at one point exactly duplicate, Adams's description of his then fiancée in a letter to Gaskell eleven years before. The second novel no doubt reflects many features of the social circle and domestic life of the Adamses. Just as Marian and her father, Dr. Robert Hooper, have long been identified as the models for Esther and her father, so Clarence King, John La Farge, and the young Elizabeth Cameron have been recognized in George Strong, Wharton, and Catherine Brooke.[4] The first novel is also biogaphically revealing, but unlike *Democracy Esther* derives from the life of Adams's inner circle and more directly represents its psychological tensions and intellectual tone.

The ultimate interest of the novel's (auto)biographical dimension lies in what it tells us of Adams's increasingly fragile enterprise as an author, his troubled attempt to publish as male historian or ostensibly female novelist the text of a redeemable America. If Esther's failure to marry reflects incompletion in the marriage of Henry and Marian Adams, it more approachably reflects those voices in Adams that resisted fusion and more distinctly anticipates the failure of *Esther*—as a novel by Frances Snow Compton—to find a readership willing to espouse it. The multifaceted marital crisis of *Esther* is for our purposes preeminently the crisis of Adams the American author in the generatively optative mood.

The story is set in mideighties New York. The choice of scene may have been dictated in part by Adams's resolve to retain his authorship's secret, but the nature of his inquiry itself makes Washington or Boston an unthinkable alternative.[5] In keeping with what had increasingly become Adams's preoccupation with his country's cultural as opposed to its narrowly political development, he appropriately set *Esther* in that city which above all others represented material success as yet unennobled by ideals. As in his previous treatment of it, the New York of the second novel is "the sink of races" (A I 248), Wall Street determining its fundamental character; but as the supreme New World secular city, New York here hosts a cast of characters who, although members of the same privileged class, entertain widely divergent opinions as to what can and cannot redeem the America of commerce and power. In the Reverend Stephen Hazard, Adams represents the view that the church, in the New World as in the Old, must as always redeem a changeless humanity from its mortal, material attachments. Through the artist Wharton, the novelist voices intimations that human character in America has begun to break free of the church's "medieval" conception of life as either happily martyred in its earthly existence or subject to eternal damnation. And in the geologist

George Strong, Adams represents what he regarded as the attitude of science: hostile to the claims of the church and attentive to the evolution of new types; by admission metaphysical ("There is no science which does not begin by requiring you to believe the incredible" [A I 284]) yet skeptical of all positive forms of belief and so unable to provide any basis for passionate affirmation.

From her blithe agnosticism and spiritual resourcefulness Esther too voices "positions," but she exists more decidedly as an emergent (cultural) expression beyond her own powers of self-articulation. As such, she figures as an object of scrutiny to the three men, all of whom are struck by her novelty—her failure to conform to the types by which religion, art, science, and (consequently) genteel American society have conservatively defined women. Wharton, the most visionary of the three, recognizes in Esther American qualities beyond reach of the Old World aesthetic that has claimed his life and work; he who is powerless to paint her likeness pronounces her "one of the most marked American types" he ever saw (A I 199). Hazard and Strong respond to her novelty by ceasing to be the creatures of their respective dogmas long enough to entertain the idea of joining Esther in marriage. But as Hazard, her one serious lover, is too deeply claimed by the church, and as Strong, her cousin, must remain always too passionlessly ironical to excite Esther's devotion, she stands at book's end without a champion: the object of a finally impotent scrutiny, isolated by the vengefully conservative workings of a complex social necessity.

The plot of *Esther*, like that of *Democracy*, turns on a courtship that culminates in ruptured relations. A young woman of twenty-five raised from the age of ten by her widowed, freethinking father, Esther meets the Reverend Stephen Hazard shortly after attending the inaugural service at his Episcopal congregation's new Fifth Avenue church. Neither the agnostic Esther nor her companion of the day, the openly atheistic George Strong, attends the service for the sake of religion but to be present at the unveiling of the extravagant neo-Gothic structure, the windows and unfinished murals of which are the work of Wharton, a friend of Hazard and Strong and Esther's art master. For Strong, interest also lies in the performance on such an occasion of Hazard, his old college friend, intellectual antagonist, and, for all their differences, fellow man of the world. Charmed by the minister's voice and eyes, Esther finds herself taking an unexpected interest in the spectacle.

Falling thereafter at Strong's instigation into the fraternal company of the three men, Esther, an accomplished, if ever "amateur," painter, is invited to help complete the transept by painting the mural of Saint Cecilia, for which her girlish cousin Catherine Brooke, freshly arrived from

Denver, is to serve as model. While Strong, present as idle observer, derides the anachronism of the proceedings, and while Wharton, a man darkly educated by a European marriage, plays at courting the innocent Catherine in the intervals between supervising the project, Hazard quietly begins to pursue Esther. Charmed in his turn by Esther's freshness and resourcefulness, Hazard finds himself professionally challenged by her comfortable agnosticism and sets out not only to win her affection for himself but also to garner her soul for the church. For her part, Esther falls in love with Hazard the man for his capacities of urbane companionship, intellectual intensity, and romantic passion. Hazard moreover possesses mystical susceptibilities that complement Esther's own. Attaching herself to his sympathetic presence in the weeks following her father's death, Esther accepts Hazard's marriage proposal in the hope that love will compel her assent to his creed. But that hope is short-lived, and her recurrent lapses into unbelief fill her with horror as she contemplates the public hypocrisy that she, as the minister's wife, will have to support—a horror compounded by the fact that her nonattendance at church is well known, and that the congregation's matriarchs abhor the match and are certain to injure Hazard for making it. Aware finally of how unwilling she is to share Hazard with his flock, she moves against her heart's desire to break off the engagement.

Although *Esther*, like *Democracy*, concludes with the heroine's dismissal of her suitor, there is the major difference that love has drawn Esther to Hazard, whereas Madeleine only entertains relations with Ratcliffe to the extent that she can conquer her fundamental aversion to his person and politics. Nothing in the end redeems Ratcliffe; but if Hazard, like Ratcliffe, cannot exist without wielding power within a deadeningly conservative power structure, he possesses qualities that inspire Esther's love, which she affirms in the novel's last line even after Hazard, desperate to hold her, has invoked the church's most belittling assumptions of the woman's constitutional weakness. Whereas Ratcliffe betrays the thinness of an overtly (if virtuoso) satiric characterization, Hazard is invested with paradoxes of personality that mark a deeper consideration. "Even at college," Strong remarks to Esther in the opening chapter, "he would have sent us all off to the stake with a sweet smile, for the love of Christ and the glory of the English Episcopal Church" (A I 191). Yet his unpuritanical cultivation and sympathy succeed to a certain point in mitigating his severity as churchman. He can sing, sketch, and recite poetry, and we are told that he was at one point enough of a poet to translate Petrarch. Hazard is sufficiently a man of the world to have for boon companions the likes of Wharton and Strong, but what distinguishes his susceptibilities from the superficial liberality of the sophisticated clergyman is his clear, if finally limited, recognition of Esther's strengths, the source for him of her attraction.

At first, Hazard's fascination with Esther has more to do with her resistance to churchgoing, her unflattering indifference to his pulpit's eloquence, which he sets out to overcome by the force and refinement of his personality. For the minister, the only conquests worth his undertaking are those of "men and women who were strong enough to have opinions of their own," and on his successful handling of Esther "he was half-ready to stake the chances of his mission in life" (A I 217). Flattered by Hazard's attentions—particularly his willingness to argue the merits of her painting before Wharton's critical assault (" 'I never knew before what it was to have a defender,' said she simply" [A I 219])—Esther permits him to dominate her judgment where superior knowledge seemed to entitle him to do so, but on specifically religious matters she holds aloof. The conviction with which she maintains her agnosticism becomes evident in the week of her father's death. When Hazard, in the vigil's final hours, offers comforts of a pastoral nature in addition to the support of his friendship, Esther easily declines. "Do not feel alarmed about me," she tells him. "Women have more strength than men." The statement, completely ingenuous, leaves Hazard stirred and disarmed, susceptible to a visionary appreciation of Esther. "Most women would have asked him for religious help and consolation. She had gently put his offers aside. She seemed to him like a wandering soul, lost in infinite space, but still floating on, with her quiet air of confidence as though she were a part of nature itself, and felt that all nature moved with her." Thus impressed, the minister confides to himself "that she could give a lesson in strength to me" (A I 263).

Such appreciation of Esther however cannot long govern Hazard's treatment of her. When she speaks soon afterward of going abroad in the spring, the minister impulsively confesses his love and makes his proposal, prevailing over her immediate objections that as a wife she must ill-suit his needs. In his moment of passionate statement Hazard dismisses the question of Esther's unbelief: "Promise to love me," he assures her, "and I will take care of the rest" (A I 268). Yet coming from his triumph, Hazard "felt that he had found a soul stronger and warmer than his own, and was already a little afraid of it" (A I 270). What draws Hazard to Esther, as he seems momentarily to recognize, is a character than can hardly be reconciled by the easy assurances of his inveterate self-confidence, but in his determination to possess her he fails to perceive that Esther cannot let him "take care of the rest" without sacrificing her strength and indeed much of her warmth, which exist for Hazard but not for his congregation. He must choose Esther over his congregation, over his plainly entrepreneurial ambitions as a clergyman, but although in moments of mental wandering he entertains flight, he can never seriously consider abandoning his rectorship. "Naturally sanguine" (Adams's chief epithet for Jefferson), Hazard instead takes for granted that Esther will "at once absorb her existence in his" (A I 294). And this leaves him ill-prepared for the lesson in strength that Esther gives him when she at last must choose between an isolation that will allow her to maintain her agnostic conception of true spirituality (one of human attachment in this life, which she had known with her father in his last hours) and what she considers the false spirituality of the church, which revolts her, as she is finally driven to confess, by its obsession with mortal flesh and the workings of a selfish, personal salvation.

Hazard loses Esther because his all-absorbing ambition blinds him to the peculiar necessity of her strength; but as churchman (and, for that matter, one of Anglican faith) he is in no position to read into her strength evidence of a new, national human order. In *Democracy*, Adams had made some attempt to create a heroine who could serve as an incarnation of national virtue. In *Esther*, he strives to create the symbol of a baffled, but aspiring, instinctively idealistic, American character, and Hazard's failure to perceive Esther in this light precisely measures his limitation. The key characterization comes toward the end of the first chapter and proceeds from the lips of Wharton, the artist and privileged seer. "Miss Dudley," he declares, "is one of the most marked American types I ever saw." After detailing the singular plainness of her mere physical attributes (her imperfect features and absence of good points excepting "her ears, her voice, and her eyes"), Wharton affirms the subtlety of her impression and the fascination it excites. "I want to know what she can make of life," Wharton declares.

> She gives one the idea of a lightly-sparred yacht in mid-ocean; unexpected; you ask yourself what the devil she is doing there. She sails gayly along, though there is no land in sight and plenty of rough weather coming. She never read a book, I believe, in her life. She tries to paint, but she is only a second rate amateur and will never be any thing more, though she has done one or two things which I give you my word I would like to have done myself. She picks up all she knows without an effort and knows nothing well, yet she seems to understand whatever is said. Her mind is as irregular as her face, and both have the same peculiarity. I notice that the lines of her eyebrows, nose and mouth all end with a slight upward curve like a yacht's sails, which gives a kind of hopefulness and self-confidence to her expression. Mind and face have the same curves. (A I 199–200)

This passage constitutes a fascinating intertextual moment in Adams's work: not only does it afford a rare view of the meditative current that served as the common source of his fictional, historical, and autobiographical writing, but it evinces the degree to which his life, married or unmarried, provided the symbology by which he shaped his major formulations of American destiny. To read Esther Dudley as a portrait of Marian Adams, a practice begun by Adams himself and that no student of this couple cannot in some manner continue, must always remain an exercise in naive and doubtful referentiality. Yet no one can deny that Esther derives from an effort on Adams's part to formulate certain intuitions pertaining to the possibilities of his nation's life, the promise and peril of the American prospect as it bore upon the cosmopolitan atmosphere of his exclusive domicile; and we do well to recognize that this effort goes back at least as far as his initial trials to describe and indeed vindicate his fiancée to Charles Milnes Gaskell. "She is certainly not handsome," Adams wrote to his British friend in March 1872, "nor would she be quite called plain"; "She knows her own mind uncommon well" but remains nonetheless "very open to instruction" (*LHA* 2:133). Writing again in May, Adams continued to meditate upon his betrothed's curious suggestion of exiguousness, self-sufficiency, and promise. "My young female has a very active and quick mind and has run over many things, but she really knows nothing well. . . . I think you will like her, not for beauty, for she is certainly not beautiful, and her features are much too prominent; but for intelligence and sympathy, which are what hold me" (*LHA* 2:137). In the same tone of apologetic fascination that Adams adopted to convey the attributes of his American bride, Wharton would later describe Esther, repeating the phrase "knows nothing well," but more boldly projecting those virtues shared by Esther and the fiancée of 1872 as expressions of an emergent if vulnerable national idealism.

In Adams's description of Marian Hooper and in Wharton's description of Esther, we see reflections of what the historian identifies as the national dilemma in 1800, when the country's "paucity of means" contrasted sharply with "the immensity" of its task (A II 23). Deprived of certain aesthetic graces and the advantages of an Old World education, Marian Hooper and Esther Dudley are distinguished by quick intelligence, of a piece with the native quickness that allowed the American people to solve their pressing material problems and to hold their own in the War of 1812. Nor is such ingenuity without its own canons of beauty. The characterization of Esther as "a lightly-sparred yacht in mid-ocean" proposes a figure of intelligence and grace abroad on an errand of immeasurable daring, a figure to which Adams would return (after Marian's death) in a chapter of the first volume of Madison's second administration, "Privateering." "Beautiful beyond anything then known in naval construction," notorious for *her* effectiveness in raids on British merchantmen, the Yankee schooner emerges as a triumphant instance of American thought, the vessel marking "the first time when in competition with the world, on an element open to all," Americans "proved their capacity to excel." But the schooner also exists as a signal female nuance in the virtually womanless *History*, transcending the customary female gender of ship reference to assume a delicate if imperious personality. Like Madeleine and Esther and the as yet unwritten Virgin of Chartres, "she could not bear conventional restraints"; and, displaying the insouciance of assured superiority, "with an open sea, the schooner, if only she could get to windward, laughed at a frigate" (A III 840). In this isolated instance of splendid realization, American character appears superlatively female.

Yet if Esther, like the schooner, manages to slip through her pursuer's fingers "at the moment when capture was sure," she does not look back to laugh. In breaking her engagement with Hazard she can expect to forfeit, at age twenty-six, her life's marital prospects, and without marriage she must feel the more keenly "her feminine want of motive in life" (A I 244). Although Hazard in the end betrays Esther and that part of himself that could respond to her strength and originality, she and Hazard both are the objects of conservative forces that could never tolerate such a union. Whereas in the *History*—in "Privateering" as in "American Ideals"—the voice of experience is embarrassed by the success of doubtful experiment, in *Esther* that voice, speaking through Esther's father and aunt, predicts with chilling accuracy the outcome of the heroine's romantic venture. The question of her marriageability troubles her father, who knows himself to be dying and who rightly supposes that after his death Esther will be prone to entertain an unsuitable match. "Poor Esther!" he reflects. "She has been brought up among men, and is not used to harness. If things go wrong she will rebel, and a woman who rebels is lost" (A I 206). Anticipating her niece's debacle, Mrs. Murray, although a woman of social prominence and an enforcer of the status quo, bitterly reflects upon what she regards as the woman's unavoidable stultification and sorrow. "Let Esther take care of her own husband," she advises Esther's father. "Women must take their chance. It is what they are for. Marriage makes no real difference in their lot. All the contented women are fools, and all the discontented ones want to be men. Women are a blunder in the creation, and must take the consequences. If Esther is sensible she will never marry; but no woman is sensible, so she will marry without consulting us" (A I 206).[6] After Hazard and Esther, consulting only their own desire, become engaged, Mrs. Murray adjusts her prophecy, declaring before Esther has resolved on her own not to marry Hazard that "the engagement will break itself up" (A I 279).

Through Mrs. Murray, the voice of genteel but bitterly dissatisfied female experience, Esther's fate is pronounced long before the fact. Thus entrapped, her novelty is stillborn, and her career as the avatar of a distinctly national type ends in the ambiguity of a necessary social isolation. Only the publication of Esther's story offers to retrieve her from obscurity and want of purpose and give her currency as a generative national idea. And it is part of the larger story that hope may lie in such publication. Adams's consciously experimental intent perhaps never reckoned the full complexity of his novel's rhetorical venture; but that venture makes for intriguing study, and to the extent that we recover it the book is redeemed from its meager plot and often weak characterizations, the defects of a novel in which too much of the action consists in intellection and the repression of sexual energy.

As if to propose that only another woman could know and retrieve Esther, Adams signed the novel Frances Snow Compton, thereby extending the fiction of the text into the rhetoric of the title page. The pseudonym merits consideration. Frances is the feminine form of the middle name of Henry's father and brother. Snow suggests the virtue of genteel womanhood but also the cool intellectuality of the author's point of view, which fixes generatively on the page to be written but fears the void to which such writing may be consigned. Compton (as Levenson suggests) could be an anglicization of Comte and would thus reflect the controversy concerning the nature of the contemporary historical phase; it is the bearing of their current epoch that Hazard, Strong, and Wharton each remains powerless to decide.[7] To the readership of 1885, "Frances Snow Compton" would not have registered as a pseudonym and hence probably would not have challenged scrutiny as a text. But the novelist does insist that we attend to "Esther Dudley," the name being central to the rhetoric of her characterization and instrumental to our consideration of her as an old or new story—the fable of a typical, compromised American womanhood or the renewable projection of a glorious, yet-to-be-realized type.

Although she is the daughter of a New York lawyer—a cavalry officer injured in the Civil War and a man of extirpated Puritan roots—Esther's name invests her with an elaborately ironic literary lineage. " 'Tell me about your cousin,' " Hazard instructs Strong in the first chapter. " 'Who is she? Her name sounds familiar.' 'As familiar as Hawthorne,' " Strong replies. " 'One of his tales is called after it' " (A I 197). "Old Esther Dudley," the fourth of Hawthorne's "Legends of the Province-House," tells the story of the supposedly last descendant of the once-eminent Dudleys, an ancient woman who for lack of connections has resided by the governor's indulgence many years in the Province House. When the British flee before the American troops during the War of Independence, she chooses to stay in the house alone and to await what she believes will be the governor's return. Years later, when the newly elected Massachusetts governor John Hancock comes to occupy the Province House, the old woman takes him at first as the king's representative. A pathological resident of a long-dead past, Esther Dudley dies on the doorstep the moment she is made to understand the irreversible fact of the new order.[8] But our (if not Hazard's) familiarity with Adams's Esther has less to do with this interesting variation of Rip Van Winkle than with her other and grander namesake—a character also out of harness, also distinguished by the misfortune of loving a minister who is her spiritual inferior, and likewise given to intuitions that mark her as one perhaps in advance of, but in any case out of sorts with, her age: Hester Prynne.

The parallels between *The Scarlet Letter* and *Esther* are numerous and mostly propose that the latter takes place in a world of clouded value and sterile refinement. Hester and Esther are both distinguished by a capacity for love and an intelligence given to moral recognition, and both are required to define themselves as socially proscribed women. Hester can do so against the harsh, if readily intelligible, protocol of life in a theocracy. Of her sin, the crime of excessive love, she stands in her own manner self-convicted and elects to live out her life on the colony's edge performing an office of consolation to those who also have been compromised, wronged, and excluded. She carries into old age the germ of a revolutionary opposition to such patriarchal codes as she has suffered under, but after her abortive attempt to escape with Dimmesdale to the Old World she is largely able to resolve her story's moral ambiguity in the paradox of the Fortunate Fall. Esther, in contrast, inhabits a materially acquisitive society that retains the church (in its ornamental high church version) as a calculated insurance of personal salvation and as a form of social regulation. The moral absolutism that Hazard spouts, lost in any case upon his emphatically worldly and pharisaical congregation, is subordinated to his campaign of laying up souls as so much otherworldly capital; in his sermon at the book's outset, he is said to take "possession of his flock with a general advertisement that he owned every sheep in it" and to have "added a general claim to right of property in all mankind and the universe" (A I 189). Never really a member of Hazard's congregation, Esther commits the social offense of accepting the minister's attentions; at the novel's end, in the eyes of a Hazard who must relinquish the idea of "owning" her, she is guilty of the mortal sin of pride. At no point does Esther stand self-convicted of anything besides her unworthiness to serve as Hazard's wife. As the novel concludes, she can claim the meager consolation of having retained her intellectual integrity, but no social role offers to mitigate the bleak prospect of an isolated life.

The lives portrayed in *Esther* are studies of energy stifled, careers without consequence, minds governed by egocentric or wavering or shapeless beliefs. For Adams, the intensity of human experience is proportionate to the conviction of the participants; at particular historical moments, ideals decide events. Some fifteen years after writing *Esther*, Adams would celebrate the Gothic Transition as just such a moment; he had already characterized the America of 1800 as bearing the marks of a procreant, popular idealism and had previously—in the ambiguous role of private secretary—felt a national ideal mobilize his youthful generation as the Union army. Early in *Esther*, Wharton speaks hopefully of the emergence of distinct American types but acknowledges the possibility that they may "come to nothing for want of ideas" (A I 199). Want of ideas that inspire conviction translates in the novel into striking incapacity for experience. If the characters live in an atmosphere that tolerates intellectual hypothesis, they submit to a system of social regulation that quashes antinomian possibility. Wharton can but feebly suggest a "next world which artists want to see, when paganism will come again and we can give a divinity to every waterfall" (A I 200); neither Hazard nor Strong can offer a model of thought and belief that does not sacrifice eros to self-consciousness. As the story culminates in broken engagement, the spiritual incapacity of what the novel presents as a privileged and gifted set of post–Civil War Americans figures above all as a paralysis of sexual passion.

It is here that we meet the most telling contrast between *Esther* and *The Scarlet Letter*. Within the firm constraints of a theocratic society, intensity could exist of a sexual as well as a religious nature, but amid the subtle repressions of a secular, intellectually sophisticated community given to self-centered pursuits, the lovers remain celibate. Passion, to be sure, receives no encouragement; in the eyes of Mrs. Murray, George Strong is the fit husband for Esther simply on the basis of what she takes to be their intellectual compatibility—their relation as cousins offering no substance for scandal.[9] For his part, the adaptable George Strong remains constitutionally incapable of passion; throughout most of the novel he promotes his friend Hazard's cause, but after Esther's final dismissal of Hazard, Strong offers himself to her as a consolation suitor, unable to comprehend the fact that Esther still loves Hazard and cannot come to marriage except by love. Between Hazard and Esther sexual passion does exist, but its expression occurs in brief flurries from which Esther promptly retreats. There is moreover the strong suggestion that no generative occasion can ever exist for them. In their first encounter, a chance meeting at a charity hospital, they enter into parental configuration amid a group of sick and dying children.

Esther does not lack passion, but she cannot find the man to define it or requite its spirituality, the husband who can save her from the deadly ennui of amateur painting, charity work, and the stifling regimen of upper-class life. Her one moment of fulfillment, the single instance when she feels well used, comes at her father's deathbed, where she successfully resolves to make her father "know, as long as he knew any thing, that her hand was in his" (A I 264). But having reaffirmed the human bond at life's edge, she hungers all the more for a living communion in which sympathy and spirituality, the force of which she had glimpsed "by the light of her father's deathbed" (A I 265), might reign. Esther and Hazard permit themselves to fantasize momentarily a fulfilling union, as both are beguiled by Esther's suggestion that they escape overseas, travel, and paint in the joy of each other's company—a moment that parallels Hester's proposal of escape in "A Flood of Sunshine." But Hazard's recollection of his pastoral duties dashes such prospects, and Esther must attempt to achieve communion with him through a willed assent to his creed. Finding herself soon in despair over her inability to reason herself into faith, at the bidding of George Strong she seizes a crucifix that has served as a prop in her studio and presses it to her breast with such violence that Strong, flustered by the emotionality (and no doubt the sexuality) of the gesture, removes the object from her grasp.[10] From here on, she can entertain no hope of becoming one with Hazard.

Nor can she invest much hope in recovering a living communion of any kind. At Niagara Falls, where the novelist lays the scene of the couple's final rupture, death increasingly comes to dominate Esther's meditation. Searching more and more for an object or force that would serve absolutely to complete her, she imagines the falls, thundering outside her window as she dresses, as the male voice of an actual divinity, "speaking" a gospel that more nearly approaches her own sense of mystery than anything in the doctrine of her churchman lover. Later, in the face of Hazard's final appeal, her eyes wander over to the cataract, and she has the sensation of "being swept over it" (A I 330). Such suicidal dreaminess marks one path of realization, in line with her despairing notion "that the next world is a sort of great reservoir of truth, and that what is true in us just pours into it like raindrops" (A I 321). Yet to the end of the book she sustains an idea of a possible "next world" that may be achieved without martyrdom. "Do you mean to separate yourself from all communion?" Hazard asks Esther after she has begun to reveal her exact hostility to church doctrine and ceremony. "If you will create a new one that shall be really spiritual," she answers the minister, "and not cry: 'flesh—flesh—flesh,' at every corner, I will gladly join it, and give my whole life to you and it" (A I 332). As Hester Prynne's literary descendant, Esther Dudley confirms the need for "a new truth" that could "establish the whole relation between man and woman on a surer ground of mutual happiness"; but Esther herself fails, at least as character, to become the "angel and apostle of the coming revolution" that Hester prophesies.[11] As character, she is defeated insofar as Hazard cannot marry her on her terms; he cannot accede to her request that he espouse the historical novelty of creating a new communion.

As martyr to the imperative of her spiritual integrity, Esther conforms to the fate of Albert Gallatin and most of the Adamses in her final isolation. Yet her martyrdom as character is necessary to her emergence, in a novel by Frances Snow Compton, as symbol: the type of an American character-to-be, which must elect to perish as a celibate possibility rather than submit to absorption in a deathly pattern of cultural repetition. But if Esther the character is to achieve success as *Esther* the book, more will be required: the novel must find a readership responsive to the requests Esther makes, a public willing to accept her as the symbol of a (re)nascent national idealism. Thus Adams carries into *Esther*'s publication the question that the text raises but cannot itself answer: whether what is genuinely original in the American character can survive the constraints of affluent respectability, which is the outcome of the nation's stunning material success, or whether it must perish for want not only of ideas (ideals) but also of the symbology that can command a national imagination. Such a symbology would indeed have to be powerful in order to preserve the intimation of historical novelty from the articulate denials of Old World religion and art and even more so to shield it from the acid glare of a science bent on reducing history to a mechanical, if (for a scientist like George Strong) ever amusing, absurdity. As we have seen throughout this study, the various negations of American exceptionalism could be as persuasive to Adams as the force of its recurrent appeal, and *Esther* maximizes that ambivalence. If under the pseudonym Adams hoped to publish the symbol of a still-eligible American type, through Wharton he expresses his doubt that such a symbol could ever exert decisive attraction over the American mind.

In view of Adams's subsequent course, Wharton's pronouncements assume a singularly prophetic resonance. More than any other character, the moody, ill-regulated painter adumbrates the troubled midcareer fluctuations of his author's thought. Like the Henry Adams of "American Ideals," Wharton hypothesizes the existence of a distinctly American character but puzzles over the subtle forms by which that character has thus far manifested its idealist leanings. With an abandon that would ill-befit his author's guise of scientific historian, but which looks ahead to the poetic license of the retired Adams, Wharton follows his intuition and thinks in overtly symbolic images. The directness with which he seizes upon a woman's image to convey his sense of what is superlatively American suggests the historian's enormous frustration with the prosaic masculinity of his materials, the political, military, and economic record failing to provide the symbology requisite to a renewable American prospect. Indeed no focal image of American aspiration comparable to the image that Wharton's remarks make of Esther would ever emerge in the *History*. Late in the work, as we have seen, Adams celebrates the American schooner as a triumph of national thought and as an imperiously female presence, but the historian hardly proposes (explicitly or implicitly) that it can serve as an enduring national symbol. By that point in the *History*, in any case, the rise of America has become increasingly subordinated to the international story of democratic leveling. Yet in the context of the novel, which was written before the *History* was even half completed, Wharton fares no better when it comes to realizing the image that Esther uniquely suggests. In post–Civil War New York, the woman as symbol is unknown and probably unknowable: although decorated in the medieval mode, the Fifth Avenue church, as Wharton complains, omits the Madonna, to him the very "heart" of a church (A I 234). Given his society's ignorance of the woman's (former) force, he can entertain little hope that a new ideal requiring a female figuration will triumph in the New World.

Through Wharton Adams begins to recognize, twenty years before writing "The Dynamo and the Virgin," that "an American Virgin would never dare command; an American Venus would never dare exist" (A I 1071). The authority he assigns to Wharton merits close attention inasmuch as it complements the authority invested in Esther on the basis of her radically different experience and mind. By background the painter is not only American but western—his youth an instance of the nation's continued "paucity of means." Beginning life as a poor boy in Cincinnati, Wharton's gifts are recognized early, but because no American academy of art yet exists he is sent to train in Europe. There, he not only learns the grand style but becomes the captive of an Old World aesthetic that projects earthly life as so much moral degradation redeemed (if at all) by a beatifying martyrdom. Wharton's distinction is that he alone of the three men has become fully subject to female attractive force or possesses experience profound enough to impeach his birthright to the American male's self-confident, scientific, entrepreneurial approach to his object of desire. Only Wharton has lost his national innocence; only he possesses the knowledge by which the New World may be distinguished, morally and aesthetically, from the Old.

Only Wharton has married—and not into the regulated gentility of American upper-class domesticity but into the bohemia of the Old World, his wife a "Parisian Pole" in whom the old pagan energies rage. Although she brings him no closer to artistic solutions for late nineteenth-century America, through her he receives education beyond Parisian academicism, and on the basis of that education he comes to recognize the need for a distinctly American expression though he is, by then, too spiritually alienated to create it. Before she is his wife she serves (quite inadvertently) as his model, a would-be suicide by arsenic whom the artist encounters at a Paris hospital that he regularly visits in pursuit of "the most extravagant subjects . . . models at moments of intense suffering and at the instant of death" (A I 251).[12] From such subjects, the epiphanic instance of a decadent civilization, Wharton derives his first success, but success on such terms is to be endlessly exacting. For by marrying his model, who had put herself in his charge after her recovery, Wharton marries his art and by so doing steps beyond such distinctions between art and life as connive in the creation of a Gothic church on Fifth Avenue. Out of touch with any prospect of a genuinely American culture, Wharton allows himself to be possessed "body and soul" (A I 251) by this woman whose one passion is "excitement," who has "the temper of a fury, and all the vices of Paris," and whose impatience with "the quiet of an artist's life" causes her to leave him after three months. Broken by her desertion, Wharton drifts to Avignon, where he reads Petrarch and learns to adore "purity and repose" (A I 252). Hazard eventually induces Wharton to return to America and accept the commission of the new church. This Wharton undertakes in good faith, only accusing the work near its completion of being no more than the "theater" of religious expression (A I 234). At this point, about midway through the novel, Wharton's wife appears on the sidewalk outside the church to extort money from the artist, and appropriately in New York spiritual estrangement becomes legal divorce, turning on momentary settlement.

Unmarried by an American legal technicality, Wharton is ostensibly free to pursue Catherine Brooke, the flirtatious Colorado orphan whom Mrs. Murray has taken under her wing. Yet his divorce remains superficial. In a spontaneous sketch of Catherine drawn just before the appearance of Wharton's wife (whom he has not seen in ten years), the fresh arrival from Denver is made to appear ten years older and is given the eyes of Wharton's original and permanent model. For her part, Catherine objects to having her features undergo the even more radical mortification necessary for her image to become a credible Saint Cecilia and yet refuses also to conform to Wharton's notion of her as a beautiful object who must be most beautiful on her western prairie. Absorbing the attentions of Wharton and the rest as so much belated education, Catherine cannot be coaxed to confess any homesickness for the West. "I like the East," she declares. "What is the use of having a world to one's self?" (A I 226). "You have the charm of the Colorado hills, and plains," scolds Wharton, her elder fellow westerner. "But you won't keep it here. You will become self-conscious, and self-consciousness is worse than ugliness" (A I 227). "Nonsense!" retorts Catherine, and she proceeds to ridicule the artist's notion that the girls (or indeed the birds, horses, and antelopes) of the West do not possess a self-regarding beauty. Catherine Brooke exists in *Esther* both as a challenge to naive assumptions as to the (western) American's purity and as an example of American character overwhelmed and tarnished by an older culture. Catherine's eastern sojourn certainly intensifies her self-consciousness: the Natural Sublime of Niagara Falls becomes, in her fancy, a self-conscious woman, and she requires that Wharton design for her "a dress which should have the soul of Niagara in its folds" (A I 318). At book's end, Europe figures as the next stop on her itinerary as she wishes to pursue the world of romance and experience for which Wharton has served as reluctant emissary.

For most readers Catherine is probably the least developed and least credible of the novel's characters; she exists most importantly as a foil to Esther, whose surface timidity contrasts with Catherine's assertiveness, and whose New England lineage gives her a more metaphysical claim to stand as an American type. "It is not a woman! It is a man!" Esther declares in vehement protest to Catherine's conceit of the falls. "No woman ever had a voice like that!" (A I 318). The distinction marks the difference between Catherine's self-possessing narcissism and Esther's need to confront, in the display Niagara Falls makes of ultimate force, the mystery of her sexual, social, and national destiny. Wharton remains correct in his designation of Esther as a preeminent study of American character; hence the most significant of the novel's several nonmarriages is that which subsists between Esther and Wharton.

Wharton recognizes that despite their master-student relationship he and Esther are practitioners of two irreconcilable schools; between himself and Esther he maintains a distance that permits him a grudging admiration of her work. Employed as Wharton's subordinate in the decoration of Saint John's, Esther insists, against the master's severer canon, on painting Saint Cecilia from the natively angelic look that she sees in Catherine's living face. Wharton, inspecting the result, draws as close as he can to an espousal of Esther. "You're quite right!" he tells the always harshly self-critical Esther.

> It's not good! It's not handled in a large way or in keeping with the work round it. You might do it again much better. But it is you and it is she! I would leave it. I will leave it! If necessary I could in a few days paint it all over and make it harmonize, but I should spoil it. I can draw better and paint better, but I can't make a young girl from Colorado as pure and fresh as that. To

me religion is passion. To reach Heaven, you must go through
hell, and carry its marks on your face and figure. I can't paint
innocence without suggesting sin, but you can, and the church
likes it. Put your own sanctity on the wall beside my martyrdom! (A I 250)

Between Wharton and Esther differences subsist that are not, finally, me-
diated by a church, least of all the Church Theological of Stephen Hazard.
An impaired American if great artist of an Old World school, Wharton
perceives Esther's distinction so exactly that he never attempts to register
her likeness and realize on canvas this superlative and vulnerable American type. Just as the angelic in Catherine could be captured only by Esther—an artist outside the dominant conservative male aesthetic—so Esther must appear to the public as the exclusive subject of the female
novelist Frances Snow Compton. By such means Adams perhaps sought to
overcome his own sense of growing impairment as a confident, if ever
critical, advocate of a prospective America.

Toward the Elegiac Mode

Even before Marian Adams's death on December 8, 1885, the novelist had
begun to regret publication of what he would afterward call "my melancholy little Esther" (*LHA* 3:34). To propose such a heroine as the shareable divination of an ideal American type had been all along a tenuous
literary venture. In November 1885, Adams implored Holt to let matters
rest with regard to the slow-to-sell novel, explaining that he "never had so
many reasons for wishing to be left in peace, as now" (*LHA* 2:636). By
August 1886, *Esther* had become for Adams an absolutely private text,
the retrospection of a personal anguish that he regretted sharing even with
Clarence King and John Hay, his closest male friends. From Japan, on
August 25, 1886, he responded with a start of pain to Hay's well-
intentioned encouragement that he give the book currency. "Perhaps I
made a mistake even to tell King about it," he writes Hay,

> but having told him, I could not leave you out. Now, let it die!
> To admit the public to it would be almost unendurable to me. I
> will not pretend that the book is not precious to me, but its
> value has nothing to do with the public who could never under-
> stand that such a book might be written in one's heart's blood.
> Do not even imagine that I scorn the public, as you say. Twenty
> years ago, I was hungry for applause. Ten years ago, I would
> have been glad to please it. Today, and for more than a year

past, I have been and am living with not a thought but from minute to minute; and the public is as far away from me as is the celebrated Kung-fu-tse. . . . Yet I do feel pleased that the book has found one friend. (*LHA* 3:34)

In the years ahead, his thought would eventually work free of such willed, and in any case never very successful, immersion in the passing moment, and he would renew under various guises his lifelong approach to an American readership. Still, what he characterizes here as his disconnection from the public would of course become a fixed assumption, a theme to which he would regularly return, and for his writing he would prefer to disallow all but the immediate readership of friends.

Through the experimental publication of *Esther* Adams had asked (as he phrased it to Holt) whether authorship without advertisement were possible, but more profoundly he had inquired into the generative occasion open to the artistic expression of his time. The ultimate object to be generated remained the America of thought and art, which alone might ennoble material achievement, but there are indications even in *Esther* that Adams had begun to perceive this ambition in a preposterous light. Wharton's wild and entirely idle scheme of building in New York a "Home of Music," a temple of the arts in which he would "create the thought of a coming world" (A I 313), satirizes the future-mindedness that Adams (admiring the forward regard of Tocqueville, Mill, and, in America, the Adamses, Jefferson, and Gallatin) had long made it his business to exemplify. Although he could never suppress his impulse to grapple with the modes of the new thought, he no doubt suspected, along with his character Mrs. Murray, that his own generation was made up of "washed-out geniuses" (A I 278) from whom a post–Civil War renaissance was not now (circa 1885) to be expected. Ending a three-month lapse in his correspondence with Gaskell in April 1886, he likened himself to "a stray monkey floating down Niagara on a hand-organ" (*LHA* 3:8), conflating the central image from *Esther* with his pathetic image of Jefferson and company as "mere grass-hoppers" floating by circumstance and adding such details as might grotesquely depict his own sense of marginalization as an American author.[13]

By the light of his widowerhood Adams began to inventory his stock of accumulated loss, broadening its meaning far beyond its immediately private context. "As I see matters now," he continues in his letter to Gaskell, "I am bothered by the conviction that the world really has suddenly made a great change; and that it is not merely I who have had a mental shock. Both here and in Europe a vast revolution seems to have occurred within a year past" (*LHA* 3:8). The change, as Adams saw it, took overt political and social form and was typified by spectacles of compulsive movement that antiquated the old liberal position; in a February 1886 letter to George Bancroft he repeated, although in a freshly catastrophic phrasing, his now standard observation that constitutional government in practice counts for less and less since "the path of 'sovereignty'—which our grandfathers called tyranny—cannot be longer blocked or impeded" (*LHA* 3:5). Yet the primary loss was that of his generation's occasion. "The future no longer belongs to us," he admonished Gaskell, naming the term of his broadened sense of bereavement. And launching in earnest upon his career of postured indifference and detached spectatorship, he professed to care little "what kind of society the world is to have; but I feel sure that it will be so different from ours that our generation will find it a bore. As you know," he continued, master of the tone that one self-ironic man of the world adopts in speaking to another, "this settles it. We become *ganaches*, and that is a role like another,—rather amusing to such as like to look on. I accept it. I always did like the theatre, though my only ambition was to write the play" (*LHA* 3:9).

Neither the Founders nor the generation schooled by the Civil War had succeeded in writing the text (or the play) of the American experiment in democratic civilization: so Adams concluded in 1886 before he had realized much more than half of his by then mostly bygone ambition as a historian. And so, as we have seen, the text by which Adams had boldly intended to name the transgenerational aspiration toward an America of thought and art became eclipsed by the metaphorics of force determinism. In view of Adams's deepening sense that the crisis in American civilization reflected the absence of a vital symbology—one that could focus the country's popular energy, deflect it from its formation as "vulgar" wealth and stockpiled armament—we must note again the failure of a female (sexual, maternal) presence to assume symbolic eminence in the *History*. In context, the female schooner exists only as an ephemeral triumph, its value as symbol qualified by the spectacle of a people uncertainly responsive to ideals and (as yet) unequal to the task of shaping their vast social force, seeming to set for democratic society the disconcerting precedent of unconscious drift. If American naval architecture united science and beauty in the suggestion of a female persona that epitomized the American's best traits, the triumph remained an isolated instance in the development of a national technology given almost wholly to the production of wealth—a technology for which the sexless dynamo would emerge for Adams as the ultimate symbol.

Increasingly, moreover, the country's vast social force appears in the *History* as making its strongest appeal to avarice. The nation, Adams recognized, could never have cohered without commerce, and to the extent that the acquisitive instinct generated the energy of success needed to eliminate the obstacles impeding interregional trade, it commands as much as any force the historian's respectful scrutiny. Yet Adams very clearly proposes that the passion to acquire became in America a rapacious, antisocial, finally irredeemable greed, and the disappearance in the *History* of the American continent as a female presence figures subtly in that proposition. In "American Ideals," the continent appears (through the license of the hypothetical democrat's utterance) as earth goddess without possible rival, "turning up to the sun's never-failing caress her broad and exuberant breasts, overflowing with milk for her hundred million children!" The historian conceded the democrat's greed but submitted that his imagination lay steeped beyond its own reckoning in utopian sentiments that responded to the land's maternal generosity: "See how she glows with youth, health, and love!" (A II 118). Nine volumes later, in "Economical Results," Adams again projects the continent as a vast, open, inviting source, but whereas in "American Ideals" he had characterized the land as mother as well as commodity, in the epilogue mater has become wholly material, a commodity indeed of an industrial and financial rather than agricultural kind: "The continent lay before them, like an uncovered ore-bed" (A III 1300). Given the studiously prosaic context—a statistical summary of the country's seventeen-year economic growth—the metaphor belies an exact rhetorical calculation. The Miltonic echo ("The world was all before them") prompts us to visualize the Americans possessing a drab, fallen, demythologized world.

Yet the *History*'s rhetoric is never overtly jeremiadical; the portents of a morally catastrophic futurity drop from a voice too scientifically abstracted to afford such consolation as was offered by a self-confidently true sight of sin. Adams accuses by implication and doubts whether history, in the last analysis, evolves by anything like a moral causality. At the end he reaffirms the American of 1815 as a figure of youth—intelligent, rapid in movement, mild in method—but with no evident resource by which to purge the inevitable "corruptions" his "relaxations" must bring, no ideal that promised to lift the mind from its immersion in material contentment. A people whose national development seemed governed by laws comparable to those that determined the formation of a crystal was hardly a people who, by the guidance of a literary elite, could author their own destiny. Elegy had always been a part of Adams's tonal repertoire, a mode that he came by as a member of a family that preserved the memory of a heroic past. But only from 1886 on did his voice become characteristically elegiac, and the loss that the *History* particularly reflects fixes the point of departure, for it involves no less than the dissolution of Adams's vocational assumption that one could clarify the nation's highest possibilities and thereby directly contribute to their attainment through the established resources of literary language. As we have seen, Adams makes for a detached and laconic elegist of Old World historiography, but he could not foreshadow his own practice's certain antiquation without making retirement, in some form, his next step as author.

In August 1890, having completed the *History*, Adams was finally at liberty to emerge from the past—that of his once-sanguine literary ambitions as well as that of his subject matter. Before him lay the gray Pacific, his chosen threshold to the life that remained. Almost at once the tone of that life established itself in the wanderer's letters home, his keenly articulated interest in the Polynesian locality alternating with expressions of unappeasable ennui—his delighted response to the land, sea, and undraped human form confounded by the sense that such did not pertain to a bereaved, middle-aged American gentleman. Only for moments in Samoa and Tahiti did his attention focus sufficiently for his restlessness to cease, but if he longed to return to Europe and America, he wished equally to escape the necessity of return. The fascination that he exerted himself to take in the surfaces of life in the South Seas did however finally become something more: a discovery of contrasts to the America that, by his lights, had indifferently formed, encouraged, and betrayed him and that from afar, in the wake of the Barings collapse, had begun to reclaim his scrutiny.

By May 1891 he had broken ground on a new book, another history, but in scale, means, voice, and aim signally divergent from the magnum opus. Known successively as *Memoirs of Marau Taaroa, Last Queen of Tahiti* (1893) and *Memoirs of Arii Taimai* (1901) or *Tahiti*, the book(s) took over a decade to assume final form; but from its start the project drew upon rhetorical attitudes and narrative methods that make *Memoirs* far more akin to *Mont Saint Michel and Chartres* and the *Education* than to the great work completed in 1890. If we trace its inception to outward circumstance, *Memoirs* seems the incidental product of a suspended itinerary. From their four months in Samoa, where they had had the chance to come face-to-face with the live remnants of island culture, Adams and La Farge passed to a Tahiti where they saw only that culture's "wreck": a much diminished, racially mixed, "Christianized" population, who had been taught over the course of the last century to wear clothes and sing hymns. In Samoa Adams and La Farge had lived the illusion of possessing "the kingdom of old-gold," particularly before the spectacle of the *siva*, a dance that celebrated the naked nubile female form; so invigorating to their "fancy" had this event proven "that no future experience," wrote Adams, "short of being eaten, will ever make us feel so new again" (*LHA* 3:291). By contrast, in Tahiti the one link to the pagan past was the old woman Arii Taimai, queen mother of the Teva clan, the ancient ruling family into whose circle Adams and La Farge gained entrance through Robert Louis Stevenson, a family friend who had been adopted by the Tevas, as the Americans themselves would later be. Adams's restlessness with a ruined Tahiti found relief in his growing intimacy with this family, and through Arii Taimai's recitation of stories, poetry, and superstitions he became increasingly interested in the details of the island's past.

If the Samoan girls helped clarify for Adams the hindrance of eros in his home culture, the pure-blooded queen, whose words had to be translated by her half-European children, provided a spectacle of loss that he found more deeply congenial, and the historian needed no more than an occasion to set to work memorializing a lost world. The work began with Adams's suggestion to Marau, Arii Taimai's eldest daughter and Tahiti's nominal queen, that she narrate what was known of the Tahitian past while he took notes, from which he would shape what would be called her memoirs. Assenting to the idea, Marau told what she knew of the island's antiquity, frequently consulting her mother; helping with translations, her sisters and brother (Tati Salmon) contributed details and variants of their own—until, as Adams wrote, he had brought the whole circle "into a condition of wild interest in history" (*LHA* 3:478). Although he had never before conducted research in quite this manner, the collaborative nature of the work must have recalled to him his seminar in Anglo-Saxon institutions, which had been similarly directed to recovering the arcana of history on the narrow scale. Yet the oral source of this primarily undocumented history personalized it in unusual ways, and Adams held to his conception of it as the memoir of a single speaker, a history that never ceased to be one person's memory, its unity requiring a voice of more or less direct witness.

As *Memoirs of Marau Taaroa, Last Queen of Tahiti*, the text opened with Captain Samuel Wallis's landfall of June 18, 1767—the first European discovery of Tahiti and the fatal moment at which exact historical knowledge of the island began—and closed about 1785, the point at which enlightened Europe, turning its attention to coming revolution, lost its faddish philosophical interest in the Tahitian state of nature. As *Memoirs of Arii Taimai*, the European arrival becomes less immediately prominent, the opening chapters given rather to clarifying island geography and genealogy, but Tahiti's bloody nineteenth-century chapter is worked out and the narrative brought up through the year 1846, when the island became a French protectorate after Arii Taimai herself brought about a truce between warring native factions. In both versions Tahitian history appears from the perspective of the aristocratic Tevas, whose hereditary leadership in the Papara districts was undermined by the European failure to perceive Tahiti's tribal system of government, which answered to no central authority, distribution of power providing the means of checking the tyrannic excesses of individual chiefs. Assuming, from the standpoint of their experience and convenience, that the islands must have a monarch, the British established the Pomares, ostensible Christian converts, in such a role; this upset the traditional restraints upon self-defining power. Not until the Pomare chief Tu, aided passively by the missionaries, had massacred much of his opposition and set out to annihilate his Teva rivals did the island rise against the unprecedented tyranny. The subordination of Tu restored some semblance of the old native power balance, but the French challenge to English influence over Tahiti reintroduced strife among the natives, and Arii Taimai could succeed in disarming her people only by promoting Tahiti's submission to France.

In both versions Adams wrote chapters of a history that he thought had already and irrevocably reached its end, and whether as Marau, the last queen, or as her mother, the principle source of what could be known of Tahiti's past, the historian created an elegiac female voice, conscious of her high if eroded station and willing to assert rhetorical prerogatives. To what extent Adams strove to capture in the diction of *Memoirs* qualities of voice that he heard in Marau's and Arii Taimai's oral accounts of island history cannot be known, but he did feel free to render as needed the speaker's persona.[14] Obvious inventions include the speaker's familiarity with writings of Western travelers to Tahiti and her conversance with Western mythology and European monarchs; such knowledge, beyond the horizon of the actual queen mother, gives the voice of *Memoirs* a certain (if affected) regal worldliness, a quality that Adams no doubt thought it should possess. But with no possible forethought, at least in the early stages, of its service beyond *Memoirs*, Adams had begun to create a point of view, a distinct tonality, as well as an English-speaking voice for the island: the alternately ironic and mournful perspective of the aged, retired witness, for whom history exists as a sequence of closed epochs. Such features as the elegiac evocation of a once-whole world or the feel that the speaker of *Memoirs* exhibits for the catastrophic movement of the recent European (as well as island) past are to reappear as important characteristics of the uncle's monologue in *Mont Saint Michel and Chartres*.

The uncle does his best to recover and give voice to the authority that the Virgin exercised over her society of worshipers and artists, but the voice of the text remains always male. In *Memoirs*, the voice is always understood to be female. Whereas Frances Snow Compton impeached the obtusely conservative male dominance of contemporary American culture only as a genteel-sounding female name, the persona of *Memoirs* exists in both versions as a historical woman who speaks with an authority conferred not only by her aristocratic station but also by her status as victim. She, like Esther, is crushed by a cultural system in which religion and philosophy do nothing to mitigate an inexorable acquisitive impulse, but the persona of *Memoirs* provides the contrast of an established, and in many respects antithetical, culture that permits the spectacle of colliding worlds. In writing *Memoirs*, Adams honed his disenchantment with contemporary Western culture, rekindled his longtime hatred of French and British imperial arrogance, and began to perceive the deeply ideological nature of the European devastation of Polynesia—the ways in which soldier, merchant, and missionary all similarly worked to replace the islander's culture with their own. As Marau and Arii Taimai he lost no opportunity to indict the objects and means of what seemed to him, from his perspective in Tahiti, a soulless, self-righteous, grasping, and increasingly ubiquitous civilization.

The speaker's characterization of "the English policy of creating and supporting a tyranny" (*T* 139) reflects not only Teva observation but the ghostwriter's own inherited animus, and the diction of *Memoirs* often belies the historian well versed in portraying the self-serving nature of British foreign affairs: "There could be but one king, and he was Tu of Pare. The chance that made Matavai the most convenient harbor for the English ships made Tu the most important person on the island to provide fresh meat for the English crews" (*T* 94). But a sharper and, in Adams's experience, fresher grievance stems from the missionaries' sanctimonious indifference to native suffering. As his characterization of the Reverend Stephen Hazard shows, Adams had begun to develop an active, principled antipathy to Protestant claims, a repugnance for much of the substance and application of church dogma; the hostility appears the more pronounced inasmuch as Wharton represents an awakened interest in the emotion of religious experience. The historian's examination of missionary diaries did more than confirm the view of the church taken in *Esther*, which dismissed contemporary intellectual Protestantism as heartless, acquisitive, and leagued with the world of money. In the face of their convert Tu's atrocities, which they regretted yet facilitated by procuring weapons—noting all the while in dispassionate detail the preparations for renewed assault—the missionaries are observed to practice a form of Christianity monstrously devoid of sympathy, in which a "Calvinistic or fatalistic view of the heathen justified or excused every possible action on all sides of every question" (*T* 143). From the perspective of Arii Taimai (the missionaries figure more importantly in the expanded *Memoirs* of 1901),

Christians are associated with hypocrisy, cowardice, massacre, treachery, and disaster specifically aimed at the Tevas.[15]

To impeach the motives and methods of European imperialism was nothing new for the historian who had studied the arrogant, acquisitive, ethnocentric character of British and French foreign policy and who had seen much the same character reappear in the American treatment of the Indian. But the iconoclasm in which Adams engages under the assumed authority of a heathen matriarch goes several steps further. In *Memoirs* he offers the Polynesian highborn woman as an achieved, and for centuries successful, cultural type. Whereas in his 1876 "Primitive Rights of Women" he had wished to affirm both the woman's strength and her place in what he represented as the traditionally indulgent "Aryan" patriarchy, in the later text he works to create the subversive image of a woman who should appear, from a British and American perspective, radically out of harness. "Women," we are told, "played an astonishing part in the history of the island" (astonishing, of course, not to Arii Taimai but to Adams and what Western readership *Memoirs* might reach).

> In the absence of sons, daughters inherited chieferies and property in the lands that went with the chief's names or titles, and these chiefesses in their own right were much the same sort of personages as female sovereigns in European history; they figured as prominently in island politics as Catherine of Russia, or Maria Theresa of Austria, or Marie Antoinette of France, or Marie Louise of Parma, in the politics of Europe. A chiefess of this rank was as independent of her husband as of any other chief; she had her seat, or throne, in the Marae even to the exclusion of her husband; and if she were ambitious she might win or lose crowns for her children, as happened with Wallis's friend Oberea, our great-aunt Purea, and with her niece Tetuanui reiaiteatea, the mother of the first King Pomare. (*T* 10)

The key to her social and political autonomy lay in what Adams insistently represents as her sexual freedom. Although the constraints of genealogy forbade her from rearing a child "not of chiefly origin," the supreme chiefess "was as free from her husband's control as any independent princess of Europe; she had as many lovers as she liked and no one made an objection" (*T* 17–18). Although not all women enjoyed such latitude, as Adams represents it, political and social power was not male by definition as in the West. Patriarchy, whether of a theocratic or oligarchic nature, could hardly exist in the absence of strong patriarchs, "and in Tahiti," Adams pointedly phrased, "old men were not much regarded" (*T* 148).

In certain passages of *Memoirs*, particularly where Adams most wants to create the impression of a distinctive voice, we may question how much Arii Taimai speaks in this prose, so much does it sound like the uncle who by 1901 had begun to talk in the initial drafts of *Mont Saint Michel and Chartres*. Here, for example, we may note the worldly breadth, the ironically self-indulgent pedantry, not to mention the "paradoxical spirit of private conversation" of the retired Henry Adams: "Even a Papara school-girl, if she reads in her history-book the story of Appius Claudius or of Tarquin, would be a little surprised to find that she knew all about it, and that Papara had a Brutus and a Virginius of its own quite as good as the Roman. The fight about a woman is the starting-point of all early popular revolutions and poetry; but as all of us, in our family, are descended from Vaiari as well as from Papara, we do ourselves no wrong by doubting whether, after all, the woman was not a pretext or even an invention to account for the outbreak of a plot" (*T* 20–21). However much the tonalities of such a passage may or may not have recalled for Adams the matriarch holding forth in her native tongue while seated on her mat in the manner of the old island queens, in Tahiti he came upon an oral historiography that clearly appealed to his own long-standing love of performative, conversational language and that may have done much to prompt the uncle of *Chartres* and the Adams of the *Education* to affect talk.

The self-validating nature of Tahitian oral history must have counted as a major source of its charm. In his earliest surviving correspondence, Adams, as we have seen, had familiarized himself with the sensation that to name is always, in whatever qualified sense, to create. By the time he wrote "Captain John Smith," he had come already to recognize that discourse largely constitutes social reality; in "American Ideals" he celebrated the extent to which even half-named illusions, if they focus a common energy, precede and accompany material enactments. After the failure of *Esther*, Adams gravitated increasingly to the position that the mathematics of force relations, rather than a poesis of desire, must finally "write" democratic history; he could thus hardly have been, in this first phase of retirement, more responsive to the pure poetry of Tahitian oral history. Recounting, as Arii Taimai, an episode that took place prior to Wallis's 1767 landing, Adams gives us to understand that the very island tradition that permits the Westerner to recover what (by Western standards) can never be more than a fragmentary or unconfirmable sequence has its own means of completing any narrative that it preserves, "but as usual tradition is indifferent to dates and details, joins together what was far apart, and cares only for what amuses it." Yet having thus implicitly impeached the story by the scientific historian's truth criteria, he proceeds to retell it as given: "*As the story is told by the people to each other*" (*T* 18; italics added). The amusement of the telling constitutes the truth criterion in what finally is more important than a truth of facts: the transgenerational rhetorical ritual that confers social identity and that makes (or once made) possible a procreant communal life.

"Primitive people," the ghostwriter observes, "seem to have kept certain stock-stories, as one keeps pincushions to stick with pins, which represent the sharp points of their history and the names of their heroes; but the pins serve their purpose in the want of writing" (*T* 21). As the one to supply the "want" of writing Adams performed a paradoxical task. Without such writing, in the alien language of the colonizer, the island past must be lost with the dying island tongue; yet to write in order (ostensibly) to preserve a history that is not so much a history as an oral tradition confirms the culture's death. Tahiti may have had its Iliad and Odyssey, as the speaker, much given to facile comparative anthropologizing, assures us, but English equivalents of native poems and songs cannot, we are told, be made, and anticipating what will become a major theme in *Mont Saint Michel and Chartres* Adams more than once refers to the impossibility of translation where "native figures have no meaning in English" (*T* 38). The writing of *Memoirs* confirmed Tahiti's entrance into history; history for Adams exists in *Memoirs* as a parable of decline. From the start this "amusement" had been a decidedly elegiac exercise, the book meant primarily as a keepsake for the old chiefess's half-European children, whose bilingualism had initiated the forgetting of the native tongue. The second version, named for the queen mother, was, however, permitted to exist as a primary document for such students of the South Seas as might find the book in the handful of American libraries to which the historian, always a member of the community of scholars, dispatched the book in 1901.

The Uncle Talks

By the time Adams spoke as the uncle of *Mont Saint Michel and Chartres*, the lessons of Polynesia had assumed a prolegomenous place in the curriculum of what had become for him a ferociously educating decade. The Baring collapse of 1890 eventuated in the Panic of 1893, prostrating an America that Adams, for all his accumulated reservations respecting the American prospect, still regarded as young and resourceful. Unnaturally depressed in his view by international fluctuations in specie, the United States easily appeared as another victim of Old World avarice, the London Rothschilds figuring as the major villains in what Henry and his younger brother Brooks thought the "gold bug" conspiracy to contract currency to the detriment of a young and necessarily expanding American economy. But if the United States suggested innocence plundered by Lombard Street capitalism as the nineties began, as the decade closed the country had assumed a vigorous Roman aspect. Not only had it elected to adopt a single gold standard, thus affirming a faith in its own capitalist potential, but it had waged a war with Spain that brought it an international sphere of influence. The triumph for Adams perhaps found its truest measure in an altered Anglo-American relation. A Britain that faced insolvency and cowered before the Germany of Kaiser Wilhelm came at last willingly, as Adams would phrase it in the *Education*, "into an American system" (A I 1051).

As a partisan student of American diplomacy, Adams at one level responded elatedly to his country's emergence as a world power, and indeed his analysis in the *Education* of Secretary Hay's Anglo-American accord not only vindicates his family's long-standing diplomatic ambition with respect to Britain but confirms his observation in the *History* that the Old World must eventually follow an American lead. Yet his elation fell always prey to saturnine reflection. At the news of Admiral Dewey's victories, the historian who had taken such pleasure recounting the triumphs of Macdonough, Decatur, and Isaac Hull cheered, but the precipitous gathering of American strength that the quick dispatch of Spain portended gave rise to a troubled consideration of the country's expanding international role. Having witnessed as "tourist" the effects of "civilisation" upon the tropics, he regretted the American acquisition of the Spanish archipelagoes, even as he judged that his country's imperial status compelled it to police them. But the fundamental danger of American success was that it might cause the New World to duplicate and intensify the corruptions that typified Old World history. For Adams, "that astounding economical upheaval which has turned America into the great financial and industrial centre of the world" constituted the decade's "greatest revolution"; far from welcoming this turnabout as a prelude to an America of thought and art, he shuddered at the thought of the opportunities it gave to "thievery and private greed" (*LHA* 4:624, 625).

Called home to Quincy after the 1893 panic to help his brothers take stock of the diminished family trust, the retired and intellectually unfocused historian came under the monomaniac spell of his brother Brooks, whose large work-in-progress, *The Law of Civilization and Decay*, had received powerful new stimulus from the summer's tumult. Under Brooks's analysis, the perplexing course of the world economy, which had seen the rapid expansion of production and markets meet the recurrent devastation of contracted credit, was reduced to a grimly evolutionary and moral fable, which pitted the producers of successive epochs against the immemorial usurer, who had emerged, in the course of the nineteenth century, as the preeminently successful type. Excited by the scope and simplicity of his brother's synthesis and its suggestion of veritable law, Henry took an active if distant part in bringing the project forward, densely annotating Brooks's efforts even after the *Law*'s 1895 publication. The work had the gratifying smack of intellectual conspiracy for the two isolated collaborators, both of whom (as Henry reports in the *Education*) "were used to audiences of one" (A I 1030). The book served the older brother by giving him a preliminary formula by which to reify his intuitions of historical impasse and by dignifying his sense of himself as rather forcibly retired. If the *Law* argued the inevitability of the centralizing goldbug, the necessary triumph of capitalist greed, it at least placed the discarded Adamses among a heroic if outmoded company: the soldiers, artists, and statesmen who, with the more humble farmers and manufacturers, had for centuries labored in the belief that they inhabited a world of comparatively fixed and intelligible values.

As evolutionary discard, retired historian, and posthumous cosmopolite, Adams discovered that he possessed a great, if oddly constrained, rhetorical latitude, and although his fuller realization of its possibilities would have to wait for the major undertaking of the *Education*, he was able to exploit that latitude brilliantly in his 1894 presidential address to the American Historical Association, "The Tendency of History," a first virtuoso performance-in-absentia. Creating, as we have seen, the fiction of a voice proceeding from an undefined point on a path of egoistic caprice "somewhere beyond the Isthmus of Panama" (D 125), the self-consciously emeritus colleague submits his views as to the likely ascendancy of a true science of history, one which should "fix with mathematical certainty the path which human society has got to follow" (D 129). Thinking no doubt of the hostile reception of Brooks's first book, *The Emancipation of New England*, that assuredly also lay in wait for the *Law*, Adams warned of the consequences of projecting a future that neither favored nor flattered the reigning social interests, and in his emerging character of self-effacing bystander he informed his profession that it must find itself in conflict with its age or cease in any real sense to exist.[16] Whether or not Adams believed that a great, revolutionizing generalization must appear from the historical discipline, or desired that it should, or even momentarily took the appearance of the *Law* as the very event is as unimportant as it is impossible to determine. As author, Adams had always sought the godlike posture that inhered in writing the truth, the law, or the future, and in the writings of the nineties and beyond, the framing of dire prophecy remained the one field in which he might vigorously pursue that ambition. To appropriate and dismiss the world in a contracted economy of terms formed part of a complex, compensatory response to his increasing sense of class and personal marginalization.

With *A Letter to American Teachers of History* this strategy would arrive at its severest statement, but even then it would remain the play of a man too paradoxical in his language to "believe" any form of words to be unconditionally true. Yet in proportion as the contemporary world became chaotic in detail he endeavored to seize upon the broadest generalizations, toying with formulas that affected definitive statement, pronouncements that coalesced in the rhetorical posture of withdrawal-in-protest from the epoch's irredeemable degradation. At Athens in 1898, having entered upon those meditations which would lead to the conceit of his twelfth-century citizenship, Adams dismissed his age in a pair of syllogisms set down "in the fewest possible words" as further annotations of the *Law*:

All Civilisation is Centralisation.
All Centralisation is Economy.
Therefore all Civilisation is the survival of the most economical (cheapest.)

. . . .

Under economical centralisation, Asia is cheaper than Europe.
The World tends to economical centralisation.
Therefore Asia tends to survive, and Europe to perish.

(*LHA* 4:557, 558)

The irony of such propositions is that they cheapen the detail of civilized experience out of existence, subordinating everything to the rhetorical act of saying the most "in the fewest possible words." As "scientist," Adams seems to be almost self-consciously vying with the banker in his effort to bring human experience under a rigid economy of terms, demonstrating indeed the worthlessness of a world in which gods and humans, work of the humblest as well as the most refined ability, the sincerest aspiration and the most faithful enterprise, are reduced to a money valuation in a contracted currency.

As he shifted his focus from a present that could exist as totality in his rhetoric only as the economizing general statement, Adams worked to recover a past that lived by virtue of its specific expenditures. Restoring to the art of Saint Michael and the Virgin what his sympathy credited as its self-denying original motive, he affirmed the popular extravagance that insisted (against the economy of Western monotheism and the Christian Trinity) upon a theologically superfluous female deity and set as a measure of an expression's value its essential resistance to translation.[17] The uncle of *Mont Saint Michel and Chartres* by no means forswears the broad or easy generalization: not only does he on occasion wantonly reduce social history to tourist sentiment, but he can never entirely restrain himself from seeing the beloved, particular expression as an expression in turn of a larger energy. To the extent that he can sustain the role of retired historian, however, Adams remains true (in his own way) to the particularities of his subject, putting (as he can) feeling before fact and sympathy before science and returning ever to an aesthetic of personal certification—one which, against his always compulsive framing of historical generalization, presumes to speak only for one self-consciously isolated, superannuated individual. The note that he strikes requires indeed that he admonish his niece-auditor not to translate his expression into her experience.

Robert Mane, the most thorough and eloquent student of *Mont Saint Michel and Chartres*, calls the volume "the most personal book [Adams] ever wrote," and although *Esther* probably surpasses *Chartres* in the psycho-sexual intimacy of its content, Mane's observation is correct insofar as *Chartres* derives its aesthetic unity from the fiction Adams creates of a scholarly, avuncular, garrulous persona.[18] Later, Adams would designate *Chartres* as the first in a sequence intended to frame a dynamic theory of history, but in its initial printing it stood to its author more as a sequel to the 1901 *Memoirs*. As the tribute to the Tevas bore the halftitle "Travels—Tahiti," so *Chartres* bore "Travels/France." Adams thus made good his intention to write (with or without the assistance of King and Hay) "a volume or two of Travels," which could be "a sort of ragbag of everything"; the omission of his name on the title page of the 1904 *Chartres* carried out the letter of his declaration to Hay in 1892 that he would "never again appear as an author" (*LHA* 3:598, 599). Here of course the anonymity had little to do with secrecy, the recipients of *Memoirs* and *Chartres* being well aware of their authorship and certainly indulgent of Adams's wish to appear exclusively within a private circle. Omission of his name from *Memoirs* was dictated by the fact that the experience (if not the English voice) belonged to Arii Taimai and her people. But not to sign a text that all of his readers would know Adams had written out of his own experience is a more complex gesture. If the omission confesses his unwillingness to enter the book as another item in the New England Adamses' catalogue of works, it nevertheless helps set the terms of familiarity on which the uncle means to entrust his confidence, for it is presently understood that the uncle and his confidante are members of the great Norman family.

In Tahiti, Adams had come face-to-face with a history that could only be told as a genealogical sequence; being native to a region of America unusually dominated by prominent families, the historian easily adopted the Teva view of the past as an affair of clans. The end of Tahitian history coincided with the termination of island genealogy as a political sequence and more specifically with the eclipse of the Tevas. To be sure, the American visitor saw in his adopted family a reflection of his New England family's political eclipse, but in the course of the nineties his intimacy with Tahitian history more subtly encouraged him to view himself as the terminus of a long genealogical sequence. The line of descent was to be traced beyond racially mongrel England to Normandy, where Adams claimed a "purer" origin among the specifically Norman portion of his "two hundred and fifty million arithmetical ancestors living in the middle of the eleventh century" (A I 345). Adams's fascination with the Middle Ages was long-standing; as early as his first tour of Europe he had exhibited a decided responsiveness to medieval architecture, and for years he sustained a scholarly interest in medieval Saxon law. In *Esther*, moreover, he had registered an appreciation of the vast difference a Madonna makes in a church. Yet it was only after Brooks, closely following Ruskin, posited the "imaginative type" of the eleventh and twelfth centuries as the antithesis of the modern "economic type" of mind that Adams discovered Normandy, and it was only after he had achieved a vivid sense of his masculine Norman inheritance that he laid claim to the Chartres cathedral as the symbol of his own people's lost feminine ideal.

His August 1895 tour of Normandy in the company of the blood-proud Henry Cabot Lodge effectively launched Adams's new career as a medievalist, his infatuation with Caen, Bayeux, Mont-Saint-Michel, and above all Coutances springing from a sudden emotion of racial identity. That emotion served to fortify Adams's sense of distinction from "the Jew" and his modern Anglo-Saxon minions and confirm a belligerence excited by Brooks Adams's philosophic anti-Semitism. Mane has shown that Lodge, a philosophic xenophobe and an activist for immigration restriction, educated Adams to the heroic view of the Norman race—"the most remarkable of all the people who poured out of the Germanic forests," as Lodge put it to his Senate colleagues in 1896.[19] Although Adams's late medievalism hardly confined itself to the proto-Fascist idolatry of the pure, primitive ancestral type, it articulated for him the differences between an actual present world and a preferred past order and gave him opportunities to indulge his conceit that he had nothing in common with his time. In the *Education* he would abandon that conceit and demonstrate that he remained perforce an active party to his age, but as born-again medievalist he spoke with the affectation of a confidential tone and as one heard, if at all, only by an initiated few.

Indeed as talker the uncle of *Mont Saint Michel and Chartres* seeks to initiate the niece into the glories of the eleventh, twelfth, and thirteenth centuries, yet he does so with every expectation of failure despite their "racial" bond. Given the collateral relation, the generational and sexual differences between uncle and niece, the fiction Adams creates of the text as a monologue brings the book's moral to an immediately sharp point of focus. Even with the inclusion of all nephews, the primary audience of *Chartres* must always remain narrow, for the book is offered as the specific legacy of the American of Norman blood, and we must not overlook Adams's subscription to national and racial distinctions and his habitual, invidious use of them in sorting the human race. But he makes the offer in the paradoxical conviction that the legatees must prove indifferent or absent.[20] In the preface, as the first order of business, Adams confesses that as author he must speak in the comparatively noncommittal tone of an uncle to a niece, the epoch being long past when an author could assume the generative position of father to his filial readers. Significantly, this book that is to develop an ethical stance with regard to preserving artistic expression in its untranslated, pure, plenary form begins with a translation of sorts involving a necessary but unequal rendering. Having opened by quoting the Elizabethan lines, "Who reads me, when I am ashes, / Is my son in wishes," Adams proceeds to alter the terminal phrasing to "niece in wishes" in order to suggest the at best distant relation of reader to author in 1904.

In so doing he arrives for the first time at a precise definition of his retired authorship, and however he might view it in the light of his vocation's evident defeat, authorship would always remain for him principally a genealogical relation. By identifying himself as uncle and not, as he would clearly prefer, father, he would appear to set boundaries to an authorial activity for which he had once sought the broadest field and by which he had hoped to foster a characteristically national life of the mind, one which would gratefully trace its line of descent from such work as his. If on completing his magnum opus in 1890 he could not claim the vast readership his ambition had called for, neither had he succeeded in creating the vital symbology required to summon the national mind into self-confident existence. At Chartres he would study an outbreak of genius that no America of thought and art had emerged to rival; in the Virgin he would find a human ideal whose equivalent American experience seemed powerless to produce. While the aesthetic project of *Mont Saint Michel and Chartres* aims at recovering the motive and feeling of a lost world's expression, the historical lesson concerns the disunity and self-destruction of a people that has forfeited (partly through material greed, partly through an irrepressible intellectual ambition) not merely the old religious aspirations, but the talismanic symbologies that drew human energy into the high communal purpose that created the "divine" art of the Virgin of Chartres. The problem of identifying, articulating, and sustaining a popular genius, of naming and imaging its ideals, of providing it with high objects to pursue, was one to which Adams had given his deepest thought as historian and novelist.

Although as author he renounces all presumption to the status of father, Adams actually defines rather loosely the limitations he sets to his activity. The device of speaking as an uncle to a niece stems from the same determination to minimize (ostensibly) his post-1890 literary ambitions that led to the paradoxically private publication of his late works. But the uncle-niece relationship cannot be as blithely minimal as Adams represents it. His very effort to put it on a casual footing gives him away, perhaps with his own connivance, for a terrible experience confesses itself in the widower's characterization of this relationship as "convenient and easy, capable of being anything or nothing, at the will of either party, like a Mahommedan or Polynesian or American marriage" (A I 341). None of his circle of nieces could have read that without instantly recalling what had befallen the uncle's marriage. Against the ideal union that Esther hungers after ("Of all things on earth," she tells Hazard on the occasion of their final rupture, "to be half-married must be the worst torture" [A I 331]), the kind of marriage that the uncle cites as analogous to the relationship between the two tourists must appear as a distinctly debased article, but the analogy nevertheless suggests that the uncle will pay court to the niece and that between the two may subsist a sublimated eroticism. Even a contemporary American niece may reflect something of the eternal woman, and Adams offers for our consideration the possibility that the uncle's words in her ear might achieve an unlooked-for germination.

Yet that consideration proceeds amid a host of discouragements. The chief is none other than the book's elegiac premise, articulated three pages into chapter 1 ("Saint Michiel de la Mer del Peril") after a description of the Norman landscape and an invocation of Wordsworth's "Intimations" ode have had an opportunity to work an effect, that in such surroundings "one knew life once and has never so fully known it since" (A I 345). Upon this sentiment Adams will build his historical thesis that in abandoning the human ideals embodied in the Norman and French communities by Saint Michael and the Virgin, Western society fell into the path of progressive disunity on which it now (1904) irretrievably finds itself. Yet the development of discouragements forms no part of the prospectus of the tour as Adams frames it in the early chapters. While the speaker establishes himself in the character of valetudinarian, he insists on his old man's privilege to be as young as he will and admonishes his companion that "the pleasure" of touring the lost Gothic world "consists not in seeing the death, but in feeling the life" (A I 438). What Adams treats as the self-evidently tragic course of history is not to distract the tourists from their principal object of pursuit: "not technical knowledge; not accurate information; not correct views either on history, art, or religion; not anything that can possibly be useful or instructive; but only a sense of what those centuries had to say, and a sympathy with their ways of saying it" (A I 397).

The phrasing affects something of the period's defiant aestheticism, yet Adams's designation of such objects confirms his abiding interest in the poesis by which societies, as he understood it, created the illusions that structured their worlds and that constituted a higher reality than the historian could ever recover in establishing merely *wie es eigentlich gewesen ist.* Although he insists that the tourists pursue the poetry and not the facts (an insistence that, as Mane has shown, Adams carried to a fault),[21] his true interest concerns the interrelation of a society's history and its art, and how certain facts give rise to a poetry that, while it lasts, exists as the preeminent fact of social life. The old spire of Chartres, Adams tells us, is worth considering "as the most perfect piece of architecture in the world," but "before taking it as art" he requires that we "take it as history" (A I 398). "Dates are stupidly annoying," he remarks in the presence of the legendary windows, "what we want is not dates but taste;—yet we are uncomfortable without them" (A I 483). In order to arrive at a sense of what the eleventh, twelfth, and thirteenth centuries had to say, he asks that we join him in forming a vivid fancy of the historical occasions that shaped their expression.

A great deal, in fact, of what those centuries say to Adams has to do with the occasions themselves, for the art's primary meaning is ultimately bound up with the circumstances, the motive, the inspiration of its creation. Hence Mont-Saint-Michel, the highest architectural expression of the male, military ideal, becomes comprehensible only as we raise the ghosts of Duke William and his men, frequent visitors to the abbey in the period of the great campaign to conquer England (that watershed in Norman-Anglo-American genealogy). Similarly, "La Chanson de Roland" can rightly be approached only as a poem performed by the Duke's jongleur after supper in the abbey refectory. Adams goes so far as to imagine such a moment in 1058, eight years before the conquest of England, when the military ideal had reached its height and the song of Charlemagne's Spanish wars served the Norman warrior as "a literal mirror," the battles recounted in the poem "scenes of yesterday and to-morrow" (A I 363). Likewise, the Chartres cathedral that we are asked to see is less the structure of 1904 than the cathedral at various stages in its building as those stages can be known through documents and inference; above all, Adams wishes to recover what he believes to have been the intellectual, artistic, and devotional drama of its completion. The apse must be seen as a problem that the architect solved only because he put himself at the full command of the Virgin, who existed for him as a factual person and whose superior genius could best guide him in the shaping of her own palace. We cannot feel the nave until we arrive at a sense of the thirteenth-century "family quarrel" between Blanche of Castile and Pierre de Dreux, donors, respectively, of the north and south transept glass, the discord of which perpetuates their enmity, which now as then is mitigated by Mary who "knows how to manage perverse children" (A I 517).

Adams's interpretation always works toward a vivid notion of the humanity that expressed itself in such manner, always reading the art for what it proclaims of its social and moral origins. But although he can never be comfortable without dates or (more importantly) exact genea-logical tables and is compulsively and conscientiously historical compared to Ruskin and Pater, in whose footsteps he distantly follows, Adams of course has very preconceived notions of what his centuries can and do say and of the character of the humanity that speaks. The sentiment that "one knew life once and has never so fully known it since" serves, again, as the book's premise. Heir (more or less consciously) to Ruskin's characteriza-tion of the Gothic genius as primitive and childlike, Adams sets out to recover the specific childhood of "his" Norman race, striking the keynote on the first page: "The man who wanders into the twelfth century is lost, unless he can grow prematurely young" (A I 343). The personages of the epoch are represented as a race acute of sense, heroic in their capacity for adventure, childlike in their imagination of deities; they are sexually pas-sionate in their devotion and uncalculatingly generous (for the most part) in their forms of worship. Adams permits no doubt of the character that he attributes to this bygone humanity, and his rhetoric of affirmation can be absolute to the point of syntactic absurdity. Generalizing personifica-tion knows no bounds in clauses such as these: "The *twelfth and thir-teenth centuries* believed in the supernatural, and might almost be said to have contracted a miracle-habit, as morbid as any other form of artificial stimulant; *they* stood, like children, in an attitude of gaping wonder be-fore the miracle of miracles which they felt in their own consciousness" (A I 573; italics added).

From a scholarly point of view this is, to be sure, holiday historiogra-phy, and well might we object to the sentimentality that speaks of "the large and simple way" (A I 363) in which the eleventh-century Norman soldier supposedly died or that ascribes to the twelfth century "the child's love of sweets" and a concern with "pain and death" on a par with that of "healthy bears" (A I 541). Problematic as such simultaneously magnifying and reductive depictions are—and puerile as we may too often find the moral intelligence of *Chartres* to be—we may honor Adams's own designation of it as something other than scholarship and accept, if with a view to a more critical pursuit, the judgment of Mane and other apologists that the book be regarded as (pure) poem.[22] If, as Adams instructs us, "what one must insist on, is the good faith of the whole people,—kings, queens, princes of all sorts, philosophers, poets, soldiers, artists, as well as of the commoners like ourselves, and the poor" (A I 579), it is largely because from the first page forward the uncle rhetorically constrains himself (if not his auditor) to make such insistences. He can hardly do otherwise than manifest his own good faith in the epoch he has chosen to espouse.

In certain respects the emeritus historian only exaggerates aspects of an established practice. Despite its scientific aesthetic, Adams's historiography had never been anything but poetic in its fundamental structure and method, and although the prose of the *History* impresses us with its caution and detachment, extravagant statements occasionally emerge from the ironic removes of its classical voice. By contrast, until the last three chapters (and even then not admittedly), science forms no part of *Chartres*'s aim, and Adams claims all along a freedom from the traditional protocol of argumentative historical discourse. If that freedom permits the indulgence of easy generalizations regarding the nature of a past people's experience, it submits by its own lights to the rigors of a lyric sympathy. Adams's prospectus is precise on this point: forswearing the pursuit of anything (immediately) "useful or instructive," it sets as our object "only a sense of what those centuries had to say, and a sympathy with their ways of saying it." Sympathy had figured as an important if covert mode of recovery in the *History*: in profound if momentary sympathy with the evident aims and probable psychology of the lost American democrat, Adams discreetly invented the text by which the democrat spoke the historian's idealized sense of him. Hedged about by a proper scientific suspicion, the democratic faith might seem to have been formulated only so that from it an as yet unearned reaffirmation might be withheld. Relieved in *Chartres* from the double burden of having to affirm an America-in-progress while grappling with the methods of a coming generation, Adams can make his point without arguing or even suspecting it if he so chooses, cultivating in himself what he assumes to have been the susceptibilities of the common people with whom he would identify his anonymous, pilgrimaging self. He affirms out of what from this standpoint is the self-evidence of (common) sympathy; sympathy of itself certifies.

Sympathy supplies meaning, indeed renders it strictly unnecessary: meaning is an evil associated with the translation that marks and enforces separation. Once we have recovered our youth sufficiently to form the large "sense of what those centuries had to say," our "sympathy with their ways of saying it" may readily expand among their various expressions, and in the atmosphere of our sympathy the old expression supplies its own sense. After the prologue to the "Roman du Mont Saint Michel," which Adams gives in the original as well as in an artlessly literal English, the uncle assures us that "anyone who attacks . . . boldly" the medieval French original "will find that the 'vers romieus' run along like a ballad, *singing their own meaning,* and troubling themselves very little whether the meaning is exact or not. One's translation is sure to be full of gross blunders," he continues, coming to the refuge from argument that marks the end of this line of reasoning, "but the supreme blunder is that of translating at all when one is trying to catch not a fact but a feeling" (A I 354–55; italics added). Later in the book, beneath his quotation of prayers to the Virgin by Dante and Petrarch, Adams refuses to translate on the grounds that such would constitute not merely blunder but sacrilege. But even in a poem that does not so intensely realize the intimation of divinity, and so may be grudgingly translated, Adams finds qualities that make the expression a touchstone of our humanity—our humanity consisting above all in our sympathy. Such a poem is the "Tombeor de Notre Dame," which concerns a monk who, lacking other talents, tumbles in the church crypt to demonstrate his devotion to the Virgin. Just as the abbot has decided to discipline him, Mary appears in order to thank the monk for the performance that has left him prostrate on the altar steps. "If you cannot feel the color and quality,—the union of *naïveté* and art,—the refinement,—the infinite delicacy and tenderness—of this little poem," asserts Adams, "then nothing will matter much to you; and if you can feel it, you can feel, without more assistance, the majesty of Chartres" (A I 604).

The majesty of Chartres consists, of course, in what Adams represents as the intense conviction of the twelfth and thirteenth centuries that the Virgin literally visited her shrine and communicated her wishes as to how it should be fashioned, so that the art, as Adams painstakingly submits, is hers. Indeed he represents this conviction as his own "firm belief," prefatory to what stands as the book's most committed certification of the Virgin's reality, its most exact intimation of the divine. "One sees her personal presence on every side," Adams affirms of the great bright absence that bears her impress.

> Anyone can feel it who will only consent to feel like a child. Sitting here any Sunday afternoon, while the voices of the children of the *maîtrise* are chanting in the choir,—your mind held in the grasp of the strong lines and shadows of the architecture; your eyes flooded with the autumn tones of the glass; your ears drowned with the purity of the voices; one sense reacting upon another until sensation reaches the limit of its range;—you or

> any other lost soul, could, if you cared to look and listen, feel a
> sense beyond the human ready to reveal a sense divine that
> would make that world once more intelligible, and would bring
> the Virgin to life again, in all the depth of feeling which she
> shows here,—in lines, vaults, chapels, colors, legends, chants,—
> more eloquent than the prayer-book, and more beautiful than
> the autumn sunlight; and anyone willing to try, could feel it like
> the child, reading new thought without end into the art he has
> studied a hundred times; but what is still more convincing, he
> could, at will, in an instant, shatter the whole art by calling into
> it a single motive of his own.[23] (A I 505)

The absolute, if ever fragile, intelligibility of the Virgin's world on such
occasions would provide Adams with a lasting measure of what on any
given occasion was the modern world's growing unintelligibility.

In the Virgin we meet the apotheosis of sympathy. Although Adams
saw the eternal woman as a sexual force, in Mary he emphasized the
maternal aspect over the erotic, for it is in the character of the mother who
loves unconditionally that Mary unites the human race. Hence Adams's
admonition that we "only consent to feel like a child." By so consenting
we become receptive to what Adams represents as the peculiar religion of
Chartres, a faith that would redeem the lost soul by restoring it to some
semblance of the primal bond between mother and child. At Chartres that
bond of ultimate sympathy constitutes the highest unity, in contrast to
which the Trinitarian God is intellectual, lifeless, divisive. The Divine
Mother "absorbs" the Trinity, abrogates the Father's bloody scheme of
atonement, indeed disputes the Fall itself insofar as she and not the Father
exists as ultimate plenitude. At Chartres the Son "is still an infant under
her guardianship" (A I 424). Not only does he, as infant, not speak,
enjoying a bond with the mother undisrupted by language and its meanings, but to the extent that he is acknowledged to progress beyond infancy,
his life remains pacific: "In the sculptured life of Christ, from the Nativity
to the Ascension, which adorns the capitals of the columns" of the central
doorway, "the single scene that has been omitted is the Crucifixion" (A I
407). Martyrdom has no necessary place in the Virgin's world. By consenting to feel like a child we enter into a maternal plenitude that would deny
the emphatically unsympathetic existence of historical life.

In *Mont Saint Michel and Chartres*, historical life figures as so much
misery, and martyrdom or common mortality is relieved by such illusions
as Saint Michael and the Virgin could give it. Oppressed always by its
physical, social, and political conditions, humanity is portrayed as meeting
its deepest anguish in the "remorseless logic" (A I 574) of a theology that,

in Adams's simplistic but poetic rendering, at once elevated the Trinity and proscribed the human, achieving logical unity but effectively consigning to nonbeing what it defined as a fallen race. Pursuing a universe intelligible to reason, the church fathers economized humanity, with which they had little sympathy, out of the system, confirming its mortal entrapment in historical life. In "Saint Thomas Aquinas," the concluding chapter, Adams treats orthodox Christian theology as the prototype of all subsequent efforts to reduce the universe to a logically demonstrable unity, a project that he at last anxiously grants is indispensable to the necessary business of policing the human race. Yet earlier in the book he duly appreciates the metaphysical nightmare produced by such demands for logical consistency and so celebrates the illogical, willful Holy Mother's embodiment of humankind's last hope. And in this he develops a recognition that he had made years before in "Primitive Rights of Women": that Mary served a popular, symbolic need that could not be satisfied by the Holy Ghost, the abstraction with which the misogynist church fathers replaced the eternal woman when they assimilated the Egyptian Trinity into Christian doctrine, manifesting a reflex later to reappear in the Anglo-American Puritan.

Taking, hypothetically, the most reductive view of the service that she provided as symbol, Adams characterizes Mary as appealing at the basest level to biological compulsion, the popular attachment to her resting "on an instinct of self-preservation"; he cites as the "surest measure" of this appeal "the enormous money value" the people of all classes "put on her assistance" when it came to securing eternal life (A I 574). But Adams never disputes the legitimacy of the popular need for the heterodox dispensation that the Holy Mother offers. By theological definition and daily practice the people may have been criminals; still, "they knew what they were, and, like children, they yearned for protection, pardon and love." To the degree, Adams suggests, that humans have a right to absolute love, they have always been ill-served by the Trinity, for "God could not be Love. God was Justice, Order, Unity, Perfection," and Son and Holy Ghost simply reflected the Father. "The Mother alone was human, imperfect, and could love; she alone was Favor, Duality, Diversity." Only she "could represent whatever was not Unity; whatever was irregular, exceptional, outlawed; and this was the whole human race" (A I 584). So Adams explains the logic of Mary as symbol, but first and last he emphasizes— and certifies—her emotional appeal to an irreducibly tragic human condition: "Mary concentrated in herself the whole rebellion of man against fate; the whole protest against divine law; the whole contempt for human law as its outcome; the whole unutterable fury of human nature beating itself against the walls of its prisonhouse, and suddenly seized by a hope that in the Virgin man had found a door of escape" (A I 596). Assembling a small anthology of her miracle literature, Adams celebrates the symbolic triumph over law, the contempt for civil and religious authority, to which her personality lent itself. Declaring that the Virgin "remains the strongest symbol with which the Church can conjure" (A I 574), he suggests that in her the eternal woman remains eternal and so preserves (rhetorically at least) a hope that in her may still be found a door of some escape.

For Adams, the door of escape remains open insofar as he can refrain from calling into the art "a single motive of his own," a condition, as he demonstrates, impossible to honor except at isolated moments. The specific project of *Mont Saint Michel and Chartres* is to summon at the urging of a decidedly elegiac *private* motive the vivid impression of a golden age through a sympathetic response to the epoch's expression; once invoked, the expression supposedly speaks only as we can forget ourselves and relinquish our designs upon it. Acceptable as we may find this paradoxical proposition as Adams's companions-in-sympathy, as readers we are always aware of a text governed by rhetorical motives that are wholly *its* own. *Chartres* remains a meditation written in modern English for a twentieth-century audience; moreover the author's pose of uncle is fraught with tensions that generate a variety of motives, not all of them consciously reckoned. Through the first ten chapters the prose mostly serves the stated object of the tour—the achievement of "a sense of what those centuries had to say, and a sympathy with their ways of saying it." But after we have completed our visit to Chartres other motives come visibly into play.

To an Adams scion, the character of childless and unmarried uncle had to constitute a confession of historical and more specifically sexual failure, and the self-consciously marginalized author-uncle of *Chartres* openly sets out in pursuit of amusements that might offer momentary compensation for a life that has evidently done little but confirm his race's alleged decline. Claiming the old man's prerogative "to be as young as one will" (A I 344), his first compensation lay in identifying himself with his puissant Norman warrior-ancestor—a gesture with distinct sexual overtones; having done that, he was prepared to retrace "the passionate outbreak of religious devotion to the ideal of feminine grace, charity and love" that occurred "in Normandy while it was still a part of the English kingdom" (A I 388). That "passionate outbreak" is his genealogical warrant to pursue the feminine ideal, in origin not a Norman but a French expression, and he establishes the male's susceptibility to the Virgin as one that confirms sexual strength. Indeed, Adams singles out the art of the Gothic Transition—the expression of that "passionate outbreak"—as the particular "object of our pilgrimage." "The quiet, restrained strength of the romanesque married to the graceful curves and vaulting imagination of the gothic makes a union nearer the ideal," the uncle tells us, "than is often allowed in marriage" (A I 372). Although the Romanesque harmonizes with even the latest Gothic (as does the choir at Mont-Saint-Michel with the north *flèche* of Chartres: "The strength and the grace join hands; the man and woman love each other still"), from this moment of accord all experience traces a decline ultimately leading to the self-conscious terminus of the uncle's occasion.

As long as the tour occupies our attention, the decline of the West remains a theme developed mostly indirectly, our purpose instead being to feel the life of the art and enter by degrees into what the architecture can conjure of Mary's presence. If we begin our pursuit of her by first recovering the emphatically male Norman warrior's sudden susceptibility to the feminine ideal, we enter her shrine at Chartres simply with the tide of "common people," sufferers without sexual self-consciousness or distinction. For the uncle, the Virgin's world becomes intelligible only as he consents to feel like a child, while in his most vivid imagination of her twelfth- and thirteenth-century worshipers (at the end of chapter 10, "The Court of the Queen of Heaven"), he has us finally adopt the perspective of the medieval female suppliant who has lost her children and who looked to Mary as a mother likewise bereaved.[24] Yet once he has declared that "we have finished our pilgrimage" and has bade us to awaken from the apparition to behold the Virgin "looking down from a deserted heaven, into an empty church, on a dead faith" (A I 522), he begins to address more and more directly the course of subsequent decay that he has attributed all along to the ascendancy of the "liberated male"—the French bourgeois and renaissance kings, the English Puritan and materialist philosophers, all of whom may be taken as precursors of what Brooks Adams called "economic man." In "The Three Queens" he turns with decided fury on the male, arguing the woman's superiority and vengefully depicting her in the character of dominatrix. Yet a different motive governs the last three chapters, in which the uncle-author reviews the twelfth- and thirteenth-century effort to arrive at God by reason (or, in the case of the mystics, by the rejection of the reflex action of reason); here the speaker identifies with the masculine temper of Abélard and the womanless, Norman-blooded, "modern" Saint Thomas Aquinas.

This complex and paradoxical transition forms the *pons seclorum* by which Adams not only returns to what he takes to be the philosophical crisis of his own epoch but prepares for the less avuncular, more professorial-father posture of authorship that is to generate the *Education*. "The Three Queens" begins with a dramatic, categorical indictment: "The scientific mind is atrophied, and suffers under inherited cerebral weakness, when it comes in contact with the eternal woman,—Astarte, Isis, Demeter, Aphrodite, and the last and greatest deity of all, the Virgin." Since the Renaissance, in Adams's rather Pre-Raphaelite view, mind has been almost uniformly scientific; hence the rediscovery of the woman requires a "revival of archaic instincts," an experience reserved for the artist alone since "the rest of us cannot feel; we can only study" (A I 523). (And yet the artist's privilege is a distinctly ambivalent one as the character Wharton illustrates it; or else it goes unclaimed, as with Saint-Gaudens, who was more apt, as we learn in "The Dynamo and the Virgin," to feel a horse or a locomotive than a woman as force.) The uncle-author of *Chartres* hesitates to identify himself as an artist yet has all along explicitly discouraged us from taking his text as conventional history. In "The Three Queens" we learn in fact that the historian is a species of the male mind that has "commonly shown fear of women without admitting it" and has tended, like the monk, to "abhor emancipated women" (A I 525). The facts, if not the legends, of the epoch's leading women thus cannot always be known. Content on his part to base his recovery on the special truth of tradition, which "exaggerates everything it touches, but shows, at the same time, what is passing in the mind of the society which *tradites*" (A I 525), Adams credits any source that supports the indomitable, peremptory, theatrical character that he is intent on ascribing to Eleanor of Guienne, Mary of Champagne, and Blanche of Castile, whose three-generation ascendancy over the temporal realm reflected the popular realization in the Virgin of an avatar of the eternal woman.

With distinct relish Adams compiles evidence of the male's emasculation during the reign of the Virgin and the queens from 1137 to 1252. Perhaps it is to preserve the notion that the Norman happily espoused the feminine ideal (as the Norman's Romanesque united harmoniously with even the latest French Gothic) that he singles out the Frenchman as the emasculated party. To be sure, Adams properly cites details of the period's iconography that bear out a sense of discordance and rivalry between the sexes, as in his analysis of the recurrent theme of Aristotle, "symbol of masculine wisdom, bridled and driven by woman" (A I 529), or as in his suggestion of the sexual politics behind the Court of Love. Yet the tourist historian's purported contempt for exact meanings translates, in "The Three Queens," into an impressionism that betrays more than anything else does motives that are decidedly his own. Adams's statement that in Lady Macbeth "Shakespeare realised the thirteenth-century woman more vividly than the thirteenth-century poets ever did" (A I 533) may serve to reinforce all of his claims of that woman's capability, indocility, energy, and decision but detracts from any serious effort to arrive at a precise sense of the epoch's temporal woman, an object that Adams conspicuously pursues in his characterization of the queens as the creators of the Court of Love and in his consideration of Nicolette and Marion. Such a remark indeed seems pointedly directed at establishing Shakespeare's prowess as a postconquest Englishman (hence part-Norman) at the expense of the thirteenth-century French poet who is unable to realize that woman who was his contemporary. Again, the Frenchman appears as the particular scapegoat for Adams's disgust with his sex.

His disgust with the male has everything to do with what he perceives as the masculine, materialist career of postmedieval history, the universal triumph of economic man, and the lost opportunity for something better that America had come to represent. The typical American, although lacking what Adams presents as the cynicism and viciousness of the French bourgeois who withdrew his capital from the cathedral when he began to doubt the true divinity of its returns, comes across as committed to the same line of thought and the same crassly material objects. Against a national mentality that demands "literal exactness and perfectly straight lines" and is convinced of an emotion's reality only when it knows "the money it cost" (A I 425, 428), the uncle would portray himself as defiantly intuitive—to the extent, at least, that he absolutely refuses to translate and insists that we feel with an intensity that renders "meaning" superfluous. But except for the poems of Dante and Petrarch and a passage from the chronicle of Joinville, Adams in fact does provide translations, including portions of Saint Francis's "Cantico del Sole," and while he endeavors to know the Virgin as the child and approach her art motiveless, his thought ever recalls him to a framing of equivalents and forms of explanation that do employ the line and the dollar figuration and that subordinate the art to a meaning that belongs wholly to a latter day.

Hence Adams's designation in the *Education* of *Mont Saint Michel and Chartres* as an attempt to establish "a fixed point" from which he could measure to his own autobiographical moment the motion of "man as a force" (A I 1117).[25] False as this assertion is to much of the spirit of *Chartres* (as well as to the comparative unpremeditation from which the book actually sprang), the scientific mind is never really absent from the uncle's discourse. In the very precincts of the Virgin's shrine he makes bold to propose that the shrine expresses something *else*, something not the Virgin. "All that the centuries can do is to express *the idea* differently:—a miracle or a dynamo; a dome or a coalpit; a cathedral or a world's fair." The "idea" here is intensely masculine: "the struggle of [man's] own littleness to grasp the infinite ... the unsatisfied, incomplete, overstrained effort of man to rival the energy, intelligence and purpose of God" (A I 439; italics added). Although Adams conjures the Virgin's presence largely by means of the reiterated insistence that we feel her "in fact" as the supreme artist of Chartres, when he is not trying to convey some sense of her immediate reality he gravitates to a conception of her as a translation of force: a force that, however officially atheistic and hence sexless, is yet male to the degree that it retains an association with the male omnipotent God whom it has come to supplant.[26] At some level Adams must have been aware of this impiety. Formulating in the *Education* the supposedly scientific aim of *Mont Saint Michel and Chartres* as the objective recovery of a humanity emotionally but also philosophically able to know its world as a unity, he conspicuously avoids his title's reference to Chartres. "Eight or ten years of study had led Adams to think he might use the century 1150–1250, expressed in *Amiens* Cathedral and the works of Thomas Aquinas, as the unit from which he might measure motion down to his own time" (A I 1117; italics added). Well might we read the gesture as an attempt to keep the shrine and his meditations there as inviolate, untranslated, as possible.

Yet if the explanation of *Chartres*'s aim that Adams gives in "The Abyss of Ignorance (1902)" misrepresents the origin and complex mood of the book, it does correspond with the direction that Adams takes in the last three chapters: "Abélard," "The Mystics," and "Saint Thomas Aquinas." What these chapters actually show is that the century from 1150 to 1250, if united in an aspiration to touch God behind the veil, was divided over the means of approach, the schoolmen and theologians opting for the slow and methodical approach through reason while the mystics and devotees of the Virgin worked to absorb themselves directly into the Absolute through a faith that suppressed the reasoning reflex. Adams sympathizes with both means and finds their tension expressive of the tragic dual-mindedness of a society that always aspired, whatever route it took, in good faith. Yet it is clear that Adams regarded the struggle to unite with (or, more ambiguously, to "rival") God as a fundamentally masculine enterprise, between man and his masculine divinity.

In dramatizing the progress of the Church Intellectual, Adams represents the Gothic Transition in a curiously different light, one which would seem to abrogate the earlier view that had seen the round arch as male and martial, the pointed as female, and their occurrence together as a nearly ideal marriage of sexual opposites. "The Transition," he now submits, "is the equilibrium between the Love of God,—which is Faith, and the Logic of God,—which is Reason; between the round arch and the pointed"; the pointed being specifically associated with Aristotle. Unable to decide "which pleases most," Adams chooses to affirm only that "the moment of balance is exquisite. The last and highest moment is seen at Chartres where, in 1200, the charm depends on the constant doubt whether emotion or science is uppermost." This assessment of Chartres's charm certainly differs from those of the earlier chapters, which absorbed the cathedral insistently in the person of the Virgin. If at Chartres doubt persists, opening our susceptibilities to the Virgin who, herself a multiple, unites a multiplicitous humanity in her defiant and heretical love, at "Amiens, doubt ceases; emotion is trained in school; Thomas Aquinas reigns" (A I 638). As "scientist" grown impatient with retirement, overly confined by the posture of uncle whose too exclusive profession had been to sympathize with a bewildering diversity of expression, Adams turns at last to Amiens and Aquinas for the epoch's most deliberate unitary expression and the one which most reflected his own philosophical desire and thus best served to frame the progress of his own ambivalent science.

Before settling into Aquinas, Adams must devote a chapter not only to the mystics' categorical rejection of the path of reason but one also to the great theologian's precursor in the way of logic, Pierre du Pallet or Abélard. In Abélard he presents the sympathetic figure of the philosophical iconoclast, the reformer whose "instincts" (as Adams, in perfect sympathy, wrote of Jefferson's) "led him to widen rather than to narrow the bounds of every intellectual exercise," and who scorned to "abstain from using his mind on any subject merely because he might be drawn upon ground supposed to be dangerous" (A II 100). As a student he was "not afraid of dabbling in forbidden fields" (A I 609); after establishing his influence in the schools as a dialectician he began to apply his disputatious and probing arts in the sensitive field of theology. As theologian he became the apostle and expositor of the Holy Ghost and for his scientific handling of this and other official mysteries was censured by the Council of Sens. The fate of this intellectual adventurer at the hands of his period's greatest vested interest surely reminded Adams of that of Galileo, which he had held up in "The Tendency of History" as the fate that awaited the uncompromising scientific historian.

So sympathetic is Adams to Abélard the well-born iconoclast, the strong mind ultimately silenced and isolated, that he downplays, even if he does not conceal, Abélard's role in the demise of the woman and his pursuit of the Godhead reduced to pure necessitarian logic. Yet if he registers no indignation over the logician's preference of the Holy Ghost to the Virgin, Adams largely concedes the justice of Saint Bernard's determination to assert the unity that comes of faith over Abélard's science. And in the chapter's opening paragraph he puts his finger on Abélard's fatal limitation in explaining Héloïse's absence from the story. This legendary romance, without which, Adams writes, the "twelfth century, with all its sparkle, would be dull" (A I 606), exhibited a disturbing imbalance; while tradition suggested that Héloïse "philosophised only for the sake of Abélard," he in his turn "taught philosophy to her not so much because he believed in philosophy or in her as because he believed in himself" (A I 607). Nothing in the twelfth century could be further than this from the example of the artists at Chartres, for not only does Abélard hold aloof from Héloïse and the attraction of the feminine ideal but from any ideal not essentially egoistic. As Robert Mane observes, Abélard's tragedy stems from his singular self-consciousness, which proved too disruptive of the epoch's emotional modes of achieving unity to be long tolerated.[27]

Still, for all of his self-consciousness his egotism is that of a "childlike time" (A I 609) and his personality for Adams remains appealingly contradictory. From his story Héloïse never entirely disappears; insofar as she is established by Abélard as "Prioress of the Oratory of the Holy Trinity" she serves symbolically to mitigate the logician's efforts to depersonalize the Godhead. So important to the book is the theme of marriage that we must pay particular attention to the passage with which the chapter concludes, taken from the condolence letter Peter the Venerable wrote to Héloïse after Abélard's death. If Adams's version of the story does not dwell on the couple's separation, it nevertheless gives us reasons to consider theirs as a kind of half-marriage, Héloïse's faith perhaps saving her from an isolation comparable to Esther's. Against the impression he creates of their unequal devotion and estrangement, Adams quotes Peter, who assures the bereaved spouse that "he to whom you are united, after your tie in the flesh, by the better and stronger bond of the divine love" rests in God, and that "He keeps him to restore him to you by His Grace" (A I 636). The passsage, for Adams, rings "with absolute passion," the more so no doubt for the private resonance of his own experience in marriage and bereavement and his long experience as a writer of condolence letters. This is one of the most affecting, uninsistent, yet devastatingly ironic moments in the book. At no point in *Mont Saint Michel and Chartres* is the tragic separation of the man from the woman so realized as here, where the future's shadow falls between the two twelfth-century historical persons.

Neither Saint Francis nor Saint Thomas Aquinas offers such complications. Strict antitheses in most respects, neither attempts a marriage that does not aim at espousing the divine thing-in-itself, and although Aquinas's "science" contrasts with the archaic animism of Saint Francis, the *Summa Theologiae*, in Adams's view, is finally no less pantheistic than the "Cantico del Sole." At the end of "The Mystics," Adams prints the latter ("too sincere for translation") as a plausible "last word of religion," and proposes Saint Francis as humankind's possible "ultimate expression" (A I 660): the eternal child who meets the creator in the Creation, loving each of its details "as a child loves the taste and smell of a peach" (A I 661). The comparison suggests the extent to which Adams viewed Saint Francis in the light of his own Quincy childhood, for he would soon be writing of his drunken childhood joy in nature and his fondness for peaches and dutiful sacrifice of the best specimens to his grandfather's science. Sympathetic as Saint Francis proves, the whole movement of the book makes clear that there comes an end to one's willingness to feel like a child just as surely as there came an end to one's personal and racial childhood. With Saint Thomas Aquinas, the thirteenth-century half-Norman theologian whose task was to "house" a society that had passed beyond the simpler unities of childhood and passionate outbreaks, Adams completes his circle of pilgrimage. His representation of Aquinas's "solution" returns him to the large subject that was proving indeed the "matter for a lifetime," as he had foreseen at the end of the second "Session," that concerned as always "the working out of the great problems of human society under all their varied conditions" (*NAR* 111:62).

How much the thought that is credited to Aquinas in the stunning if troubled last chapter actually resembles the untranslated original has been in fact persuasively challenged. Heavily indebted as Adams was to secondary sources in his architectural and literary chapters, he had nevertheless spent time in and about the buildings and had sustained direct contact with the texts. As for the epoch's intellectual edifice, however, "he never," as Robert Mane writes, "actually visited the church," obtaining his knowledge of medieval metaphysics from commentaries.[28] This presents no real problem in the story of Abélard, for despite Adams's lengthy dramatization of Abélard and William of Champeaux sparring over their respectively nominalist and realist proofs of God, the moral of Abélard finally concerns the dead ends (intellectually and politically) of his enterprise and his falling out of relation with the eternal woman. But with Aquinas, who of course never married and whose logic flourished at Mary's expense, there exists almost no life that is not thought. It matters greatly, therefore, that Adams (to all appearances) never opened the *Summa Theologiae* and that of Aquinas's five proofs of God, with which he would have had to become familiar through his secondary sources, he represents only the most purely physical—that which argues God's existence from motion.[29] But having thus constrained the breadth of Aquinas's thought at a distance from the original texts, Adams still is not finished: in working from mere excerpts of the one proof of God's existence, Adams mistranslates, as Michael Colacurcio has shown, the key word *movens*, usually rendered "mover," to "motor": " 'I see motion,' said Thomas:—'I infer a motor!' " (A I 667).[30] He thereby absorbs Aquinas's specialist meaning into the problematically mechanistic universe of a later day. Nowhere else in *Mont Saint Michel and Chartres* is an expression of the Gothic age so dominated and distorted by a contemporary motive.

For that reason, "Saint Thomas Aquinas" reveals that the tour, having begun in elegy, inevitably subserved a somber reckoning of that world that the uncle (if not the niece) practically never leaves. Yet that sense of inevitability supplies the chapter's force. If Adams gives us an Aquinas who too obviously reflects his own anxieties with regard to the impasses of Western thought, an Aquinas who translates much too readily into a vocabulary of force determinism (itself a translation of Calvin), he nevertheless creates a hero animated by his own lifelong excitement in the constructive intellectual task as well as one made tragic by his own maturing sense that the most masterful text structures human society much less than ambition dared hope. By visualizing Aquinas as the architect of a theological cathedral Adams is able to introduce a dramatic action into the intellectual materials with which his volume must conclude, the learned doctor's task none other than to raise an edifice capable of housing God and humanity in one "harmonious home" (A I 665). This, for Adams, has been the task of Western thought ever since its social and intellectual currents broke away from the channel in which the Virgin briefly held them and exists in the present of his own text as the categorical imperative of science, philosophy, and history as well as the lurking obsession of such literary work as he might undertake in retirement. The interest of Thomism lies at once (paradoxically) in its "astonishingly scientific method" (A I 689), which makes the theologian a contemporary of Haeckel and Clerk Maxwell, and in its implicit, self-effacing faith, which keeps Thomism "medieval" in that term's best sense, preserving it from "the corruption and pollution" of the coming "enlightened Europe" (A I 691).

But for a single difficulty, Thomism, in Adams's rendering, even subdues the world's troubling multiplicity, seeing all phenomena as "a simple emanation from God" (A I 674). God is conceived as the Prime Motor with which the human "conductor" remains congruent as long as it "elects" to return the energy passing through it (which only ostensibly belongs to it to spend as it chooses) to the motive source. By regarding the cathedral as a dynamic equilibrium (which of course requires that he blur the distinction between electricity and gravity), Adams constructs a literary cohesion between the electrical and architectural analogies; playing admittedly fast and loose with the theology proper, he returns us ever to the heroic conception of Saint Thomas Aquinas engaged in the drama of building his church from its foundation in God upward to the central tower of church dogma and the spire, the human will to converge. After celebrating the apparent success of each stage of the Church Intellectual's construction, Adams proceeds to qualify the success, adducing reservations that always come back to whether humanity can be held to such an arrangement—whether it can be induced to agree to the small, undignified if redeeming place that the architecture reserves for it. Once the cathedral has been built, its success rests on the perilous conditions that "Faith," not science, "alone supports it" and that humanity consent to become the "many-sided, voluntary, vanishing human soul" aspiring to God that the church spire represents (A I 695, 692).

Were it not for its inconstant human complement the cathedral would stand. And the trouble with humanity, in Adams's estimate, is that it requires socially and morally an omnipotent, judging God but must insist on its individual free will, its status as an independent energy faced with moral choice. In "Les Miracles de Notre Dame," Adams championed the outlawed human multiple and the woman whose love created a familial unity beyond law, but after the waning of the feminine ideal's attractive force, human freedom, for Adams, becomes a grotesque spectacle that repels sympathy. "Satire," he had bitterly observed at the end of his discussion of *Roman de la Rose*, "took the place of worship. Man, with his usual monkey-like malice, took pleasure in pulling down what he had built up" (A I 571–72). A humanity that had evolved a magnificent art in what it had felt to be the neighborhood of its God resumed its bestial affinities, and Adams presents subsequent history as a self-serving exercise of human will unennobled by ideals. The political conclusion that he draws is emphatic. "A church which embraced, with equal sympathy, and within a hundred years" expressions ranging from the Virgin and Saint Francis to Saint Thomas Aquinas "was more liberal than any modern state can afford to be." In the alarmist mode of his correspondence with Brooks he avers that "such elasticity long ago vanished from human thought" (A I 675).

Turning over, in this mood, the contradiction between God's omnipotence and human freedom, Adams frankly scorns the idea that anyone "ever seriously affirmed the literal freedom of will," affirming that the contradiction "always must exist, unless man either admits that he is a machine, or agrees that anarchy and chaos are the habit of nature, and law and order its accident. The agreement," he continues chillingly, "may become possible, but it was not possible in the thirteenth century nor is it now" (A I 685). Without human thought's old "elasticity" there exists, evidently, no liberality, no middle ground between order and anarchy, and mechanism, he submits, is more sympathetic than chaos. From this position of altogether contracted sympathy comes the astonishing comment that "Saint Thomas was working for the Church and the State, not for the salvation of souls, and his chief object was to repress anarchy" (A I 685). In a subsequent passage that aims at translating the doctrine of grace into the electrical analogy that he has drawn of Thomism, Adams graphically portrays how indifferent the Aquinas of this reading must prove to the salvation of individuals who are merely parts in the machine:

> Supposing the conduction to be insufficient for a given purpose; a purpose which shall require perfect conduction? Under ordinary circumstances, in ninety-nine cases out of a hundred, the conductor will be burned out, so to speak; condemned, and thrown away. This is the case with most human beings. Yet there are cases where the conductor is capable of receiving an increase of energy from the Prime Motor, which enables it to attain the object aimed at. In dogma, this store of reserved energy is technically called Grace. In the strict, theological sense of the word as it is used by Saint Thomas, the exact, literal meaning of Grace is "a motion which the Prime Motor, as a supernatural cause, produces in the soul, perfecting free-will." It is a reserved energy, which comes to aid and reinforce the normal energy of the battery. (A I 688)

Again, by translating *movens* to motor, Adams perpetuates *his* motive even as he purports to be giving an "exact, literal meaning."

In the end Adams does not so insistently vilify the human but honors as he must the persistent human effort to order the universe. This effort constitutes the mythos he would impart from one generation to another; translation subserving tradition, as that is possible. All along he has claimed a share of the "common" person's perspective, to be one with the average pilgrim who has had to feel and believe where reason fails, and that pose is not entirely disingenuous. The chaos of human experience has gathered despite the continuous intellectual effort to preserve the dogma of organic unity; the demise of that dogma must finally be attributed to "the universe itself which presented different aspects as man moved" (A I 695). Adams absolves his own generation specifically, telling the niece that "your parents in the nineteenth century were not to blame for losing the sense of unity in art" (A I 694). Far from merely serving as a tool of repression, Thomism figures in the last pages above all "as art": the "most complete expression" of human aspiration, even though tragically "unsatisfied, incomplete, overstrained" (A I 695, 439), and as such catastrophic. The overambitious, partly fallen Beauvais, not the mathematically perfect Amiens, emerges here as the proper material counterpart to the *Summa Theologiae*. So the final image of Thomism, and the epoch that it closes, restores the human figure in its good, if tragically uncertain, faith. Logic can only support aspiration:

> If Faith fails, Heaven is lost. The equilibrium is visibly delicate beyond the line of safety; danger lurks in every stone. The peril

of the heavy tower, of the restless vault, of the vagrant buttress; the uncertainty of logic, the inequalities of the syllogism, the irregularities of the mental mirror,—all these haunting night-mares of the Church are expressed as strongly by the gothic Cathedral as though it had been the cry of human suffering, and as no emotion had ever been expressed before or is likely to find expression again. The delight of its aspirations is flung up to the sky. The pathos of its self-distrust and anguish of doubt, is buried in the earth as its last secret. You can read out of it whatever else pleases your youth and confidence; to me, this is all. (A I 695)

The book thus ends on the note of personal certification but also in the suspicion that such sympathy for the tragically divided and limited human being may not (yet) cross the *pons seclorum* between uncle and youthful niece.

The splendid last paragraph exhibits Adams's commitment to a process of writing—and hence a rhetoric—that insistently undermines the certitudes and closures in which the speaker wishes to take shelter. The conclusion returns us particularly to a thought that had occurred to the uncle as he stood before Mont-Saint-Michel, to which he had hoped to come as to an ancestral "cradle of rest"—that "when you look longer at it, you begin to doubt whether there is any repose in it at all" (A I 349). What Adams registers as the architecture's lack of repose materializes as his own text's restlessness, the vagrancy of the verbal cathedral magnifying that of the stone. If art at the last does not turn into history, it remains always historical, part of a continuous paradoxical discourse. Having succeeded in establishing several possible versions of "a fixed point," Adams's inquiry would return now to America—womanless, perhaps, but not without its curious modes of regeneration—and the twentieth century as it was to be met there.

7

Henry Adams's Bequest

The Widower as Historian

OF THE VARIOUS motifs that animate *Mont Saint Michel and Chartres*, none recurs more insistently than that of the Gothic expression's exceptionality in the course of human experience. The achievement, Adams assures us, holds ever aloof from our reflex effort to know it as part of a sequence. The "twelfth-century windows break the French tradition. They had no antecedent, and no fit succession" (A I 469). The thirteenth century offers "a beauty not always inherited, and sometimes not bequeathed" (A I 352). "The immense structure" of Saint Thomas Aquinas's *Summa Theologiae* "rested on Aristotle and Saint Augustine at the last, but as a work of art it stood alone, like Reims or Amiens Cathedrals, as though it had no antecedents" (A I 665). And in the book's closing paragraph, Adams declares that the cathedral's anguish and aspiration are proclaimed "as no emotion had ever been expressed before or is likely to find expression again" (A I 695). The nonsequential uniqueness of the expression requires an irregular and singular study: if we "want to know what Churches were made for," we must return to Chartres "on some great festival of the Virgin" and give ourselves up to it; and for this we must "come alone! That kind of knowledge cannot be taught and can seldom be shared" (A I 441).

By such insistence would Adams share some part of his sense of the expressions' miraculous character—the genius by which "the infinite rises into a new expression, always a rare and excellent miracle in thought" (A I 441). As miracle it defies sequence; it cannot and indeed must not admit of mere evolutionary explanation, the historian's prediction-in-retrospect. It is rather as debacle that it enters history—history conceived as a decreation that in the end excepts nothing, translating all phenomena as variously expressing the equalization of cosmic force. In the *History*, the question of whether American experience would prove miracle or debacle remained rhetorically open, the moral catastrophe implicit in the failure of the Republican visionaries suspended by the seemingly uniformitarian and still (as of 1890) strictly unforeseeable evolution of democratic society. In *Mont Saint Michel and Chartres*, however, history for Adams has assumed a decidedly postcatastrophic tone. Meditated in the uncle's rhetoric of terminated genealogy, human experience appears uncertain only in the details of its protracted self-demise.

Even more marked by the discontinuous instance is the experience inscribed in the *Education*. Metaphors of force determinism are thus invoked more systematically to explain the incoherence of history—history, that is, as an idealistically conceived human construct or reading of experience assuming some form of divine providence. Only as progressive decreation, Adams shows us, does history obviously cohere. Yet, as we have seen, the *Education*'s rhetoric does not proceed from a self-confirmed point of genealogical termination: the text as published book resists the conviction that posterity will not learn from the past, that future society cannot still elect the history it would inhabit. The present of the speaker's occasion is at once post- and precatastrophic—located, in the scheme of the dynamic theory of history, between irruptions of force in a period marked by frantic adaptation to the increasingly volatilized human environment. Although Adams can form little material notion of his future reader, to the very real degree that he wishes to bear toward that reader a redeemingly generative relationship, the *Education* cannot insist that the future is absolutely void. The new century, in the *Education*, is both catastrophe and possibility, and we do well to note that behind his prognostications of the increasing sexlessness of the American citizen, or behind the ersatz mathematics of the dynamic theory, Adams abstains from any steady or detailed seeing of the America to come. Not surprisingly (the *Education* is after all an exercise in retro- as well as prospection) the mood of *Mont Saint Michel and Chartres* now and then claims him; so he writes, much as he had written of the epoch belonging to the Virgin and the three queens, of a sixteen-year "reign" "during which Mrs. Cameron and Mrs. Lodge led a career, *without precedent and without succession*, as the dispensers of sunshine over Washington" (A I 1024; italics added). The book's closing paragraphs seem particularly to avert themselves from the prospect of a future and a broad anonymous readership, absorbed as they are in the passing of the three friends, King, Hay, and Adams, whose succession remains uncertain at best. Whether we take "Nunc Age" or the 1916 preface as the book's "final" note, we find that note one of studied hesitation.

In assessing Henry Adams's bequest—especially as that bequest is framed by that last hesitant testament, the 1918 *Education*—we come back repeatedly to the proposition that history is too discontinuous to support those acts of bequeathal which Adams at every stage of his career envisioned as the ultimate image of successful authorship. Moreover we come back to that proposition with an irony that foregrounds our very readership, for to assess that bequest is in certain respects already to accept it, to grant its claim on our attention, and to refute (however tentatively) Adams's own suspicion that his word must prove alien to the coming public. The fact of our readership alone constitutes a first (if least) measure of Adams's success, but our readership is apt to proceed from our share in the broader concern of his life's project, and it is by what his project dialogically contributes to our own that his success is finally to be measured. If the twentieth century seems ultimately more continuous than Adams foresaw, it is not simply because he pushed his vision of historical discontinuity to what for him were the furthest imaginable extremes, but because civilization has not yet chosen or chanced to implement its perfected capacities for self-destruction. The fact that he speaks to us with continued urgency suggests that he is our predecessor precisely because he remains our contemporary. If his appeal lies in his extremity, in his sense of an immediately imperiled public life, it lies as well in his example of historical consciousness striving for coherence against the conviction that our common resource for this essentially public work is radically diminished, if not bankrupt. His bequest is that of the disinherited man of means, the *Education* being at once the record of disinheritance and the inconclusive trial of those means which remain to him—and, through him, perhaps to us.

Those means, as Adams repeatedly reminds us, are those fundamentally of his great-grandfather's generation. Like John Adams, the great-grandson beheld the crippling ironies (the vice and unreason, the organized avarice, the catastrophic politics) of an "enlightened Europe," and *Mont Saint Michel and Chartres* distantly reflects Karl Marx's reading of the postmedieval period as the dissolution of ancient communal unities in an all-out formation of a market economy. Nevertheless, the light of his neoclassical republican heritage always shone for him, and as he witnessed the U.S. government rapidly expand as an imperial power at home and abroad, the scion ever honed his sense of the hypocrisy with which nineteenth- and twentieth-century leaders invoked the "pure" revolutionary-period doctrines. An old man in the first years of the twentieth century, the belated child of the eighteenth remains nowhere more true to certain idols of the Enlightenment than in his habit of holding humanity accountable for the course its history takes, in his conviction that moral and rational capacities alone make possible modern (as opposed to medieval) social life, or in his depiction of the irrational and therefore corrupt behavior of concentrated power. Skeptical of any doctrine that requires the abiding reasonableness or essential intelligibility of humanity and its world—suspicious indeed of the efficacy of his abashedly Newtonian "literary language"—he still never manages to abandon the idea that public life can be redeemed only by such emergency action as must proceed from a shared capacity for rational self-reflection that can translate into concerted action operating toward the restraint of power. The dynamic theory may project humanity as doomed without the "miracle" of a sudden evolution in the power of the human brain, but the *Education* irresistibly lends itself to an aspiringly rational discussion of collective experiences and options to be conducted by the brain trust as constituted in the 1907 (or 1918) present.

The *Education*, in short, ventures, even as it profoundly suspects, the ultimate rationality of the dialogic process. And it is in this that we feel at once Henry Adams's inheritance and his signal disinheritance. Enact as he must certain eighteenth-century assumptions as to the secular reformability of the world, he does so as one deprived of his share of confidence in the American background's supposedly enabling resource. At times he attributes his disinheritance to the scrupulous conservatism of his extinct "class," which had been too patriotic, too republican to embrace the unreflective pragmatism, the overwhelmingly monetary canon of success that had produced the dominant American tone. Class in Adams's usage is of course practically synonymous with clan, the Quincy Adamses, whose self-interrogation and propensity to take "retrograde" positions predisposed its sons to withdrawal from the material game of life, despite being bearers of the best cards. Cohesive and fateful as the Adams family is portrayed to be, however, it too manifests discontinuities that Henry Adams would more particularly impress upon us. As son, he looks back on a father whose "perfect poise" and "intuitive self-adjustment" (A I 746) marked him as a family anomaly more than his failure to become president and whose modest aloofness to both good and bad fortune was a trait that the next generation neither inherited nor acquired. "He stood alone," writes Henry of Charles Francis Adams. "He had no master—hardly even his father. He had no scholars—hardly even his sons" (A I 745). The motif of disinheritance, of nonsequentiality, of the sometimes miraculously, but much more often absurdly, isolated instance, is hardly a matter of singular examples. The *Education* as a whole emerges as a sustained allegory of disinheritance, and from our perspective that allegory exists as the ironic genealogy of the son- , daughter- , or contemporary-in-wish who is Adams's common reader.

We have seen that some divergence from family practice had been necessary for the literatus to define his own Adamsian vocation. As Charles Francis Adams's son, Henry had carried, much as his father had, a free pass, "good for this generation only," and Madeleine Lee's scorn of Americans who should say "Abraham is our father" (A I 25) reflects the liberation of the son of Abraham established in Washington as a man of letters, prepared to reclaim his inheritance at a distance. Although never one to renounce all consideration to which his name entitled him, it was as the privileged American sensible of losing his "common," ideological birthright to invent self and world—a birthright secured by such national fathers as Jefferson, Gallatin, and John and John Quincy Adams—that Henry began to concern himself with paternity on a cosmic scale. His sense in old age of a cold, unapproachable, sadistically absent God-the-Father could not help but exaggerate the gulf he describes as having always subsisted between Charles Francis Adams and himself. Yet for much of his life he exhibited little practical need for theological certainty; as long as his work could go forward on the assumption that his authorship participated in the fostering of a great national order, he remained much less subject to the sensation of a universe devoid of reason and direction. By the time he came to write *Mont Saint Michel and Chartres* and the *Education*, however, his perspective had greatly altered. For Henry Adams the elegist, earthly genealogy satisfactorily cohered only in the now bygone conviction of its divine propinquity: the perception of God as "feudal *seigneur*" (A I 368), or holy mother, or, in its severely intellectual "Thomist" form, as direct act of creation—the soul, essentially a divine emanation, having "no father or mother" (A I 673).

Adams the elegist treats that conviction as an experience absolutely of the past, and in treating it so, projects contemporary humanity as small, contemptible, isolated, and sorrowful, the alternately depraved and hapless creature of its technology. The sorrow which that projection held for Adams may be gathered from the fact that throughout his career he returned to the notion that earthly generation, assured of its innate vitality—its biological and cultural capacity to invent—creates its own world, realizing a distinct, if mostly unwritten, social order, and in so doing abides in the sensation of the divinity's nearness.

Had not that sensation once been known in America? For the Henry Adams of the early 1880s, it had been possible to conceive the Jeffersonian democrat as undertaking his material tasks with the sense that he strove not simply for personal gain, but against the immemorial tyranny that had characterized human institutions; plausibly, the frontiersman in his wilderness responded to the earth as to an absolutely accessible goddess. His paternity was not at issue: he had created himself in conjunction with the New World where the eighteenth-century glorification of man had spawned a practical if uncodified religion, and where the citizen's material achievements vindicated the seeming irrationalism by which he dismissed his European genealogy. For such comparatively innocent experience post–Civil War America offered no ground. As members of a society in which shared ideals, compelling purpose, and the possibility of a "really spiritual" communion are not possible, Esther and her circle provide a kind of inverse example and may be taken to define the conditions in which Adams found himself while at work recovering the bygone Jeffersonian democrat. Amid the constraints of genteel Manhattan, Hazard can fleetingly perceive Esther as "a part of nature itself," but because no man comes forward after *her* father's death to espouse her and the visionary order she may embody, Esther feels herself to be "a solitary bird," able to see "on her aërial path . . . no tie more human than that which bound her to Andromeda and Orion" (A I 263, 264). For Esther the human tie, loving and procreant, would have satisfactorily answered for the divine, and her social isolation figures as a cosmic alienation and absurdity. The passage foreshadows the *Education* and the late essays, where the moral emptiness of the astronomer's heaven would serve as a dominant existential metaphor.

Esther, as we have seen, turns upon the loss of the marital occasion. For the narrator of the *Education*, the marital occasion lies in the past: the past of the twelfth and thirteenth centuries, but also the past of 1872 to 1892, the narration's twenty ostensibly missing years. Now and then we are permitted to see traces of Adams's once sanguine nationalist ambition, but the appointed failure of America to espouse such ideals as the reformer-historian might project becomes evident in the portentous closing paragraphs of "Quincy (1838–1848)," where the death of John Quincy Adams, in bringing an end to Henry's boyhood, marks also the first intimation of the consolidating power that had already antiquated the ideals that proceeded from Quincy's puritanical deism. This failure is made explicit in "Rome (1859–1860)," where the narrator sights the young Henry Adams "on the steps of the Church of Santa Maria di Ara Coeli" and invites us to contemplate the would-be historian against the old man's crushingly retrospective knowledge: that the empire, in its inexplicable failure as in its millennial ambition, "was going to be America" (A I 803). Into his various careers—private secretary, reformer, teacher, and historian—the Adams of the *Education* reads the historicist crisis that had surfaced in his earliest essays as well as in the *Gallatin* and *Democracy* and that had darkened the experiment of *Esther* and deflected the idealism in which the *History* was originally framed; but in the *Education* he achieves for the first time a sustained articulation of that crisis, recognizing it precisely as an "Evolution which did not evolve" (A I 931). Conceiving the breakdown of nineteenth-century idealism as a loss of providential directionality (genealogy) in human movement, he portrays his life less as the attempt to generate, through a tireless authorship, an America of thought and art, than as the steady loss of all acceptably transcendent principles of unity, old and new—without which supposedly no career of his had ever begun in earnest.

The preoccupation with unity is thus ultimately cosmogonic and casts Adams in the role of perennial son, whose efforts to trace his origin compound his sense of fatherlessness. "To an American in search of a father," he writes in "Darwinism (1867–1868)," "it mattered nothing whether the father breathed through lungs, or walked on fins, or on feet" (A I 930). Yet if nineteenth-century science coldly refuted the God of Scripture, its evidence had hardly cohered in a new cosmogony—a new text on the authority of which an American scientific and literary elite could set about creating a renascent human order. For the young Henry Adams, as depicted by the narrator of the *Education*, the evidence did seem to point to a true, if as yet unwritten, genealogy, but the story appeared to be lost in something very like a corrupt and discontinuous text. "On the further verge of the Cambrian," beyond the Siluria of one's "grinning" ancestor, the *Pteraspis*, "rose the crystalline rocks from which every trace of organic existence had been erased" (A I 929). The void to which the search for origins led coalesced with the void toward which the meditation of ends increasingly tended. Perhaps those very rocks of Wenlock Edge had come to mind as Adams contemplated, in writing the last pages of the *History*, the furthest verge of democratic evolution.

What Adams reads as an act of erasure, perpetrated as it were by an invisible hand, defines the catastrophe of the post-Darwinian historian: his loss of all grounds for believing that he might someday succeed in restoring to human history its orderly descent from the originating One, and with them the mandate to create a supreme secular order. Herein lies the first condition of disinheritance, indeed all precedent of a discontinuous historicizing: the loss not only of the moral law but of its evident reflection in such physical law as offered (in the manner of Newton's principles) some ultimate image of harmonic coherence. The *Education*'s necessarily egocentric historiography detects discontinuity on the large and small scale, indeed registers events as erasures: much of the book's fame rests in the fact that it requires the reader to "miss" two decades in the turn of the page between "Failure (1871)" and "Twenty Years After (1892)," but we are also asked to consider Adams's undergraduate years at Harvard as an "autobiographical blank" (A I 770). In a remark that Adams attributes to John Hay, who gazes upon the Washington scene from his window on Lafayette Square, the Civil War (that signal experience of a generation) itself fades from the page of common memory: "There is old *Dash* who broke the rebel lines at *Blank*burg!" (A I 1017; italics added). "History," Adams had written in *Chartres*, "is only a catalogue of the forgotten" (A I 373), but in the *Education* it appears more precisely as a record of the process of forgetting—the mind waking at life's end "to find itself looking blankly into the void of death" (A I 1140). Beneath this process Adams meditates a history most acutely memorable as de-creation: the death of Louisa Adams Kuhn, avatar in the *Education* of the "eternal woman" (A I 799), remains always "the last lesson,—the sum and term of education" (A I 982), which leads to the apocalyptic moment in which Mont *Blanc* "looked to him what it was,—a chaos of anarchic and purposeless forces" (A I 983) radically inimical to the human desire for coherence.

The horror of Louisa's death is compounded in the telling by the fact that her instance, far from being without succession, must absorb the horror of Marian's. Again, Adams establishes his sister's mortality as the first in an unwritten, but (at least for the 1907 readership) understood, sequence, which renders absurd anything resembling an anthropocentric cosmogony: "*For the first time*, the stage-scenery of the senses collapsed; the human mind felt itself stripped naked, vibrating in a void of shapeless energies, with resistless mass, colliding, crushing, wasting and destroying what these same energies had created and labored from eternity to perfect" (A I 983; italics added). Having burdened his text with the task of accounting for the absurd deaths of two brilliant American women in the flower of life, we can hardly wonder that the rest of the *Education* should prove womanless or that Adams should remark that in American society "the reproductive sources lay hidden" (A I 1126). Louisa's death, symbolically the debacle of the American woman and hence the key to the loss of the marital occasion, occurs in a chapter monitorily entitled "Chaos (1870)." Coming one chapter before the book's (and life's) self-designating midpoint, it portrays Adams's intitiation into what in retrospect he would entertain as the anarchic phantasm of the post-Newtonian universe—nature conceived as "supersensual," "parricidal" force (A I 1068).

"In plain words," he would write in "The Grammar of Science (1903)," "Chaos was the law of nature; Order was the dream of man" (A I 1132). Chaos—the ostensible and indeed perhaps actual condition from which the historian had repeatedly endeavored to rescue the story of human experience—emerges, in the *Education*, as the specific negation of the woman.[1] Insofar as the woman is presented as the chief source of a renewable, inheritable, habitable order, this contributes a note of absolute loss to the *Education*'s larger story. In what is perhaps his ultimate condemnation of the male, Adams in this same chapter suggests that "the dream of man" had been approached only in the parthenogenesis by which the woman "conceived herself and her family as the center and flower of an ordered universe which she knew to be unity because she had made it after the image of her own fecundity" (A I 1139).[2] The utopian conception of her world, in which nature and order are one, excludes the adult male or rather includes his conspicuous absence; this conception (like that of Esther) is of course the figure of a self-recriminating male imagination. Unable to idealize the male and female in anything like an Edenic pairing, Adams appears to condemn the male as capable only of half-marriages and as exhibiting his deepest (and most disastrous) tendencies in his transition from the worship of goddesses to the technological cultivation of his own omnipotence. How could Adams have conveyed more profoundly the loneliness, the widowerhood, of the male intellectual estranged from all forward-looking ideals? In the end, the woman, for him, has been essentially "killed" by the supersensual chaos that the man has released into her sphere and that neither the biology nor the symbology that prompted her to rule (if only in accordance with a former dream of man) could contain or resist.

A view of history as progressively de-creative assured one measure of continuity. "Nature," Adams remarks in "Nunc Age (1905)," "has educated herself to a singular sympathy for death" (A I 1178), and in *Mont Saint Michel and Chartres* he had noted sympathetically "the lines of gratitude" that Saint Francis on his deathbed added to the "Cantico del Sole" "for 'our sister death,' the long-sought, neverfound sister of the schoolmen, who solved all philosophy and merged Multiplicity in Unity" (A I 661). The chaos sighted in the *Education* did not admit of such essentially maternal personification—chaos after all had proved to be the negation of his sister; nor does the entropy thesis of *A Letter* anywhere assume the air of consolation. Adams's momentary warmings to the coherence of death hardly comport with the spectacle of a cosmos that is impersonal, wasting, and absurd; to the degree that he remains in life his impulse is to resist such coherence. The dynamic theory of history must begin by supposing "that the forces of nature capture man" (A I 1153), but Adams's sermon proceeds in the conviction that humanity's one chance lies (as ever) in assimilating those forces to the human dream of a moral order. Again, that one chance seems to require no less than an instantaneous reformation of mind, which would save it from breaking apart amid "the next great influx of new forces" (A I 1175). Adams is far from sanguine about the likelihood of such a miracle. As historian he has lived to record a phase in which he believes the mind to have "already entered a field of attraction so violent that it must immediately pass beyond, into new equilibrium, like the Comet of Newton, or suffer dissipation altogether, like meteoroids in the earth's atmosphere" (A I 1173). Yet he compulsively studies and protests against the spectacle not so much of his own as of his kind's death.

The dynamic theory of history (like *A Letter to American Teachers of*

History) makes for a troubled and ironic, if in the end genuine, protest against the universe of death. In it Adams begins, as rhetorically he was ever wont to do, by positing humanity reductively, first as a mechanical, only secondarily as a moral, force, before going on to calculate the possibility that the species may succeed in preserving the moral order that in the best of circumstances it had never fully achieved and that seemed likely under pressure to metamorphose into a mere "despotism of artificial order which nature abhorred" (A I 1138). We need not look far to find a precedent for the totalizing sweep of this theory: explanations of human experience that dwarfed the human to an ineffectual atom figured in Reformation thought, and the New England jeremiad, while affirming the redemptive course of history and the requirements which that course imposed on human conduct, pointedly recalled auditors to a sense of God's omnipotence. "A historical formula that should satisfy the conditions of the stellar universe" (A I 1064) proves however to be at cross purposes with the impulse to avert the final catastrophe of mind, for not only does it make a history responsive to human intervention theoretically improbable but suggests, as the revision of an earlier theology, that a chaotic, because godless, omnipotence is the just desert of a depraved, because godless, humanity. Adams of course is well aware that his theory must constitute an ambiguous protest against death. If, at his venture's start, "his associates in history condemned such an attempt as futile and almost immoral" (A I 1064), the historian himself concedes in the end that his attitude may be "profoundly unmoral" as it "tended to discourage effort," even as he stood by his intention and avowed all along "to encourage foresight and to economise waste of mind" (A I 1178). The paradox attests to the logical difficulty of his position, but it also confesses a tenuous sympathy for the broad, unknown audience that his vocation and subject required.

That audience remains the American public, and although as a matter of realistic expectation Adams reduces that quantum to an elite actual readership, he comes up against the same problem of an unreflecting citizenry that he had as a contributor to the *North American Review*. Early and late the public figures in his text as the doubtfully regenerative force that the text would provoke and instruct, but in the *Education* the benefit of the doubt must constantly vie with the accumulated skepticism of the intervening years. National character as it appears in the *Education* is the evolved creature of State and Wall streets, and although it still retains a comparative moral purity, that purity seems all but lost as potential social force. "The American mind had less respect for money than the European or Asiatic mind, and bore its loss more easily; but it had been deflected by its pursuit till it could turn in no other direction." And with tacit reference to the *History*'s supposed failure, Adams adds that the American mind "shunned, distrusted, disliked, the dangerous attraction of ideals, and stood alone in history for its ignorance of the past" (A I 1020). In "American Ideals," the Jeffersonian democrat's more or less willful ignorance of the past had been credited with affording him the capacity for illusion needed to generate "the energy of success"; but the superlative ignorance that Adams imputes to the American of 1907 consigns the American of a less primitive epoch to a singular failure, the immensity of his material means rendering grotesque his paucity of national aims. Ill-equipped to sustain its own call for ennobling ideals, the *History* had concluded with the image of a public gravitating toward just such a failure.

Against its own unanswerable argument that humanity is doomed, the *Education* manages to hypothesize a door of escape; but it only remotely seeks to restore a national ideal, to renew hope in the eligibility of an America of thought and art. The text divides too much between apologia and warning, embarrassed, as we have seen, by its want of self-evident social purpose. Proportionate to Adams's embarrassment is his hostility to the public; the "new American" whom he must reach if he really is to address a national public figures as an unlikely audience for a latter-day jeremiad, an implausible candidate for a son-in-wish. This American indeed appears only as a third, conjectural person beyond the monologue's assumed circle of hearing and is treated with studied, if not genuinely scornful, aloofness. As though parodying the aristocrat's invocation of genealogy, this person, we are told, "showed his parentage proudly; he was the child of steam and the brother of the dynamo"; he had put thought and art as well as his presumed liberty as an American citizen aside to become, in a new feudal arrangement, "the servant of the powerhouse" (A I 1146). His material self-content was disturbed only by an unreflecting will-to-power. This new American stood as an ironic descendant of the "new order of man" that the historian had celebrated at the beginning, and hollowly reaffirmed at the end, of the *History*; having unsympathetically projected this citizen as a machine, Adams has abandoned those positions from which he might detect "the beatings of a heart" beneath his surface. He can hardly write in the expectation that this citizen will read his story with the sympathy he himself has pared so thin, but then he ventures little confidence that beyond his private circle he will be read at all. At his authorship's uneasy terminus, he could preserve some hope that his text would reach the rare mind that can purposively react, but he could affirm only that the text had "served one purpose— that of educating *me*" (LHA 6:112).

Despite his long-standing retirement from naive eighteenth-century notions of authorship, Adams considered self-education that did not have as its object the education of a public practically unconscionable. The public aim of the *Education* therefore survives the text's erasure of the very ideology that prompted Adams to write in ultimate consideration of the commonweal. The wonder of the *Education* is always that the text came to exist publicly in spite of its massive self-contestation. Given what Adams recognized all along (and conceded by his writing of the 1916 editor's preface) as the *Education*'s inevitable publicity, the "privacy" of the text remains a rhetorical problem, not at all dismissed by the claim that as historical relativist the protagonist sought only "to invent a formula of his own for his universe" (A I 1151), still less by the suggestion that the author meant the *Education* as "a kind of esoteric literary art" (*LHA* 6:63). If his generational cohort William James criticized the matter of the text for being "esoteric,"[3] Adams, who was always troubled about the *Education*'s viability as a public statement, feared that the book's elaborate symbology was even more dubiously shareable. Precisely where he endeavors to frame his broadest "scientific" generalizations about a collective historical experience, he must resort most patently to a historiography of personal certification. Turning, in the collapse of all "objective" models of historical succession, "at last to the sequence of force," the protagonist-historian finds himself "reduced to his last resources" (A I 1069): namely, his mind's evident attraction to the various manifestations of force, past and present, which has become the one persuasive way for that mind to comprehend history as a sequence. Public as its aim may be, that mind could know its attraction and arrive at a mode of stating it only through a self-reflexive poesis.

As poetic language that will not translate into logical, much less mathematical, argument, the historian's testament takes the form of a personal but aspiringly public reverie. Throughout the book, brief imagistic resolutions serve to punctuate a paradoxical, closureless discourse—the compulsive and seemingly purposeless discussion that Adams identifies satirically as the Conservative Christian Anarchist's (anti)Hegelian calling. Expository as the book is, Adams invests little confidence in any mere sequencing of ideas, manifesting a consciousness that the text's appeal must lie in the persuasiveness of its imagery and symbolism. "Unity is vision," he affirms in "Twilight (1901)," and although unlike the child, who "will always see but one," the old man looks out upon a world in which "even the stars resolve themselves into multiples" (A I 1084), Adams turns repeatedly to visual metaphors in order more singularly to *see* his sense. "Images are not arguments," he very rationally concedes at the beginning of "A Law of Acceleration (1905)," "rarely even lead to proof, but the mind craves them" (A I 1167). It craves them as it craves resolution and unity: meaning as image is meaning and mind momentarily contained. Even the comet, figure of velocity and imminent disintegration, offers the linguistically multivalent (if indeed not yet disintegrative) mind some measure of repose.

Images—more accurately, a rhetoric that draws frequently upon visual metaphor—always dominated Adams's writing more than logical exposition. We have seen that in his 1868 review of Sir Charles Lyell's *Principles of Geology* he had objected to the absence of truths that appealed to the imagination in the geographer's prose. A part of Adams always suspected that "truth" lay as much in the power of a visual symbol to compel assent as in the cautious exposition of statements regarding the nature of "objective" reality.[4] To invoke (again) the Aristotelean distinction, Adams was always much more the rhetorician than the dialectician, despite his cultivation (early and late) of a scientific aesthetic, his posture of disinterested inquiry. Ever responsive to the poetry of large scientific generalization, the historian probably always despaired of scientific method, no more persuaded that it led to truth than he was convinced that reform politics led (unassisted) to a purified state. He who wrote of the diseased members of the body politic, of a democratic ocean, of a schooner that laughed at her pursuers, of a woman whose face was like the sails of a yacht, of the Virgin in glass, of the cathedral's perilous equilibrium, needed little encouragement to retrieve his education in images. While, as late as the final chapters of the *History*, the image served to embellish a truth presumed to transcend discourse, in the *Education* it has become the most vivid means of conjuring the sensation of knowable reality. The life achieves its sharpest resolution as disparate impressions: a yellow kitchen floor, the steps of Ara Coeli, a straggling caravan, a darkening prairie, a comet.

But as a rhetorical artifice that acquires in context a multifaceted symbolic life, the least complicated image resolves at last into multiples, drawn into a play of meanings that no image or idea can finally resolve in a persuasively transcendent unity. Considered in toto, the life takes shape as "a succession of violent breaks or waves, with no base at all" (A I 1005), which moves "the historian" toward the resolution of his narrative in metaphors for accelerating and disintegrative change—an ambivalent resolution at best. The failure to arrive at the sensation, much less the substance, of the unmoving One is proclaimed by the irreconcilable character of the *Education*'s focal expression, the Dynamo and the Virgin. In this ultimate instance of half-marriage the two terms unite to suggest the death of the vital unitary symbol, "the *absence* of the Virgin's unity," as John Carlos Rowe observes, revealed "in the very image of the hollow

Dynamo."[5] The composite figure articulates the de-creative tendency of history in its postmedieval phase, realizing symbolically the great contrast that the text aims to focus as a tract in search of a historical paradigm. As rhetoric, it enacts the loss of such symbols as once supported the conviction of unity—the sensation, that is, of a life redeemed from the common waste of historical existence. Recalling Adams's once-cherished ambition to frame a publicly consequent symbology of renewal, we can hardly believe that it would have much pleased him to learn that the Dynamo and the Virgin have proven to be the best-known expression of his varied and voluminous authorship, although it certainly could not have surprised him.

Yet finally it is Adams's compulsive authorship, belying the conceit of an already posthumous author, that emerges as the *Education*'s grandest symbol or, if one prefers, example. This, to be sure, forms the core of his bequest. Alternately heroic and mock-heroic, the elderly Henry Adams appears in the *Education* as one preeminently given to research and writing, and throughout the second half, the text relentlessly mythologizes the process of its composition. It is therefore essential that we comprehend the Dynamo and the Virgin as an act of recognition on the part of a protagonist "reduced to his last resources," the retired author whose hobbyhorse scholarship culminates in "Mont Saint Michel and Chartres: a study of thirteenth-century unity" and "The Education of Henry Adams: a study of twentieth-century multiplicity" (A I 1117). David L. Minter is right in distinguishing the Adams of this text as a "man of interpretation" who in the wreck an inherited design must improvise a workable, if fragmentary and in the long run unenduring, order; and although the author-as-image dissolves (resolves) spectacularly into multiples, the text at once portrays and submits itself as the product of a committed authorship.[6] The historian-protagonist who sets himself to the task of writing the text that we are supposed to be reading is, to be sure, but one facet of the character Henry Adams; more problematically, he exists as the ironic projection of the narrative voice that, in its turn, does not always coincide with the Henry Adams who distributed the 1907 *Education* accompanied by various and contradictory statements of intent. Yet these authorial guises do converge in the assumption of an interpretive office, even as the interpretive activity all but goes to pieces in the absence of a self-evident public rhetoric.

In the absence of an established public relation, the interpretive activity faces its greatest danger: the reflex dissolution of the instinctive conviction that the self is a unit whose multiplicity converges in the language of its conscious, authorial will. "Nearly all the highest intelligence known to history," Adams writes in "The Abyss of Ignorance (1902)," "had drowned itself in the reflection of its own thought" (A I 1115), but the narcissism of the neoclassical or romantic thinker might at least trace the lineaments of a Creator in its sublime incompletions. As the textual fragmentation of Henry Adams amply demonstrates, knowledge of unity as the self was perilous, and in the "new psychology" the protagonist-historian finds unwelcome confirmation that the ego comprises multiple personalities, being "nothing but a dissolving mind" (A I 1116) decomposing in a cosmos devoid of God. Impelled as we have continually seen by a distinctly social imperative—"the anarchist bomb bade one go on" (A I 1114)—the elderly student in pursuit of synthesis must confront all sorts of evidence that he may be finally no more exempt than the bomb-thrower from the claims of "the sub-conscious chaos below" (A I 1116). The synthesis (the dynamic theory with its law of acceleration) itself figures the ego as comet or "man-meteor," and the author-protagonist specifically as "the runaway star Groombridge, 1838, commonly called Henry Adams" (A I 1151)—an object that may or may not defy the laws that appear to dictate its dissolution. The problematizing of the author is relentless. We must keep in view all the more the fact that these multiples of Henry Adams resolved sufficiently to materialize in acts of publication: the two first editions of the *Education*, which in time became a singular, if in interpretation ever a multiple, bequest.

The absence of a self-evident ("eighteenth-century") public rhetoric—of an assured, all-purpose "literary language"—has of course not impaired the *Education*'s dialogic eligibility; if anything, the hesitant and self-refractive egocentricity from which Adams's public pronouncements emerge has overwhelmingly favored the book's reception among twentieth-century readerships. The status of such "private" expression as would speak on behalf of a shared experience is after all a public problem not peculiar to Henry Adams; as Adams himself was aware, many writers before him, and as we are aware, many writers since, have sought in self-study a language to compel a renascent public consciousness. We may defer for the moment the question of Adams's ultimate success, but we cannot too often insist that the lessons of the *Education*, and of Adams's work generally, are never separable from the irresolutions to which his efforts to speak publicly always came. From the manikin of his deconstructed selfhood Adams proves unable to alienate the "heroic" motive to save the republic in which he still, in 1907 and in 1918, might chance to live, and the perseverance of his vocation goes far to explain his enduring appeal. His observation that in America "the reproductive sources lay hidden" becomes in the face of his incessant practice an affirmation that those sources do exist, beneath and beyond his language's ability to locate and name them and in spite of his symbology of genealogical rupture and progressive sterility. But his persuasiveness lies as well in his exacting scrutiny of the historical field in which that redemptive motive must work and in his sobering sense of the constrained potential of the gifted individual. The *Education* submits itself as an example of emergency historicizing and even (more tentatively) as a regenerative stock of historical knowledge. But it offers itself also as a memento mori, viewing individual ambition and duty against the horizon of death—that death which must claim, alike, the most and least sanguine of Americans.

The last chapter, "Nunc Age (1905)" (which may be translated "now go" or "now act"), reestablishes the degree to which the bequest despairs of posterity, but more than that we are made to feel the speaker's sense of his own absolute, if comparatively small, mortality. Here the protagonist appears not so much as author-historian as "traveller in the highways of history," arriving once again in New York, "an older man" than his father had been when the ex-minister brought his family home in 1868. The New York of this chapter represents a sort of climax to that city's recurrent appearance in his work as a symbol of power unennobled by ideals, scarcely contained by a technological, not to say moral, intelligence: "The cylinder had exploded, and thrown great masses of stone and steam against the sky" (A I 1176).[7] To the observer at his club window, the spectacle is that of Rome under Diocletian without the prospect of a Constantine the Great. In these pages Henry Adams, the self-consciously "old type" of man, affects withdrawal before the prospect of the new man, the new American, "with ten times the endurance, energy, will and mind of the old type," the new messiah for whom the New York corporations "were ready to pay millions at sight" (A I 1176). The American who had failed in his search for a father need not look here for a son.

From New York he passes on to a Washington enlivened by Roosevelt's battling of the trusts and corporations, the "new power" that Adams had known in youth as State Street and that now more than ever, notwithstanding the opposition of a president whom Adams had earlier characterized as "pure act" (A I 1101), "tore society to pieces and trampled it under foot" (A I 1177). Already cited with Lodge as an example of the law that "a friend in power is a friend lost," Roosevelt can still tenuously figure as a son-in-wish; as we have seen, he was one of the younger men who received a copy of the 1907 *Education*. But in the last pages Adams concerns himself more with writing the obituary of his generation—that idealistic, renovating, empire-building force whose defeat was to be read in the careers of King, Hay, and Adams. Only an insistent fraternal tenderness intervenes to suggest the exemption of John Hay, who dies amid uncompleted tasks after having brought the world "for the first time in fifteen hundred years" in sight of "a true Roman *pax*." Considering the context, it is impossible to believe that Adams meant readers to take this extravagant statement at its word: surely it is the delicate equilibrium of the (near) accomplishment that Adams most wishes to impress upon us. The alternative to the *pax* is world war, the "catastrophe" that the deceased Hay "need not repine at missing" (A I 1180). Adams's conceit, in the book's concluding sentence, of returning with his friends in 1938 to review the world's progress toward a reign of peace excites in him nothing more profound than a shudder.

Hay's uncompleted tasks mirror the "avowedly incomplete" status of the *Education* and Adams's other attempts to formulate a theory of history; both reflect the fragmentary accomplishments of Gallatin, Jefferson, the Presidents Adams, and Saint Thomas Aquinas—the fate of all heroic intellection. The protagonist's final posture is one of "submission and silence" (A I 1177); word of Hay's expected death throws him "into the depths of Hamlet's Shakespearean silence," which the text glosses as his wordless "assent to dismissal" (A I 1181). This "final" posture has been, as we have seen, a recurrent one: preeminently that of the bereaved husband and retired author, we see its antecedent in the younger brother baffled as to a precise mode of entry into his country's public sphere. Its origin surely lies in that spectatorial self which Adams created the moment he first took pen in hand. The rule of silence would only become absolute with his death in 1918. Still, amid the compulsive rush that frequently characterized the language of his "posthumous" years, there was a silence that he clearly heard and wished to profess as his, as if his language were yet another event passing before the spectator behind the veil. At the end of "Buddha and Brahma," the Rajah affirms, with Gautama's blessings, that

> Life, Time, Space, Thought, the World, the Universe
> End where they first begin, in one sole Thought
> Of Purity in Silence.
>
> (A I 1201)

But as one who could not "fly the world," Adams's being was ever caught up in the event of his language; in such lines he contemplated repose from a life that could not silence, and so could not complete, itself.

In the bronze effigy that marks the Adams grave site at Rock Creek Cemetery, the widower contemplated more nearly this repose. The *Education*'s closing image of Henry Adams implicitly aspires to the silence and withdrawal of Saint-Gauden's "eternal figure" (A I 1021), which as literary image appears in "Twenty Years After (1892)"—the story's midpoint —as a last lesson in artistic expression and religious feeling. The figure speaks to the wish to be absolved of history, language, generation: as

Adams testily explained to Roosevelt in 1908, the form was meant "to exclude sex and sink it in the idea of humanity" (*LHA* 6:198). In the end one was a son, father, or husband by mere accident of relation. The hooded manikin would transcend the world of such relations, yet it betrays no eagerness to put off its human form. If it held out to Adams the prospect of unity—a completed marriage, a perfected absence—nevertheless, as public statement, "the interest of the figure was not in its meaning, but in the response of the observer" (A I 1021). So speaks the text of the monument, which Adams directed in his will to be left ever uninscribed. Such too would be the generative interest of this author, who had made himself over into the absence of his text.

Response

In an editorial entitled "The Holy War," George Harvey, Adams's distant successor to the *North American Review* editor's chair, opened the December 1918 issue by greeting the new order that had commenced with the November armistice. "The cost can never be reckoned," he affirmed, "nor, in compensation, the gain. Slowly but irresistibly, as the Phoenix of a new civilization emerges from the ashes of destruction, the forces of humanity compelled to unite in crushing the powers of evil will crystallize into a world fraternity whose one God will be, no longer the King of kings,—for kings shall be no more,—but the Heavenly Father of all mankind."[8] Thus twenty-one years before the German invasion of Poland did a common sentiment speak, voicing its aspiration in a rhetoric so mummified as to reveal the vitality in the tiredest phrase of Henry Adams—a Henry Adams who since March had been ashes.

Toward the end of that issue, concerned almost exclusively with the war and the subsequent politics of peace, appeared one of the earliest reviews of the *Education*. Bringing expectations shaped by the example of John Stuart Mill to the book entitled, in its first trade release, *The Education of Henry Adams: An Autobiography*, the anonymous reviewer displayed the perplexity of a reader whose perusal failed to turn up a sensibly straightforward text. "Just what did Adams intend by this narrative," which, despite its theme of education, hardly commended itself as "collateral reading" in any curriculum and which was "so much more comprehensive than most autobiographies, that are *not* stories of education?" Sidestepping the difficulties of engaging his question, the reviewer represents Adams's story as distinctly dated, its paradox attributable to the benighted conditions of Adams's as it were distant epoch, identified as 1850 to 1914, the year the late war began. "Without undue optimism," the reviewer offered, "one may say that the moral atmosphere of the time—except insofar as it was illumined by the heroism of the Civil War—was murkier than that of today." In the clarity earned by an American-won Great War, the nervous temptation to be cheerful turned smug. "A nice little boy," averred the reviewer, "had not half the chance that he has nowadays." Against what he read as Adams's "mathematical, and hence avowedly relative" idea of life, the reviewer commends what he asserts to be the common man's effort to set "a bound to mathematical complexity," the citizen's attempt to establish "a fundamental law based not on a theory of government but upon public opinion as something deep, much overlaid indeed by the shifting sands of thought, but finally solid."[9] We have seen how a young Henry Adams, sanguine and despairing in the illusive clarity above the smoke of his own generation's war, agonized duly over the phantom of public opinion in his day's *North American Review*—a connection the reviewer nowhere makes.

In protest to such optimism ("the outlook for civilization is murky" [*D* 115]) and as a corrective to the *Education*'s regrettable mix of "science with society," which he felt obscured the marrow of brother Henry's philosophy, Brooks Adams brought out *The Degradation of the Democratic Dogma* in November 1919. The volume with the thumping title collects "The Tendency of History," "A Letter to American Teachers of History," and "The Rule of Phase Applied to History," prefaced by Brooks's own lengthy "The Heritage of Henry Adams." The latter places Henry's work as a kind of afterword in a sequence commencing with the idealistically democratic aspirations of John Adams and George Washington and ending in the violent disabusal of John Quincy Adams's failed presidency—the catastrophe, in Brooks's estimate, not only of a family and a nation but of all humanity's democratic hopes. Confirming, with a rigid literalism all his own, Henry's (rhetorical) reduction of history to the moral of *A Letter*, Brooks reduces Henry's "meaning" to the meager conclusion that Brooks himself (with Henry's help) had long ago reached: that "man" existed "as a pure automaton, who is moved along the paths of least resistance by forces over which he has no control"—a reversion, as we are told, "to the pure Calvinistic philosophy" (*D* vii–viii). Reading the "Rule" (which he misrepresents as a work conceived after *A Letter*) as "an attempt by means of a mathematical formula" (*D* 114) to presage the catastrophic transformations of an accelerating society, Brooks establishes his brother in the character of scientist, crediting him with foreseeing a new level of activity in 1917, the year the United States entered the war. Intolerant of language that did not thus reduce, Brooks was in his own way as insensible as the reviewer in *North American Review* to Henry's anguished recognition that mathematical discourse—that "paradise of endless displacement" (*A* I 1135)—must remain for one of his education and purpose always unintelligible, if indeed not pernicious.

Treatment of Henry Adams as the author of prophetic scientific texts was continued by his first biographer, James Truslow Adams, a New Yorker whose bloodline traced to Maryland rather than New England but whose saturnine nature put him in sympathy with the New England Adamses he voluminously chronicled. Writing in the early moments of the Great Depression, the biographer fully endorsed the historian's late experiments in predictive historiography: "The attempt to do exactly what he did will undoubtedly some day have to be undertaken again," and although with the accumulation of new evidence "there may be a shift in the ground, Adams will yet remain the first pioneer" in the monist correlation of all knowledge. James Truslow Adams's biography was written to accompany an edition of Henry Adams's collected works; this was a prohibitively expensive project during such hard times and the short biography alone made it into print. "Adams himself," noted the biographer in his preface, "would have enjoyed the irony of the fact that the very breakdown of our economic system—whether temporary or not—which he predicted a generation before it occurred has precluded the possibility of publishing his own *Works* for the time being on the scale contemplated."[10] No doubt he would have savored the irony but only as a slender relief from the debacle's horror.

An instructive contrast is to be found in the response of Carl Becker, a professional historian who no doubt spoke for much of the guild in his notice of the *Education* appearing in the April 1919 *American Historical Review*. In his generous appraisal of Adams's accomplishment, Becker brackets for salutary neglect the mathematics and metaphysics ("this meaningless philosophy of history") by which others simplistically espoused or dismissed Adams's text. Preferring to read the *Education* as an "apologia pro vita sua," Becker judges the book as "fascinating" throughout, "particularly perhaps in those parts which are not concerned with the education of Henry Adams." The limits of his sympathy with the book are made clear by what he identifies as the "chief question" that the *Education* leaves with the reader: Why did Henry Adams regard his "enviable" life as a failure? For Becker, the envy of Adams's life is large and multifaceted, but centers in the nine volumes of national history that "rank with the best work done in that field by American scholars."[11] Sixteen years later Becker amplified his praise, pronouncing that in the *History* one meets a work "which for clarity, tight construction, and sheer intelligence applied to the exposition of a great theme, had not then, and has not since, been equalled by any American historian." By contrast, to Becker the *Education* was frequently unclear and suffered from loose construction.[12]

To be sure, Becker did not speak for all professional historians; Charles Beard, for one, would come sufficiently under the spell of "philosophy of history" to claim that Brooks Adams's *Law* merited inclusion "among the outstanding documents of intellectual history in the United States and, in a way, the Western World."[13] Yet the exception mostly proves the rule. Prior to the appearance of such seminal work as Hayden White's *Metahistory: The Historical Imagination in Nineteenth-Century Europe* (1973), the unchallenged consensus of American professional historians had been to regard philosophy of history as excrescence, whereas now it is more apt to be met as an integral and indeed fascinating part of the poesis and rhetoric of (historical) writing. A self-designated "political historian" following Becker's lead, William Dusinberre in *Henry Adams: The Myth of Failure* (1980) has recently enlarged upon the thesis that the *History* constitutes Henry Adams's most realized accomplishment and that it must count as the great success of a man who was given all his life to morbid self-deprecation and who regrettably made failure the all-engrossing theme of his late, flawed works.[14]

The professional historian's insistence that we pay homage to the Adams of the *History* corrects what since the *Education's* 1918 publication has been the tendency (encouraged of course by the *Education* itself) to read the book as the essential, rather than the supplemental (if culminating), text of Adams's prolific career. In his brief review of it in the May 23, 1919, London *Athenaeum*, T. S. Eliot showed how easy it was to moralize about the text and the life without a single reference to Adams's prior accomplishment as a historian. Later, in "Gerontian," the poet would derive from the *Education* not only phrasings but the existential dilemma in which an emblematically old man meditates on the amorally regenerative and destructive forces of nature and history; in reviewing the *Education* for a British readership, however, Eliot portrays Adams as a rather philistine pursuer of "what, upon a lower plane, is called culture," a pursuit that "left him much as he was born: well-bred, intelligent, and uneducated." Beginning with the observation that John Adams was "said to be descended from a bricklayer," the review patronizes the great-grandson's text as the expression of a regional mind stultified by its two dominant characteristics—conscientiousness and skepticism. Overlooking the historical consciousness and social concern that inform the *Education*, Eliot reduces Adams's quest to one that failed because it resisted the consummate aesthetic resolution; seeking education "with the wings of a beautiful but ineffectual conscience beating vainly in a vacuum jar," Henry Adams remained "unaware that education—the education of an individual—is a by-product of being interested, passionately absorbed." Adams's concern with education that far transcended that of "an individual" goes entirely unnoticed, obscured by Eliot's comparison of Adams to the novelist Henry James, who possessed "the sensuous contributor to the intelligence" that Adams, to the impairment of his education and art, allegedly did not.[15]

Eliot's evident distaste for Henry Adams the historian was shared by Van Wyck Brooks and Lewis Mumford, who in pointedly rejecting the expatriate pattern strove to extract from the national experience a "usable past." But Brooks and Mumford both saw that in order to be usable, the past had to be recovered as a history dominated by images and examples capable of exerting mythic appeal to the unrealized creative energies of a complacent public; the writing of such history required the artist more than the historian. In the Henry Adams who pursued, as historian, an America of thought and art, the perilous divination of prospects from retrospects had already undergone a scrupulous test, but the lesson was mostly lost upon the exponents of a renascent national culture who came of age with the first world war. Mumford, in *The Golden Day: A Study in American Expression and Culture* (1926), focuses solely on the aged Adams who, he writes, could "picture a whole and healthy society" only with reference to the past and who could not, in looking to the future, put "desire and imagination, with their capacity for creating form, symbol, myth, and ideal, on the same level as intelligence."[16] In "The Literary Life in America" (1921), Van Wyck Brooks represents Adams as one who possessed the vision to see that his generation required an idealistically minded school to start new influences but who lacked the faith or fortitude to found it, as he might well have done had he signed *Democracy*. His failure, according to Brooks, lay in his hesitation to embrace the literary life, to venture the risk of becoming an artist, to appear as such in the public eye. In *Sketches in Criticism* (1932), Brooks claims that Adams himself "never clearly saw, what we can see, that he was by nature an artist" and that it was more the "family conscience" than "the instinct of the artist" that directed Adams into the "toilsome paths" that produced the *History*.[17]

For Van Wyck Brooks, the *History* would hardly exist, and he would write always of Adams's career as one in which the accomplishment was never as certain as the wasted effort. Still, in his elegiac *New England: Indian Summer, 1865–1915* (1942), he spells out the *Education*'s importance to the literary generation who came of age at the Great War's outbreak and who in its aftermath would have none of the blandishment proffered by the *North American Review*'s editor. "The *Education*," writes Brooks, "with its acrid flavour, struck, during the war-years, the note of the moment. It appealed to the younger generation, who felt themselves adrift, and who were in revolt against their past." Far from appearing as an evolutionary discard, "Adams, for many, seemed an older brother" in his disgust with the sterilities of American life.[18] We may judge the appeal to have been strong, forcing personalities as disjunct as Brooks and Eliot to come to terms with it and contributing a note of anguish to the poetry of Eliot and the prose of Hemingway and Fitzgerald.[19] Less frequently did the older brother offer to this generation a model of pragmatic striving. In *Main Currents in American Thought* (1930), Vernon Louis Parrington presents Adams as "an honest man and an able," one of the few authentic sources of light in the Gilded Age. Devoting in his turn scarcely a paragraph to the *History*—which he thought too narrowly political—Parrington singles out *Mont Saint Michel and Chartres* in particular for praise: not only did it stand as a forerunner of his own generation's indictment of the acquisitive society and anticipate his own generation's desire for organic community, but it did so with exemplary tenderness and wisdom. For Parrington such an achievement counted much more than Adams's experiments in scientific history, which bore in any case the flaw of disregarding the economic springs of action.[20] Noting the extent to which "Adams anticipated the writers of the twenties," Granville Hicks in *The Great Tradition* (1935) enlarged considerably on Parrington's reservation. Not only did Adams preach "the general futility of action and the particular helplessness of political effort," but he also indulged himself in the production of "elaborate generalizations, not in order to influence the age in which he lived but merely to amuse himself."[21] Nothing could have been more counterrevolutionary.

In the first three decades after Adams's death, response to his work nearly always came back to the question of his self-alleged failure. This is hardly surprising, as response to Adams's lifework inevitably took as its point of departure the *Education*, not only a text meant to provoke response but also one that had been promoted by the circumstances of its 1918 appearance to the status of a best-seller. Even Carl Becker, familiar as he was with Adams's previous accomplishments as a historian, had to pause before the *Education*'s large-scale erasure of a major career in the assertion of that career's failure. Although failure has long ceased to be the exclusive focus of Adams's critical readership, the response must always return to this theme. The *Education* remains the portal through which most readers discover Henry Adams's writing, if indeed they discover the writing that preceded and followed the *Education*, and it is in this work that failure on a millennial scale (a theme that darkens the earliest surviving letters and that haunts the visionary sympathies of "American Ideals") becomes all-engrossing, implicating author and reader alike in an uncertain and anxiously incomplete textual relation. Whereas we are apt now to view that failure as shared, enacted by a discourse increasingly cognizant of its own inadequacy to state its problem and increasingly self-interrogative of its dialogic viability, the earlier response tended to treat the matter with reference to the faithlessness and perversity—or, inversely, the heroism and genius—of Adams the historical person. The person, the supposed origin of the text, assumed a life of his own apart from, and greater than, the text that had largely served to project Adams's multiple public images.

In Carl Becker's estimate, Henry Adams's career was anything but a failure, and Adams's self-judgment was attributable to his sense of having exerted as author no appreciable influence on the course of American affairs. In Becker's fundamentally comic vision, the alleged failure was a gifted and fabulously successful man's wayward conceit, the consequence of unreasonable expectations to be traced to the peculiar family background. For Ivor Winters, who like Becker superlatively (if by his own admission inexpertly) praised the *History*, the failure came down to Adams's perverse and irresponsible abandonment of the modes of rational understanding, a moral weakness that led to "the radical disintegration of a mind."[22] In thus condemning the later Henry Adams, Winters enlarges upon a judgment handed down in 1919 by Paul Elmer More, equally, if rather more coolly, scornful in his attack upon what he too takes to be Adams's willful obscurantism.[23] In spite of Winters's dismissive arrogance—his terror in the presence of the assertively multivalent text—one must concede a certain rightness to his affording Adams first place in the rogue's gallery of *The Anatomy of Nonsense* (1943), where the historian's inmates are poets (Stevens, Eliot, Ransom), authors who had likewise written beyond the bounds of a narrowly rationalist and moralist notion of language. But it took the larger imagination of men like Robert E. Spiller and R. P. Blackmur to see that such language reflected more than individual perversity and that the failure that Adams's text argued and enacted pertained to a collective experience.

Although attempts had been made by Brooks, Mumford, Parrington, and Hicks to contextualize Adams in the broad framework of literary and intellectual history, only with Robert E. Spiller's "Henry Adams" in *Literary History of the United States* (1948) would the long career that ended in failure assume the magnitude of a canonized national expression. As Spiller represents them, the questions that Adams puts to the student of literary history are emphatically public and, in the postwar America of the midtwentieth century, as urgent as ever: "Why had man once more failed? What new conditions made the hope for perfection again seem vain?" Like Van Wyck Brooks, Spiller assesses Adams in the light of the 1918 *Education*'s postwar reception and the disillusionment in which a generation "gradually discovered" the book's "voice to be its own." But unlike Brooks, whose ambivalence to Adams suggests that he found the precursor's pessimism too immovable and, as such, too potentially persuasive, Spiller recognizes the dialogic element of Adams's discourse, its saving capacity to submit its conclusions to the reflection of others. "No idea, feeling, or experience," Spiller writes of Adams, "was complete until it had been thrown back to him from the sounding board of another's consciousness." Although Spiller's account of Adams's career relies overmuch on the life pattern offered by the *Education*, he astutely identifies the "discovery of an authentic and adequate medium of expression" as the "life's quest." And with regard to the necessitarian arguments of Adams's late work, Spiller wisely cautions against "assuming a finality in Adams' logical position." In Adams's most imaginative and hence most enduring accomplishment, the bringing together of the Dynamo and the Virgin, we receive "the impression of work still in progress" rather than that of a perfected form; its incompletion, Spiller implies, requires the reader's conscious, constructive participation.[24]

Less easily compassed is R. P. Blackmur's response, which takes the form of articles and chapters of a perhaps aptly uncompleted book written over a twenty-five-year period. Between 1931 and 1955, Blackmur would progress from discovering in his own voice an affinity for Adams's that went so far as to mimic the *Education*'s rhetoric to an affirmation of the power of human discourse that defined itself against Adams's denials of that power by citing what Blackmur considered the capacity of Adams's symbols to articulate and (at least emotionally) unify human experience.[25] In "The Expense of Greatness" (1936) Blackmur established the terms of his lengthy pursuit of his subject. Commending Adams to us as "a mountain to be mined on all flanks for pure samples of human imagination," specimens whose greatness lies in their ability to exert at once an attractive and disseminative force on the minds that engage them, he exalts Adams as one who achieved such failure as concludes only the supreme intellectual effort. His was "failure in the radical sense that we cannot consciously react to more than a minor fraction of the life we yet deeply know and endure and die."[26] Adams achieved such failure in pursuit of unity, a foredoomed quest, as Blackmur characterizes it, urged by the radically disintegrative tendencies of modern society—a quest taken up by one who had had to withdraw to the peripheries of his society to prevent the waste of his talents.

In his sequence of chapters entitled "The Virgin and the Dynamo," Blackmur essentially retells and revises the *Education* and the late speculative essays, reconstituting Adams the narrator and Adams the protagonist as the tragic and finally heroic artificer of unifying symbols. Adams's task as defined by Blackmur is deeply rhetorical in motive: "a deliberatedly undertaken program of what Kenneth Burke would call symbolic action by one man against the infinite forces that drive upon and within him."[27] Of Adams's many expert readers few have approached Blackmur's appreciation of the intricate, interactive life of Adams's later symbology. But his projection of Adams as "one man against the infinite forces that drive upon and within him" overly magnifies Adams's own less insistently romantic conception of the protagonist's quest in the *Education*'s second half, and the characterization prevents him from inquiring deeply into the social existence—the authentically rhetorical dimensions—of Adams's symbolic action. Blackmur's Adams is a distinctly mythic conception, built almost exclusively upon the *Education*'s testimony; because he sees Adams as an example of the modern artist, the symbolic action of the work prior to *Mont Saint Michel and Chartres* remains for Blackmur ever ancillary. And as the modern artist is by definition neglected, isolated, and essentially absolved of his social and economic complicity, Blackmur nowhere seriously attempts to identify a community for which Adams's symbolic action can conceivably be consequential.

The first book-length interpretive studies bearing the imprimatur of the academic press appeared in the early 1950s. Max Baym's *The French Education of Henry Adams* (1951), an influence study that somewhat overstates the case of the French origin of Adams's ideas and attitudes, celebrates Adams as the first great American literary man of the world, through whom "cosmopolitan culture at last made its full entry into these United States."[28] William Jordy's *Henry Adams: Scientific Historian* (1952) aims at examining Adams's temperamental attraction to a science of history that, as Jordy shows, was not only often bad science but also, particularly in the late works, history distorted for the purpose of dramatizing human moral failure. This study admirably places Adams's work in the context of its scientific and historiographic antecedents, but Jordy's recurrently querulous tone measures the degree to which contextualization per se fails to explain the multivalent rhetoric of Adams's historiography. Recognizing that Adams throughout life "stopped short of final solutions," and that readers "who refuse to enter into the paradoxical spirit" of Adams's discourse "had best seek another author," Jordy ultimately regards Adams's inability to arrive at some positive unitary conviction as failure in an absolute sense, traceable to the enigma of Adams's "perverse" personality.[29]

For the generation whose historical consciousness evolved in permanent reference to the twin mushroom clouds that ended the second world war in Japan, new urgency lay in Adams's vision of a society overwhelmed by the forces it had recklessly released from the natural world. If his despair seemed precisely to prophecy the despair of those who were in the position to contemplate the actual instruments by which civilization as they knew it could be brought to an end, his persistent attachment to the ideals of eighteenth-century rationalism (particularly that of decentralized political power) appealed to the American intellectual's perennial sympathy with the idea of republican virtue. At the same time, Adams's effort to unify an intractable experience by the symbolic resource of his art satisfied that same intellectual's modernist prejudice that affirmation comes most credibly from an avowed and skeptical egotism, which experientially and experimentally creates its own characteristic expression. Robert A. Hume's *Runaway Star: An Appreciation of Henry Adams* (1951) and J. C. Levenson's *The Mind and Art of Henry Adams* (1957) testify to such historical and intellectual conditions and bear an urgency that far transcends mere academic consideration of the subject. Both proceed from the conviction that Henry Adams's art and example speak intimately to the spiritual climate of midtwentieth-century America, and both books aspire to put Adams within reach of a general educated public. The shorter *Runaway Star* makes of Adams in the end "a symbol of the tragic valor possible to man as he fronts infinity and finds it void of all certain promise but his own"—a symbol much like that which Blackmur makes of Adams and not unlike that made by Levenson in the *Mind and Art*.[30]

Levenson is easily the most forthright when it comes to stating the public value of Henry Adams, author and symbol. Indeed he begins the *Mind and Art* by declaring that "Henry Adams offers to his fellow Americans the richest and most challenging image of what they are, what they have been, and what they may become."[31] The opening sentence suggests that this image (or those images) may be set down in the pages that follow with a singular precision, but Levenson's study, a landmark interpretation of Adams's work, pays too rigorous attention to the subject's complexities to make entirely good on that suggestion. At once an intellectual biography and a comprehensive commentary on the works, the *Mind and Art* brings an exacting scholarship to the task of re-creating a usable national past, and the text's distinction lies equally in Levenson's critical penetration and in his implicit conviction that criticism exists as a social praxis whose mandate is to focus shared value. Positing a heroic strain in the personality of Henry Adams—the artist who preserves against the chaos of history the resource of the twelfth-, thirteenth-, and, more importantly, eighteenth-century past—Levenson explores, yet ultimately defines as inessential, Adams's less acceptable sides: Adams the anti-Semite, the malicious author of *A Letter*, the corrupting influence on George Cabot Lodge. At thirty years' distance from its publication, we can see that Levenson's study begs the question customarily begged by criticism that glorifies the alienated artist as a redemptive influence: By what agency does the artist act on culture, particularly that which extends beyond the horizon of a politically marginalized literary elite? Published initially by a trade press, and attempting to render unobtrusive its purely scholarly apparatus, the *Mind and Art* does make a bold attempt to assimilate into a general readership and thereby serve as a means of extension.

For Ernest Samuels, Henry Adams likewise exists preeminently as an artist, although certainly one whose national and geopolitical concerns invest his work with particular relevance to the cold war era. The first volume of Samuels's deservedly acclaimed critical biography appeared in 1948, the second in 1958, and the third and last in 1964. An explicit aim of *The Young Henry Adams* was to rescue the historical man and many-sided author from the *Education*'s "strangely blighting shadow"—from the self-distortions of one who unjustifiably represented his life as a failure. Although Samuels identifies himself as a non–New Englander with only qualified admiration of "the Brahmin view of life," he honors like Levenson the eighteenth-century republicanism of Henry Adams's Quincy heritage, valuing it particularly for its exacting endorsement of the democratic cause, and he admires his subject as a man who remained true to the idealism of that heritage long after much of its dogma appeared dated.[32] If he agrees with Brooks Adams that Henry "was never quite frank with himself or with others," and if he concedes that his subject's mind betrays "the grip of many prejudices and contradictions," Samuels affirms nonetheless that that mind was "a terrifyingly honest one."[33] Although Samuels richly contextualizes this mind in the social and intellectual milieu of its times, his Henry Adams too achieves ultimate stature as symbol. "For all the oppressiveness of his cultivated misanthropy," writes Samuels in the preface to *Henry Adams: The Major Phase*, "he is modern man writ large." This man manages to triumph with his humanity mostly intact. Facing the dissolution of common belief and the assertion, in increasing magnitude, of irresponsible power, Samuels's Adams, author and man, sufficiently conquers his despair to exert himself in favor of virtue and, despite a chronic sadness, ever sustains the instinct for joy that makes possible the life-affirming act.[34]

The response to Adams that has followed in the last two decades has tended more to refine than to challenge the heroic view of him established by Blackmur, Levenson, and Samuels and to leave undisturbed his status as the celebrated embodiment of classical republicanism and undaunted modernity. Book-length studies have tended to focus on particular aspects of his work: Vern Wagner's *The Suspension of Henry Adams: A Study of Manner and Matter* (1969) explores the style of Adams's language and makes the case of its comic genius, while John Conder's *A Formula of His Own: Henry Adams's Literary Experiment* (1970) examines the late masterpieces with a view to the thematic, pedagogical, and rhetorical strategies that arguably bind the two texts as a unit. In *Symbol and Idea in Henry Adams* (1970), Melvin Lyon creates a taxonomy of the images that structure Adams's thought. In *The Force So Much Closer Home: Henry Adams and the Adams Family* (1977), Earl N. Harbert examines Adams's work as the expression of the larger unity of the family, a coherence that

Harbert rightly documents in the intertextuality of the family writings. Wagner, Conder, and Harbert reveal a fascination with the rhetoric of Adams's language, suggest the inadequacy of analyses that focus mainly on the symbolic resolutions achieved (or not achieved) in Adams's texts, and Harbert has addressed in detail the specifically pedagogical strategies of the *Education*.[35]

By degrees the emphasis in Adams scholarship has shifted from the elevation and study of Henry Adams the author-icon to a closer examination of how his works function textually and rhetorically. As this survey has shown, serious attention to the ironic and paradoxical—the "avowedly incomplete"—nature of Adams's language commenced with the accounts of Blackmur and Spiller; without the benefit of a theoretical sense of the text, Wagner in turn focused upon Adams's suspension of meaning in paradox, insisting insightfully, if perhaps too patly, on his resolution of contradiction in humor. With the increasingly disciplined awareness of the modes by which language constitutes social reality, attention to the dynamics of Adams's text has become absorbing. In *The Interpreted Design as a Structural Principle in American Prose* (1969), David L. Minter designates the Adams of the *Education* (the protagonist merging with the narrator and author) as the "man of interpretation": a figure whose primary activity is hermeneutic and who improvises almost as a secondary concern variant and ever-provisional simulacra of order and meaning.[36] Building on Minter's analysis, but with an emphasis on the text focused by Derrida, John Carlos Rowe in *Henry Adams and Henry James: The Emergence of a Modern Consciousness* (1976) depicts Adams as engaged with at least partial self-consciousness in the de-centered poesis of the text but unable to enter the Nietzschean and Derridean "joyous release" of thought unbounded by a transcendental signified.[37] From the Lukácsian perspective of *Seeing and Being: The Plight of the Participant Observer in Emerson, James, Adams, and Faulkner* (1981), Carolyn Porter rightly insists that Adams's writings be viewed as participation (albeit disaffected) in the broader social enterprise of creating meaning. Given her premises, Adams perhaps too inevitably resolves as an example of the bourgeois impasse of reified consciousness, but her analysis properly restores Adams's text to a world of social and economic nexus.[38]

My aim in this study has not been particularly iconoclastic. Like many of Adams's readers, I too have been drawn to his work for what it seems to embody (even if in fossilized form) of an old "republican virtue," a public-mindedness that, deflected from the immediately political realm, strove to create a language of national renascence. Against a moral skepticism that formalized itself in his pose of the detached observer, Adams ever sustained the desire to create a publicly disseminative language that might palpably participate in shaping the America to come. The vocational commitment to create such a language met with the repeated failure of its objects and the evasiveness of a commanding symbology. Undoubtably the vocation's greatest (and always in part unconscious) "failure" lay in Adams's inability to decide what an America of thought and art must be: a unity of empire, dominated by a single set of cultural formulas translating all "rival" expressions into its own privileged terms, or a unity of love, a spiritual communion in which space was reserved for the human (sexual, cultural) other—the regenerating and unforeseeable miracle for which the other was ever the source. Still, the commitment to create a language (a door of escape) open to the saving possibility lives—however problematically, however hysterically—in the *Education*, and even its troubled inversion in *A Letter* may be taken as a measure of that commitment's persistence. If I have opposed any tendency in the previous critical representation of Adams, it is that which, by enshrining him as a postromantic, protomodernist artist, obscures the Adams who throughout life sought (as pedagogue, moralist, and mythmaker) a generative relation with a broad readership. Ultimately this Adams, a disabused historicist but still a historicist by reflex, would have to insist upon unity, without which in some more or less theological form no public moral aspiration was for him conceivable.

Adams's desire to create a language of national renascence should prompt, in this last decade of the twentieth century, qualified sympathy at best: too often has the nationalist sentiment amounted to nostalgia and the self-righteous exercise of power. Given, however, the technology and political hegemony of American civilization (to everyone's peril so very incomprehensible in scope), the effort to sustain a critical discourse that can specify the dangers if also the potential that lies in the power at American disposal cannot be incidental to our survival. Can Adams materially assist us in this effort? Does our reading of his work contribute to the purposiveness we would (re)invest in the history we inhabit? Does his text submit itself to the renewal of shared possibility? The answer to these questions is I think yes: the ongoing lesson of Adams's work lies not only in his lifelong attention to the tendencies of political and technological power—most specifically to the tendency of power to distort and reconstitute "constituted" government and social relations toward unwritten, irrational, and incomprehensible ends—but also in the monitory impasse to which he came as the committed publicist of this problem. But our yes requires one focal qualification: that we admit—as Adams, for all the evidence of his practice, never unequivocably could—that history remains always a human construct, even if too frequently it is one determined by interests and discourses difficult to call to account. As a human construct, history may be constituted by a poesis that precedes and indeed inscribes us, but we cultivate our paralysis if we thereby conclude that it does not solicit our participation as responsible authors—authors, that is, who are cognizant of the dialogical character and consequence of our texts and who elect to conceive discourse as crucially (if only relatively) susceptible to ideological self-consciousness and moral self-review.

Whereas I have emphasized the generative motive of Adams's authorship, I would restore finally Henry Adams the iconoclast, the Henry Adams whose paradoxical discourse resists translation into any of its own multiple projections of unity (to say nothing of those of his readers) and the Henry Adams whose voice in retirement assumed with a certain bitter satisfaction the position of the "other." The distance between the reader's "one" and the textual "other" who is Henry Adams is never easily, never entirely, bridged; but requiring as it does an ironic enactment of tradition, one's bridge-making can afford a genuine, if unusually self-critical, sense of commonality. He who affirms in much of his writing that the best features of our common life arise from a poesis of desire assures us also that this poesis perishes under the tyrannies of the modern condition and that with it dies the possibility of a common life. Adams's discourse projects in the end the possibility of an unregenerate void, and his reader ought never to forget that his language smashes (as it can) the idol of the author-reader relationship. If some seventy years of critical reading have restored Adams to his end of that ideal, it is largely through the instruction that he makes ironically available to us, which urges us after all to believe in the poesis of a shared discourse, even in the absence of an underlying sense of direction in public history. Properly, then, our "completions" of Adams's text proceed only in an awareness of the unforeseeability, the historical fragility, of the enterprise, and with a continued sense of the void he saw always at the edge of his word.

Notes

Introduction

1. White, *Metahistory*, p. 41.
2. The terms "historicist" and "historicism" are given various and conflicting definitions. My usage follows that of Allan Megill, for whom "historicism" economically denotes "*any* attribution of directionality to history, whether or not that directionality is seen in specifically developmental terms" (*Prophets of Extremity*, p. 265).
3. Samuels, *Henry Adams: The Major Phase*, p. 352.
4. Particularly as he develops it from *The Archaeology of Knowledge* onward, Foucault's concept of discourse is slippery and protean, and I make no attempt to apply it (in any of its forms) directly in my analysis of Adams's work. Yet Foucault's view that language constitutes reality as a system of contending power relations can be of use in understanding Adams's attempts to reconstitute American public reality, present and future, through his writings. In invoking Bakhtin, I have in mind not merely the Henry Adams who wished his texts to engage in a generative public dialogue but the Adams who tended to abstract himself from the multiple contending voices at play in his text, refraining as author from any simplistic attempt to privilege certain meanings over others.
5. Although, as Bercovitch points out, "Adams's manikin extols the national past while pointing steadily toward the cosmic void" (*American Jeremiad*, p. 197), the rhetorical project of the 1907 *Education* in particular (as I argue in Chapter 2) vigorously resists that void as the terminus of national experience.
6. In 1980 James M. Cox announced, "*The Education of Henry Adams* remains a neglected book in American literature" ("Learning through Ignorance," p. 198), and, although he meant primarily to draw attention to the fact that the literary curriculum as shaped by the New Critics tended to exclude such a text, the assertion retains its rightness. With the massive critical attention in recent years to autobiography and other forms of nonfiction prose, the *Education* may now be better known, but the nature of the book's rhetoric is such that it is always apt to read as a neglected book—an urgent message that the speaker delivers in the conviction that it will go for the most part unheeded.

Chapter 1

1. Much earlier in life, Adams the correspondent did have ambitions of reaching audiences beyond the designated recipients of his letters and the circle of

mutual friends with whom his letters were often shared. Such ambitions were subject to repudiation and reespousal: in 1900 he urged Elizabeth Cameron to destroy his letters to her, but in 1915, less than two and a half years before his death, he asked her to edit their correspondence as a memorial to the old life of Lafayette Square (see Chapter 3, under the subheading "Correspondence"). During his time in the South Seas, where he wrote some of his longest and best letters, it was no doubt refreshing for him to write to a known, select, contemporary readership after he had just finished the monumental *History*, which spoke to what had become for him a progressively alienated projection of a general and largely future audience.

2. Adams reported to John Hay, January 23, 1884, that "Trollope has amused me for two evenings. I am clear that you should write autobiography. I mean to do mine. After seeing how coolly and neatly a man like Trollope can destroy the last vestige of heroism in his own life, I object to allowing mine to be murdered by anyone except myself" (*LHA* 2:532).

3. Adams of course was hardly alone in his troubled response to the promise of science. Among his contemporaries, the Mark Twain of *A Connecticut Yankee* and *The Mysterious Stranger* offers a particularly interesting parallel.

4. The best-known statement of this idea is Roland Barthes, "The Death of the Author," in *Image-Music-Text*. Variously deconstructed, the author still manages to persevere as a category of critical discussion. Before a reading of texts identified with the names Lévi-Strauss and Rousseau, Jacques Derrida very properly warns us that "the names of authors ... have here no *substantial* value" (italics added) and "indicate neither identities or causes" (*Of Grammatology*, p. 99). Yet they would nonetheless appear to indicate loci of complicity, as he very shortly goes on to list a series of proper names preceded by the appositive, "the sustainers of the discourse" (p. 102). For his part, Michel Foucault confirms the operationality of the author's name if not the subject to which it ostensibly refers. While he calls in the *Archaeology* for the "suspension" of such traditional discursive unities as book and oeuvre "designated by the sign of a proper name" (pp. 21–31), in "What Is an Author?" he remarks that "the name of the author remains at the contours of texts—separating one from the other, defining their form, and characterizing their mode of existence" (*Language, Counter-Memory, Practice*, p. 123). For Foucault, the idea of the individual author is a concomitant of the text's emergence as commodity. For Fredric Jameson, a more systematic student of the materiality of cultural formation, the author is but a guise of the bourgeois "centered subject" and must constitute a prime example of reification under capitalism. But unreal as the subject is held to be, it exists "as a mirage which is also evidently in some fashion an objective reality" (*Political Unconscious*, p. 153). With a view finally to what Mikhail Bakhtin invokes as "the great and anonymous destinies" of discourse (*Dialogic Imagination*, p. 258), in this study I retain Henry Adams as more than a merely nominal unity—retain him, that is, as a "live" if ever complicit and ultimately disappearing author. Granted that he assumed his authorial office amidst the strong currents of predetermined discourses, I retrieve him as one who was not without decided (if necessarily limited) ideological self-consciousness and as one who could exert moral choice in the face of his historically constrained textual options.

5. The editors of the Belknap edition of Adams's letters identify "the only

chapter of one's story for which one cares" rather positively as *Esther*; under *Esther* they have indexed a page reference to the March 8, 1886, letter to Holt.

6. Twelve years earlier, in a letter to Gaskell, Adams had used some of the phrasing by which he characterizes Esther to describe his then-fiancée, Marian Hooper. This coincidence and the novel's motif of unrealizable marriage are explored at length in Chapter 6.

7. For a concise exposition of Adams's intellectual and moral inheritance, see Harbert, *The Force So Much Closer Home*, chapter 1, "The Great Inheritance."

8. Adams's scientific historiography chiefly derives from Comte and Spencer. His transitional methods and the moral drama they depict, however, are the original products of his application (as the self-conscious scion of a founding American family) of European historiography to his own troubled national heritage.

9. The opposition between Old and New world, culture and nature, time and space, which Adams endlessly plays upon, has of course recently received extensive attention in such works as Sacvan Bercovitch, *The American Jeremiad*, and David W. Noble, *The End of American History*.

10. See Levenson, *The Mind and Art of Henry Adams*, pp. 208ff.

11. For Adams to continue to regard the United States as an exceptional historical possibility may be thought in some ways highly consistent with the "prophecy" of the *History*'s epilogue. The American mandate, from Puritan times onward, always had two possible outcomes: success or failure proportional to the millennial opportunity. What complicates this view, however, is the apparent exclusion of a rhetoric of moral causality from the epilogue's prophecy, which suggests that human virtue makes no difference in what is a predetermined social course. We may read that exclusion as a deliberate refinement of the American jeremiad or, more confidently, as the bleak rhetoric that a confused Adams sincerely offers in the name of science. "The Tendency of History" (1894) and *A Letter to American Teachers of History* (1910) seem much closer to deliberate refinements. See n. 21.

12. Samuels, *Henry Adams: The Major Phase*, pp. 77–78.

13. As the youngest brother in the fourth generation of his family's prominence, Brooks felt perhaps most acutely the lateness of the Adamses' hour. His disappointments as of 1893 (at age forty-five) ranged from chronic ill-health to the hostile reception of his first book, *The Emancipation of Massachusetts* (1887), and his inability to affect the course of either Republican or Democratic party. Temperamentally and intellectually, Brooks lacked Henry's breadth; his thought ran, howbeit obnoxiously to his fellow New England intellectuals, along the established economic, Spencerian, and racist lines of the day. See Anderson, *Brooks Adams*, for an appreciative but not uncritical treatment of the younger brother's career.

14. Because of its close attention to the Columbian Exposition's contradictory expressions, the best study of the fair is Reid Badger, *The Great American Fair: The World's Columbian Exposition and American Culture*. See particularly chap. 16, "A Confusion of Symbols." In "Myths, Machines, and Markets: The Columbian Exposition of 1893," Justus D. Doenecke usefully discusses the social context of the fair and the dimensions of American life it did not represent.

15. Henry Nash Smith, *Virgin Land*, p. 188. See also Noble, *End of American History*, chap. 1.

16. Turner, *Early Writings*, p. 228.

17. Sullivan, *Autobiography of an Idea*, pp. 317–26. Mumford, *The Brown Decades*, pp. 141ff. Wright, *Autobiography*, pp. 147, 149–52. More recent assessments have challenged such strictures, vindicating Burnham and the board of architects on the grounds that they promulgated, during a time of haphazard and explosive urban development, fundamental notions of civic planning. See Burg, *Chicago's White City*, pp. 307–8. With some persuasion Badger has argued that the exposition, in all of its contradictory expressions, always remained a peculiarly Victorian institution, reflecting the culture without itself exerting major influence (*Great American Fair*, p. 118). Major or minor, its influence has been and continues to be real inasmuch as the fair constituted an event that persistently lends itself to reinterpretation.

18. Burg, *Chicago's White City*, p. 191.

19. As Samuels notes, Adams in the *Education* "exercised the poetic license of retrospect and chose the Chicago World's Fair of 1893 to symbolize the revelation of the new force of electricity, reading back into his experience the troubled ignorance about the nature of electricity that he was later to feel in the Great Hall of Dynamos in the Paris Exposition of 1900" (*Henry Adams: The Major Phase*, pp. 382–83).

20. According to Brooks Adams, Henry wrote "The Tendency of History" "as a sort of preface or introduction" (*D* 96) to *The Law of Civilization and Decay*, which was to appear in spring 1895. Although its statements clearly transcend that occasion, it could certainly have served in that capacity.

21. Inverted, that is, if we assume with Bercovitch that the American jeremiad's distinctive feature lies in *its* inversion of "the doctrine of vengeance into a promise of ultimate success, affirming to the world, and despite the world, the inviolability of the colonial cause" (*American Jeremiad*, p. 7). Not only would Adams appear to restore the doctrine of vengeance, but he would appear to do so with a particular vengeance of his own. From the prospect of apocalypse he would strip any hint of moral signification; from the jeremiad, any overt moral motive. The implied "moral" is that the world is too far gone to engage on moral grounds, a motif that Adams resumes in the *Education* and pushes to an extreme in *A Letter to American Teachers of History*. Such rhetoric is perhaps always to some degree morally operative, although its accomplishment can be at times only vaguely measured as so much inconclusive resistance to its own overt conclusion—that "silence is best."

Chapter 2

1. Henry Adams to Lucy Baxter, March 25, 1890: "No amount of Stoicism can prevent one from hankering, not for the future but for the past. . . . I dread the decline of powers, and wish the moment were past when I could still say to the passing moment—Verweile doch, du bist so schön!" (*LHA* 3:231). Shortly after his brother John's death in 1894, he wrote to Charles Milnes Gaskell: "I have certainly no reason to think that any of us are stronger than he. My own nerves went to pieces long ago. My inference is therefore that I need not bother myself about anything beyond five years hence. I may calculate on not outlasting the

century" (*LHA* 4:215). Hypochrondriac that he was, he was persistently able to seize the vitality of his old age. In December 1899 he wrote to Brooks Adams: "One lives in constant company with diseased hearts, livers, kidneys and lungs; one shakes hands with certain death at closer embrace every day; one sees paralysis in every feature and feels it in every muscle . . . and, through it all, we improve; our manners acquire refinement; our sympathies grow wider . . . we should almost get to respect ourselves if we knew of anything human to respect" (*LHA* 5:66).

2. James, *Selected Letters*, pp. 242–43.

3. See Chapter 1, n. 1.

4. Charles published a scathing anonymous review of *The Life of Albert Gallatin* in the *Nation* and criticized the *History* as a work-in-progress on matters of word-choice, tone, and method. See Samuels, *Henry Adams: The Middle Years*, pp. 64–66, 386, 395. The effusive response of Charles Francis Adams, Jr., is quoted in *LHA* 6:48, n. 1.

5. Samuels, *Henry Adams: The Major Phase*, p. 332.

6. See ibid., p. 334.

7. On Adams's "several economic identities," see ibid., pp. 123–24.

8. This has been a tendency in the work of Adams's most significant seminal critics: Blackmur, Samuels, and Levenson. One sees it too in more recent studies by Melvin Lyon, John Conder, and John Carlos Rowe.

9. James, *Selected Letters*, p. 243.

10. This letter, dated March 20, 1909, is not reprinted in *LHA*. See Henry Adams, *Henry Adams and his Friends*, ed. Cater, pp. 649–50.

11. Harbert, *The Force So Much Closer Home*, p. 147.

12. Brooks Adams, "The Heritage of Henry Adams," p. 103.

13. Quoted in Samuels, *Henry Adams: The Major Phase*, p. 336.

14. James, *Selected Letters*, pp. 242–43.

15. Jameson, *Historian's World*, pp. 136, 138.

16. In the same years that Adams developed a historical thesis based on the second law of thermodynamics, James Harvey Robinson argued the pertinence of the social, as opposed to the physical, sciences to the historical discipline. A proponent himself of "scientific" history, Robinson wrote that "it is essential . . . for everyone dealing with the past to understand that history can never become a science in the sense that physics, chemistry, physiology, or even anthropology, is a science" given the "appalling" complexity of historical phenomena (*The New History*, p. 61). For a discussion of the varieties of "science" that the progressive historians brought to their historiographies, see Hofstadter, *The Progressive Historians*, pp. 41–43.

17. Quoted in Samuels, *Henry Adams: The Major Phase*, pp. 333–34.

18. Quoted in ibid., p. 335.

19. Roosevelt to Henry Cabot Lodge, January 28, 1909, *Letters of Theodore Roosevelt*, 6:1490.

20. Of his troubled relations with Theodore Roosevelt, Adams wrote: "With him wielding unmeasured power with immeasureable energy, in the White House, the relation of age to youth,—of teacher to pupil,—was altogether out of place; and no other was possible" (A I 1101).

21. One is struck by the number of commentators who have affirmed the *Education*'s unity while conceding the book's unruliness. "Failure," writes William

H. Jordy, "is the paradoxical unity in Adams' thought. Imagine his thought without the unifying theme. Loose ends would appear everywhere" (*Henry Adams: Scientific Historian*, p. 256). But Jordy, in the last statement, as much as concedes that they do. "The narrative," writes J. C. Levenson, "leads to the unification of sense and intellect in art—the one choice Adams saw as somehow opposed to death" (*The Mind and Art of Henry Adams*, p. 325). Yet, Levenson continues, of the "half a dozen ways to get to his conclusion" that Adams employs, each "was interesting, but the series became an intricate confusion" (p. 333). Similarly, Ernest Samuels states in *Henry Adams: The Major Phase* that "one is obliged to agree with [Adams] that the 'form' of the *Education*, its inner architecture, ultimately breaks down; the didactic and narrative elements resist artistic fusion" (p. 352). But he speaks later of the text as dialectically unified. With "A Dynamic Theory of History" and "A Law of Acceleration," Samuels writes, "Adams came full circle in the Platonic dialectic of his book, ending with what he initially postulated, the dichotomy that 'ran through life'" (p. 394). Ultimately, Samuels affirms that the *Education* is artistically unified as well: revisions indicate that Adams "had a keen sense of the artistic unity of the work" (p. 570). The tendency to read the *Education* as a unified text is reflected in two recent articles by critics distrustful of the dogma of textual unity. Employing Emile Benveniste's categories of person and discourse, James Goodwin argues that "the non[third]-person form of address in the *Education* reflects an abdication of individual power, of political agency and of historical responsibility. The lesson taught through the *Education*'s rhetoric, form of narration and theory of history is one of submission and 'passive obscurity' in the face of historical destiny" ("*The Education of Henry Adams*: A Non-Person in History," p. 135). While Goodwin's reading is astute, it does not sufficiently distinguish the rhetorical occasions of the *Education* from the occasion of *A Letter to American Teachers of History* and thus cannot hold up when considered in the light of the *Education*'s pre-1918 publishing history. Like Goodwin, Hayden White (in "Method and Ideology in Intellectual History") approaches the *Education* dialogically but ahistorically. Thus: "Adams' text is anything but an invitation, explicit or implicit, to a renewal of any *dialogue*. Its suppression of the expected voice of the dialogistic mode of discourse, that 'I' which implies the existence of a 'you' to participate in the verbal exchange by which meaning is to be dialectically teased out of the words used as medium, is enough to suggest as much" (p. 303). Yet, White admits, were he to continue his commentary, his "aim would be not to reduce all of these messages to a single seemingly monolithic position that could be condensed into an emblematic paraphrase, but rather to show the myriads of different messages emitted, in terms of the several codes in which they are cast, and to map the relationships among the codes thus identified . . . which would locate the text within a certain domain of the culture of the time of its production" (p. 305). Such a location of the text, simultaneously a location of the text's reader/reading, *is* dialogic; the matter of invitation is moot. The *Education*'s "myriad of different messages" has been and will continue to be read in ways that inevitably privilege particular configurations and that inevitably realize the reader's desire to read the text unitarily—in toto life-affirming or bleakly nihilistic.

22. Thus we cannot rest with such apparently plausible conclusions as those of Judith N. Shklar, who writes that Adams's final discovery was that not only his

education but "all education was pointless" and that the "very idea of an education that prepared young people for success was a delusion" (*"The Education of Henry Adams* by Henry Adams," p. 60).

23. Samuels, perhaps loosely, refers to the "Platonic dialectic" of the *Education* (see n. 20). Levenson sees in the *Education's* final chapter a calculated pedagogical antagonizing of the student/reader. "He did not mind seeming crusty, and he had motive for killing off his self-projection in sympathy as well as in story. The title of the last chapter is 'Nunc Age.' The teacher tells his pupil, 'Now go make your career.' As he explained at the beginning of the work, the manikin's function was to be a means to education: 'Once acquired, the tools and models may be thrown away.' If the student is to make his way in the world, he must let go the hand of his guide and proceed alone" (*The Mind and Art of Henry Adams*, p. 348). In *"The Education of Henry Adams*: The Confessional Mode as Heuristic Experiment," Earl N. Harbert finds the *Education* governed by a calculated heuristic: "The author acts as teacher rather than narrator and uses his own confessional as a carefully censored casebook example" (p. 222). This is substantially true, although Adams's Socratic end probably came in and went out of view in proportion to his ability to visualize educable readers. All too often he could not.

24. "The general reader of the 'Education,'" wrote Mabel La Farge, "may admire or criticise what the book contains. The 'nieces' are especially interested in what has been omitted. But here they pause at the sacred portals of silence, and the ground becomes delicate to tread. Twenty years are passed over—years that were the most joyful, as well as the most sorrowful of the Uncle's life. The *glorious* years were still to come, at the end" ("A Niece's Memories," pp. 6–7).

25. Blackmur, *Henry Adams*, p. 86.

Chapter 3

1. In his introduction to the *Life*, which he anthologized in *The Shock of Recognition*, Edmund Wilson described it as a "dreary and cold little book" in which Adams "turns the poor young man into a shadow, and withers up his verse with a wintery pinch" (p. 744), a judgment that Samuels in *Henry Adams: The Major Phase* calls unfair to "Adams's critical acumen or to his forebearance" (p. 511). As Samuels notes, the book was well received by the Lodge family. There were perhaps limits to self-effacement in Adams's writing about a man upon whom he had left such a stamp. As J. C. Levenson forcefully comments, when "Lodge uttered his second-hand convictions on the degradation of modern society, the failure of the American man, or the need for art to be bad in order to succeed, the Adamsish phrases make the older man seem to have been a corrupter of youth" (*The Mind and Art of Henry Adams*, p. 386).

2. Samuels notes that most reviews of the *Poems and Dramas* neither examined nor alluded to the *Life*, leading him to judge that it was generally withheld from notice. See *Henry Adams: The Major Phase*, p. 512.

3. See Bailyn, *Ideological Origins*, chap. 1, "The Literature of Revolution." For a recent discussion of the public language of pre-revolutionary America, see Robert A. Ferguson, " 'We Hold These Truths': Strategies of Control in the Literature of the Founders." Ferguson writes illuminatingly of the Founders' "faith in the

text to stabilize the uncertain world in which they live" (p. 4), and of the dialogic manner by which their documents were produced. "In making a finished text, the eighteenth-century man of letters distributes private drafts to a large circle of friends for advice before publication" (p. 9); such a process produces public texts which are distinctly "consensual" at the expense of individual differences among author and advisers (p. 20). We do well to read the agonized eccentricity of Adams's late writings in the light of such a model.

4. See Samuels, *Henry Adams: The Major Phase*, pp. 100, 606.

5. Henry Adams to H. A. Bumstead, February 1, 1910: "Mr Jameson has just brought me your comments on my attempt to understand the alphabet of physics . . . I assure you that the task of learning two or three new languages and modes of thought at once, when one is past seventy years old, and has nothing but books to teach one, is desperate enough to excuse loud cries for help" (*LHA* 6:305). Although the one extant version of the "Rule" incorporates revisions made after the writing and circulation of *A Letter* (1910), from the letter (dated January 1, 1909) that Adams drafted to his American Historical Association colleagues to accompany the "Rule," we can see that it forms part of an argument and rhetorical project that antedates the desperation that *A Letter* represents.

6. Adams's high opinion of Franklin the diplomatist is evident in his review of Bancroft's *History*, reprinted in *Sketches for the North American Review*.

7. Levenson rightly observes that in the "Rule" Adams appeals "to wonder rather than to catastrophic terror" (*The Mind and Art of Henry Adams*, p. 361).

8. Theory of light may of course be taken metaphorically to mean theory of knowledge, the systematic epistemology (established in view of a verifiably ultimate reality) without which no theory of history could possess for Adams enduring value. But, as Adams certainly knew, basic epistemological questions were raised by the post-Newtonian effort to propose an explanation of light as a wave rather than a corpuscular phenomenon. The effort involved one of the monumental problems of nineteenth-century science—that of the ether. In the persistent failure of researchers to verify the latter's existence, the mechanical universe lost its status as (probable) absolute description of physical reality, and scientific explanations became more widely recognized as the hypotheses that experimenters had long held them to be. For a discussion of the ether and its place in Adams's thought, see Jordy, *Henry Adams: Scientific Historian*, pp. 220–55.

9. In *American Literature and the Universe of Force*, Ronald E. Martin discusses the common nineteenth-century assumption "that a term such as *force* had a real and existent referent" (p. 7) and examines Adams's perception of "the relationship of cause and effect as absolutely necessitous" (p. 105). As Martin observes, Adams's tendency to reify scientific hypothesis constrained his "scientific" thought to the logic of "naive determinism" (p. 106). Jordy usefully discusses Adams's reification of the scientific concept as a resistance to the "phenomenalist's view of science" that worked by "conveniences" and suspended the question of the real. Most egregiously for Adams the historian, this meant that "the history of science was not that of the progressive discovery by ingenious investigators of aspects of an ultimate reality" (*Henry Adams: Scientific Historian*, p. 232).

10. The second law of thermodynamics is present in the "Rule" (Gibbs's theory is based on it) but hardly as an absolute law of dramatized tyranny. Jordy's analysis of the science and scientism of the *Education*, the "Rule," and *A Letter*

remains the most detailed, but Melvin Lyon rightly draws attention to Jordy's exaggeration of the second law of thermodynamics' centrality to the *Education* and the "Rule" (*Symbol and Idea*, p. 305).

11. The alarming imprecision of Adams's terms ("vital energy," the "evolutionist" doctrine of progress) and his reducive misrepresentation of his "authorities" (particularly Ostwald, Dastre, Haeckel, and Bergson) are discussed by Samuels, *Henry Adams: The Major Phase*, pp. 478ff. For an examination of Adams's haphazard research, see Jordy, *Henry Adams: Scientific Historian*, pp. 217–19.

12. The marginalia in Adams's scientific texts document vividly what was for him the difficulty of dialogic entrance. In a copy of Lucien Poincaré's *La Physique moderne, son évolution*, he wrote in reference to a discussion of the ether, "Is it possible that this chapter conveys a clear idea to anyone?" See Jordy, *Henry Adams: Scientific Historian*, pp. 229, 233–36.

13. The phrasing suggests that there is something remarkable, even authoritative, in the pessimism of the female poet; it also suggests that Adams had particular women in mind. Ernest Samuels proposes Elizabeth Barrett Browning: "*Perhaps* he was thinking of *Aurora Leigh* and its record of misfortunes" (letter to the author, May 26, 1987).

14. Of *A Letter*'s rhetorical indeterminacy, Levenson writes: "The old hell-fire preachers had used their catastrophic rhetoric for the purpose of converting those who would give heed, whereas even the best-intentioned readers of the *Letter* are forced to ask, Conversion to what? To deterministic science or vitalistic thought? To university reform or cowed silence? To co-operative effort or delusion with democracy? And one feels that Adams would only have answered with the counter-question, Conversion of whom?" (*The Mind and Art of Henry Adams*, p. 374).

15. By Jordy's count, nineteen letters (excluding the letter and two postcards from William James as well as the responses of his other regular correspondents) commenting on the substance of *A Letter* exist in the Adams estate—a slight response considering the fact that Adams distributed somewhere between two hundred fifty and five hundred copies. Of the nineteen comments, none "was favorable" or went beyond "a polite discussion of some point raised by Adams" (*Henry Adams: Scientific Historian*, p. 247). No doubt the least satisfactory responses were those suggesting the dated irrelevance of Adams's thought. "I am constantly astonished," wrote Arthur T. Hadley, political economist and president of Yale, "to find how much less the younger men of today are caring for a certain kind of scientific romancing than did the men of twenty years ago" (p. 245). Frederick Jackson Turner's American Historical Association presidential address of 1910 confirmed the general disinterest in history as thermodynamics, dismissively mentioning the topic in passing. A reply from Ellsworth Huntington, the Yale experimental geographer, "pointed out the antiquated character" of Adams's solar theory and the obsolescence of his climatology, which did inspire Adams to "explore the new realm of environmental geography" (Samuels, *Henry Adams: The Major Phase*, p. 487). The pursuit however remained fragmentary and inconclusive.

16. James, *Selected Letters*, p. 264.

17. From a letter of February 3, 1910, to Elizabeth Cameron not reprinted in *LHA*. See Henry Adams, *Letters*, ed. Ford, 2:533.

18. Chalfant, *Both Sides of the Ocean*, pp. 280–81.

19. Of the generation of Bancroft, Prescott, Motley, and Parkman, David Levin writes: "Membership in [the] literary aristocracy did not mean being a professional writer. The New England man of letters was a gentleman of letters, trained for some other, more 'useful' profession and usually practicing it" (*History as Romantic Art*, p. 4). By the time Adams came of age, however, the line between professional and gentleman had somewhat blurred. As Emerson redefined him, the man of letters was a popular (if not yet professional) figure, a poet wary of absorption in the past, a lyceum speaker who addressed the present democratic crisis. Nathaniel Hawthorne (always admired by Adams) had done much to make the professional man of letters respectable, if not aristocratic, by conservative standards. Nevertheless, as a man of letters, Adams (who came from a family that was not, by Boston standards, precisely aristocratic) was attracted to the earlier gentlemanly type and like "Prescott, Motley, and Parkman made gestures toward the law" (ibid., p. 4).

20. "Two Letters on a Prussian Gymnasium" would ultimately appear in the October 1947 *American Historical Review*. For an account of Henry Adams's intriguing absence from the pages of the *Atlantic*—and of what that absence suggests of Adams's early sense of his authorial vocation—see Charles Vandersee's excellent article, "Henry Adams and the *Atlantic*: Pattern for a Career."

21. Quoted in Samuels, *The Young Henry Adams*, pp. 51–52.

22. *A Cycle of Adams Letters, 1861–1865* (1920), edited by Worthington Chauncey Ford, prints a good selection of Henry Adams's letters in the illuminating context of the family wartime correspondence.

23. Charles F. Adams, Jr., and Henry Adams, *Chapters of Erie and Other Essays*, p. 3.

Chapter 4

1. Inspired by such works as Gordon S. Wood's *The Creation of the American Republic, 1776–1787* (1969) and J. G. A. Pocock's *The Machiavellian Moment: Florentine Political Thought and the Atlantic Republican Tradition* (1975), much has been done in the last twenty years to define the role of classical republican ideas in the development of American ideology. A recent issue of *American Quarterly* (37, no. 4) usefully reviews past work in this field and delineates new directions. The conflict Adams faced was paradigmatic: attached (as a man of republican sympathies) to ideals that could only be realized in a society that had achieved a state of repose, he yet endorsed and sought (as a liberal, free-trade man) to facilitate the economic expansion that the country's ongoing settlement required but that inevitably created new wealth and destabilized older balances of power.

2. Brooks, *Three Essays on America*, pp. 214, 215.

3. As Richard Hofstadter has shown in *Social Darwinism in American Thought*, the fatalism encouraged by Herbert Spencer and his followers deeply affected the intellectual and political tone of post–Civil War America, confirming the more privileged classes in their disregard of the social injustice that accompanied laissez-faire capitalism. Generally Adams was a party to this confirmed disregard; but, although he toyed with some of the most extreme forms of mechanistic

determinism, they never failed to revolt him, and he never succeeded in ridding himself of the wish to believe that a nation could deliberately choose and shape its history.

4. In the *Education*, Adams himself claims that the *North American Review*'s circulation "never exceeded three or four hundred" (A I 934), an estimate that F. L. Mott accepts for the period prior to the editorship of Adams, who appears to have increased circulation to 1,200 before the review was sold to Allen Thorndike Rice (Mott, *History of American Magazines*, 2:247). See nn. 13, 16.

5. John Quincy Adams, *Lectures*, p. 72.

6. This style is perhaps most consistently at its best in "The New York Gold Conspiracy," an article that may be no more rhetorically certain of its ultimate aims than any of Adams's early work but that was written quite specifically to exasperate the Erie influence in England where Adams all along intended to publish it. Writing of events too inherently outrageous to allow for much bombast, Adams was able to focus his language and realize his argument (that corporate power endangers popular institutions) in his skillful narration of the comic horror of Gould's and Fisk's schemes.

7. Carolyn Porter reads such moments as part of "a recurrent pattern of *forced* retreat to higher ground" (*Seeing and Being*, p. 175; italics added); my reading of Adams's development as an author emphasizes the element of choice involved in his increasingly philosophical and poetic engagement of his concern. But Porter is certainly right in observing that as Adams "was pushed back from immediate participation" in the political realm, "the scope of his imagined power widened" (pp. 175–76).

8. Translated as "what actually happened," the determination of which constituted the objective of the documentary historiography of Leopold von Ranke and his school.

9. In his review of Bancroft's *History of the United States from the Discovery of the American Continent*, vol. 10, Adams approves of the elder historian's course as one that has become increasingly cautious. "No doubt Mr. Bancroft entertains as ardent a faith now as forty years ago in the abstract virtues of democracy and 'the gentle feelings of humanity,' but time and experience have tempered this faith with a more searching spirit of criticism than was fashionable in the days of President Jackson" (*Sk* 151).

10. Harbert, *The Force So Much Closer Home*, p. 40.

11. What was thought to be the resistance of the *North American Review*'s readership to Darwin's evolutionary theories is reflected in the cautious and conciliatory tone adopted in two articles printed during Adams's tenure as editor: Chauncy Wright's "The Genesis of Species" (July 1871) and W. D. Whitney's "Darwinism and Language" (July 1874).

12. It is thus not surprising that Samuels and Harbert arrive at divergent yet equally plausible conclusions as to which geological school Adams champions— Samuels maintains that he stands by Agassiz (*The Young Henry Adams*, pp. 165–66) while Harbert argues that his "real sympathies lay with Lyell and uniformitarianism" (*The Force So Much Closer Home*, p. 40).

13. As late as 1907 Adams remained uncertain of the practicability of this ambition. "The circulation of the *Review*," he writes in the *Education*, "had never exceeded three or four hundred copies, and the *Review* had never paid its reason-

able expenses. Yet it stood at the head of American literary periodicals; it was a source of suggestion to cheaper workers; it reached far into societies that never knew its existence" (A I 934). But in the very next chapter he suggests that one of the disincentives of writing for E. L. Godkin's *Nation* was "that he should find there only the same circle of readers that he reached in the *North American Review*" (A I 943). He could never abandon the idea that the *North American Review* exerted a profound if mostly indirect influence, yet he was never satisfied that it actually did so and that it reached a public beyond a minority elite.

14. Samuels, *The Young Henry Adams*, pp. 227–28.

15. E. L. Godkin, "The *North American Review* for January," *Nation* 22 (February 17, 1876): 118–19.

16. According to F. L. Mott, Adams gave the *North American Review* "more 'bite' than it had had for a long time—perhaps more than it had ever had before" (*History of American Magazines*, 2:248). But the real coup in the quarterly's history was the accomplishment of Allen Thorndike Rice, Adams's successor, who bought the review from Osgood in 1877, converted it to a bimonthly and then a monthly, incorporated material of broader appeal, and purged the writing of its antiquated style. The revolution was complete when Rice moved the editorial office to New York, out of the orbit of Boston and Harvard. (See Mott, *History of American Magazines*, 2:260; 3:31.)

17. See Samuels, *The Young Henry Adams*, pp. 265–66.

18. Edward Chalfant has recently questioned whether Adams had any part in two articles that have long been thought to be efforts in which he collaborated: "The 'Independents' in the Canvass," which Chalfant argues to have been entirely written by Charles Francis Adams, Jr., and "Von Holst's History of the United States," which he thinks should be wholly attributed to Henry Cabot Lodge (*Sk* 236–42). Whereas the evidence that Charles wrote "The 'Independents' " with at most minimal editing on the part of Henry seems convincing, I think that we may take Adams at his word when he declares of "Von Holst's History of the United States" that the "last two pages are *my* centennial Oration." Chalfant doubts whether Adams could really accept the thesis that the Constitution "made a nation" and suggests that "authorship attested in print by two persons" is "extremely different from authorship attested in print by one person" (*Sk* 241). Yet, as I have argued, the nature of Adams's work as teacher, scholar, and editor was highly collaborative during this period, and his thought, although guided and even confined by family doctrine, did not seek the repose of closed arguments. But even if "Von Holst's History of the United States" is entirely the product of Lodge, Adams's cosignature indicates his serious if experimental subscription to its thesis. It is well to recall that as late as 1876, Adams's published writings had all appeared in the collaborative context of journals or coauthored books; he had yet to develop the more singular authorial identity that comes of the comparative isolation involved in writing a single-author book.

19. J. C. Levenson provides a valuable analysis of the novel's uncontrol: "An excessive sense of horror" disrupts the achievement of "satiric detachment," "irony turning into monstrosity" (*The Mind and Art of Henry Adams*, p. 88).

20. "There are few more interesting contrasts of character in our history," wrote Adams, "than that between the New England President, with his intense personality and his overpowering bursts of passion . . . and 'the Genevan,' as the

Aurora called him, calm, reticent, wary, never vehement, full of resource, ignoring enmity, hating strife. Perhaps a combination of two such characters, if they could have been made to work in harmony, might have proved too much even for the Senate; and, if so, a problem in American history might have been solved, for, as it was, the Senate succeeded in overthrowing both" (*G* 411).

21. Adams's depiction of New England's trials during the embargo seeks its explanation in Darwinian metaphor. "New England, hostile to the government, and dependent more immediately on commerce than her neighbors, resisted, revolted, and gasped convulsively for life and air. Her struggle saved her; necessity taught new modes of existence and made her at length almost independent of the sea. Virginia, however, friendly to the government and herself responsible for the choice, submitted with hardly a murmur, and never recovered from the shock; her ruin was accelerated with frightful rapidity because she made no struggle for life" (*G* 380).

22. Samuels comments perceptively with regard to the rhetorical bearing of this particular letter. "To Lodge it was another veiled warning, which he would not—or could not—heed, as Adams found out to his deep distress" (*Henry Adams: The Middle Years*, p. 64).

23. Quoted in ibid., p. 66.

24. Eugenia Kaledin suggests that Marian Adams may have collaborated in some of the writing of *Democracy* and that, in less direct modes, she may have contributed to both *Democracy* and *Esther* (*Education of Mrs. Henry Adams*, pp. 9–10). It may not, therefore, be exaggerating to say that those novels publish a voice that is partly that of a woman and that the novelist's ambiguous gender reflects an intimately and often unconsciously dialogic process of composition.

25. This is the rendering offered by the editors of the Harvard *Letters of Henry Adams* (2:360).

26. Samuels, *Henry Adams: The Middle Years*, p. 72.

27. Inasmuch as discussion in *Democracy* and *Esther* figures to the virtual exclusion of images of nonverbal action, the novels seem particularly to bear out Bakhtin's proposition that "the human being in the novel is first, foremost and always a speaking human being" (*Dialogic Imagination*, p. 332) amid the novel's restless heteroglossia. And given what has commonly been observed as the thinness of Adams's characterization (an observation usually registered as a criticism, edged by contrasting his characterization with that of James), the novels readily lend themselves to Bakhtin's assertion that "the speaking person in the novel is always, to one degree or another, an *ideologue*, and his words are always *ideologemes*" (p. 333). The complexity of the ideologemic interaction is not necessarily proportional to a character's "realization," and we cannot do justice to these fascinating texts until we suspend the novel's ability to project character as a major criterion of success. As I hope my analyses of Adams's fiction show, the interest of the novels' dialogic life far transcends the three-dimensional verisimilitude that Adams's characters (particularly when compared to those of James) typically lack.

28. Samuels, *Henry Adams: The Middle Years*, p. 86.

29. Cf. Adams's equivocal disavowal of his remarks in "The Tendency of History" on the principle that "silence is best": "I have not ventured to express any opinion of my own; or, if I have expressed it, pray consider it as withdrawn" (*D* 133); also, his insistence that Brooks Adams not dedicate *The Law of Civiliza-*

tion and Decay to him: "My destiny—or at least my will, as an element of the social mass in movement—lies in silence, which I hold to be alone sense. Even my name, on a dedication, talks too much to please me" (*LHA* 4:284). The confidentiality of Nathan Gore's utterances also anticipates Adams's late sequence of privately published texts.

30. Levenson, *The Mind and Art of Henry Adams*, p. 88.

Chapter 5

1. The readers of the privately printed draft volumes of the *History* were George Bancroft, C. F. Adams, Jr., John Hay, Carl Schurz, the industrialist Abram Hewitt, and the financier Samuel Ward. Although three of the readers had themselves written history, the group was anything but narrowly specialist and therefore gives us a strong sense of the intelligent general readership Adams hoped to reach.

2. By his own admission, Morse tacitly encouraged Adams to write the biography of Burr in order not to discourage him from writing *John Randolph*. Although Morse would later explain to Adams that Henry O. Houghton disapproved of Burr's inclusion in the Statesmen Series, he and Houghton were in agreement all along that the series was no place for a biography of the infamous traitor. See Ballou, *The Building of the House*, pp. 342–43.

3. Morse appears to have consulted Adams on occasion about potential authors for the American Statesmen series (see *LHA* 2:425, 452, 472–73, 479; 3:248–49), but at no point did Adams's recommendations eventuate in a commission. Three of Adams's associates did, however, write for the series: Henry Cabot Lodge, Daniel C. Gilman, and Carl Schurz. (Adams had hoped Schurz might write the *Gallatin*, but the former Missouri senator was to author the two-volume *Henry Clay*.) A description of the American Statesmen Series appearing in the Houghton Mifflin 1899 *Catalog of Authors* confirms that the series was aimed at rewriting American history from a distinctly northern perspective. "The principle adopted by the editor has been to make such a list of men in public life that the aggregate of all their biographies would give, in this personal shape, the history and the picture of the growth and development of the United States, from the beginning of that agitation which led to the Revolution until the completion of that solidarity which we believe has resulted from the civil war and the subsequent reconstruction" (pp. 154–55).

4. See Samuels, *Henry Adams: The Middle Years*, pp. 207–9.

5. Adams's particularly charged memory of the Battle of Malvern Hill may be gauged by his July 19, 1862, letter to Charles Francis Adams, Jr. (*LHA* 1:307–9).

6. "The imps of perversity, contradiction, and paradox," writes Samuels in *Henry Adams: The Middle Years*, "colored his own vision, and he knew it and wittily apologized for them. He attacked these traits in Randolph as if by the very violence of his assault he might uproot them in himself" (p. 200).

7. "In truth," wrote Adams to John Hay in June 1882, "I rather grudge the public my immortal writings. I neither want notoriety nor neglect, and one of the two must be imagined by every author to be his reward. My ideal of authorship would be to have a famous *double* with another name, to wear what honors I

could win. How I should enjoy upsetting him at last by publishing a low and shameless essay with smutty woodcuts in his name!" (*LHA* 2:463).

8. Adams's highly detailed recollection of *Tom Jones* is suggested by his September 22, 1867, letter to Gaskell (*LHA* 1:552–53).

9. Adams provides an extended, satiric gloss to "strict construction run riot" as he proceeds to opine that "on such principles it would not have been difficult to prove that Congress could lay no imposts at all, because, in the sense contended, no possible impost could be uniform; one or another class of people might always be exempt from its burden, unless light, air, and water could be made dutiable; but granting that Randolph was correct, he might at least have consoled the petitioners by telling them that a means of evading the difficulty existed; that to obtain their object they need only go to the President and invoke the treaty-making power which brought Louisiana, all its inhabitants and all their property, real and personal, through the custom house, made them all citizens, and gave them special privileges of foreign trade, without offense to the Constitution, or authority from an act of Congress" (*R* 123–24).

10. Although he appears to allude to Randolph's fairly well-known sexual impotence, Adams does not venture beyond innuendo: "Some private trouble weighed on his mind, and since he chose to make a mystery of its cause a biographer is bound to respect his wish" (*R* 247). Earlier in the book Adams had likewise referred to "some mental distress" under which Randolph had suffered late in his first term as congressman. "There is talk even of a love affair," the biographer writes significantly, "but it is very certain that no affair of the heart had at any time a serious influence over his life" (*R* 45). Insofar as he portrays Randolph as crushed by the masculine intellectuality of Luther Martin, Adams hardly needs directly to invoke Randolph's alleged sexual weakness.

11. In his account of congressional discussion in the wake of the embargo's evident failure, the historian would again marvel over Randolph's verbal power: "With all John Randolph's waywardness and extravagance, he alone shone among this mass of mediocrities, and like the water-snakes in Coleridge's silent ocean his every track was a flash of golden fire" (*A* II 1188).

12. See Samuels, *Henry Adams: The Middle Years*, pp. 202–3.

13. In two parts, under the pen name "Housatonic," "A Case of Hereditary Bias" appeared in the *New York Tribune* on September 10 and December 15, 1890. The author was William Henry Smith.

14. In *The American Compromise: Theme and Method in the Histories of Bancroft, Parkman, and Adams*, Richard C. Vitzthum challenges the notion that the *History* is programmatically scientific. "Although the countless metaphors in the *History* which oppose inertia or static mass to activity, motion, and efficiency have sometimes been explained in terms of Adams' committment to science, it seems more likely that they were inspired by the same kind of activism that is obvious in the writings of the New England historians who preceded Adams. These and many other metaphors with a scientific ring are no more prevalent in the *History* as a whole than those taken from other areas of human experience— for example, the many figures based on breaking waves or blowing winds, on military combat, on biblical or classical mythology, or on the drama and especially on Shakespeare. Adams seems to show no special preference for scientific imagery. Like all the other kinds in the *History*, it serves a largely illustrative, rather than

thematic, function" (p. 156). Vitzthum's observation valuably emphasizes the literary nature of Adams's enterprise in the *History*; still, there is no denying the scientific aesthetic that dominates the *History*'s heterogeneous metaphoric.

15. Concise discussions of the variant and problematic meanings of "scientific history" may be found in Hofstadter, *The Progressive Historians*, pp. 35–43, and Jordy, *Henry Adams: Scientific Historian*, pp. 1–6.

16. Valuable analyses of Adams's documentary methods appear in Jordy, *Henry Adams: Scientific Historian*, pp. 53–56, and Vitzthum, *The American Compromise*, pp. 177–206.

17. Both Jordy (*Henry Adams: Scientific Historian*) and Samuels (*Henry Adams: The Middle Years*) provide good accounts of the impact of Comte and Spencer on Adams's thought.

18. Jordy, *Henry Adams: Scientific Historian*, p. 81.

19. See Chapter 4, n. 3. The prestige and pervasiveness of the various forms of social Darwinism and their profound and paralyzingly conservative effect on political and social thought are concisely addressed in Richard Hofstadter's well-known *Social Darwinism in American Thought*. In *American Literature and the Universe of Force*, Ronald E. Martin more specifically examines the career of force determinism in American expression.

20. Samuels, *Henry Adams: The Middle Years*, pp. 358–60.

21. Vitzthum (*The American Compromise*) rightly emphasizes Adams's determination to preserve the original language of the document and, hence, of the historical experience and provides a highly illuminating analysis of Adams's variant modes of assimilating (through the signaled and unsignaled paraphrase) source material into his historical narrative. See particularly pp. 182ff.

22. Henry Adams's inclusion of John Adams in the human movement that expressed itself in the election of Jefferson entails a bold rendering of the great-grandfather, one clearly meant to separate the democratic virtue of John Adams (that which made him a "true American") from the dross of his antidemocratic sentiments. As Gordon S. Wood has shown, the second president's antidemocratic phase dominated his later career. "Once the hopes of 1776 were dissipated, Adams set for himself the formidable task of convincing his countrymen that they were after all 'like all other people, and shall do like other nations.' In effect he placed himself not only in the path of the American Revolution but in the course of the emerging American myth" (*Creation of the American Republic*, p. 571). If in his turn the grandson was prepared to reaffirm that Americans were more like other people than was popularly supposed, he preserved for his own use the American myth and did so the more decidedly by assigning his great-grandfather a signal place in it. The differences between John Adams and the Henry Adams of the initial volume of the *History* may be measured by what appears to be the great-grandson's specific objection to one of John Adams's dismissive assertions. The United States, John Adams asserts in a letter to Benjamin Rush, is "more Avaricious than any other Nation that ever existed" (ibid., p. 574). To which Henry Adams counters: "Avarice against avarice, no more sordid or meaner type existed in America than could be shown on every 'Change in Europe" (A II 119).

23. This is George Hochfield's reading of the *History*. See Hochfield, *Henry Adams: An Introduction and Interpretation*, p. 62.

24. In *Henry Adams: The Middle Years*, Samuels suggests that Adams, at least

while at work on the *Gallatin*, principally saw "in Jefferson the mirror of his own weaknesses, his aversion to rough combat, his love of abstract generalizations, and his own Hamlet-like indecision" (p. 49) and that he preferred to identify himself with the more courageous Gallatin. But insofar as Gallatin never so precisely mirrored his own habits as thinker, writer, and conversationalist—particularly his fatal attachment to a language of inconclusion and paradox—there were clearly limits to such identification. By the time he began composing the *History*, Adams had come largely to accept the validity and strengths of such "weaknesses" as he shared with Jefferson. As Samuels later remarks, the historian "seemed to hold the mirror up to himself as he dwelt on Jefferson's complex sensibility" (p. 388). For a useful survey of Adams's ambivalent treatment of Jefferson in the *History*, see Dusinberre, *Henry Adams: The Myth of Failure*, pp. 115–20.

Chapter 6

1. In the *Education*, however, Adams strikes a conciliatory note that contrasts sharply with the arrogant self-sufficiency displayed in the letter to Gaskell. "Although everyone cannot be a Gargantua-Napoleon-Bismarck and walk off with the great bells of Notre Dame," he writes in "Quincy (1838–48)," "everyone must bear his own universe, and most persons are moderately interested in learning how their neighbors have managed to carry theirs" (A I 724).

2. Holt, *Garrulities*, p. 139.

3. The *History* and the records from which it was written are virtually womanless. The appearance of a woman in those historical documents that Adams compiled in pursuit of the Jeffersonian period was a refreshing event, or so we might gather from the attention he pays to Mrs. Francis James Jackson, wife of a very badly treated and hence short-term British minister. She is described as "a fashionable Prussian baroness with a toilette" (A III 83); "her comments on American society," Adams tells us before quoting them, "had more value than many official documents in explaining the attitude of England toward the United States" (A III 112).

4. Samuels alludes extensively to the probable models of the characters in *Esther*. See Samuels, *Henry Adams: The Middle Years*, pp. 238ff.

5. To be sure, Adams's setting of the action in New York accords—as the editors of the *Letters* suggest—with his determination to baffle those who might be in a position to identify the "real-life" originals of his fictional characters and from them the novel's author (*LHA* 2:509). Those in the best position to reach behind the veil were of course the very members of the Adams inner circle (Hay, King) who had been in on the secret of *Democracy* but who were not immediately entrusted with that of *Esther*. Millicent Bell, perceptively analyzing the many shortcomings of the second novel, writes that Adams's "natural audience was a private group of friends. His novels, like his deft and affectionate letters, seem to have been written for the diversion of these select companions—for whom a book like *Esther* would be the merest topic-outline of long-shared thought and experience" ("Adams' *Esther*," p. 104). As Adams's secret and experimental publication of the novel makes clear, and as the book read in the context of his other work confirms, nothing could have been further from the author's intention, although

one may perhaps count among the novel's failings its tendency to give the impression of being meant exclusively for a private circle.

6. Cf. Clarence King's charge, reported in "Free Fight (1869–1870)," that nature had twice blundered. "Except for two mistakes, the earth would have been a success. One of these errors was the inclination of the ecliptic; the other was the differentiation of the sexes, and the saddest thought about the last was that it should have been so modern" (A I 966).

7. See Levenson, *The Mind and Art of Henry Adams*, p. 199.

8. Bell gives the allusion to "Old Esther Dudley" what I find to be a less plausible but still intriguing reading, admissible under the rule of paradox that customarily governs Adams's text. Observing that Hawthorne's Esther Dudley had been "faithful to the death," Bell asks whether there may be "a sense in which Adams' Esther Dudley is the keeper of a vanished authority, that of the Puritan conscience, which required the act of virtue without promise of salvation?" ("Adams' *Esther*," p. 108).

9. Mrs. Murray is by no means a simple conception. Her failure to advocate the urgings of the heart not only reflects her alliance with the conservative forces of her society but also her chronic intellectual stultification. A childless social matriarch, she supplies an illustration of the half-married state; her observations reflect a conviction that marriage cannot long subsist on the romantic forms of love. "If I were a girl again," she remarks at one point, "I would much rather a man should ask for my head than my heart" (A I 220).

10. Levenson rightly identifies this as the book's climax (*The Mind and Art of Henry Adams*, p. 202).

11. Hawthorne, *The Scarlet Letter* in *Novels*, pp. 344–45.

12. One of the terrible ironies of *Esther* is that Wharton's model, a would-be suicide, should anticipate those tendencies in Adams's model that were very shortly to be realized. Following the death of Dr. Robert Hooper, Marian Adams, unlike the fictional Esther after the death of her father, could not resist such invitations of nonbeing as Esther contemplates in the current of the Niagara River above the falls. Having authored in part the text of his wife's breakdown and his marriage's dissolution, Adams must have looked upon his second novel as an instance of astonishing penetration and mortifying shortsightedness.

13. Cf. Henry Adams to Barrett Wendell, March 12, 1909: "My favorite figure of the American author is that of a man who breeds a favorite dog, which he throws into the Mississippi River for the pleasure of making a splash. The river does not splash, but it drowns the dog" (*LHA* 6:237).

14. On Adams's reworking of the stiffly translated transcripts of Arii Taimai's oral history into the voice he created for her *Memoirs*, see Samuels, *Henry Adams: The Major Phase*, p. 104.

15. Although commonly regarding himself as a man of a superlative racial extraction, Adams in *Memoirs* genuinely disputes the claims to racial superiority on which Western imperialism has perennially justified its actions and early in the book subjects the solemn pronouncements of Aryanism to satire. The ghostwriter has Arii Taimai utter the following pungent witticism: "We believe ourselves to belong to the great Aryan race—the race of Arii—and our chiefs were Arii, not kings" (*T* 7).

16. Brooks Adams claims that Henry wrote "The Tendency of History" "as a sort of preface or introduction" to the *Law* (*D* 96). See Chapter 1, n. 20.

17. On the force-economy centered in the "fetish-power" of the Christian cross, see the *Education*, chap. 33, "A Dynamic Theory of History (1904)," particularly pp. 1158ff.

18. Mane, *Henry Adams on the Road to Chartres*, p. viii.

19. Ibid., p. 90.

20. This is particularly borne out by Adams's response to his brother Brooks when the latter, praising *Mont Saint Michel and Chartres* as the "crowning effort of our race," urged him "to publish an edition and let it be sold" (quoted in *LHA* 5:669). "Thousands of people exist who think they want to read," replied Henry in a letter dated June 5, 1905. "Barring a few Jews, they are incapable of reading fifty consecutive pages, or of following the thought if they did. . . . There are already some fifty copies [of *Chartres*] afloat, and I'll bet ten to one that half of them have not been once read. Yet they've been given only to the most appreciative and cultivated personal friends" (*LHA* 5:668).

21. On Adams's very sketchy and at times downright erroneous descriptions of his architectural sites, see ibid., pp. 113–52. Mane is right to credit the inventiveness of some of Adams's errors—particularly that which led Adams to ascribe to Mont-Saint-Michel a marvelous little room (Le Chartrier) that does not in fact exist (ibid., pp. 121–22).

22. Ibid., p. vii.

23. The sequence of personal pronouns in this passage is noteworthy: "Anyone can feel it . . . you or any other lost soul . . . anyone willing to try . . . he could, at will, in an instant, shatter the whole art by calling into it a single motive of his own." Beginning by emphasizing the art's universal accessibility—"Anyone . . . you or any other lost soul"—he concludes the passage with a doubly alienated "he": divided from the art at the first stirrings of self-conciousness (a self-consciousness, indeed, that exists *as* the third person) and divided from the reader who has been invited by the "anyone" and the "you" to unite in what becomes at last an impossibly self-forgetting experience.

24. "Never sympathetic with the masses of working men," Eugenia Kaledin comments, "Henry Adams found women to be his main source of identity with the powerless in the democracy he was always striving to understand" (*Education of Mrs. Henry Adams*, p. 10).

25. For a reading that assumes—as mine does not—a dialectical and rhetorical unity to subsist between *Mont Saint Michel and Chartres* and the *Education*, see John Conder, *A Formula of His Own: Henry Adams's Literary Experiment*.

26. "All the steam in the world could not, like the Virgin, build Chartres," affirms Adams; yet "both energies acted as interchangeable forces on man, and by action on man all known force may be measured. . . . Symbol or energy, the Virgin had acted as the greatest force the western world ever felt, and had drawn man's activities to herself more strongly than any other power, natural or supernatural, had ever done; [but] the historian's business was to follow the track of the energy; to find where it came from and where it went to; its complex source and shifting channels; its values, equivalents, conversions" (A I 1074–75). The "historian's business" presents a contrast to the touring uncle's pleasure.

27. Mane, *Henry Adams on the Road to Chartres*, p. 216.

28. Ibid., p. 211.

29. Colacurcio, "The Dynamo and the Angelic Doctor," p. 702.

30. Colacurcio writes: "*Movens* is, in form, a verbal noun; as such it points first of all to activity; it describes a being as an agent rather than as a nature. Thus *mover*, in the accepted philosophical jargon, signifies any being which acts in any way whatever to produce motion (change) of any sort whatever. *Motor*, on the other hand, with its unmistakable materialist and mechanist suggestions, is clearly inappropriate to Thomas' notion of God as Pure Spiritual Act. One suspects that not even Aristotle, who has been accused of offering a so-called 'physical proof,' of a God who does not at all transcend the material world, could be accused of dealing in 'motors'" (ibid., p. 701).

Chapter 7

1. Ernest Samuels has drawn attention to the frequent recurrence throughout the *History* of the word "chaos"; historical actors and historian alike repeatedly confront an experience that repels political shaping and moral explanation. See *Henry Adams: The Middle Years*, p. 369.

2. The mythic conception of the woman in these lines bears a striking resemblance to Hazard's perception of Esther as "a wandering soul, lost in infinite space, but still floating on, with her quiet air of confidence as though she were a part of nature itself, and felt that all nature moved with her" (A I 263). In both instances the figure of "feminine" self-possession serves as a reproach to the designing, self-regarding, interventionist male.

3. James, *Selected Letters*, p. 243.

4. Adams's sense of the force of visual images is made explicit in his discussion in the *Education*, chap. 33, of the fetish-power of the cross and the crescent. In *Esther*, the heroine is understood to be lost to Hazard's faith when the cross which she presses to her breast (on George Strong's dare) fails to compel her assent.

5. Rowe, *Henry Adams and Henry James*, p. 124.

6. Minter, *Interpreted Design*, pp. 6, 130ff.

7. The figure, one of arrogance and chaotic assertion, contrasts with Adams's figuring (in the last paragraph of *Chartres*) of the cathedral's delighted, anguished aspiration.

8. *NAR* 208:803–4.

9. Ibid., 921, 922, 929.

10. James Truslow Adams, *Henry Adams*, pp. 205, iii.

11. Becker, "*The Education of Henry Adams*," pp. 434, 424, 433, 426.

12. Becker, *Everyman His Own Historian*, p. 166.

13. Beard, Introduction to *Law of Civilization and Decay*, p. vii.

14. Dusinberre, *Henry Adams: The Myth of Failure*, p. 4.

15. Eliot, "A Sceptical Patrician," pp. 361–62.

16. Mumford, *The Golden Day*, p. 221.

17. Brooks, *Sketches*, pp. 198–99.

18. Brooks, *New England*, p. 490.

19. The impact of the *Education* on Hemingway and Fitzgerald is addressed by George Monteiro in "The Education of Ernest Hemingway."

20. Parrington, *Main Currents*, pp. 225, 217.

21. Hicks, *The Great Tradition*, p. 139. A very thorough Marxian analysis would more deeply probe the evident privatization of Adams's intellectual pursuits.

22. Winters, *Anatomy of Nonsense*, p. 68.

23. In 1921, Paul Elmer More wrote that "the tragedy of Adams's education is that of a man who could not rest easy in negation, yet could find no positive faith to take its place" (*A New England Group*, p. 140).

24. Spiller, "Henry Adams," pp. 1080, 1093, 1096, 1099, 1103.

25. Blackmur portrays himself in an Adams-like third person in his 1928 essay, "Politikon."

26. Blackmur, *Henry Adams*, pp. 3, 4.

27. Ibid., p. 28.

28. Baym, *French Education*, p. ix.

29. Jordy, *Henry Adams: Scientific Historian*, pp. 158, 159.

30. Hume, *Runaway Star*, p. 238.

31. Levenson, *The Mind and Art of Henry Adams*, p. 1.

32. Samuels, *The Young Henry Adams*, pp. viii, xi.

33. Samuels, *Henry Adams: The Middle Years*, p. ix.

34. Samuels, *Henry Adams: The Major Phase*, p. ix.

35. Harbert, "*The Education of Henry Adams*: The Confessional Mode as Heuristic Experiment."

36. "The man of design," Minter writes, "participates in modern man's continuing faith in design, in careful planning and concerted devotion as a means of assuring success; the man of interpretation participates, on the other hand, in modern man's tendency, especially in his art, to make interpretation—both as historical recounting (historical narrative) and as imaginative translation (artistic narrative)—a means of taming unexpected and unacceptable failure" (*Interpreted Design*, p. 6). Such "taming" in Adams's case ultimately takes the form of a narrative about one man's effort to tame the chaos that envelops him in the failure of received design. "Because the *Education* is the story of a man whose 'accidental education' prepares him for the act of telling it," Minter writes, "it is finally the story of its story" (p. 133).

37. "The manikin of the *Education*," Rowe writes, "is the archetype for the modern man of interpretation, a figure condemned to the unreliability of his language" (*Henry Adams and Henry James*, p. 129). To be sure the manikin is that, but it is also the reflection of a Henry Adams whose historicality resists the absorption of even his own archetypes—a Henry Adams who is always multiple, other. "As Derrida has suggested," Rowe continues, "man must experience such a condition with either a joyous release or an anxious dread." But Adams in the end cannot be held to this strict either/or: in the florid dramatizations of dread that characterize his late correspondence and books, we can certainly detect an element of joy, a gusto revived in the renewed if sardonic occasion for writing. Adams the writer sought out, and gloried in, conditions that required virtuoso paradoxical discourse. Despite (in Rowe's words) the "apocalyptic tone" of the late writings, it is very possible to see Adams's ongoing practice as partaking in substance of "that

Nietzschean affirmation . . . that one detects in Henry James" (p. 129). At the same time we ought not to trivialize Adams's authentic dread: What writer of his generation labored under a heavier burden of Enlightenment doctrine or had achieved a greater martyrdom in the way of historicism? What writer had a firmer grasp of the social dissolutions that paralleled the increasingly manifest unreliability of language or had a keener sense of the political violence not to be checked by the literary artist's Nietzschean affirmation?

38. Porter, *Seeing and Being*, pp. 201–2.

Bibliography

Works by Henry Adams

Only those works by Adams not previously cited in Abbreviations follow.

A Cycle of Adams Letters, 1861–1865. 2 vols. Edited by Worthington Chauncey Ford. Boston: Houghton Mifflin, 1920.

The Education of Henry Adams. Edited by Ernest Samuels. Boston: Houghton Mifflin, 1973.

Henry Adams and His Friends. Edited by Harold Dean Cater. Boston: Houghton Mifflin, 1947.

The Letters of Henry Adams. 2 vols. Edited by Worthington Chauncey Ford. Boston: Houghton Mifflin, 1938.

The Life of George Cabot Lodge. In *The Shock of Recognition*, edited by Edmund Wilson. New York: Farrar, Straus and Cudahy, 1955.

"Two Letters on a Prussian Gymnasium." 1859. *American Historical Review* 53 (October 1947): 59–74.

Other Works

Adams, Brooks, "The Heritage of Henry Adams." In *The Degradation of the Democratic Dogma*, edited by Brooks Adams. 1919. Reprint. New York: Peter Smith, 1949.

———. *The Law of Civilization and Decay: An Essay on History*. 1896. Reprint. New York: Vintage Books, 1955.

Adams, Charles F., [Jr.], and Henry Adams. *Chapters of Erie and Other Essays*. Boston: James R. Osgood, 1871.

Adams, James Truslow. *Henry Adams*. New York: Albert and Charles Boni, 1933.

Adams, John Quincy. *Lectures on Rhetoric and Oratory*. 2 vols. Edited by J. Jeffery Auer and Jerald L. Banninga. New York: Russell and Russell, 1962.

Anderson, Thornton. *Brooks Adams: Constructive Conservative*. Ithaca: Cornell University Press, 1951.

Badger, Reid. *The Great American Fair: The World's Columbian Exposition and American Culture*. Chicago: Nelson Hall, 1979.

Bailyn, Bernard. *The Ideological Origins of the American Revoluton*. Cambridge: Harvard University Press, 1967.

Bakhtin, M. M. *The Dialogic Imagination*. Translated by Caryl Emerson and Michael Holquist. Austin: University of Texas Press, 1981.

Ballou, Ellen B. *The Building of the House: Houghton Mifflin's Formative Years*. Boston: Houghton Mifflin, 1970.

Barthes, Roland. "The Death of the Author." In *Image-Music-Text*, translated by Stephen Heath. New York: Hill and Wang, 1977.

Baym, Max I. *The French Education of Henry Adams*. New York: Columbia University Press, 1951.

Beard, Charles A. Introduction to Brooks Adams, *The Law of Civilization and Decay: An Essay on History*. 1896. Reprint. New York: Vintage Books, 1955.

Becker, Carl. "*The Education of Henry Adams*" (review). *American Historical Review* 24 (April 1919): 422–34.

———. *Everyman His Own Historian*. New York: F. S. Crofts, 1935.

Bell, Millicent. "Adams' *Esther*: The Morality of Taste." In *Critical Essays on Henry Adams*, edited by Earl N. Harbert. Boston: G. K. Hall, 1981.

Bercovitch, Sacvan. *The American Jeremiad*. Madison: University of Wisconsin Press, 1978.

Blackmur, R. P. *Henry Adams*. New York: Harcourt Brace Jovanovich, 1980.

———. "Politikon." *Hound and Horn* 2 (1928–29): 49–60.

Brooks, Van Wyck. *New England: Indian Summer, 1865–1915*. New York: E. P. Dutton, 1942.

———. *Sketches in Criticism*. New York: E. P. Dutton, 1932.

———. *Three Essays on America*. Edited by James R. Vitelli. New York: E. P. Dutton, 1970.

Burg, David F. *Chicago's White City of 1893*. Lexington: The University Press of Kentucky, 1976.

Chalfant, Edward. *Both Sides of the Ocean: A Biography of Henry Adams. His First Life—1838–1862*. Hamden, Conn.: Archon Books, 1982.

Colacurcio, Michael. "The Dynamo and the Angelic Doctor: The Bias of Henry Adams' Medievalism." *American Quarterly* 17 (Winter 1965): 696–712.

Conder, John J. *A Formula of His Own: Henry Adams's Literary Experiment*. Chicago: University of Chicago Press, 1970.

Cox, James M. "Learning through Ignorance: *The Education of Henry Adams*." *Sewanee Review* 88 (April–June 1980): 198–227.

Derrida, Jacques. *Of Grammatology*. Translated by Gayatri Chakravorty Spivak. Baltimore: Johns Hopkins University Press, 1976.

Doenecke, Justus D. "Myths, Machines, and Markets: The Columbian Exposition of 1893." *Journal of Popular Culture* 6, no. 3 (Spring 1973): 535–49.

Dusinberre, William. *Henry Adams: The Myth of Failure*. Charlottesville: University Press of Virginia, 1980.

Eliot, T. S. "A Sceptical Patrician." *Athenaeum*, May 23, 1919, pp. 361–62.

Ferguson, Robert A. " 'We Hold These Truths': Strategies of Control in the Literature of the Founders." In *Reconstructing American Literary History*, edited by Sacvan Bercovitch. Cambridge: Harvard University Press, 1986.

Foucault, Michel. *The Archaeology of Knowledge*. Translated by A. M. Sheridan Smith. New York: Pantheon Books, 1972.

———. *Language, Counter-Memory, Practice*. Translated by David F. Bouchard and Sherry Simon. Ithaca: Cornell University Press, 1977.

Godkin, E. L. "The *North American Review* for January." *Nation* 22 (February 17, 1876): 118–19.

Goodwin, James. "*The Education of Henry Adams*: A Non-Person in History." *Biography* 6, no. 2 (Spring 1983): 117–35.

Harbert, Earl N. "*The Education of Henry Adams*: The Confessional Mode as Heuristic Experiment." In *Critical Essays on Henry Adams*, edited by Earl N. Harbert. Boston: G. K. Hall, 1981.

———. *The Force So Much Closer Home: Henry Adams and the Adams Family.* New York: New York University Press, 1977.

Harvey, George. "The Holy War." *North American Review* 208 (December 1918): 801–4.

Hawthorne, Nathaniel. *Novels*. Edited by Millicent Bell. New York: Library of America, 1983.

Hicks, Granville. *The Great Tradition*. New York: Macmillan, 1935.

Hochfield, George. *Henry Adams: An Introduction and Interpretation*. New York: Barnes and Noble, 1962.

Hofstadter, Richard. *The Progressive Historians: Turner, Beard, Parrington*. Chicago: University of Chicago Press, 1968.

———. *Social Darwinism in American Thought*. Boston: Beacon Press, 1955.

Holt, Henry. *Garrulities of an Octogenarian Editor*. Boston: Houghton Mifflin, 1923.

Houghton Mifflin. *A Catalog of Authors*. Boston: Houghton Mifflin, 1899.

Hume, Robert A. *Runaway Star: An Appreciation of Henry Adams*. Ithaca: Cornell University Press, 1951.

James, William. *The Selected Letters of William James*. Edited by Elizabeth Hardwick. Boston: Nonpareil Books, 1980.

Jameson, Fredric. *The Political Unconscious*. Ithaca: Cornell University Press, 1981.

Jameson, John Franklin. *An Historian's World: Selections from the Correspondence of John Franklin Jameson*. Edited by Elizabeth Donnan and Leo Stock. Philadelphia: American Philosophical Society, 1956.

Jordy, William H. *Henry Adams: Scientific Historian*. New Haven: Yale University Press, 1952.

Kaledin, Eugenia. *The Education of Mrs. Henry Adams*. Philadelphia: Temple University Press, 1981.

Kaplan, Harold. *Power and Order: Henry Adams and the Naturalist Tradition in American Fiction*. Chicago: University of Chicago Press, 1981.

La Farge, Mabel A. "A Niece's Memories." In *Letters to a Niece and Prayer to the Virgin of Chartres*. Edited by Mabel A. La Farge. Boston: Houghton Mifflin, 1920.

Levenson, J. C. *The Mind and Art of Henry Adams*. Boston: Houghton Mifflin, 1957.

Levin, David. *History as Romantic Art*. Stanford, Calif.: Stanford University Press, 1959.

Lyon, Melvin. *Symbol and Idea in Henry Adams*. Lincoln: University of Nebraska Press, 1970.

Mane, Robert. *Henry Adams on the Road to Chartres*. Cambridge: Harvard University Press, 1971.

Martin, Ronald E. *American Literature and the Universe of Force*. Durham: Duke University Press, 1981.

Megill, Allan. *Prophets of Extremity: Nietzsche, Heidegger, Foucault, Derrida*.

Berkeley: University of California Press, 1985.

Minter, David L. *The Interpreted Design as a Structural Principle in American Prose.* New Haven: Yale University Press, 1969.

Monteiro, George. "The Education of Ernest Hemingway." In *Critical Essays on Henry Adams,* edited by Earl N. Harbert. Boston: G. K. Hall, 1981.

More, Paul Elmer. *A New England Group and Others.* Shelburne Essays, 11th ser. Boston: Houghton Mifflin, 1921.

Mott, Frank Luther. *A History of American Magazines.* 5 vols. Cambridge: Harvard University Press, 1938–68.

Mumford, Lewis. *The Brown Decades: A Study of the Arts in America, 1865–1895.* New York: Dover, 1931.

_____. *The Golden Day: A Study in American Expression and Culture.* New York: Boni and Liveright, 1926.

Noble, David W. *The End of American History.* Minneapolis: University of Minnesota Press, 1985.

Parrington, Vernon Louis. *Main Currents in American Thought.* 3 vols. New York: Harcourt Brace, 1930.

Pocock, J. G. A. *The Machiavellian Moment: Florentine Political Thought and the Atlantic Republican Tradition.* Princeton: Princeton University Press, 1975.

Porter, Carolyn. *Seeing and Being: The Plight of the Participant Observer in Emerson, James, Adams, and Faulkner.* Middletown, Conn.: Wesleyan University Press, 1981.

Robinson, James Harvey. *The New History: Essays Illustrating the Modern Historical Outlook.* 1919. Reprint. Springfield, Mass.: Walden Press, 1958.

Roosevelt, Theodore. *The Letters of Theodore Roosevelt.* 8 vols. Edited by E. E. Morison. Cambridge: Harvard University Press, 1952.

Rowe, John Carlos. *Henry Adams and Henry James: The Emergence of a Modern Consciousness.* Ithaca: Cornell University Press, 1976.

Samuels, Ernest. *The Young Henry Adams.* Cambridge: Harvard University Press, 1948.

_____. *Henry Adams: The Middle Years.* Cambridge: Harvard University Press, 1958.

_____. *Henry Adams: The Major Phase.* Cambridge: Harvard University Press, 1964.

Shklar, Judith N. "*The Education of Henry Adams* by Henry Adams." *Daedalus* 103 (Winter 1974): 59–66.

Smith, Henry Nash. *Virgin Land: The American West as Symbol and Myth.* Cambridge: Harvard University Press, 1950.

Smith, William Henry ["Housatonic," pseud.]. "A Case of Hereditary Bias." *New York Tribune,* September 10 and December 15, 1890.

Spiller, Robert E. "Henry Adams." In *Literary History of the United States,* edited by Robert E. Spiller, Willard Thorp, Thomas H. Johnson, and Henry Seidel Canby. New York: Macmillan, 1948.

Sullivan, Louis. *The Autobiography of an Idea.* 1924. Reprint. New York: Dover, 1956.

Turner, Frederick Jackson. *The Early Writings of Frederick Jackson Turner.* Edited by Fulmer Mood. Madison: University of Wisconsin Press, 1938.

Vandersee, Charles. "Henry Adams and the *Atlantic*: Pattern for a Career." *Papers on Language and Literature* 7, no. 4 (Fall 1971): 351–73.

Vitzthum, Richard C. *The American Compromise: Theme and Method in the Histories of Bancroft, Parkman, and Adams*. Norman: University of Oklahoma Press, 1974.

Wagner, Vern. *The Suspension of Henry Adams: A Study of Manner and Matter*. Detroit: Wayne State University Press, 1969.

White, Hayden. *Metahistory: The Historical Imagination in Nineteenth-Century Europe*. Baltimore: Johns Hopkins University Press, 1973.

———. "Method and Ideology in Intellectual History." In *Modern European Intellectual History*, edited by Dominick La Capra and Steven L. Kaplan. Ithaca: Cornell University Press, 1982.

Wilson, Edmund. Introduction to Henry Adams, *The Life of George Cabot Lodge*. In *The Shock of Recognition*, edited by Edmund Wilson. New York: Farrar, Straus and Cudahy, 1955.

Winters, Ivor. *The Anatomy of Nonsense*. Norfolk, Conn.: New Directions, 1943.

Wood, Gordon S. *The Creation of the American Republic, 1776–1787*. Chapel Hill: University of North Carolina Press, 1969.

Wright, Frank Lloyd. *An Autobiography*. 1932. Reprint. New York: Horizon, 1971.

Index